Librarian's Guide
to Online Searching

Librarian's Guide to Online Searching

Cultivating Database Skills for Research and Instruction

Fifth Edition

CHRISTOPHER C. BROWN AND
SUZANNE S. BELL

 LIBRARIES
UNLIMITED™
An Imprint of ABC-CLIO, LLC
Santa Barbara, California • Denver, Colorado

Copyright © 2018 by Christopher C. Brown and Suzanne S. Bell

Library of Congress Cataloging in Publication Control Number: 2018011054

ISBN: 978-1-4408-6156-7 (paperback)
       978-1-4408-6157-4 (ebook)

22 21 20 19 18   1 2 3 4 5

This book is also available as an eBook.

Libraries Unlimited
An Imprint of ABC-CLIO, LLC

ABC-CLIO, LLC
130 Cremona Drive, P.O. Box 1911
Santa Barbara, California 93116-1911
www.abc-clio.com

This book is printed on acid-free paper ∞
Manufactured in the United States of America

Contents

Foreword

When I submitted the completed manuscript of the fourth edition of this book, I sent my longstanding and wonderful editor, Barbara Ittner, a note saying, "Here it is: the fourth edition, and I think the best. I'm good with it. But I don't have another one in me." Soon after the book came out, I retired from my day job as an academic reference librarian. A year later found me also retired from my online teaching position. I have been deeply (and happily) engaged in quite different priorities and interests ever since.

But the *Librarian's Guide* must go on! More than a year ago, Ms. Ittner started asking me, "If not you, then who?" It was agonizing not to have any good answers to that question, and my relief—nay, joy!—was profound when she told me she thought she had the right person. E-mails were exchanged, and in short order, I knew that Barbara had indeed found the right person in Prof. Christopher Brown. Eventually, we were all able to meet in person, and I told him, "It's your book now. Make it your own."

And he did just that. Using the analogy of rehabbing an old house, he has taken it right back to the foundations and rebuilt it. It is now totally revamped and refreshed, up to date, and "with all mod cons," as the Brits say. It is immediately evident to me that Prof. Brown brings to this text much deeper and richer knowledge across librarianship, and he has technological skills that are, again, deeper and more formal than I could ever aspire to. To highlight some examples of the excellence awaiting you, the examples in the book are more "library oriented," such as the use of a MARC record to demonstrate database structure and fixed vs. iterating fields in chapter 2.

There are a number of new chapters. The one on government information resources demonstrates Brown's expertise and ease in that area; it is a chapter only a longtime expert in the field could write. Other new chapters include one devoted exclusively to controlled vocabulary, one on the major vendor interfaces that gets into all the new features common nowadays, and a timely one devoted to discovery services.

In addition to new chapters, you will also find many more and a much wider range of databases discussed throughout the book. I found the chapter on statistics especially notable in this regard, but all the chapters now include some new databases. Before I put faculty into a panic ("Oh no! *Everything* is different. I'll have to redo my whole syllabus!"), let me quickly add that the same databases are featured in the "subject" chapters, but now from the vendors that are more widely used (which will no doubt come as a very pleasant development). The "old standards" are then augmented with additional important resources in the topical area. There is more attention throughout to Gale databases, plus those from Readex, Adam Mathew, and others. Throughout the book, you will also find a wider range of exercises in which government information sources are given equal footing with all the other types of resources.

Rather than a tedious review of the literature, Brown takes a more useful "news you can use" approach in the chapter on users (formerly "Focus on People," now "User Behaviors and Meeting Information Needs"). His guide to having a "brainstorming session with yourself" is invaluable, whether you are a new library student or an established professional.

If you are an MLIS faculty member who has used previous editions of this text, yes, you will need to make some adjustments in your syllabus. But the effort will be well worth it, because I think you will find the overall tone of this new edition very appealing: Prof. Brown is simply more scholarly and has a wider and greater depth of experience than I. There is an academic rigor here that I could never hope to attain and what I can only express as an "embeddedness" in the profession that is evident in every example, every discussion. He digs deeper into the topics throughout the book, from "How Databases Work," to "Humanities Databases" (which gets into primary sources, e-books, and nontextual databases), to the addition of a thorough glossary at the end.

Like a house, Christopher Brown has rebuilt this book and made it his own. I know I leave it—and you, gentle readers—in the best of hands. Welcome to the all-new *Librarian's Guide to Online Searching*, fifth edition.

Suzanne S. Bell
Rochester, New York

Preface

This book is not intended to be a thorough survey of all existing databases available to libraries. It cannot even cover all vendors. These would be impossible tasks, as there are hundreds of vendors offering thousands of databases of both primary and secondary source materials. This book covers the basic principles of databases, their structure, how to search them, and a survey of databases in various academic fields.

This fifth edition roughly follows the chapter organization of the fourth edition. This was done intentionally to make it easier to use in classroom settings. I know how challenging it can be to have to hunt for assigned readings when updating syllabi. But there are some exceptions, because several chapters have been added. I now devote a full chapter to controlled vocabulary. A chapter on government information addresses the many resources available for census and statistics, legislation and legislative histories, and navigating documents from the three branches of the U.S. government. An entire chapter is now devoted to Web-scale discovery tools. These have been ubiquitous in medium to large academic libraries and have features that need to be explained. A point of continuity with previous editions, Suzanne Bell has graciously offered to reprise her role as author for the chapters on database evaluation and teaching at the end of the book.

Carrying on the tradition of the fourth edition, additional exercises, search tips, and tutorials will be available on the publisher's Web site at http://www.abc-clio.com/books.librariesunlimited.com/Librarians-Guide-to-Online-Searching. This will be updated periodically with the inevitable database changes.

Are librarians still needed? Are the tools currently in use by librarians to bring information to match up to user needs—by these tools I mean online databases—still necessary?

In 2017, a research report produced by Pearson, Nesta, and the Oxford Martin School looked at employment prospects for all of the 772 occupations tracked by the U.S. government and considered trends and prospects for future demand. The occupations of librarians, curators, and archivists were placed in the top 10 of occupations with the greatest probabilities of future demand (Bakhshi et al. 2017). Why do you think that librarianship ranked so highly? I think it has everything to do with technology, that is to say—databases. Databases and the ability to search them and to teach and explain them to others makes librarian professions valuable to all who seek the information it takes to get ahead in their professions, studies, and all areas of their lives.

The U.S. government agrees with this assessment. The *Occupational Outlook Handbook* job outlook for librarians from 2016 to 2026 is estimated to have a 9 percent growth rate. Although this government source does not specifically tie this growth to databases, it does say that there will be a continuous need "for librarians to manage libraries and help patrons find information" (U.S. B.L.S. 2017). At least part of this growth could be attributed to skills with understanding and teaching database skills.

If there is a library-related text more in need of frequent revision than one about online databases, I don't know what that book would be. Across all disciplines, databases have evolved with new features. New entrants into the market are changing the way discovery happens. Corporate spinoffs and purchases of online products can make one's head spin. New mapping products are transforming business and social science research. Web-scale discovery tools are becoming ubiquitous in academic libraries. These are just a few of the trending machinations in the realm of library databases.

Readers of this book should come away with a thorough background of how databases work; how they are constructed and, in the case of some databases, how they transitioned from the legacy print world to an online environment; how technologies within databases can interact with other products such as bibliography citation services, outbound linking to full-text content, and social media mentions; and the methods used by libraries to provide access to licensed content from anywhere in the world.

The scope of the book is limited to databases typically used in academic and public libraries, with the requisite skills necessary to search them effectively.

This fifth edition roughly follows the chapter organization of the fourth edition. This was done intentionally to make it easier to use in classroom settings. I know how challenging it can be to have to hunt for assigned readings when updating syllabi.

The first six chapters cover database basics: what databases are and how they came about, how they work in layman's terms, consideration of underlying vocabularies that prove essential to the ultimate goal of finding "all and only" the relevant information, and seven basic tools necessary for effective searching. Preserved from the fourth edition is the valuable "Searcher's Toolkit," with the same seven essential tools necessary for effecting searching.

Chapters 7 through 13 provide a discipline-specific focus and such special topics as bibliographic tools, statistical databases, and the relatively new Web-scale discovery services. Chapter 14 shifts the focus to user needs and how they can be met with the vast array of online products. Serving as a point of continuity with previous editions, Suzanne Bell has graciously offered to reprise her role as author for the chapters on database evaluation and teaching in chapters 15 and 16.

Several chapters have been added. I now devote an entire chapter to controlled vocabulary. A chapter on government information addresses the many resources available for census and statistics, legislation and legislative histories, and navigating documents from the three branches of the U.S. government. An entire chapter is now devoted to Web-scale discovery tools. These have been ubiquitous in medium-to-large academic libraries and have features that need to be explained.

Since the fourth edition, there have been many changes to the library information industry as well as to databases themselves. The newly formed Clarivate Analytics has acquired *Web of Science* and the EndNote bibliographic formatting software from Thomson Reuters. EBSCO and ProQuest have both been building up their e-book holdings, with EBSCO acquiring Gobi (formerly YBP Library Services) and ProQuest acquiring Coutts Information Services. Vendors have been adding to primary-source offerings. Gale's *Early Arabic Printed Books* is a prime example of this. Incorporation of social media into data analytics and search results themselves can be seen with integration of alternative metrics into some databases and a new database, *voxgov*, built largely around federal government social media mentions.

For faculty using the book in library and information science classrooms, chapters contain both examples of how to search databases as well as examples that can be assigned as homework in classes. I have used variations of these examples in my classroom teaching over the years, and hopefully others teaching database searching will find them useful as well.

The work is also designed for library practitioners: professionals, paraprofessionals, and anyone providing reference services in libraries. But it will also be of use to researchers independently pursuing studies who desire a more in-depth view of today's database technologies and how discovery can best be accomplished.

References

Bakhshi, Hasan, Jonathan M. Downing, Michael A. Osborne, and Philippe Schneider. 2017. *The Future of Skills: Employment in 2030*. London: Pearson and Nesta. Accessed November 5, 2017. https://www.nesta.org.uk/sites/default/files/the_future_of_skills_employment_in_2030_0.pdf.

U.S. Bureau of Labor Statistics. 2017. *Occupational Outlook Handbook*. Accessed November 5, 2017. https://www.bls.gov/ooh/education-training-and-library/librarians.htm.

Acknowledgments

Special thanks go to Suzanne Bell, the author of the first four editions of this book. Suzanne has been a tremendous encouragement to me as I take over "her baby" and has offered much input and made many suggestions throughout the process. I know I cannot adequately fill her shoes and the path she has so clearly set forth in the previous editions of this book.

I also thank the hundreds of students I have had in the classes I have taught since 1999 through the University of Denver's Library and Information Science program. They have clarified the way I teach database searching and continually kept me on my toes.

Kim Dority has been an encouragement for two decades, first as an instructor in the university's LIS program and also as being the one who introduced me to Barbara Ittner of Libraries Unlimited.

The University of Denver's Main Library, where I have worked since 1999, provided ample leave time, including a summer sabbatical, to allow for completion of this book.

1
Introduction to Library Databases

Databases have become almost magical. Fuzzy searches, fast results, full text mining, concept maps, text to voice, spell checking, and vocabulary control—but how did we get to this point? What historical precedents in library science and information-seeking behaviors brought about our current state of searching and, more importantly, of discovery?

A Brief History of Information Access before Databases

Before databases, there were library catalogs and print indexes. Library catalogs usually consisted of wooden drawers of catalog cards housed in handsome wooden cabinets. The cards in these cabinets would typically be accessed by author, subject, or title. If you were looking up an author, you would need to invert the name so that the last name (family name or surname) appeared first. This indirect ordering of names is the way cards were filed and accessed in alphabetical order. East Asian names could be filed in their normal order, as Chinese, Japanese, and Korean last names are first as a matter of culture.

A lot of work went into creating and maintaining card catalogs. Cards had to be typed one card at a time. Then they had to be filed. Each library item required a set of cards, one for each access point. In the simplest of cases, there might be a single author card, a title card, and up to three subject cards. In cases where the books required more description, cards could be more than a single card. Multiple cards might be required to accommodate contents notes, complex series titles, and other added entries. Card catalog drawer space quickly filled up when that happened. But that was the precomputer way of life in libraries of the early to mid-20th century.

Articles were also accessed very differently. Indexes to periodical articles were published in print volumes, making the use of library space very different from today's patterns. Users clustered around index tables and reference book stacks where periodical indexes were shelved. The tedious task of accessing indexes one year at a time was extremely time-consuming. In some cases, cumulative indexes would merge 5–10 years of information together, making the work just a bit less onerous.

Let's take a hypothetical case of a student trying to research a topic in the 1970s before computers had taken over as the primary access method for library research. Let's say that we are researching the sinking of the *Titanic*. First, we want to find resources from the popular press. We access the green volumes of *Readers' Guide to Periodical Literature*. As the *Titanic* incident occurred in 1912, we would need to search all years from 1912 through the present day (in the 1970s). There are cumulated editions for some years of *Readers' Guide*, so that saves us a bit of time. We discover the subject entry is *Titanic (Steamship)*, and after going through many physical volumes, we have uncovered over 100 citations that we may want to consult.

Next, we decide to find more scholarly resources, so we consult the *Bulletin of the Public Affairs Information Service*, which is cumulated annually. This indexing service began in 1915, so we miss the earliest years. We then move on to *America: History and Life*. This index was published from 1964, but a retrospective volume covers 1954–1963. After tediously going through these volumes, we find only four relevant articles.

H. W. Wilson, publishers of the *Readers' Guide to Periodical Literature*, also published the *International Index to Periodicals*, which goes back to 1907. This index went through several title changes, including *International Index*, *Social Sciences & Humanities Index*, and then split into the *Social Sciences Index* and the *Humanities Index*. After hefting these volumes around for several hours, we come up with just over a dozen more citations.

Now that we have painstakingly written down several dozen citations (more than we need), we need to see whether our library owns the journals that contain the articles and especially the specific years cited. This entails walking over to the card catalog drawers and looking up journal titles to find the holdings and the call numbers so we can walk to the shelves to get the print journal articles. The library will likely lack some of the journals we need, which is why we had to write down more citations than we will end up using. If we really need articles that the library does not own, we can request an interlibrary loan. This process may take an additional 4–8 weeks.

After going to the shelves, we pull the relevant serial volumes, perhaps marking the first pages with index cards. Then, going over to the photocopy machines, we can feed coins into the slot to make copies. This entire process consumes an entire afternoon. And, of course, now we need to go back to the dorm room to read all these things. All of this could have been done today with databases in perhaps a half hour or less, printouts included.

What started out as an additional way to access journal indexes—the online database—has become the sole method of searching everything. So transformative have databases become that reference collections have decreased their footprint, often to only a few shelves, Web sites have become the focal point of access, and library guides are now indispensable to understanding and accessing research and scholarship. To be a reference librarian means being a database expert in today's library environments, whether in a school library, a public library, or in an academic library.

No longer are databases just the online catalog and article indexes, they are now statistical portals, sound and video platforms, and an entrée to the world of primary sources. While vendors have endeavored to simplify interfaces by presenting the ubiquitous single search box, librarians need to know how these products work (or sometimes don't work) so that we can leverage resources to better serve our clientele.

But are today's databases too good? Robots and automation are taking over many fields. The semantic Web is becoming more sophisticated, and search engines such as Google are getting better at uncovering relevant resources all the time. Will there come a day when librarians will no longer be needed as intermediaries? I certainly hope not.

Let me offer some evidence that librarians will still be needed for some time to come:

- Librarians are uniquely equipped to assist users in navigating the ever-growing number of online database products.

- Librarians are equipped to bridge the gap between high-tech databases and database users. That's why you are reading this book!

- Researchers need to find "all and only" the relevant research, but too often sophisticated, automated search engines return much more. The trained searcher can teach users the best search techniques.

This book serves as an introduction and learning tool for today's variety of databases, from the simple online catalog to the complex statistical portal.

Progression from Citation-Only Resources to Full Text

The print index world was one of "citation only" resources (often referred to as A&I, or abstracting and indexing). It's difficult to name databases today that only provide citations and do not also contain full text. Users now are so accustomed to retrieving full text, or at least links to full text, that they are nonplussed when they encounter a database that only serves up citations without it.

The big three vendors (Gale, EBSCO, and ProQuest) have A&I database products, but because these products integrate with other full-text products on the same vendor platform, full text from other products bleeds through to the products without full text.

An example of this is the *Bibliography of Asian Studies*. Indexed items without full text will only have links to a library's link resolver so that users can see whether they can find full text through another database, or use the magic of OpenURL technology to place an interlibrary loan request. But for a subset of materials, full text magically appears in the form of PDF icons. This is bleed through from other EBSCO databases to which the library subscribes and is a major advantage of having large vendor aggregators in the first place or subscribing to many databases from the same aggregator.

Another example is *Anthropology Plus*, another product on the EBSCO-host interface. This is a combination of the Royal Anthropology Institute's *Anthropological Index* combined with Harvard University's *Anthropological Literature* database, originating from their Tozzer Library. ProQuest's *Periodicals Index Online* is an example from the ProQuest world. The most obvious index-only tool is actually the library online catalog in each of our institutions.

Now that we have fully entered the computer age and have migrated from print indexes to computer databases, either links out to full text or the full text itself can reside within databases. Thus, user expectations have evolved along with the technologies.

Physical Analogs

Many of our current databases have their beginnings in the print world and survive today as online continuations of long-standing print indexes. Other databases were "born digital," meaning that they were created for the first time in digital format, with no print version as a precursor. Why is it important to know whether there is a physical analog and what the title is? I suggest the following reasons:

- Sometimes the physical precursor had features that the database version does not have. This might include browsing features or other functions that aid in accessibility.

- We can appreciate the tedious work of previous generations of librarians, catalogers, and indexers.

- If a database becomes unavailable, either because of technical problems or because of budget cuts, we could consider using the print version.

- Identifying physical versions can enable us to free up shelf space in reference collections or in book stacks generally.

Here are a few examples of selected online databases with physical analogs (table 1.1).

Databases and Their Scope

Not only do we need to discover what databases are available to us (freely or for a fee), but we need to know what is in those databases so that we can select the appropriate one. An important prerequisite to searching any database is understanding its scope of coverage. To users, all Web-based information seems flat; that is, everything seems to be equal in value. When we understand the scope of a database, contours start to appear. By scope, we mean the topics covered by the database; what kinds of materials are included (e.g.,

Table 1.1. Examples of Physical Analogs.

Database	Physical Analog(s)
AccessUN (Readex)	*Check List of United Nations Documents* (1946–1949); *United Nations Documents Index* (1950–1973); *UNDEX. United Nations Documents Index* (1970–1978); *UNDOC, Current Index United Nations Documents Index* (1979–1996); *United Nations Documents Checklist* (1996–1997); *United Nations Documents Index* (1998–)
ERIC (several providers)	*Current Index to Journals in Education* (CIJE), journal articles *Resources in Education* (RIE)—ED documents; materials in the ERIC fiche set
ProQuest Congressional	*CIS Index to Publications of the United States Congress*; *CIS Annual*; *CIS U.S. Serial Set Index*
ProQuest Dissertations and Theses	*Dissertation Abstracts International*; *American Doctoral Dissertations*
PsycINFO (several providers)	*Psychological Index*; *Psychological Abstracts*
PubMed (National Library of Medicine with Medline version from several providers)	*Index Medicus*, cumulated in *Cumulated Index Medicus*
Sociological Abstracts (ProQuest)	*Sociological Abstracts* (Cambridge Scientific Abstracts)

dissertations, scholarly articles, book chapters, popular magazine content); dates of coverage (e.g., 1980 to present, 1600–1900); and other areas.

Scope is so important that we are devoting an entire chapter to it. Without a thorough knowledge of the scope of a database, you won't know whether the database is appropriate for the topic, why results are not found when searching, or how to search effectively for materials.

Where to Find Scope Information about a Database

Sometimes database scope information is clearly stated; other times, it is more difficult to discern. *World News Connection (WNC)* from East View Information Services is a prime example of a database that doesn't clearly state its scope of coverage. Government documents librarians would likely know the history and origin of this database, but the vendor just provides this statement:

A powerful online subscription service bringing news from around the world, translated into English, typically within 24–72 hours from the time of the original publication or broadcast. The information is obtained from newspaper articles, television and radio broadcasts, online sources, conference proceedings, periodicals, and non-classified reports. This information is collected and translated by and for the U.S. Government.

This is an extremely inadequate statement of scope. Although this database was previously offered by Dialog (now a ProQuest company), the U.S. government ordered aggregators to stop offering it (Conkling 2014). But the *World News Connection* scope note as presented by East View does not mention this fact. We have to search Google like this, "site:edu "world news connection," to discover what this database is really all about. After foraging around through several library guides, we have discerned a few things about *World News Connection*.

World News Connection is a continuation of the news gathering efforts of the Foreign Broadcast Information Service, originally started by the United States Office of Strategic Services (OSS) in 1941, later taken over by the Central Intelligence Agency (CIA), and then by the U.S. State Department. It was originally issued in paper format (along with microform distribution to some libraries). Paper and microfiche dissemination ended in 1996.

World News Connection is the online format that was disseminated after tangible distribution stopped. Then, to the disappointment of government documents librarians, *WNC* was completely discontinued as of December 31, 2013. It would have been helpful if the vendor had mentioned these points on its Web site, but it failed to do so.

Here are some places to look for scope statements:

- Database main page or help page. If the database is fee-based, you will only get to this page if you are a subscriber.

- Vendor sales information on the company Web site. Simply search the database name and you shouldn't be far from vendor sales information.

- Library guides authored by knowledgeable reference librarians. As an example, *Access UN* is a database offered on an older Readex interface. Although the database help screen describes in detail what is covered, it doesn't discuss the print indexes that had been physical analogs or versions of this content before it went online as a database. But by searching Google like this, "site:edu accessun," I am able to find out more about the scope of this database.

- Correspondence with the vendor. In some cases, vendors don't have all the information you need easily available, such as journal titles lists. You may need to write to a sales representative to get more complete scope information.

Scope: Dates of Coverage

It is important that you become very familiar with coverage dates. Many professors recommend that students search *JSTOR* for scholarly journal content, not realizing that *JSTOR* in many cases is a "moving wall" of content and does not include the recent three to five years of content (JSTOR 2017). It would be useless to search a historic e-book collection, such as *Early English Books Online (EEBO)*, for information on network computing. See chapter 9 for a chart providing date coverage for databases of early e-books.

Another reason dates of coverage can be important is in the case of aggregators that, because of contract restrictions, must place embargos on journal content. Larger libraries generally have electronic resource management systems (ERM or ERMS) that assist in providing dates of coverage for each content provider. Figure 1.1 shows a journal with up-to-date full content from the publisher, but embargoed content from an aggregator.

Scope: Materials Indexed

Today's databases contain all kinds of materials found in libraries, including primary source materials, such as archival holdings that are unique to a particular archive; journal holdings; newspaper content (sometimes available as full-text broadsheets, including advertisements, and other times only as HTML text of article content); sound recordings (in plain English: music); full text of books, both rare and common; government publications, from parliamentary proceedings to congressional hearings to

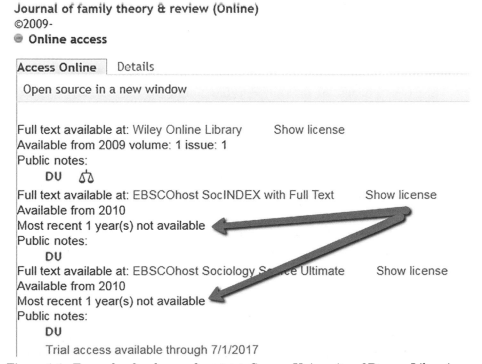

Figure 1.1. Example of embargoed content. *Source:* University of Denver Libraries.

agency reports; and data sets from international organizations or government bodies.

Some databases have cover-to-cover indexing of journals, whereas others may have only featured scholarly articles.

Scope: Availability of Peer-Reviewed Content

Many databases have an automatic link to limit search results to "academic" or "scholarly" or "peer-reviewed" publications. But what does this mean, and how can databases automatically do this limit?

Peer-reviewed journals, also known as scholarly or academic journals, follow a review process that adds a degree of rigor to the publication process. There are several types of peer review, but all of them involve the paper being submitted to readers familiar with the discipline and thus having the authority to critically evaluate the content and to pass judgment as to the worthiness of the publication for the intended journal. When I teach peer review to incoming university students, I do so by comparing an academic journal to a general magazine publication. "Who writes for general magazines?" I ask. Students respond by saying, "Journalists, professional writers." Then I ask, "Who writes for scholarly journals?" Responses are usually, "Professors, expert researchers, and people with degrees after their names." These responses are all correct. At this point, I say, "So magazines are written by professional writers who do not have much expertise in the field, and peer-reviewed journals are written by experts in their field who may not be good writers."

As publishing peer-reviewed content is a point of pride for the publishers who do that, they make it quite clear which of their journals are worthy of that distinction. Some vendors then use that information to populate a "peer-reviewed" field in their databases, doing this work "in-house."

Some databases let another database, like *Ulrichsweb*, do the limiting to peer-reviewed content. ProQuest owns Bowker, and Bowker publishes *Ulrich's Periodicals Directory* and its online version, *Unrichsweb*, so many ProQuest products rely on the historically curated Ulrich's content to assist with the peer-reviewed limiter.

Here is an example of how the peer-reviewed limit might be used. A researcher wants to find a journal to publish her article. "I need to find which journals would be appropriate to submit a qualitative policy analysis to and whether there are models for how those articles are composed in those journals."

The first thing I did was to search *Ulrichsweb* for the subject term "policy analysis." No results. Next, I tried just the term "policy"; still no results. I'm a bit puzzled. I then did a keyword search for the words "policy analysis" and got nearly 5,000 results, more like what I was expecting. After examining a few of the more academic of these titles, I discovered that the subjects are very broad. The relevant subjects seem to be either political science or public administration. These are almost useless in terms of pinpointing the subject in this case, but they can be helpful in ruling out policy analysis in the realm of education or social work, areas that are not of interest to my researcher.

Now that I understand how subjects work, I am ready to build up a much better search. I decide to retain my keyword terms, policy analysis, and the subject descriptor public administration. I click the limiters (fixed field limits) for "active" and "academic/scholarly," and I narrow the results to "peer reviewed." I now retrieve 157 titles that I can review for editorial policies and other matters (see figure 1.2).

Ulrichsweb gives you the scope of the journal and editors' names. You could just Google the journal you are interested in to get author instructions and policies.

There is a danger in relying on databases to tell us which articles are peer-reviewed. Although a journal may tend to have peer-reviewed content, this does not mean that 100 percent of the articles indexed within that journal are necessarily peer-reviewed. There may be editorials, notes or comments on previous articles, book reviews, announcements, or other indexable content that isn't actually peer-reviewed. The student must be careful to ensure that what a database marks as scholarly or peer-reviewed actually is. In the example below from *Academic Search* (figure 1.3), we see that the article "Birds of the Air" is designated as coming from a scholarly/ peer-reviewed journal, but in fact this is a poem.

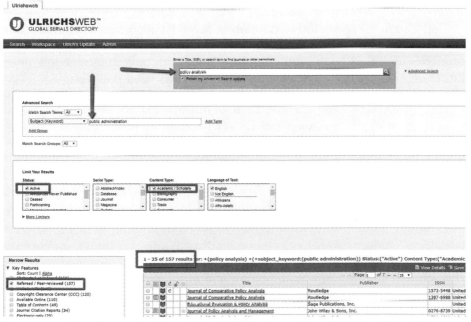

Figure 1.2. Searching *Ulrichsweb* for scholarly journals and their policies. The screen shots and their contents are published with permission of *Ulrichsweb* and ProQuest LLC. Further reproduction is prohibited without permission.

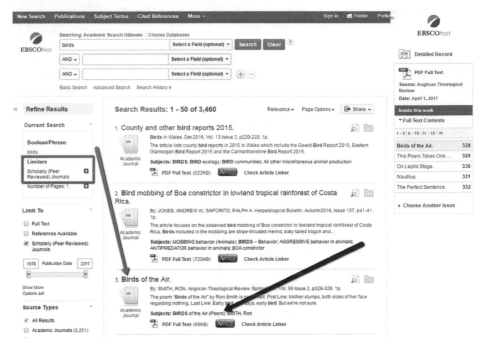

Figure 1.3. *Academic Search* limited to peer-reviewed content. ©2017 EBSCO Industries, Inc. All rights reserved.

Scope: Countries and Languages Covered

Although most available databases favor English-language materials and are Western-centric, an increasing number of databases cover other countries and other languages. Some are searchable only in foreign language interfaces. Examples of this include Gale's primary source materials in their stunning database, *Early Arabic Printed Books*, which can be searched in Arabic. ProQuest's *East Europe/Central Europe Database* includes materials in most of the languages of Eastern and Central Europe and can be searched in the original languages.

Scope: Breadth and Depth of Coverage

Breadth of coverage of a database refers to the entire range of subject content, dates of coverage, and countries and languages included. How broadly a database searches is important to advanced researchers because they need to know what they are *not* surveying. Are they covering American scholarship only or also international scholarship? Is it only English-language content (and, if so, only American or also those of Canadian, British, Australian, or other English-speaking countries) or other languages as well? Are these languages only European or also Asian languages? Are book chapters covered? What about conference papers? Are dissertations and theses included? What dates of publications does the database index? Does it include only scholarly journal articles or also nonacademic? These

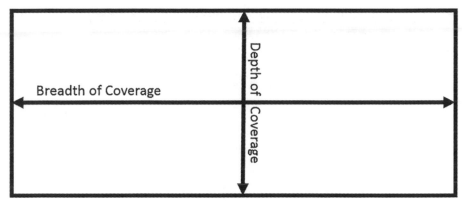

Figure 1.4. Depth vs. breadth of database coverage illustrated.

are just some examples of the many breadth questions that need to be addressed.

Depth of coverage refers to how deeply the database is capable of searching. Can it search just in the metadata or can it also search down into the full content, that is, the full text of textual documents? Some databases may include full text of selected journals, but is that full text indexed by default? Are journals indexed exhaustively or only selectively?

The simple illustration in figure 1.4 helps us to focus on these important issues.

With all these scope considerations in mind, let's examine some of the variations of databases available across the wide spectrum of vendor and publisher interfaces.

- A&I or citation-only databases. As previously mentioned, there are fewer databases than ever before that have no full text.

- Linked full-text databases. If your library subscribes to content from a database that has the full text to a citation, then that full-text availability will bleed through to the database that, in and of itself, has no native full text.

- Full-text databases. This seems to be the only category that users truly understand. Because they own their content, publishers will nearly always have complete full-text availability. Aggregators will have varying levels of full text, sometimes with embargo periods of several weeks to several months, and sometimes several years, before they are allowed to offer full text for certain types of content.

Exercises

1. Go through the databases in your library's list of databases. Which databases are A&I only (in other words, they have no full text within the database itself, even if they may link out to full text)?

2. Select five databases from your local library's database list. For each of these databases, fill out these scope considerations:

- What are the dates of coverage?
- What materials are indexed (journal articles, books, conference papers, dissertations, newspaper articles, etc.)?
- What languages and countries are covered?
- Is the content peer-reviewed?
- Is the full text available within database? Are there links out to the full text? Is the full text searchable?
- Extra credit: Does the database have a physical analog? If so, what is the title?

References

Conkling, David. 2014. "World News Connection and ProQuest." Blog post, March 10. https://wikis.library.tamu.edu/display/ERAnnounce/2014/03/10.

Hart-Davis, Guy. 2015. *Learn Excel 2016 for OS X*. 2nd ed. New York: Apress (distributed by Springer).

JSTOR. 2017. "JSTOR's Moving Wall: Archive vs. Current Definitions." Accessed November 28, 2017. https://support.jstor.org/hc/en-us/articles/115004879547 -JSTOR-s-Moving-Wall-Archive-vs-Current-Definitions.

Suggested Reading

Cleveland, Ana D., and Donald B. Cleveland. *Introduction to Indexing and Abstracting*. 4th ed. Santa Barbara, CA: Libraries Unlimited, 2013.

2
How Databases Work

The magical qualities to which we alluded in the first chapter need to be explained. We hardly see all the layers upon layers of technology working together. In this chapter, we examine the standards that underlie many of the technologies, the way databases are constructed, how information is stored in databases, indexing processes, the reasons for databases to fail, and how all these technologies work together to bring full text to the user's desktop.

Standards within Librarianship

It's reassuring to know that librarianship is all about standards. We don't just make things up as we go; we follow established conventions and protocols. The American Library Association has a list of dozens of standards on topics that include academic libraries, access, buildings, cataloging, ethics, information literacy, interlibrary loan, reference services, special collections, and many more (http://www.ala.org/tools/guidelines/standards-guidelines). But what we'll focus on here are the standards that relate directly to the way databases work. The National Information Standards Organization (NISO) continually works on updating standards and recommended practices. NISO is a nonprofit organization whose standards are accredited by the American National Standards Institute (ANSI). Many of the library-related standards listed in table 2.1 are joint ANSI/NISO standards.

Each of the standards listed in table 2.1 has something to do with online library databases: from the display of information fields and records, to the linking of full text from competing information providers, to the formation of bibliographic citations and output, to citation management software. Other standards track statistics for online database usage and full-text access, underlying structures of controlled vocabularies, and permanent linking to content.

Table 2.1. Selected Standars in the Library Database Realm.

Standard	Notes
MARC Record Standards	Library of Congress (https://www.loc.gov/marc)
Resource Description and Access (RDA)	Library of Congress (https://www.loc.gov/aba/rda)
ISO 2108:2005	Information and documentation; International Standard Book Number (ISBN)
ANSI/NISO Z39.2-1994	Information Interchange Format
ANSI/NISO Z39.7-1995	Library Statistics
ANSI/NISO Z39.9-1992	International Standard Serial Numbering (ISSN)
ANSI/NISO Z39.14-1997 (R2002)	Guidelines for Abstracts
ANSI/NISO Z39.19-1993	Guidelines for the Construction, Format, and Management of Monolingual Thesauri
ANSI/NISO Z39.50-2003 (S2014)	Information Retrieval: Application Service Definition & Protocol Specification
ANSI/NISO Z39.71-1999	Holdings Statements for Bibliographic Items
ANSI/NISO Z39.84-2000	Syntax for the Digital Object Identifier
ANSI/NISO Z39.85-2001	The Dublin Core Metadata Element Set
ANSI/NISO Z39.88-2004 (R2010)	The OpenURL Framework for Context-Sensitive Services
ANSI/NISO Z39.93-2014	Standardized Usage Statistics Harvesting Initiative (SUSHI) Protocol
Knowledge Base and Related Tools (KBART)	http://www.niso.org/workrooms/kbart
Open Discovery Initiative (ODI)	http://www.niso.org/workrooms/odi
NISO Alternative Assessment Metrics (Altmetrics) Initiative	http://www.niso.org/topics/tl/altmetrics_initiative
Digital Object Identifiers (DOIs)	http://www.doi.org/factsheets.html
ORCID	Distinguishes one researcher/author from another (https://orcid.org)

Librarianship has always had standards; but the more we invoke technology, the more standards come into play. Those that seek to search databases effectively need to have a basic understanding of and appreciation for these underlying standards.

Think a bit about how database standards work:

- Standards build upon other standards (standards as building blocks).

- Standards allow for identification of resources (standards as identifiers).

- Standards allow for disambiguation of similar things (standards as clarifiers).

- Standards allow for interlinking (standards as collaboration tools).

Although most standards are not well-known to the public at-large, other standards are well-known and are clearly instantiated in our culture. The International Standard Book Number, or ISBN, is an example of a nearly universally understood standard.

Field, Records, and Tables

Before you begin to learn to search online databases, you need to understand how they work and their underlying structures. Perhaps the easiest way to learn about databases is to build upon what most people likely already know, Microsoft Excel. When you open a blank Excel document, you notice a series of empty boxes, referred to as cells or fields. The cells can take on various characteristics: number, currency, accounting, short or long date, time, percentage, fraction, scientific, or text. In Excel, the format of the data in the cell affects both the display of the data as well as how the data can be searched.

A date cell, or field, can be displayed in a variety of ways, such as 1/1/2018; Jan. 1, 2018; January 1, 2018; 1 January 2018; and so forth. Excel stores dates in an efficient manner, with January 1, 1900, being represented by the number "1" and January 1, 2019, being stored as "43464"—the number of days from January 1, 1900 (Hart Davis 2015). The display of the date is merely a cultural convention for user convenience. This just happens to be the way Excel stores dates. Library databases may store dates in a different manner. My point is that you need to have an understanding of underlying information storage. Having this background enables you to know how to retrieve information from databases.

Like Excel, databases store information in various formats, including textual, date, numerical, currency, and additional formats to handle images, video content, and sound files. In online library databases, most fields will be textual in nature and contain such information as author(s); title; source title (e.g., journal name); subject and keywords; and abstract. Because these fields vary in terms of length, they are considered "variable-length fields." This means that the amount of data can be flexible, although not infinite. The other type of field is less exciting but very powerful: fixed fields. Fixed fields economize space in a database. They are also a shorthand way of referring to a limited number of possibilities. For example, "eng" is a common fixed field value for an item in the English language.

A database record consists of a collection of fields. Figure 2.1 shows an example of data exported in rows and columns. The rows represent records in a database. In this case, the data is economic census data downloaded from the *American FactFinder* database. The entire figure is a table; rows 12–20 are individual records, and each box is a cell. The columns are fields containing the same kinds of information all the way down the column.

	Geographic area name	2012 NAICS code	Meaning of 2012 NAICS code	Year	Percent	Number of es	Establishmer	Number of en	Annual payro	Production, d	Productio		al cost of	Total value of	Value added	Capital expen
10												**Field**				
11					**Record**											
12	Colorado	21111	Oil and	2012				367,096	4,322	8,206	588,982	3,...1,154 (r)	12,472,627	5,942,990 (r)	6,741,517 (r)
13	Colorado	21211		2012	0		2,219	182,172	3,823	152,896	311,004	1,103,947	863,558	70,915
14	Colorado	21222	Gold ore	2012			747	58,100	546	1,571				
15	Colorado	21223	Copper,	2012	0 (r)	3	0	26	D	D	30	D	D	D	D	2,429 (r)
16	Colorado	21229	Other	2012	0	9 (r)	4 (r)	1,040 (r)	D	D	1,708 (r)	D	D	D
17	Colorado	21231	Stone	2012	0 (r)	55	11	620	29,324	442	925	21,417	38,456	D	65,131 (r)	D
18	Colorado	21232	Sand,	2012	0 (r)	49	7	497	23,719	D	631	14,307	D	D	10,592	D
19	Colorado	21239	Other	2012	0	7	3	903	38,010	D	1,516	35,251	D	D	276,534	D
20	Colorado	21311	Support	2012	0 (r)	653	169	18,074	1,190,064	13,602	26,523	910,759	990,969	5,000,683	5,985,786 (r)	976,072 (r)

Figure 2.1. Information downloaded from American FactFinder showing data in rows (like individual records in online databases) and columns (like database fields).

Levelling the reading gap: A socio-spatial study of school **libraries** and reading in Singapore.

Authors:	Loh, Chin Ee. National Institute of Education, Nanyang Technological University, Singapore, chinee.loh@nie.edu.sg
Address:	Loh, Chin Ee, chinee.loh@nie.edu.sg
Source:	Literacy, Vol 50(1), Jan, 2016. pp. 3-13.
Page Count:	11
Publisher:	United Kingdom : Wiley-Blackwell Publishing Ltd.
Other Journal Titles:	Reading: Literacy & Language
Other Publishers:	United Kingdom : Blackwell Publishing
ISSN:	1741-4350 (Print) 1467-9345 (Electronic)
Language:	English
Keywords:	reading, social class, Singapore, socio-spatial, case study, school **libraries**
Abstract:	This article takes a comparative socio-spatial approach at the intersection of social class and reading politics to provide a fresh way of examining school reading policies and practices, unearthing previously hidden spaces of inequity for reading intervention. The juxtaposition of two nested case studies in Singapore, one of an elite all-boys' school and another of a co-educational government school with students in different academic tracks, revealed inequitable practices, specifically in the designs and uses of school **library** spaces between schools serving different social classes. The study argues that attempts to design reading interventions should move away from the view of student-as-problem to structure-as-problem in order to discover new perspectives for reading intervention. Additionally, this study demonstrates how foregrounding social class in educational research is necessary for effective design of educational strategies that aim to transform education and society by narrowing the gap between students from different social classes. (PsycINFO Database Record (c) 2016 APA, all rights reserved)
Document Type:	Journal Article
Subjects:	*Reading; *School Based Intervention; *School **Libraries**; *Social Class
PsycINFO Classification:	Curriculum & Programs & Teaching Methods (3530)
Population:	Human Male Female
Location:	Singapore
Grant Sponsorship:	Sponsor: Nanyang Technological University, National Institute of Education (NIE), Office of Educational Research (OER), English Language and Literature Academic Group, Singapore Grant Number: 8/13 Other Details: Start-Up Grant Recipients: No recipient indicated
Methodology:	Nonclinical Case Study
Format Covered:	Electronic
Publication Type:	Journal; Peer Reviewed Journal

Figure 2.2. *PsycINFO* record (EBSCO) showing variety of fields. ©2017 EBSCO Industries, Inc. All rights reserved.

This representation of fields and records is very much like how data lives in online databases.

Now that you have a basic introduction to records and fields, let's consider their underlying structure in the context of an online database record. Take a look at figure 2.2, a record from *PsycINFO* (EBSCOhost interface).

You see a record with a series of fields labeled with field names (Authors, Address, Source, etc.). There is a way for you to view a bit more of the data stored in the database fields. By using the EBSCOhost "Export" feature and selecting "Direct export in RIS format," you can see some additional information (figure 2.3).

```
TI- Levelling the reading gap: A socio-spatial study of school libraries and reading in Singapore.
AU- Loh, Chin Ee
AF  Loh, Chin Ee, chinee.loh@nie.edu.sg, National Institute of Education, Nanyang Technological University, Singapore
AD- Loh, Chin Ee, chinee.loh@nie.edu.sg
SO- Literacy
S2- Reading: Literacy & Language
VI- 50
IP- 1
SD- Jan, 2016
YR- 2016
PM- Jan, 2016
PG- 3-13
PC- 11
SP- 3
PU- United Kingdom : Wiley-Blackwell Publishing Ltd.
P2- United Kingdom : Blackwell Publishing
PN- 11
SN- 1741-4350, Print
SN- 1467-9345, Electronic
DO- 10.1111/lit.12067
LA- English
KP- reading
KP- social class
KP- Singapore
KP- socio-spatial
KP- case study
KP- school libraries
SU- Reading; School Based Intervention; School Libraries; Social Class
AB- This article takes a comparative socio-spatial approach at the intersection of social class and reading politics t
MJ- Reading; School Based Intervention; School Libraries; Social Class
CL- Curriculum & Programs & Teaching Methods (3530)
PO- Human (10)
PO- Male (30)
PO- Female (40)
LO- Singapore
GR- Sponsor: Nanyang Technological University, National Institute of Education (NIE), Office of Educational Research (
MD- Nonclinical Case Study
PT- Journal
PT- Peer Reviewed Journal
AT- Journal Article
MT- Electronic
RD- 20151214
LU- 20160418
AN- 2015-55718-001
FR- 47
FR- Y
CP- Published by John Wiley & Sons Ltd.. UKLA. 2015
UR- http://du.idm.oclc.org/login?url=http://search.ebscohost.com/login.aspx?direct=true&db=psyh&AN=2015-55718-001&site
```

Figure 2.3. *PsycINFO* record with fields exported in a tagged format. ©2017 EBSCO Industries, Inc. All rights reserved.

Notice that information from the "population" fields (with field tag "PO" in figure 2.3) contains a greater degree of detail in the exported record above. The real values stored in the three PO fields in the database are apparently not "human," "male," and "female" but rather "10," "30," and "40." That's because it takes less space to store these numerical values than to store the meaning of the values. These values are fixed field values rather than variable-length field values.

Imagine if all database information were in a simple text file with no delineation of differences of information type. Keyword searching could certainly be done across all of this, but important distinctions such as name as author versus name as subject of article would be lost. Articles about a particular company could not be distinguished from articles that simply mention the name of a company. Author affiliations could not be distinguished from other mentions of colleges, universities, or research institutes. This is where the value of information stored in fields comes in.

Databases are based on standards, and they have an underlying structure. Without this structure, all the information would be just like a pile of books in a heap: lots of information there, but no way to figure it out. These structural divisions, or fields, are arrays of information patterns organized logically. Authors and creators are kept in one kind of box. Title is kept in another, and so on.

In the "old days" of library databases, searching a database was very expensive. Library-related searching was often mediated by a professional librarian so that users would not incur as much cost. In the mid-1990s, an online database might cost $30 to $60 per hour just to run searches, and then anywhere from $0.75 to $1.00 per record just to retrieve the records with abstracts (Jacsó and Tenopir 2001). No full text, just abstracts! With prices like that, searchers really needed to know the structure of fields and how to search them. The economics of things forced the issue. Librarians, not information seekers, did the searching so as to save money.

Today, some databases provide more extensive documentation about what fields contain what information and how they can be searched. For example, figure 2.4 shows an excerpt from a document about searchable fields within the ProQuest *Library Science Database*.

Online library databases were high-priced and highly valued in the 1980s and early 1990s, but users received less access for more cost. Today, universities bear the brunt of the pricing, and the high cost of database

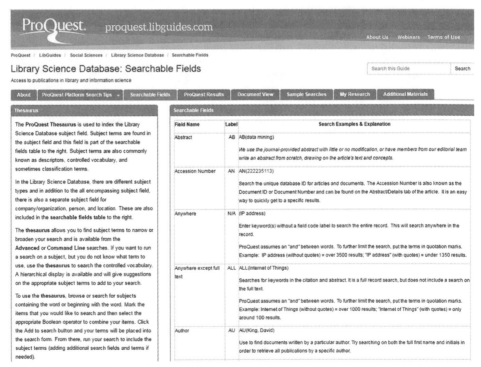

Figure 2.4. Details of database fields and how to search them. (*Source:* https://proquest.libguides.com/librarysciencedatabase/fields. The screen shots and their contents are published with permission of ProQuest LLC. Further reproduction is prohibited without permission).

access is masked by the "big deals" entered into by universities and colleges that can afford them. Rather than subscribing to selected, relevant journal titles, these package deals offer many more titles, for a similar charge, but a high percentage of the titles may be out of the library's scope of interest. As a result, access has greatly increased, but, sadly, users generally have little appreciation for the high costs and have become sloppy in their search practices. Hopefully, this brief background provides an appreciation for the technologies available today for maximizing retrieval and relevancy.

Exploring Field Code Consistency

Publisher databases and databases that come from a single issuing source (e.g., *ERIC, Medline, Agricola*) tend to have consistency in field codes. Large database aggregators have a tougher job. They attempt to unite into a single interface a variety of records from various sources that have differing field tags. This is necessary because of the varying content. A business database may necessitate the use of Standard Industrial Classification (SIC) codes or North American Industrial Classification System (NAICS) codes that a literature database does not need.

To illustrate this point, I did a search in *Business Source Complete* for online databases. Here are some of the records that showed up near the top of the results that contain differences in fields displayed (with bolded field labels highlighting variations in fields):

Record 1:

Title: Considerations and Benefits of Implementing an Online Database tool for Business Continuity

Authors

Source

Document Type

Subject Terms

Author-Supplied Keywords

Abstract

Author Affiliations

ISSN

Accession Number

Images

Record 2:

Title: The Cue-of-the-Cloud Effect: When Reminders of Online Information Availability Increase Purchase Intentions and Choice

Authors

Source

Document Type

Subject Terms

Author-Supplied Keywords

NAICS/Industry Codes

Abstract

Author Affiliations

ISSN

DOI

Accession Number

Publisher Logo

Images

Record 3:

Title: Online Inventory Seeks Workers (cover story)

Authors

Source

Document Type

Subject Terms

Geographic Terms

People

Abstract

ISSN

Accession Number

Record 4:

Title: CORRECTION [A correction to article "45 Fast Financial Fixes" that was published in September 2016 issue is presented.]

Source

Document Type

Subject Terms

Abstract

Full Text Word Count

ISSN

Accession Number

Record 5:

Title: Closing the Skills Gap: Key Learnings for Employers and Job Seekers

Authors

Source

Document Type

Subject Terms

Company/Entity

Abstract

Author Affiliations

ISSN

DOI

Accession Number

Publisher Logo

In each representation of a record, the title is shown, followed by the field labels contained in the rest of the record. The record numbers in the field representation are not the order of records in the search results; they are used for ease of reference in the discussion.

Note the variation in fields present in the five records. Record 2 contains two fields not present in record 1 (NAICS/Industry Codes and DOI). Record 5 has a Company/Entity field, but no NAICS field. Record 4 is the only record that contains Full Text Word Count, although that is theoretically possible from each of the records. It should be obvious that EBSCO's *Business Source* database collects records from many different sources and combines them into a single database. This is not a flaw, it's just something you need to keep in mind when searching.

Variable-Length Fields

To understand how library databases work, let's start with more familiar territory: records from the library catalog. Although it is not so easy to see the "under-the-hood" display from most databases, most online library catalogs provide easy access to machine-readable cataloging (MARC) records. This will assist you in understanding the important distinction between variable-length fields and fixed fields.

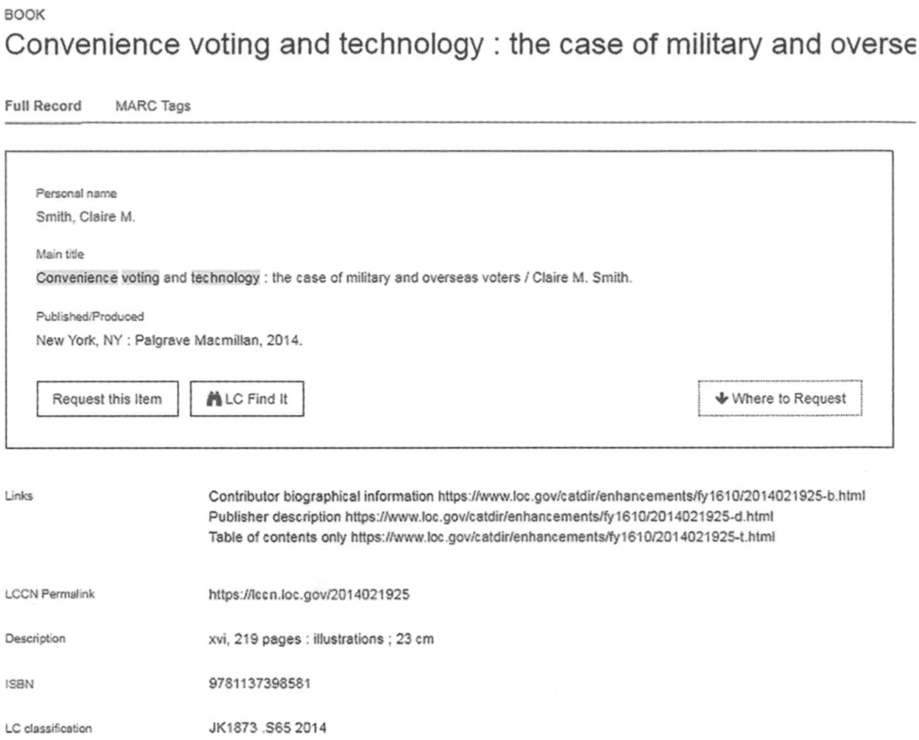

BOOK

Convenience voting and technology : the case of military and overse

Full Record   MARC Tags

Personal name
Smith, Claire M.

Main title
Convenience voting and technology : the case of military and overseas voters / Claire M. Smith.

Published/Produced
New York, NY : Palgrave Macmillan, 2014.

Request this Item	🔍 LC Find It	⬇ Where to Request

Links   Contributor biographical information https://www.loc.gov/catdir/enhancements/fy1610/2014021925-b.html
                                 Publisher description https://www.loc.gov/catdir/enhancements/fy1610/2014021925-d.html
                                 Table of contents only https://www.loc.gov/catdir/enhancements/fy1610/2014021925-t.html

LCCN Permalink   https://lccn.loc.gov/2014021925

Description   xvi, 219 pages : illustrations ; 23 cm

ISBN   9781137398581

LC classification   JK1873 .S65 2014

Figure 2.5. Standard view of a catalog record from https://catalog.loc.gov/.

Let's take a record for a book from the Library of Congress's online catalog as an example (figure 2.5).

What you see in figure 2.5 is a user-friendly representation of selected fields from a catalog record. There are many more fields than are shown in this card catalog–like view, and to fully understand how fields work, you need to look at the underlying MARC record for this book (figure 2.6).

Note the field tags to the far left. The 000 series fields are for control numbers and various fixed field information that is addressed in the next section. The remaining fields are all variable-length fields of various kinds. The 100s are main entry fields for various kinds of authorship identification and disambiguation. The 200s are for title and edition statements. The 300s are for physical description or related administrative purposes. Series statements are found in the 400 fields. 500 fields are reserved for various kinds of notes. Added entries of various types and linking data occupy the 700 and 800 fields (Library of Congress 2017). But even this representation of the data is not the way the information is stored in the database.

To see how the data are really stored, we need to look at the raw MARC record, as seen in figure 2.7.

Here we see numbers and letters all run together with no line breaks. Before trying to make some sense of this record, which is in "MARC communication format," make note of the labeled MARC fields we saw in figure 2.6 above.

```
000     02309cam a2200361 i 4500
001     18185400
005     20160909095707.0
008     140612s2014    nyua     b    001 0 eng
906     __      |a 7 |b cbc |c orignew |d 1 |e ecip |f 20 |g y-gencatlg
925     0_      |a acquire |b 1 shelf copy |x policy default |e claim1 2015-04-30
955     __      |b re23 2014-06-12 |i re23 2014-06-12 to Dewey |w xl03 2014-06-16 |a xn11 2
010     __      |a  2014021925
020     __      |a 9781137398581
040     __      |a DLC |b eng |c DLC |e rda |d DLC
042     __      |a pcc
050     00      |a JK1873 |b .S65 2014
082     00      |a 324.6/5 |2 23
100     1_      |a Smith, Claire M.
245     10      |a Convenience voting and technology : |b the case of military and overseas
264     _1      |a New York, NY : |b Palgrave Macmillan, |c 2014.
300     __      |a xvi, 219 pages : |b illustrations ; |c 23 cm
336     __      |a text |b txt |2 rdacontent
337     __      |a unmediated |b n |2 rdamedia
338     __      |a volume |b nc |2 rdacarrier
504     __      |a Includes bibliographical references and index.
505     0_      |a Introduction : "my polling place is my living room" -- Who are UOCAVA vo
650     _0      |a Absentee voting |z United States.
650     _0      |a Transnational voting |z United States.
650     _0      |a Soldiers |x Suffrage |z United States.
650     _0      |a Voting |x Technological innovations |z United States.
856     42      |3 Contributor biographical information |u https://www.loc.gov/catdir/enhan
856     42      |3 Publisher description |u https://www.loc.gov/catdir/enhancements/fy1610/
856     41      |3 Table of contents only |u https://www.loc.gov/catdir/enhancements/fy1610
```

Figure 2.6. MARC record view (with no word wrap). *Source:* https://catalog.loc.gov/.

```
02309cam··2200361·i·
45000010009000000050017000090080041000269060045000679250062001129550215001740100017003890200018004060
40002800424042000800452050002200460082001600482100002100498245010200519264004700621300004500668336002
60071333700280073933800270076750400510079450500610000845650003601485650004101521650003901562650005401160
185601070165000840101701603000930185418185400201603090957 07.0140612s2014···nyua····b····001·0·
eng····a7bcbccorignewd1eecipf20gy-gencatlg0 aacquireb1 shelf·copyxpolicy·defaulteclaim1··
2015-04-30··bre23·2014-06-12ire23·2014-06-12·to·Deweywxl03·2014-06-16axn11·2015 05 11 P copy
rec'd., to CIP ver.fre13·2015-05-20·Copy·1·Barcode·00431342017·to·Calmtre13·2015-05-20·Copy·2·
Barcode··00431342005·to·Discard··a··2014021925··a9781137398581··aDLCbengcDLCerdadDLC··
apcc00aJK1873b.S65 201400a324.6/52231·aSmith, Claire·M.10aConvenience·voting·and·
technology·:bthe·case·of·military·and·overseas·voters·/cClaire·M.·Smith.·1aNew·York,·NY·
:bPalgrave·¶
Macmillan,c2014.··axvi,·219·pages·:billustrations·;c23·cm··atextbtxt2rdacontent··
aunmediatedbn2rdamedia··avolumebnc2rdacarrier··aIncludes·bibliographical·references·and·
index.0·aIntroduction·:·"my·polling place is·my·living·room"·--·Who·are·UOCAVA·voters?·--·The·
development·of·military·and·overseas·voting·rights·in·the·U.S·--·Evaluating·voting·policy·success·:·
aggregate·outcomes·--·Evaluating·voting·policy·success·:·voter·satisfaction·--·Defending·votes·:·the·
unique·problems·of·military·voters·--·Voting·technology,·privacy,·and·security·concerns·--·The·future·
of·convenience·voting·for·overseas·and·domestic·voters·--·Appendix·I:·Chronology·:·significant·events·
in·the·development·of·military·and·overseas·voting·--·Appendix·II:·Changes·in·electronic·transmission·
methods·and·voting·outcomes,·2012·vs.·2008.·0aAbsentee·votingzUnited·States.·0aTransnational·
votingzUnited·States.·0aSoldiersxSuffragezUnited·States.·0aVotingxTechnological·
innovationszUnited·States.423Contributor·¶
biographical·informationuhttps://www.loc.gov/catdir/enhancements/fy1610/2014021925-
b.html423Publisher·descriptionuhttps://www.loc.gov/catdir/enhancements/fy1610/2014021925-
d.html413Table·of·contents·onlyuhttps://www.loc.gov/catdir/enhancements/fy1610/2014021925-t.html¶
```

Figure 2.7. "Raw" MARC record.

001	020	264	650
005	040	300	650
008	042	336	650
906	050	337	650
925	082	338	856
955	100	504	856
010	245	505	856

Now look at this marked-up version of figure 2.7 with field tags in bold (figure 2.8).

What you notice in the larger, bolded numbers section is an exact representation of the field labels previously noted. Following the section with all the numbers is all the textual information from the MARC record run together. By now, it should be obvious what is happening. The beginning section specifies which fields are present in the record and what the starting and stopping points for that field are. This information is sufficient to tell an integrated library system (ILS) how to display the record—when a field starts and where it stops and the next field begins.

Some variable-length fields may iterate, that is, there may be more than one instance of the field. Consider the field that contains subject headings

02309cam 2200361 i

4500**001**000900000**005**001700009**008**0041000269**06**004500067**925**00620011
2**955**021500174**010**001700389**020**001800406**040**002800424**042**00080045205
0002200460**082**001600048**2100**002100498**245**010200519**264**004700621**300**00
4500668**336**002600713**337**002800739**338**002700767**504**005100794**505**064000
845**650**003601485**650**004101521**650**003901562**650**005401601**856**010701655
856009201762**856**009301854-18185400-20160309095707.0-140612s2014
nyua   b   001 0 eng - a7bcbccorignewd1eecipf20gy-gencatlg-0 -
aacquireb1 shelf copyxpolicy defaulteclaim1 2015-04-30- bre23 2014-
06-12ire23 2014-06-12 to Deweywxl03 2014-06-16axn11 2015-05-11 2 copy
rec'd., to CIP ver.fre13 2015-05-20 Copy 1 Barcode 00431342017 to
Calmtre13 2015-05-20 Copy 2 Barcode 00431342005 to Discard- a
2014021925- a9781137398581- aDLCbengcDLCerdadDLC- apcc-00aJK1873-
b.S65 2014-00a324.6/5223-1 aSmith, Claire M.-10aConvenience voting and
technology :bthe case of military and overseas voters /cClaire M.
Smith.- 1aNew York, NY :bPalgrave
Macmillan,c2014.- axvi, 219 pages :billustrations ;c23 cm- atext-
btxt2rdacontent- aunmediatedbn2rdamedia- avolumebnc2rdacarrier- -
aIncludes bibliographical references and index.-0 aIntroduction : "my
polling place is my living room" -- Who are UOCAVA voters? -- The
development of military and overseas voting rights in the U.S --
Evaluating voting policy success : aggregate outcomes -- Evaluating
voting policy success : voter satisfaction -- Defending votes : the
unique problems of military voters -- Voting technology, privacy, and
security concerns -- The future of convenience voting for overseas and
domestic voters -- Appendix I: Chronology : significant events in the
development of military and overseas voting -- Appendix II: Changes in
electronic transmission methods and voting outcomes, 2012 vs.
2008.- 0aAbsentee votingzUnited States.- 0aTransnational votingzUnited
States.- 0aSoldiersxSuffragezUnited States.- 0aVotingxTechnological
innovationszUnited States.-423Contributor
biographical information-
uhttps://www.loc.gov/catdir/enhancements/fy1610/2014021925-b.html-42-
3Publisher description-
uhttps://www.loc.gov/catdir/enhancements/fy1610/2014021925-d.html-41-
3Table of contents only-
uhttps://www.loc.gov/catdir/enhancements/fy1610/2014021925-t.html

Figure 2.8. MARC Communication Format view of record (text enlarged and bolded to show numeric field labels).

or descriptors. There will likely be more than one subject for an individual record. These fields are iterating fields. However, certain other fields do not iterate. Control numbers are a unique way to identify a record within a database. One and only one such number is necessary. The 245 title field in a MARC record never iterates. Iterating fields are a crude way that flat databases can look a bit like relational databases.

Relational databases can represent information in one-to-one relationships, as Excel spreadsheets do, as well as one-to-many relationships. Microsoft Access is an example of a relational database that is relatively easy to set up. However, because online library databases are not currently stored in relational tables, we don't need to get into that at this point.

To summarize, variable-length fields contain the textual information that we can read and understand without external aids. They convey the basic author/creator, title, descriptions, publication information, and subject terms.

Fixed Fields

To see how fixed fields work, you can examine the Library of Congress's online manual *MARC 21 Format for Bibliographic Data* (Library of Congress 2017). Part of a MARC record, known as the *leader*, contains letters or numbers that are stored in precise positions. These character positions, together with the codes that carry meaning, are a space-saving way of conveying information that otherwise would take up a lot more space. To illustrate this, here are possible values (in this case letters) that can occupy space "06 - Type of record":

06 - Type of record
    a - Language material
    c - Notated music
    d - Manuscript notated music
    e - Cartographic material
    f - Manuscript cartographic material
    g - Projected medium
    i - Nonmusical sound recording
    j - Musical sound recording
    k - Two-dimensional nonprojectable graphic
    m - Computer file
    o - Kit
    p - Mixed materials
    r - Three-dimensional artifact or naturally occurring object
    t - Manuscript language material

In addition to book records, records for other information formats also have fixed fields, and they can convey many kinds of information. Fixed field data can contain audience age groupings; intended audience; material types;

publication types; language; population group (whether human or animal or male, female, or transgender); and methodology—all examples from the *PsycINFO* database. They can contain historical eras (as *Historical Abstracts* and *America: History and Life* do). Most limiters or facets that appear with search results will be data extracted from fixed field data. One of the wonderful features of current databases is their ability to leverage this fixed field data by producing limiters. What is really happening in these cases is that extra benefit is being derived from the many long years of following standards.

Online Database Indexing

Perhaps the easiest way to think about online database indexing is to consider how indexing worked with print periodical indexes. Print indexes were typically arranged by author and subject, and perhaps other access points as well.

To really oversimplify things, there are basically two kinds of indexes in the print world: inward-facing indexes and outward-facing indexes. Inward-facing indexes are the kind you see in indexes in the back of a book. Words and concepts within the book are indexed for ease of access. The author's nomenclature and word preferences are kept, as there is a single voice throughout the book (as long as it is not an edited book with different chapters by various authors).

The outward-facing index (e.g., a journal article index) does not adhere to the word choices of a single author; it must unify various concepts under a single subject term. For example, suppose you have an article where one author prefers to use the term "road" and another article with a different author whose preference is the term "highway." Indexing would endeavor to bring these concepts together somehow, typically by preferring one term over another and having a "see" reference from the unauthorized term over to the authorized term. Online indexing does the same thing.

An index is only as good as the skill of the indexer. It's just a reality of language. Although we can look to indexes, print or online, as a kind of authority, they are only as authoritative as the person doing the indexing. We have to ask whether the indexer truly understood the article or chapter being indexed.

We have been discussing indexing of subjects, but there is another aspect of indexing when it comes to computer access and speed. To make the content of databases discoverable, computerized indexing processes must occur. Let's make an analogy to a directory of names, such as a print telephone directory. If the directory contains 50,000 unsorted names, you may need to read through most of the names before you find the one you are looking for. Indexing makes order out of chaos by sorting in alphabetical order so that you can jump to the relevant section. Computer indexing likewise has complex referencing systems of indexing so that users can quickly access database content.

We don't search the Internet "live" in real time. When we visit a search engine, such as Google, we are really searching Google's indexing of the

Internet. It takes Google much time to scour Web content, collect it, and index it for fast retrieval. The same thing holds true for library databases. It would simply take too long if we had to wait for live searching of database content. The information is compiled, compressed, and indexed for quick retrieval.

Database Updating

Database content is added incrementally. This is important to understand for a number of reasons. If you are waiting to find out new articles covered by a favorite journal, then an online index would not be the quickest way. Rather, daily monitoring of the journal's Web site would be the best way. It may take a month or two for database content to reflect newly published content. The records may not show up immediately because they need to be properly indexed. Not only does basic metadata need to be created—describing such things as author/creator, title, pages of print, or size of digital file—but subject metadata needs to be added by professional indexers. Some database content is added in stages. For example, *PubMed* includes articles from medical journals soon after they are published, but the full indexing with medical subject headings (MeSH) are not added to the records until sometime later. There is more on this in chapter 10.

If currency of information is of prime importance to a researcher, then the best thing to do is to monitor a specific journal's Web site daily. Don't wait for databases to load content or for Google Scholar to catch it. At least it's not like the old days of waiting for the U.S. Mail to deliver print journal copies to the library!

When Databases Fail

Databases will fail. I don't mean when the power goes out or when a server is down for maintenance; I'm talking about problems with the data within the database itself. There are many possible reasons for failure, so this list is only some of the possibilities.

Incomplete Data Loads

Missing records often occur when libraries migrate their catalog data from one integrated library system (ILS) to another. They also can occur when loading vendor records into a local ILS. I have experienced this myself when loading tens of thousands of vendor-supplied records from the Early English Books Online (EEBO) into our local catalog (III Sierra at that time). For whatever reason, records may have offending data in a field that the ILS record loader rejects.

The same kind of thing can happen with vendor databases, especially those that load data on a regular basis from multiple sources. The big three aggregators, Gale, EBSCO, and ProQuest, all experience hiccups with the sources that supply them with data. Vendors are always responsive and thankful when librarians contact them and point out these errors.

Incomplete or Corrupt Indexing

On September 13, 2017, I searched the *Ingenta Connect* database for a review written by Amy Hoseth on Google Scholar in the *Charleston Advisor* journal. No results were found. Yet, I have the article on my computer, and I can clearly browse to the January 2011 issue that contains the review by Hoseth. I rechecked my search by author: no results. I searched again by title: again, no results. Of course, I don't know the reason for this omission, but it's a reminder that indexing and databases can sometimes let us down.

Let's face it: no database is perfect all the time. Database corruption happens on occasion. When I have notified database vendors of problems, they are generally quick to resolve things. Without naming names, several years ago, I noticed an apparent import problem with several databases where every subject entry had an extra "nnnn" appended to every subject. I do have an exact screen capture of this situation, but I don't want to embarrass the vendor. Here is an exact representation of that error (bold added):

> Title: Ilford move secures black-and-white future
> Source: British Journal of Photography, v. 152 (March 9, 2005) p. 5
> Descriptors: Ilford Ltd.; Black and white photography. **nnnn**
> ISSN: 00071196

In some cases, the "nnnn" was appended to the previous word without intervening punctuation or space, meaning that the indexing of individual words was corrupted. Fortunately, this mistake was corrected across many thousands of records soon after I reported it.

In another situation with a news database, there were no articles for the subject "Russia" for the early 2000s. This was an obvious case of records not being properly loaded or indexed. I contacted the company, and the situation was resolved shortly afterward. The point is that nearly any time you have a data migration or data import, loss or indexing errors are possible. This is understandable in a world where data were created under different conditions over time. This is something to keep in mind the next time your library is considering migrating to a new ILS.

General Downtime

Not only do databases occasionally contain corrupted data, but in larger academic libraries with hundreds of databases, it is probably safe to say that at least one database is down or not properly accessible at any given time. This may be because of problems on the vendor's side, problems with the library proxy system, or other general problems. It's just a fact of the world we live in. It's one of the trade-offs of having all the advantages of instant online access to information, as opposed to having the time-consuming endeavor of looking up information in print indexing tools. It is not uncommon for databases to be down for weeks or months before anyone even notices that there is a problem.

Defaults

Having examined the underlying structures of online databases, let's cover the considerations when searching databases as well as the technologies that enable them to work together. Many databases have a simple search box with the option of doing more advanced searches if desired. Advanced searching generally provides a search box for searching within a specific field. But most basic search boxes are actually searching a combination of fields. Of course, they often don't tell you that. You, the database expert you are now becoming, have to figure that out for yourself. When you search with the initial search box, you are searching the default search fields.

Defaults are used for your database search experience if you do nothing—that is, if you just enter terms without changing anything—no selecting of fields from the pull-down menus or selecting check boxes for limiters. But which fields are being searched and which fields are not being searched when you use the default settings? Very often, search engines don't say.

Some databases are set to search metadata only by default. That is, they search basic fields, such as author, title, subject, abstract, or summary, but not the numerical fields (e.g., ISBN, ISSN, DUNS number, NAICS number) nor the full text (if that option is available within the database). Examples of such databases are most of the EBSCOhost databases, such as *Academic Search*, *Business Search*, and H.W. Wilson databases that now run under the EBSCOhost interface. These EBSCOhost databases have the option of searching full text, but the user needs to intentionally make that change; it is not the default. On the other hand, some databases do, in fact, search full text by default. An example of this is ProQuest's *Dissertations and Theses Global* database, which searches "anywhere" by default. Defaults make a huge difference in the number of retrieved results. In this case, users need to intentionally change the search scope to "anywhere except full text" to search metadata only.

Another consideration is how the Boolean operators (see chapter 4) operate by default. In the EBSCOhost platform, by default, plurals are searched when singular forms are entered (as if you had entered an OR search), as long as they are not enclosed in quotes.

How do you know which fields are searched in the default search? Very often, vendors don't even state this in their documentation. Yet, it is important to know which fields are searched by default and which ones are not. We need to develop a test for this.

Let's take EBSCO's *Academic Search* as an example. From the advanced search form, you might notice that if you do nothing (the default), the pull-down menu reads "Select a Field (optional)," but there are also other fields by which you could search (figure 2.9).

Which of these fields is searched by default? Is "TX All Text" searched? Is "AU Author" or "ISSN"? You would assume that "AB Abstract" would be indexed by default, as that is such an important field in conveying the "aboutness" of the items being indexed, but would "TK Ticker Symbol" in the above example be searched? In other words, is the "TK Ticker" field also indexed by default? How can you know?

To figure out which fields are, in fact, searched by default, we can set up a matrix of all fields within the database to keep track of what we find. Table 2.2 shows fields that are available to be searched via the pull-down menu in EBSCO's *Academic Search* database.

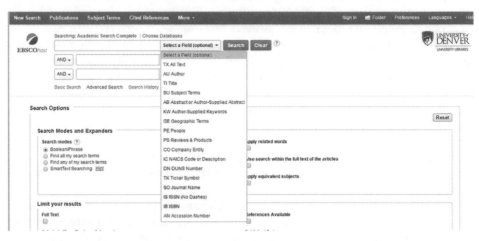

Figure 2.9. *Academic Search* pull-down menu shows available fields to search. ©2017 EBSCO Industries, Inc. All rights reserved.

Table 2.2. Setting up test for default fields from EBSCO's *Academic Search database.*

Field Label	Searched by Default?
TX All Text	[all fields in this column to be filled in by you]
AU Author	
TI Title	
SU Subject Terms	
AB Abstract of Author-Supplied Abstract	
KW Author-Supplied Keywords	
GE Geographic Terms	
PE People	
PS Reviews & Products	
CO Company Entity	
IC NAICS Code or Description	
DN DUNS Number	
TK Ticker Symbol	
SO Journal Name	
IS ISSN (No Dashes)	
IB ISBN	
AN Accession Number	

We need to set this up as a controlled experiment. For control purposes in our experiment, we need to find a field in this case that can be searched but that is unique to each record in that database. The only field that will be unique among all the records in this database will be the "AN Access Number." Let's select a record for this test that will have many of the fields we need to test, including the company-related fields. Let's take the record in figure 2.10 as our example.

Note that the accession number is 77572646. This will serve as our control mechanism. If you search for "77572646" in just the "Accession Number" field, you should get one and only one record, and that is indeed the case (figure 2.11).

Now, let's test to see if the accession number itself is indexed by default. To do this, you need to keep your first line, the "AC Accession Number" search, which is our control, but then add the access number in the default ("Select a Field") pull-down menu option (figure 2.12). Notice that the "AND Boolean" operator is being used, meaning that both the search statement on the first line of the form and that on the second line must be true.

Before you hit "Search," let's think about what is about to happen. If you retrieve this record, you will know that the accession number is in fact indexed in the default fields, as we already know that the accession number searched with the "AN" field tag retrieves only that one record, and adding a further condition to that will either prove or disprove which fields are searched in the default field search. If, however, no results are returned, then you will know that the accession number is not searched by default. Now hit "Search." You get the message: "No results were found." You can

Figure 2.10. Setting up a test to see which fields are searched in the default field search. ©2017 EBSCO Industries, Inc. All rights reserved.

conclude that the accession number is not searched by default. Think about it: why would it need to be? Every accession number is unique, so adding this data to the default search index adds nothing and only makes the default index larger for no reason.

Now let's run this same test for other fields, beginning with "TX All Text." We first need to find a string of text to test. I now open the PDF file and look for a string of text that doesn't cross over to a second line (so that my search is not obscured by line returns or strange characters). I select the string of text

Figure 2.11. Performing the default field test, phase I. ©2017 EBSCO Industries, Inc. All rights reserved.

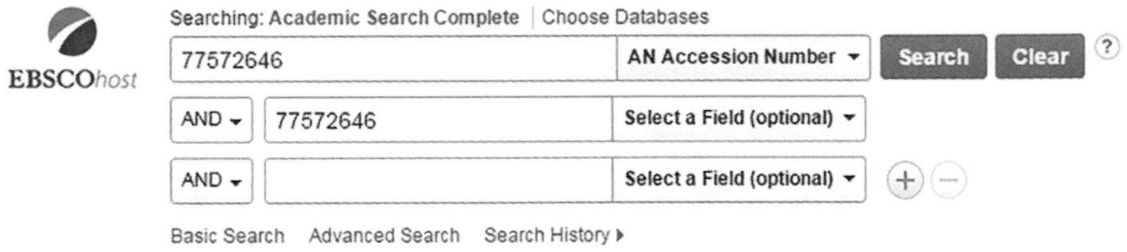

Figure 2.12. Performing the default field test, phase II. ©2017 EBSCO Industries, Inc. All rights reserved.

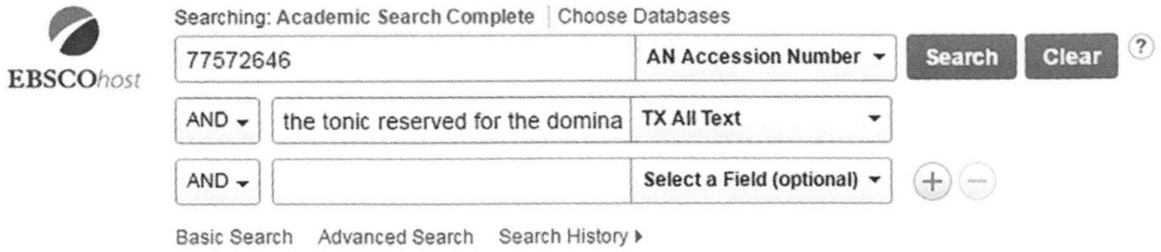

Figure 2.13. Performing the default field test on another field. ©2017 EBSCO Industries, Inc. All rights reserved.

"the tonic reserved for the dominant. Beethoven, however, did often attempt" found way down on page 89 of the article. Just to make sure that this string of text is properly indexed, I first set up my search like this (figure 2.13):

First, I always make sure that my test will work with the specific field being tested, especially when testing for full text. Sometimes full-text searches do not work properly because of faulty unchecked optical character recognition (OCR) or because of strange characters that may affect how a search will be executed. "Gremlin" characters (not a reference to fictitious mischievous creatures that cause machines to malfunction, but rather to hidden characters in an electronic text, such as a soft hyphen or line break, or even not-so-hidden characters that may have unpredictable results in searching, such as #) often cause searches within quotation marks to fail. This will tell us whether the full text is properly indexed in the database. If we retrieve this one article, we are then ready to test for the text in the default search.

Now for the test. With the accession number set as our control mechanism, we now change the pull-down menu selection from "TX All Text" to the default "Select a Field (optional)." After hitting the "Search" button, we get "No results were found," meaning that the EBSCOhost search interface does *not* search the full text of articles by default. This is a very important discovery, and the results make total sense.

Now we need to perform the same test for other indexed fields. It makes sense for the title field to be indexed by default, and indeed it is, as are the author and various subject fields (table 2.3).

Table 2.3. Sample form for testing default database fields in Business Source database.

Field Label	Searched by Default?
TX All Text	No
AU Author	Yes
TI Title	Yes
SU Subject Terms	Yes
AB Abstract of Author-Supplied Abstract	[you figure it out]
KW Author-Supplied Keywords	[you figure it out]
GE Geographic Terms	[you figure it out]
PE People	[you figure it out]
PS Reviews & Products	[you figure it out]
CO Company Entity	[you figure it out]
IC NAICS Code or Description	[you figure it out]
DN DUNS Number	[you figure it out]
TK Ticker Symbol	[you figure it out]
SO Journal Name	[you figure it out]
IS ISSN (No Dashes)	[you figure it out]
IB ISBN	[you figure it out]
AN Accession Number	No

Now I will leave it up to you to test the other fields to see whether they are indexed by default or not using the same method I have laid out in table 2.3.

Why is doing this important? If you want to know why searches succeed or fail, you need to know how search engines execute their searches. You need to have confidence when you tell users that a database either contains the information they need or it does not. You need to know the scope of databases and how searches are performed within that scope.

What Are Keywords Anyway?

Keyword searching is very often the default type of search across most search engines. It is the most common kind of search performed by users and even by librarians. But what is a *keyword search*? What are we really searching when we perform this kind of search? Keyword searching is very powerful, especially when you consider that it is a relatively new convention. Think about keywords in the context of the history of searching. For journal articles, indexes were historically the only way to access article content. Most indexes could be accessed by author, title, or subject. In the days of print journal article indexes, there simply was no keyword searching; the only access points were authors, titles, or subjects.

In the computer age, that all changed. You can presently search across most metadata fields with keywords, not merely authors, titles, and subjects. This truly transformed the way searching can be done. Let's take Gale's *Academic OneFile* as an example. When you enter this database, you are presented with a single search box in the basic search interface. When you enter keywords into the search box, what is really happening? To really see what fields are being searched by a default keyword search, you need to perform the tedious testing we just demonstrated in the preceding section on defaults. Aside from the more obscure fields, you can be assured that a keyword search will find information from author, title, abstract, and subject fields.

However, some databases have a very different default. Several ProQuest databases have the default field as "Anywhere." As previously noted, searches in ProQuest *Dissertations and Theses Global* have the default field set to search anywhere—that is, in the metadata and in the full text. For this reason, a keyword search will produce an almost "Google-like" number of results. Doing a search for "cats" in this database brings back 362,106 results. The problem is that the keywords will be found either in the metadata, in the full text, or in both. But if I flip my search to "Anywhere except full text – ALL," I get 10,373 results. This is still a lot of results but only a fraction of the more universal search, and it produces records that are more likely about the topic being searched rather than merely having a passing mention of the term.

Control Numbers

Control numbers take us back to our discussion on standards earlier in this chapter. Imagine how difficult it would be to search for information on a complex company with many subsidiaries. We need some kind of standard control number to help us disambiguate the situation. *Hoovers Online* database, owned by Dunn & Bradstreet, assigns proprietary control numbers they call a data universal numbering system (or DUNS number, which also reminds us of their name) to uniquely identify a company, a company headquarters, and a subsidiary. These control numbers can then be used to more effectively search for precise company information in such databases as EBSCO's *Business Source Complete*.

Authors are nearly impossible to provide authority control over in magazine and journal articles. There are simply too many authors, too little information about the authors, and too little time to do all the identification and disambiguation necessary for the level of control that the Library of Congress's authority file has for book authors. But the ORCID (Open Researcher and Contributor ID) control numbers can be a way to get closer to "all and only" materials authored by a particular author. Look up these control numbers on the official Web site at orcid.org. Then use the ORCID control number to search *Web of Science*, one of the few databases where one can search by this control number. In the future, I think ORCID numbers will be increasingly used in database searching for the important task of keeping track of authors.

Most people even outside of libraries are familiar with International Standard Book Numbers (ISBNs). There is however a problem with ISBNs and with using them in searching databases. ISBNs serve the book trade industry better than they serve the library community. First, ISBNs refer to a particular manifestation of a work: paperback, clothbound, or electronic. The same work may have multiple ISBNs. This can help when ordering books, but it is often not the best way to search for users who simply need a work and don't care about the manifestation. Second, there are two systems of numbers: a 10-digit number, or ISBN10, and the newer 13-digit number, or ISBN13.

In table 2.4, you see various editions of Stephen King's novel *The Shining*. Some records have an ISBN10 and others an ISBN13. The final digit is a "check digit" used to detect errors in data entry. In the ISBN13s, the first 3 digits are currently 978. The remaining 9 digits are identical in the 10-digit ISBN and its 13-digit counterpart of the same manifestation; they are shown in bold.

The best practice is to search ISBNs as a last resort, unless you need to find a specific imprint or manifestation of a work.

International Standard Serial Numbers (ISSNs) are control numbers to uniquely identify journal titles. There are two journals with the title *International Peacekeeping*. One is published in London, and the other is published in Hingham, Massachusetts. But the ISSN is an easy way to distinguish between them when searching, 1353-3312 versus 1380-748X.

I generally consider the ISSN to be a more reliable control number than the ISBN for general library searching. ISSNs do a better job of uniquely identifying journals or other serial content. There are some considerations to keep in mind. One is that the ISSN was not developed until the 1970s, so not all older serials have had ISSNs retrospectively assigned to them. In addition, different ISSNs are assigned for different formats, such as a print serial and the electronic version.

ISSNs are very useful in tracing the history of academic journals. One simple example is the journal *Canadian Psychologist*. From 1950 to 1974,

Table 2.4. ISBNs for Stephen King's The Shining.

0385121679	1977 Doubleday 1st edition (450 pages)
978**0385121675**	Same with ISBN 13
0345806786	2013 First Anchor books trade paperback edition (659 pages)
978**0345806789**	Same with ISBN 13
0307743659	2012 1st Anchor books mass market edition (659 pages)
978**0307743657**	Same with ISBN 13
0743437497	2002 Pocket Books, juvenile audience (505 pages)
978**0743437493**	Same with ISBN 13
0743424425	2001 Pocket Books (683 pages)
978**0743424424**	Same with ISBN 13

the ISSN was 0008-4832. But the title changed to *Canadian Psychological Review* in 1975, and a new ISSN was assigned, 0318-2096. The *WorldCat* database (the fee-based version, not WorldCat.org) is especially useful in these situations. A field in the record for *Canadian Psychologist* contains this information:

Succeeding Title: Canadian psychological review; (DLC) 75644700; (OCoLC)2242008; 0318-2096

See the ISSN number in that record? It's the "0318-2096." *WorldCat* is probably the most helpful resource in tracking down these title changes. I have encountered times when a serial has split into more than a dozen separate serials and later back to a single title again. Without the aid of ISSNs, this kind of research would be next to impossible to figure out. We'll discuss the *WorldCat* database more fully in chapter 12.

Digital Object Identifiers (DOIs) are a standard for uniquely identifying articles. The initiative was launched by the International DOI Foundation in 1998 and first launched in 2000 (IDF 2017). A DOI is generally used to point to anything on the Internet, but we most often see it used for online journal articles or e-books. It is commonly used by journal publishers. Here is an example of a DOI: 10.1007/s00018-017-2560-7. One easy way to resolve a DOI is to go to the official Web site at http://www.doi.org. DOIs can be pasted into the search box, and you will then be directed to the publisher's version of the article.

A couple of points should be noted here. First, simply resolving a DOI will generally allow access if users are on campus and the campus library subscribes. If a library uses a proxy service, remote users will need to know how to proxy the DOI so that they can be granted access from off campus. Second, although your campus library may provide access to the article, the access might be though an aggregator rather than through the publisher. To work around this, users can either search the title of the article in their discovery tool, if there is one, or look it up in Google Scholar, assuming that the institution has allowed Google Scholar to show local holdings.

Table 2.5. Control Numbers Commonly Used in Online Library Databases.

Code: D U N S Number (or DUNS Number)
Code lookup or information: http://www.dnb.com/duns-number/lookup.html
Selected databases using this code: *Business Source* (EBSCO); *ABI / Inform*
    (ProQuest); *Hoovers Online*

Code: ORCID ID
Code Lookup or Information: https://orcid.org (Elsevier)
Selected databases using this code: *Scopus*; *Web of Science*; *IEEE Xplore*

Code: ISBN
Code lookup or information: http://www.lookupbyisbn.com
Selected databases using this code: Many

Code: ISSN
Code lookup or information: http://www.issn.org
Selected databases using this code: Many

Code: SIC
Code lookup or information: https://www.osha.gov/pls/imis/sicsearch.html
Selected databases using this code: *Standard & Poor's NetAdvantage*;
    ReferenceUSA

Code: NAICS
Code lookup or information: https://www.census.gov/cgi-bin/sssd/naics/
    naicsrch?chart=2017
Selected databases using this code: *Business Source* (EBSCO); *ABI / Inform*
    Collection; *Business Insights: Global* (Gale)

Code: DOI
Code lookup or information: http://www.doi.org
Selected databases using this code: *ScienceDirect* (Elsevier); *Wiley Online Library*;
    SpringerLink; *SciFinder*

Code: *PubMed* ID (PMID)
Code lookup or information: https://www.ncbi.nlm.nih.gov/pmc/pmctopmid
Selected databases using this code: *Medline* (various vendors); *PubMed*; *Biological*
    Abstracts; *IEEE Xplore*; *Web of Science*

Code: Patent Number (U.S.)
Code lookup or information: https://www.uspto.gov/patents-application-process/
    applying-online/patent-number
Selected databases using this code: *SciFinder*; Google Patents; USPTO Database;
    Web of Science (cited patents)

Code: CAS Registry Number
Code lookup or information: https://www.cas.org/content/chemical-substances/faqs
Selected databases using this code: *SciFinder*; *Biological Abstracts*

DOIs use the handle system to assign permanent URLs to objects. All DOIs begin with a primary prefix of "10." (IDF 2017. DOIs are a requirement for inclusion in some citation systems. APA, Chicago, and Turabian citation styles require the inclusion of a DOI, if there is one. Don't expect every scholarly journal article to have a DOI.

Table 2.5 lists some of the control numbers commonly used in online databases.

Suite of Technologies

Libraries today have a suite of technologies to make things work. These technologies include databases, proxy services to control access, aggregated databases, reference linking (OpenURL services), electronic resource management (ERM) systems, integrated library systems (ILS), library management systems (LMS), discovery tools, digital and institutional repositories, and link resolver technologies. Check your library's Web site or ask a reference librarian about the best ways to enhance your database-searching experiences.

In this section, we will discuss several of these technologies in the context of online databases.

Proxy Services

Libraries need a way to allow access to licensed databases to which they have subscribed. Usually, colleges and universities register their Internet domain with the vendor. In the case of the University of Denver, that would be du.edu. Anyone who is on campus, whether accessing via a hardwired connection (rare these days) or over wireless, will be accessing through the university's domain. But what about off-campus, remote, and distance education students? One of the popular technology solutions for these situations is to run licensed database content through a proxy service. This allows users to authenticate with their institutional credentials and ensures that only users covered under the vendor contract can gain access.

Two examples of proxy services include EZproxy (an OCLC product) and Web Access Management (WAM), owned by Innovative Interfaces Inc. (III). An EZproxy URL will be formed like this:

> **http://du.idm.oclc.org/login?url**=http://www.jstor.org/stable/4450851
> http://www.jstor.org.**du.idm.oclc.org**/stable/4450851

The first URL is a prepend URL, meaning that it is added before the resource URL. The second one is a translated URL.

A WAM URL for the same resource looks like this:

> http://0-www.jstor.org.**bianca.penlib.du.edu**/stable/4450851

I call this a "wraparound" URL because the proxy elements wrap around the URL, as denoted in bold above.

There are several reasons why library database searchers need to know something about proxies. The first concern is communicating with off-campus patrons. Imagine you are helping a remote library user over a chat interface. All your communications with them will need to include a proxied URL for licensed resources to ensure that they will be able to log in with their credentials. You need to be able to instantly recognize the proxy elements so that you can tell whether there is one. I also recommend testing the proxy you send to ensure that it actually works.

A second reason relates to the way proxies tend to behave with citation services such as RefWorks, EndNote, or similar citation management software. Take a close look at the citation generated by a citation management program:

> Wang, Hei-Chia, Che-Tsung Yang, and Yi-Hao Yen. 2017. "Answer Selection and Expert Finding in Community Question Answering Services." *Program: Electronic Library and Information Systems* 51 (1): 17-34. doi:10.1108/PROG-01-2015-0008. http://www.emeraldinsight.com.du.idm.oclc.org/doi/10.1108/PROG-01-2015-0008.

Notice that, in addition to the DOI, the citation includes a URL with an EZproxy component embedded within the link. The problem is that only people associated with the University of Denver will be able to access this resource. This is completely unhelpful. You must take the proxy element out of the URL. Actually, I would argue that you shouldn't even include a URL because the DOI is sufficient. URLs to information on the open Web may change or cease to work. But in the context of a scholarly journal article, online is just a format. It makes no difference if a user accesses the article in print, microform, or online format. Thus, inclusion of a URL is superfluous and may even be misleading. We will discuss citation software in greater depth in chapter 14.

Permalinks

Databases are complex, and those who program them have the difficult task of streamlining code and ensuring that their products execute that code efficiently. One of the side effects of all these layers of technology is that database URLs are often extremely long and cumbersome. Not only that, they are often transitory in that they are customized for the computer you are using. Features users want, such as saving records, remembering search histories, and preserving user preferences, require some kind of user ID, either temporary or permanent. This usually affects the URL, and thus makes the URL nonreusable.

The permalink, sometimes called a *durable URL*, is a solution to this problem. Even complex databases, such as the U.S. Census Bureau's *American FactFinder*, now have permalinks available to link to specific tables. This really helps when trying to undergird a grant or business proposal with exact numbers. Here are some examples of permalinks from various vendors:

- EBSCO *Academic Search*:

  http://search.ebscohost.com/login.aspx?direct=true&db=a9h&AN=47275080&site=ehost-live&scope=site

- ProQuest Central:

  https://search-proquest-com.du.idm.oclc.org/docview/1931154924?accountid=14608

- HeinOnline:

  http://www.heinonline.org/HOL/Page?handle=hein.journals/juraba
  45&start_page=225&collection=journals&id=235

- Academic OneFile (Gale):

  http://go.galegroup.com/ps/i.do?p=AONE&sw=w&u=udenver&v
  =2.1&id=GALE%7CA55937503&it=r&asid=f9abd16a835ca8a
  5edb74

Looking over these permalinks, in some of them you can discern accession numbers (EBSCO and ProQuest), shorthand for journal titles (Hein), reference to page numbers (Hein), and combinations of letter and numbers that can only mean something to a computer (Gale). These URLs should persist when users want to revisit the items at a later time or pass them along to a colleague.

We cannot discuss permalinks apart from proxy services. If you are e-mailing a durable URL to a patron, you may also need to proxy the permalink, making it a bit longer.

Originating URLs and Resultant URLs

Have you even noticed how library databases sometimes have extremely long URLs? The primary reason for this is that the vendors want users to have positive searching experiences. By setting up a temporary database session, the user can save articles to a folder, retain search histories, and perform other useful tasks. Registering and logging in to the database often allows for additional features, such as saving records over time and maintaining search preferences. But for all these things to work, a database session needs to be encoded in the URL. This causes URLs to be long.

You can observe this URL lengthening upon entering these databases. For example, the initial or originating URL to enter *WorldCat* is

> http://du.idm.oclc.org/login?url=http://newfirstsearch.oclc.org/
> dbname=WorldCat;autho=100113122;done=referer;fsip

But upon entering, a session ID is assigned to the search session and is encoded in the URL:

> http://newfirstsearch.oclc.org.du.idm.oclc.org/WebZ/FSPrefs?entit
> yjsdetect=:javascript=true:screensize=large:**sessionid=fsa
> pp2-50615-jak7fu91-5y5hwk**:entitypagenum=1:0

I call this a "spawned" URL. Notice the bolded session information in the URL string above. It is important to understand this, because the URL will not work for other people. In fact, it will likely fail the next day for the initial user as well. Not only do initial URLs change, but individual article URLs very often change as well. The way to get around this is to use the permalink feature within the database.

OpenURLs

One of the most exciting technologies of the last 15–20 years has been OpenURL technology. What started as the creation of Herbert Van de Sompel of the University of Ghent, Belgium, blossomed into a standard (ANSI/NISO Z39.88-2004) that allows users to discover full text from competing publishers (Van de Sompel and Beit-Arie 2001).

OpenURLs are called "open" because they do exactly what you do not want to do with your banking information. Private transactions need to be encrypted so that sleuths cannot get your log-in and password information and drain all your money. OpenURLs do just the opposite: they pass along all the content information through a URL that is almost humanly readable.

In the early days of databases, when there often was no full-text access directly through the database, OpenURLs were necessary. It was a way for aggregator databases to locate content in either other aggregator products or in publisher portals. These days, OpenURLs are less necessary, as it is very common for the full text to be present.

Let's take a look at a typical OpenURL (figure 2.14).

The element in the box in figure 2.14 is what I call the "head." The remaining part of that long URL is what I call the "tail." Notice that it is possible to read the citation directly from the URL.

atitle (article title) = History of information science

aulast (author last name) = Burke

date = 2007

epage = 53

issn = 0066-4200

stitle (short title) = Annu Rev Inform Sci

title (journal title) = Annual Review of Information Science and Technology

volume = 41

A "head transplant" can be done so that the URL is resolved against a different library service, that is, from another institution. For example,

https://du.alma.exlibrisgroup.com/view/uresolver/01UODE_INST/openurl?url_ver=Z39.88-2004&url_ctx_fmt=info:ofi/fmt:kev:mtx:ctx&rft_val_fmt=info:ofi/fmt:kev:mtx:journal&rft.atitle=History+of+information+science&rft.auinit=C&rft.aulast=Burke&rft.date=2007&rft.epage=53&rft.genre=article&rft.issn=0066-4200&rft.spage=3&rft.stitle=ANNU+REV+INFORM+SCI&rft.title=ANNUAL+REVIEW+OF+INFORMATION+SCIENCE+AND+TECHNOLOGY&rft.volume=41&rfr_id=info:sid/www.isinet.com:WoK:WOS

openURL "head"

Figure 2.14. Structure of an OpenURL.

the head from the University of Northern Colorado Library's OpenURL resolver is

http://xt9lp6eh4r.search.serialssolutions.com/?

This OpenURL prefix can be substituted for the University of Denver head in figure 2.14, and we would then have a URL that would resolve to a different library.

In this chapter, we have covered necessary technical territory for understanding the "under-the-hood" aspects of library databases. From fields, both fixed and variable-length, to records, to indexing of databases, we discovered that everything is based on standards. Things can go wrong with databases, especially as database problems are not visibly apparent and are often only discovered by the observant searcher. We also discussed some of the interwoven technologies that work behind the scenes to allow access.

Exercises

1. Using the form in table 2.2 and adapting it as necessary, find out which fields are indexed by default in EBSCO's *Business Source* database. You will need to do the diagnostic tests described in this chapter.

2. To explore the depth of ProQuest field tags, spend some time in the ProQuest LibGuides: https://proquest.libguides.com/proquestplatform. By clicking a database name and then exploring the searchable fields, you can see how these many databases differ from one another.

3. Examine other databases to which your library subscribes. Which ones have permalinks, and which ones don't need to have them because the database links will work without a permalink?

4. Go to your library's online catalog and pull up any book record that is not in English. Now go to the MARC record view for that book. Can you see variable-length fields that iterate in that record? Which fields are they? Can you see the three-letter fixed field for the language of the book in the record?

References

DOI International Foundation. 2017. *Factsheet: Key Facts on Digital Identifier System*. Accessed December 29, 2017. https://www.doi.org/factsheets/DOIKeyFacts.html.

Jacsó, Péter, and Carol Tenopir. 2001. *Content Evaluation of Textual CD-ROM and Web Databases*. Englewood, CO: Libraries Unlimited, 2001.

Library of Congress. 2017. *MARC 21 Format for Bibliographic Data*. Update No. 25, December 2017. Accessed December 29, 2017. https://www.loc.gov/marc/bibliographic.

Van de Sompel, Herbert, and Oren Beit-Arie. 2001. "Open Linking in the Scholarly Information Environment Using the OpenURL Framework." *New Review of Information Networking* 7, no. 1: 59–76.

3
Controlled Vocabularies

One of the core skill sets of being a librarian is being able to analyze an object and to use a few words to tell the world what the object is "about." In the early days of cataloging, long before computer technology, catalogers needed to capture the "aboutness" of books so that they could be found by subject. Each book had a set of catalog cards containing descriptions and subject analysis. For each subject devised, another set of cards would need to be created and filed so that they could be found. There was a tension in this exercise. On the one hand, there was the desire to create as many subject access points as possible to make the books more findable, and, on the other hand, there was the realization that the more subject access points created, the more time would be needed to type the cards, and the more space would be required to store more card catalog cabinets to hold all those cards. A compromise between more subject terms and less space was the pre-coordinated subject heading. A cataloger could use a single access point to refer to multiple semantic notions with a great degree of specificity.

A few examples of some pre-coordinated Library of Congress subject headings from the book records show how these headings work:

State government publications—Colorado—Bibliography—Catalogs

Shore birds—Habitat—United States—Data processing

Shakespeare,William,1564–1616—Adaptations—Historyandcriticism—Periodicals

Each of the subject headings happen to have four distinct semantic notions.

Indexers had the same tension when it came to the task of indexing periodical articles. More subject terms are desirable, but then you need to have more entry points within a print index to accommodate them. The more access points you have, the more paper is required for printing, the thicker your index volume is, and the more money it costs to print the index. Early indexers resorted to a similar solution: use pre-coordinated subject terms to capture the aboutness of articles.

Why Control?

Before we start looking at basic search tools, we need to discuss control. I often say that librarians are control freaks (I mean this in a very good sense). We like to classify things, categorize, analyze, and organize the world. Not that my office is organized, mind you. Some of us may have neat desks, but at the very least we want to be able to find things—and information.

You likely became familiar with the Dewey Decimal Classification System in high school and maybe later with the Library of Congress Classification System—systems that were all about where books live on shelves. A book can only be shelved in one place. But in the digital world, we are not limited by space. A digital object does not have to live in a single place, as required by a physical object. It can live in multiple places. Alongside the traditional classification systems have come online schemes that allow for many descriptive terms for the thing we are describing. Cloud systems have introduced social tagging so that professional indexers and catalogers are no longer the only ones who get to do the classifying. But there is still a place for exactness and expertise in a subject area. For example, we want our medical doctors to be able to find out what is wrong with us and to locate information to remedy things with as much precision as possible. If we are ever involved with the legal system, we pay attorneys to fight for our rights and expect that they can retrieve information on our behalf with speed and accuracy. Control mechanisms are behind the metadata that allow for this to occur.

Controlled Vocabulary: To Use or Not to Use?

There are times when use of controlled vocabulary makes complete sense, and other times when a more general keyword search strategy makes the most sense. There are reasons why you would need to use available controlled vocabulary, and there are also reasons for just doing keyword searches.

Here are some reasons to use controlled vocabulary:

- You need greater precision in your search results.
- You want to follow the accepted nomenclature for a given field.
- You want to minimize "noise" and false drops in search results.
- You need to bring together synonyms for similar concepts.

And here are reasons to go beyond controlled vocabulary (keyword searches):

- You really need to search for nomenclature of individual authors.
- Indexers are not perfect; they may miscategorize articles.
- Controlled vocabularies lag behind culture and technology.
- Not all records in a database have had controlled vocabulary applied yet.

While keyword searching is by far the most popular method of searching, there are times when more precision is necessary. An undergraduate student needing to find sufficient resources for a five-page paper on trends in accounting only needs to find perhaps four or five peer-reviewed scholarly articles on the topic. They don't need everything, only something on the topic. However, a master's or PhD student needs to do a thorough literature review to find everything on a topic. Failure to find everything would be embarrassing at their defense and in reviews of subsequent publications. Simply put, the high school student or undergraduate student needs to find something; the doctoral student needs to find everything. Thus, precision in searching is an essential feature to employ.

Controlled vocabulary is finding its way into popular culture in ways that could not have been predicted several years ago. *Wikipedia*, the free online encyclopedia, has a lot of positive things going for it. While we don't like to see students relying on *Wikipedia* content for their scholarly research papers, there are many librarians and university professors who create content for it. *Wikipedia* itself is built on standards of controlled vocabulary. We have likely all seen disambiguation pages. There is even a Chris Brown disambiguation page (https://en.wikipedia.org/wiki/Chris_Brown_(disambiguation)). No, there is no page in *Wikipedia* for Chris Brown the librarian, but there are pages sorting out the singer, various athletes with the name, and others.

In addition to the disambiguation pages, *Wikipedia* has its own manual of style (https://en.wikipedia.org/wiki/Wikipedia:Manual_of_Style) with rules for punctuation and capitalization, dates and times, grammar and vocabulary, and other markup-style matters. As of mid-2017, there were 282,483 disambiguation pages. The ANSI/NISO document uses the term *mercury* to illustrate disambiguation, so it is interesting for us to see how the *Wikipedia* database handles these ambiguities in its disambiguation page (see https://en.wikipedia.org/wiki/Mercury). In addition to mercury (element), Mercury (mythology), and Mercury (planet), there are also seven fictional characters, four literature references, numerous references to music and other media, eight companies with Mercury in their name, four people with either the first or last name "Mercury," and further disambiguation in fields of science and technology, transportation, sports, and other areas. This is quite an impressive guide for keeping things straight. It illustrates how control of terminology has become important in popular culture and can assist us in understanding its use in databases.

Kinds of Control

One of the most powerful sets of tools in the quest for finding the "all and only" are controlled vocabularies. It is helpful to break down controlled vocabularies into various types.

Subject-Specific Controlled Vocabularies. Subject-specific controlled vocabularies have been created by authoritative associations or indexing companies that more or less follow international standards for thesaurus construction. Examples of this are the *Thesaurus of ERIC Descriptors*, *Thesaurus of Psychological Index Terms*, and the *Thesaurus of Sociological Indexing Terms*.

General Controlled Vocabularies. General controlled vocabularies are not designed for any one discipline, but broad enough to cover all possible topics. The attempt to be universal in scope means that subject-specific vocabulary is not favored, but rather more general or universal terms are selected instead. The clearest example of this is the *Library of Congress Subject Headings* (*LCSH*).

Computer Back-Generated Controlled Vocabularies. The large aggregated databases hosted by EBSCO, Gale, and ProQuest generally feature what appear to be controlled vocabularies. But these vocabularies are "back generated" after the fact by the vendors. They harvest and collect existing subjects from subject fields; do a degree of merging, de-duplication, and normalization; and then present their back-generated list of terms. This is not the same process as was done in the first two steps, where subject descriptors or subject headings were carefully applied by humans at the time of indexing. This is done through the magic of computers. In a sense, this is a giant "smoke and mirrors" endeavor.

As an example of this process, consider this situation from EBSCO *Academic Search*. A student performs a subject search for "California AND teenagers" (see figure 3.1).

Notice that this record has a subject term for *teenagers*. But according to the abstract, this article is not at all about teenage human children, but the high juvenile mortality of the San Clemente sage sparrow. We can easily imagine how this error occurred. EBSCO, in an effort to bring together everything in its database about teenagers, did a global search that included the term *juvenile* and then applied the subject term *teenagers* to those records. An indexer in the life sciences, if building up this record in the traditional

Shifting Threats Faced by the San Clemente Sage Sparrow.

Authors: HUDGENS, BRIAN[1] hudgens@iws.org
           BEAUDRY, FREDERIC[2]
           GEORGE, T. LUKE[3]
           KAISER, SARA[4]
           MUNKWITZ, NICOLE M.

Source: Journal of Wildlife Management. Aug2011, Vol. 75 Issue 6, p1350-1360. 11p. 4 Charts, 6 Graphs.

Document Type: Article

Subject Terms: *WILDLIFE research
                 *HABITAT (Ecology)
                 *TEENAGERS
                 *POPULATION dynamics
                 *AMPHISPIZA

Geographic Terms: SAN Clemente Island (Calif.)
                    CALIFORNIA

Author-Supplied   adaptive management
Keywords: Amphispiza belli
                  California Channel Islands
                  global climate change
                  island endemic
                  population viability analysis
                  San Clemente sage sparrow

Abstract: Threats to a species' persistence are likely to change as conservation measures reduce some threats, while natural and anthropogenic changes increase others. Despite a variety of potential underlying mechanisms, extinction threats will be manifested through one of the 3 components of population dynamics: reducing population growth potential, increasing population variability, or lowering the population ceiling. Consequently, effective management can be guided by monitoring programs and population models that examine each of these components. We examined the potential for a coupled monitoring and modeling effort to guide management of species-at-risk while accounting for evolving risks using the case study of the threatened San Clemente sage sparrow (Amphispiza belli clementeae). Originally listed due to a low population ceiling imposed by severe habitat loss, we found that the major threat to San Clemente sage sparrow persistence has shifted to low population growth potential driven by high juvenile mortality. We further found that successful mitigation of high juvenile mortality will shift the primary threat to drought frequency, which is predicted to increase on San Clemente Island as a consequence of global climate change. The latter shift is a consequence of the boom-bust ecology exhibited by San Clemente sage sparrows in response to rainfall-likely a common characteristic of short-lived terrestrial vertebrates in arid environments. Our ability to successfully recover this species hinges on a comprehensive monitoring and modeling program incorporating all 3 components of population dynamics informing changes in management priorities to reflect shifting threats. Our study indicates that the next critical step to recovering sage sparrows is to understand and mitigate the causes of high juvenile mortality. In response to these predictions, the United States Navy has funded a radio-telemetry study to determine the cause(s) of juvenile mortalities. [ABSTRACT FROM AUTHOR]

Figure 3.1. Evidence of automatic subject term assignment.

way, would never have assigned the subject term *teenagers* to this record. This illustrates the difference between the point-of-indexing application of controlled vocabulary and the attempts of vendors to enhance their products.

Two Types of Subjects:
Headings vs. Descriptors

There are two basic types of subjects: subject headings and subject descriptors. It is very important to understand the differences between these two schemes. To understand the differences, we need to look back into a bit of library history. In the late 1800s and early 1990s, the Library of Congress began the long evolution of its *Library of Congress Subject Headings* (Stone 2000). This was a pre-coordinated controlled vocabulary, which means that catalogers coordinate the "aboutness" of a subject by encapsulating the overall subject of materials. For example, a work may be about Japan's foreign relations with the United States. In this case, a pre-coordinated heading would be both "Japan—Foreign Relations—United States" as well as "United States—Foreign Relations—Japan." In both cases, we see three separate semantic notions on the same line: Japan, another for the United States, and a third for the notion of foreign relations.

The pre-coordination of headings meant that subjects could be assigned in an economical manner. When cards had to be filed in card catalogs, each additional assigned subject heading required an additional set of cards. It made sense to have one set of cards for "Japan—Foreign Relations—United States" and another set for "United States—Foreign Relations—Japan."

While the *subject headings* approach with one or more semantic notion per heading served its purposes in the precomputer era, it is not the preferred type of subject term employed in most current online databases. The *subject descriptor* model is used instead.

Subject descriptors have only one semantic notion per term. The terms may contain several words, including complex terms, qualifiers, and other words to disambiguate one term from another, but there is only one semantic notion per term. This is what we observe in the major thesauri, such as those for *ERIC*, *PsycINFO*, and *Sociological Abstracts*.

When searching subject descriptors, it is the searcher who coordinates the terms, a postcoordination process. This can be done using Boolean operators, as we will discuss in chapter 4.

Over the years, I have found that students who take the time to read the 172-page ANSI/NISO Z39.19 standard about the construction of controlled vocabularies have a greater understanding and appreciation for the process of establishing and applying such controlled vocabularies (ANSI/NISO 2010).

Thinking about the differences between subject heading and subject descriptors, let's consider the practical differences. In the early days of subject cataloging, when cards had to be individually typed and filed, it made sense to follow a "rule of 3" whereby generally no more than three subject headings would be assigned (Weihs and Intner 2016). When I first started working in the reference department of Cornell University's main library in 1986, the combined card catalog for all the university libraries took up a huge room with thousands of drawers containing catalog cards. Imagine how much more real estate would have been required if catalogers had assigned subjects using a subject descriptor approach instead of a subject heading scheme with multiple notions pre-coordinated.

Subject Headings

Let's take a more in-depth look at the differences between subject headings and subject descriptors. The easiest place to find subject headings is in the library catalog itself, as this is the legacy inventory system and finding aid for libraries. In figure 3.2, we see a book with five subject headings:

1. Masó, Mireya, 1963 – Exhibitions

2. Nature – Effect of human beings on – Antarctica – Exhibitions

3. Human beings – Effect of environment on – Antarctica – Exhibitions

4. Art and science – Exhibitions

5. Antarctica – In art – Exhibitions

These five headings were pre-coordinated by catalogers and contain a lot of information, both about the subject and the geographic locations that are the focus of the work.

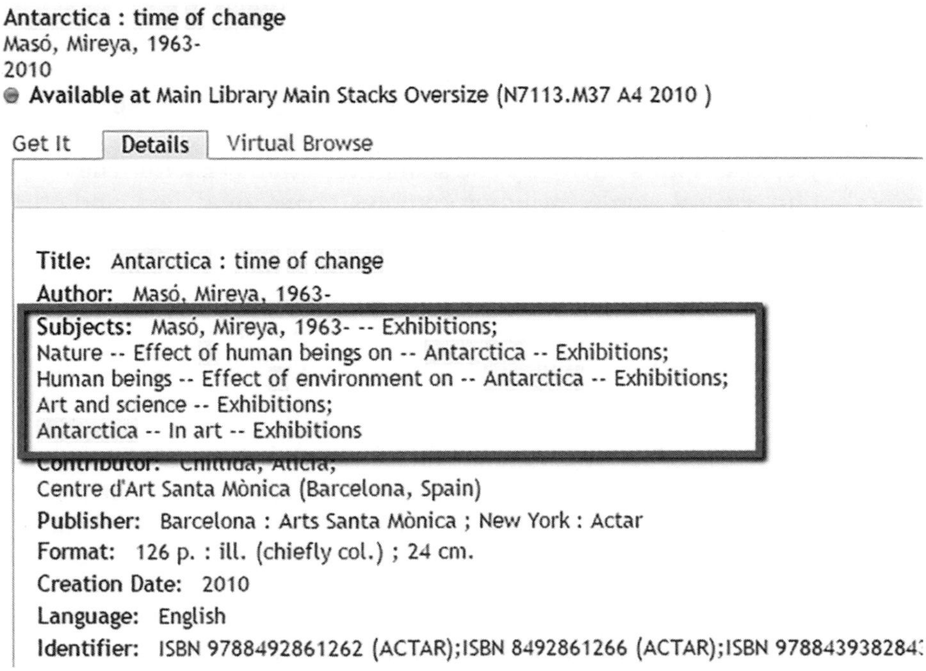

Antarctica : time of change
Masó, Mireya, 1963-
2010
● **Available at** Main Library Main Stacks Oversize (N7113.M37 A4 2010)

Get It   │ **Details** │ Virtual Browse

Title: Antarctica : time of change
Author: Masó, Mireya, 1963-

Subjects: Masó, Mireya, 1963- -- Exhibitions;
Nature -- Effect of human beings on -- Antarctica -- Exhibitions;
Human beings -- Effect of environment on -- Antarctica -- Exhibitions;
Art and science -- Exhibitions;
Antarctica -- In art -- Exhibitions

Contributor: Chillida, Alicia;
Centre d'Art Santa Mònica (Barcelona, Spain)
Publisher: Barcelona : Arts Santa Mònica ; New York : Actar
Format: 126 p. : ill. (chiefly col.) ; 24 cm.
Creation Date: 2010
Language: English
Identifier: ISBN 9788492861262 (ACTAR);ISBN 8492861266 (ACTAR);ISBN 978843938284:

Figure 3.2. Example of multiple subject headings in local online catalog.
University of Denver online catalog. Used with permission.

It is clear that there are multiple semantic notions in each of these headings (separated by the long dashes). It is a characteristic of *Library of Congress Subject Headings* to allow one or more separate semantic notions in a single heading. This allows for economy of space in the record layout, and in the old days of card filing, it allowed for fewer catalog cards to be typed and economy of space in the catalog drawers. In an online catalog environment, the subjects generally contain hyperlinks so that users can search for other materials under the same heading. When we click the link for the heading "Antarctica – In art – Exhibitions," we see that the link executes a new search for us (a *backlink*) to discover all the records in the database that have this pre-coordinated heading (figure 3.3).

While academic libraries are more likely to use *Library of Congress Subject Headings*, public libraries are more likely to use *Sears List of Subject Headings*. Dating back to its first edition in 1923, the system looks very much like *LCSH*. But it is less robust, existing in a single fat volume as opposed to the *LCSH*'s five large volumes.

Subject Descriptors

While most catalogs continue adding and maintaining pre-coordinated subject headings in records, most online databases take a different approach. Rather than employ subject headings with one or more semantic

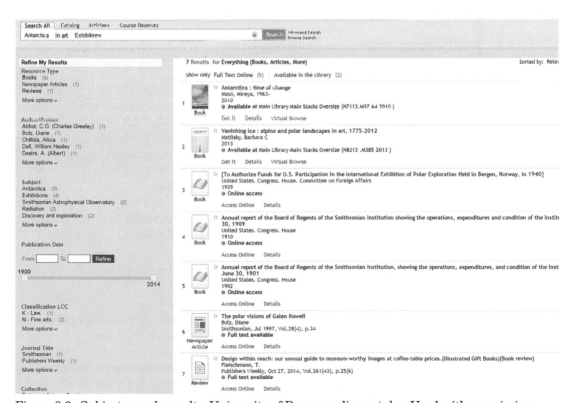

Figure 3.3. Subject search results. University of Denver online catalog. Used with permission.

Subject Heading Exercise

An excellent place to begin is with the familiar: your local online library catalog. The *Library of Congress Subjects Headings* are likely used in your local catalog. Of course, we could consult the *Library of Congress Subject Headings* books to determine headings to search by, but these are not generally as available as they were 20–30 years ago. So, we need a different strategy. We are going to first search by keyword, then examine some relevant records, and then redo the search with more accurate *LCSH* terms.

Let's say you are assisting a student who is trying to find books about censorship during the U.S. occupation of Japan. You start by doing a keyword search in the local catalog:

censorship AND japan AND occupation

After examining a few results, you notice that these subject headings seem relevant:

Japan -- History -- Allied occupation, 1945–1952
Censorship -- Japan -- History

You can now redo your searches. First, you search with both subjects together:

(Japan -- History -- Allied occupation, 1945–1952) [as subject]
AND (Censorship -- Japan -- History) [as subject]

In the search, you placed the two subject heading strings within parentheses, followed by "[as subject]" to denote that you should search these headings as subjects in your respective online catalog systems. The precise search syntax will vary, depending on your local online catalog. But the point is to go through the exercise of initially finding records with simple keyword searches, followed by more informed and exact searching by subject headings.

If your library does not have many materials on this topic, try the same strategy using *WorldCat* (either the subscription-based First-Search *WorldCat* or the freely available WorldCat.org). There will be more on *WorldCat* in chapter 12.

notions, they use subject descriptors, with one and only one semantic notion per descriptor. Let's take a look at some databases that employ subject descriptors.

For their controlled vocabulary, the *IEEE Xplore* database makes use of the *INSPEC Thesaurus*. Here are the subject descriptors for an article titled "Prediction of Rising Stars in the Game of Cricket":

- learning (artificial intelligence)
- pattern classification
- sport

Notice that each of these formal descriptors contains one and only one semantic notion, not multiples ones, as we see with subject headings. But in this case, using the *INSPEC Thesaurus* does not capture some of the key elements from this article, most notably the fact that it is about the game of cricket. Because the formal *INSPEC Thesaurus* does not have terms for games, *IEEE Xplore* makes use of several additional fields. These fields contain terms that are not controlled by a thesaurus, and we don't know if they are controlled at all or if they are just randomly assigned. What we do notice is that each of these three schemes have only a single semantic notion.

IEEE Keywords

- games
- proposals
- mathematical model
- measurement
- databases
- machine learning algorithms
- social network services

INSPEC: Noncontrolled Indexing

- cricket game
- classification
- discriminative machine learning algorithms
- generative machine learning algorithms
- categorywise assessment
- rising star prediction
- international cricket council rankings

Author Keywords

- cricket
- machine learning
- online social databases

- prediction

- rising stars

The author keywords are commonly found on the first page of articles, usually just after the abstract. If the author doesn't know what the article is about, then we are all in trouble!

The *ERIC* database also uses a thesaurus. Let's see this in action by consulting the online *ERIC* thesaurus. In the ProQuest interface, the descriptor "Parent Student Relationship" looks like this (figure 3.4):

Sometimes the vendor's implementation of a thesaurus in an online database is confusing. For help, compare this to the same entry in the print analog, the *Thesaurus of ERIC Descriptors* (table 3.1).

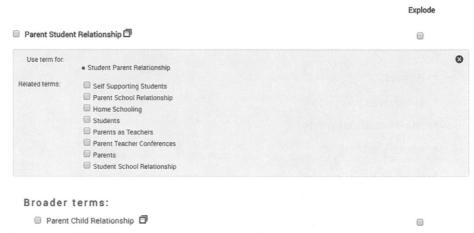

Figure 3.4. ERIC Thesaurus under ProQuest interface. The screen shots and their contents are published with permission of ProQuest LLC. Further reproduction is prohibited without permission.

Table 3.1. Layout of the Print *ERIC* Thesaurus Entry for *Parent Student Relationship*.

Parent-Student Relationship	**SN**
Relationship between parent and child that focuses on the child's role as student (Note: Prior to Mar80, the use of this term was not restricted by a Scope Note.)	UF
Student-parent relationship	BT
Parent-child relationship	RT
Home schooling Parent-school relationship Parent-teacher conferences Parents Parents as teachers Self-supporting students Student-school relationship Students	

You see each of the elements represented. The order is a bit different, but all items are the same. The formal relationships between terms are clearer in the print version. "SN" is scope note, an optional note to tell indexers when to apply a term. "UF" stands for used for. Since "Student Parent Relationship" is not an authorized *ERIC* term, that fact is noted in the record for the authorized term. Under the entry for "Student Parent Relationship," there will be a cross-reference for the authorized term. "BT" is a broader term, and "RT" is a related or parallel term.

An alphabetical outlay of *ERIC* terms shows that authorized and unauthorized terms are interfiled in alphabetical order (figure 3.5).

The authorized subject descriptors have check boxes to their left, and the option to "Explode" (which will be explained later). The unauthorized

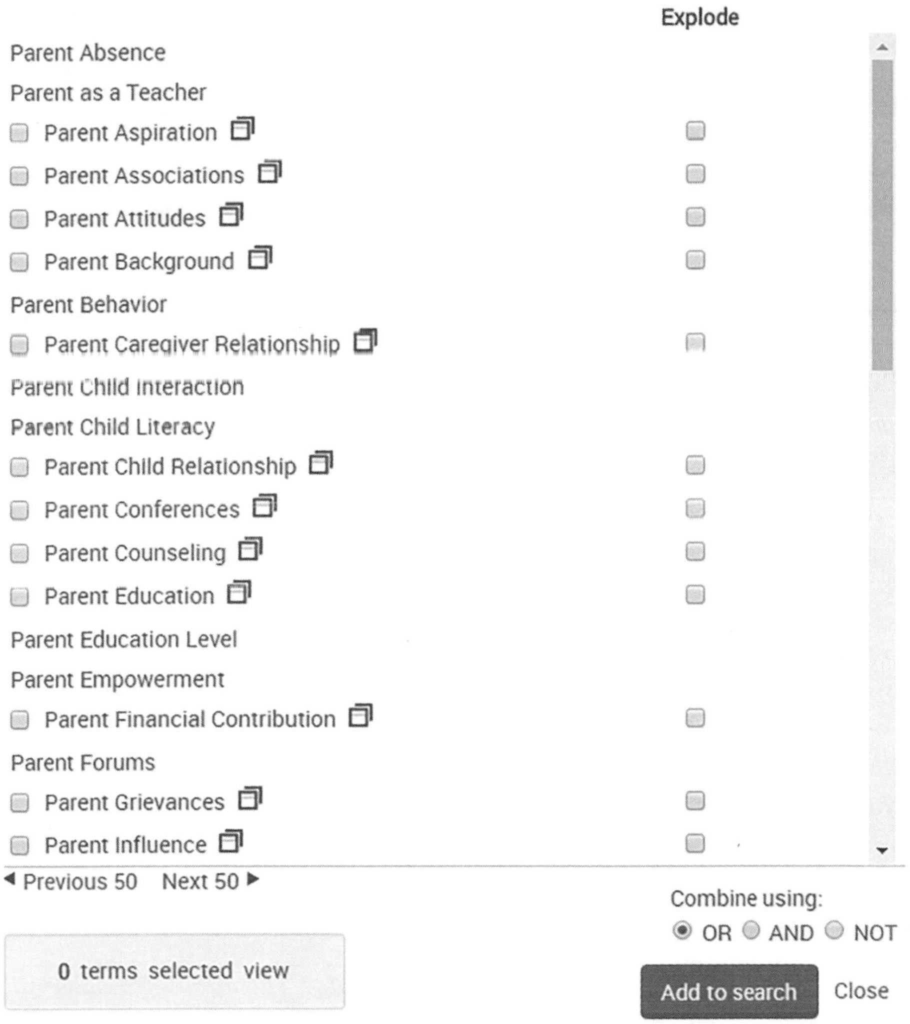

Explode

Parent Absence

Parent as a Teacher

☐ Parent Aspiration ⧉   ☐

☐ Parent Associations ⧉   ☐

☐ Parent Attitudes ⧉   ☐

☐ Parent Background ⧉   ☐

Parent Behavior

☐ Parent Caregiver Relationship ⧉   ☐

Parent Child Interaction

Parent Child Literacy

☐ Parent Child Relationship ⧉   ☐

☐ Parent Conferences ⧉   ☐

☐ Parent Counseling ⧉   ☐

☐ Parent Education ⧉   ☐

Parent Education Level

Parent Empowerment

☐ Parent Financial Contribution ⧉   ☐

Parent Forums

☐ Parent Grievances ⧉   ☐

☐ Parent Influence ⧉   ☐

◀ Previous 50   Next 50 ▶

Combine using:
◉ OR ○ AND ○ NOT

0 terms selected view

Add to search   Close

Figure 3.5. ERIC thesaurus (ProQuest) showing authorized and unauthorized descriptors. The screen shots and their contents are published with permission of ProQuest LLC. Further reproduction is prohibited without permission.

terms have no check boxes, but clicking the term will take users to the authorized term.

Best Practice: When you take the time to discover subject headings or subject descriptors, take the time to search them with appropriate field tags, not merely as keywords.

Databases with Thesauri

As seen in the examples above, it is not uncommon for the premier database in a given field to have its own thesaurus. These are very often created by associations or agencies that are responsible for indexing records for their print and online indexes. This makes sense, as it takes a very serious commitment to maintain and update a major thesaurus project. Many of these tools have a previous life in the print world and have migrated nicely over to the online database era. Not every database has a thesaurus associated with it. They typically use computer technologies to generate indexes automatically. Although this is not the same level of authority as a thesaurus, it may likely be good enough given that entire full texts can be searched as well in a high percentage of cases.

Table 3.2 shows a selected list of databases that use online thesauri, along with references to their print versions.

Table 3.2. Examples of databases with thesauri and their print analogs.

Database	Thesaurus in Database	Print Version
Agricola	NAL *Agricultural Terms*	NAL *Agricultural Terms*
Congress.gov (history of bills)	*Legislative Indexing Vocabulary* (in use 1973–2008). Legislative Subject Terms (a more compact list) was used from 2009 onward. (LOC 2017)	*Legislative Indexing Vocabulary*
Engineering Village *Compendex*	*EI Thesaurus*	*EI Thesaurus*
ERIC	*Thesaurus of ERIC Descriptors*	*Thesaurus of ERIC Descriptors*
IEEE Xplore	*INSPEC Thesaurus*	*INSPEC Thesaurus*
INSPEC	*INSPEC Thesaurus*	*INSPEC Thesaurus*
ProQuest Congressional	CIS *Thesaurus of Index Terms*	CIS *Thesaurus of Index Terms* [loose-leaf]
PsycINFO	*Thesaurus of Psychological Index Terms*	*Thesaurus of Psychological Index Terms*
Sociological Abstracts	*Thesaurus of Sociological Indexing Terms*	*Thesaurus of Sociological Indexing Terms*
United Nations Official Document System	*UNBIS Thesaurus*	*UNBIS Thesaurus*

This is just a sampling of the many thesauri that exist. There are many interesting thesauri not necessarily connected with online databases typically seen in libraries. One of these I find interesting is the *Macrothesaurus for Information Processing in the Field of Economic and Social Development*. I have often referred to both the print and online versions of this thesaurus when giving instruction to those in economic and regional development fields who are trying to develop their own local thesauri.

Other Kinds of Authority Control

In the book world, where the library catalog is the finding aid, we have become accustomed to several kinds of control: control of subjects through some kind of subject heading scheme, control of authors through name authority files, and control of titles (e.g., titles of series) through title authority files. The *Library of Congress Authorities* database (authorities.loc.gov) contains each of these elements. These systems work well for books because there are fewer of them when compared to magazine, newspaper, and journal articles. In the book world, it is relatively easy to determine who the authors, editors, and other contributors actually are, as there is usually sufficient information available to do so.

Now think about the situation in the realm of journal articles. Article databases often only give initials for given names of authors. We don't know the full names. Sure, someone could take the time to examine every PDF or HTML full text from the journals just to see whether the full form of the names could be recovered. But then there would be the realization that there is no name authority file for journal authors. Sometimes names may be entered differently, whether intentionally or not. This situation is so out of control that most databases make no attempt to straighten out authors. It is up to the researcher to try to figure it out. If one is fortunate, a resume or curriculum vitae (CV) of an author might be posted online that lists all publications of that author. Now think about how much worse the situation is for magazine and newspaper articles.

When it comes to control, one database stands out as the ultimate in control. I am referring to Readex's *United States Congressional Serial Set* database. Not only are subjects controlled in this database, but so is almost everything else. It would be very unusual for an article database to exercise name control for every author of every article in a database. But for this database, Readex has researched every personal name ever mentioned within the nearly 16,000-volume *Serial Set*. This makes it a research gem. Every individual name in the *Serial Set* is indexed, with birth and death dates for disambiguation, if known. This is a great boon for genealogists. While we do not expect this to be the norm for databases, it must be called out as an exemplary model.

Figure 3.6 shows the indexing for personal names mentioned in the full text of each volume. Also, notice the tabs for subjects; congressional acts; geographic location; publication categories (e.g., annual reports, hearings, impeachment materials, executive department publications, presidential communications, treaties); congressional standing committees; and session of Congress.

Figure 3.6 Readex Serial Set with evidence of control over every name mentioned.
© Readex, a Division of NewsBank, Inc. Used with permission.

Controlled vocabulary also exists for subjects (as you might expect). But there is also control for acts of Congress (laws of the United States). This is important, as an act will often be mentioned in an informal manner; the controlled vocabulary will bring together all these mentions in a more unified manner. Acts are arranged first by general category and then by act name.

One of my favorite control features in this database is the indexing of geographic locations. The unified form of entry for place names, county names, and natural features such as mountains, rivers, parks, and wilderness areas makes this an extremely valuable tool for historians. Users will also notice control mechanisms for congressional standing committees (with dates active for ease of reference); publication category (including annual reports, legislative reports, and hearings); and session of Congress.

It can easily be said that this database is an authority in itself. It is not constructed with back-generated data and thrown up on the Internet. It is very carefully constructed and is deserving of the centerpiece of research on Congress.

Databases such as the Readex *U.S. Congressional Serial Set*, with its extensive research and multiple control mechanisms, are rare these days. The norm is for automatically generated indexes that are quickly generated and often marked with strange, unintended consequences, as will be illustrated next.

Databases with Back-Generated Indexes

Some aggregator databases create indexes through automation, first by extracting data from various fields and then merging it into a single index. These are produced with little human intervention, and a lack of cleanup is often evident in the finished product. Nevertheless, there is some value to this process, as these indexes can provide insight as to database scope and content. We often see back-generated indexes for fields other than subject.

EBSCO

To see these back-generated indexes in action, we can look at EBSCO-host's *Business Source* database, which has indexes for author, author-supplied keywords, company entity, document type, DUNS number, entry date, geographic terms, headings, ISBN, ISSN, language, NAICS code or description, people, publication name, reviews and products, thesaurus terms, ticker symbol, and year of publication. Browsing the year of publication index allows us to see how many publications are in the database for each year. A browse by document type reveals the distribution counts of each document within the database, from over 14 million articles, to a count of only one each for the document types of anecdote, book summary, diagram, illustration, reprint, riddle, and transcript. These indexes are further examples of back-generated data, where the vendor extracts each value for a field and reconstitutes it as an index with database frequency counts. While every effort is done to make this clean and error free, evidence remains that this is a computer process and not a human process. For example, the following entries exist in the author index within *Business Source*:

> brown jr., g. e 1 entry (note the space between the initials)
> brown jr., g.e 2 entries (no space between the initials)
> e", daniel psenny (yes, that's literally how it reads)
> h liu (listed in index as if last name were "h" and the first name
> were "liu," but examining the article shows that the "h" is an initial
> of a given name)

These back-generated indexes may be helpful on some levels, but it should be kept in mind that these are really a "smoke and mirrors" computer process that should not be confused with the careful practices that librarians have done over the years in cataloging and indexing materials with great care and precision. Luckily, many vendors seem to be moving away from these back-generated indexes, perhaps for these reasons.

EBSCO is implementing what it calls its Comprehensive Subject Index (CSI). This controlled vocabulary was originally based on *Library of Congress Subject Headings*, but it is being continually modified beyond *LCSH* (EBSCO n.d.). It will be interesting to see how these developments can enhance subject access.

ProQuest

ProQuest's indexing is harder to find within the basic interface. It is context-sensitive and must be accessed from within the advanced search module. Once a field tag is selected, users will see a "lookup" feature for that field. From within *ProQuest Central*, for example, when doing a lookup for a subject, you see subjects like those below, giving evidence of back-generated, less-than-clean data:

adult; aged; aged, 80 & over; cell differentiation; diagnosis, differential; female; gene expression regulation, neoplastic; humans; immunohistochemistry; japan; male; middle aged; predictive value of tests; sensitivity & specificity

Yes, believe it or not, that is a single "subject." If you viewed the record from which this heading came, you might have a fuller understanding of how this massive subject came to be.

To further demonstrate what is obviously going on, that is, automatic extraction of data with insufficient cleanup, you see these index entries, obviously for the same person (also note the use of lower case for each of these name entries):

d'amato, alfonse
d'amato, alfonse m.
d'amato, alphonse
d'amato, sen. alfonse m.
d'amato, senator

We could keep doing this for each of the indexes within *ProQuest Central*, but by now you hopefully get the idea.

Gale

Gale has a "Browse by Discipline" feature in its *Academic OneFile* database. Searching for "D'Amato," as we did above for *ProQuest Central*, shows that Gale is attempting to exercise some control over the extracted data. We see two entries with "see" references:

D'Amato, Alfonse Marcello
    See D'Amato, Alfonse M.
D'Amato, Alphonse Marcello
    See D'Amato, Alfonse M.

Then, under the authorized entry, "D'Amato, Alfonse M.," we see numerous subdivisions, including the following:

Appointments, resignations and dismissals (8)
Appreciation (1)
Behavior (10)
Beliefs, opinions and attitudes (27)
Cases (2)

Compensation and benefits (2)
Contracts (1)
Death of (1)
Discipline (1)
Donations (1)
Economic policy (119)
Elections (3)

It seems that Gale is intentionally attempting to go to a subject headings approach, bucking the general trend in modern online databases to prefer subject descriptors. It remains to be seen whether this strategy is sustainable and whether it works for them.

Aggregators, like Gale, have the challenging task of creating indexing for items that they never "touch" like a book cataloger does. There is little that can be done to really control authors in an authoritative manner. Think for a second about author authority control in an online catalog context. Careful research is performed by the Library of Congress to create and maintain authority records (Library of Congress 2011). This is a mammoth project, but it does not include journal or magazine articles, only books and other whole formats. So then, what's up with databases that contain author indexes, giving the impression that someone is actually creating and maintaining author authority records for authors of journal articles?

Of course, the aggregators have a difficult task. This section is not intended to beat up on them. We just want to show how the data are organized in their attempts to exercise control in the easiest and most cost efficient manner.

Exercises

1. Read the *Guidelines for the Construction, Format, and Management of Monolingual Controlled Vocabularies* (ANSI/NISO 2010). It's rather long, but you will greatly benefit from it.

2. Go to the *ProQuest Congressional* database. Using the "find terms" feature, try to determine whether this database uses subject headings (one or more semantic notions per term) or subject descriptors (only one semantic notion per subject term).

3. Go to *ABELL: Annual Bibliography of English Language and Literature*. What kinds of subject terms does this database have? Do they appear to be principled and based on something like ANSI/NISO standards, or do they appear to have been created in some other manner? Besides subject terms, what other indexes does *ABELL* have?

4. Go to the *GeoRef* database (*GeoRef* is also part of the *GeoScienceWorld* database). Are geographic terms used in the subject thesaurus? If so, discuss the relationships between terms.

5. Go to the Readex *United States Congressional Serial Set* (if you have it). Are geographies included in the subject thesaurus? Where did

the geographies go? Is there evidence of control over the way the geographic entries are formed?

6. Your topic is "driverless cars." Find out what the controlled-vocabulary terms are in (a) *IEEE Xplore* engineering database (uses the *INSPEC* thesaurus; to access this, go to "advanced search" and search with "*INSPEC* Controlled Terms" from the pull-down menu); (b) *Academic Search*; (c) *ProQuest Central*; and (d) Gale's *Academic OneFile*.

7. Now do the same thing as in number 6 in the same databases for the concept of "tablet computers."

References

ANSI/NISO. 2010. *Guidelines for the Construction, Format, and Management of Monolingual Controlled Vocabularies.* ANSI/NISO Z39.19 2005 (R2010). Baltimore: National Information Standards Organization. Accessed December 29, 2017. http://groups.niso.org/apps/group_public/download.php/12591/z39-19-2005 r2010.pdf.

EBSCO. n.d. "What Is EBSCO's Controlled Vocabulary?" Accessed November 19, 2017. https://help.ebsco.com/interfaces/EBSCO_Guides/General_Product_FAQs/ What_is_EBSCOs_Controlled_Vocabulary.

Library of Congress. 2011. "Library of Congress Names." Accessed November 28, 2017. http://id.loc.gov/authorities/names.html.

Library of Congress. 2017. "LIV—Legislative Indexing Vocabulary." Accessed November 28, 2017. https://www.congress.gov/help/legislative-glossary#glossary_legislati veindexingvocabulary.

Stone, Alva T. 2000. "The LCSH Century: A Brief History of the Library of Congress Subject Headings, and Introduction to the Centennial Essays." *Cataloging & Classification Quarterly* 29, no. 1-2: 1–15.

Weihs, Jean, and Sheila S. Intner. 2016. *Beginning Cataloging.* 2nd ed. Santa Barbara, CA: Libraries Unlimited.

Suggested Readings

Gross, Tina, and Arlene G. Taylor. 2005. "What Have We Got to Lose?: The Effect of Controlled Vocabulary on Keyword Searching Results." *College & Research Libraries* 66, no. 3: 212–230.

Gross, Tina, Arlene G. Taylor, and Daniel N. Joudrey. 2015. "Still a Lot to Lose: The Role of Controlled Vocabulary in Keyword Searching." *Cataloging & Classification Quarterly* 53, no. 1: 1–39.

Beyond the Textbook

Carrying on the tradition of the fourth edition, additional exercises, search tips, and tutorials will be available on the publisher's Web site at http://www.abc-clio.com/books.librariesunlimited.com/Librarians-Guide -to-Online-Searching. This will be updated periodically with the inevitable database changes.

4
The Searcher's Toolkit: Part 1

What Searching Is All About

This may seem obvious, but when you approach a database, you are looking for information. Simplistically, there are two ways to approach the information quest: searching and browsing. Databases are generally so large that you encounter them through a mysterious blank search box. Some databases also allow users to browse information based in the logical structures of the database. But either way, the main goal of the quest is finding "all and only" the relevant information. If we all knew exactly how to frame a question so that we could achieve this goal, then a book like this wouldn't be necessary. But the reason for asking questions is that we don't know the answers. It's only when you perfectly know the answers that you can perfectly frame the questions.

By continuing the *Searcher's Toolkit* from previous editions of this book, the hope is that you will find these seven basic tools as a memorable and helpful set of instruments in your repertoire of search skills. These tools are becoming less important when searching with search engines such as Google, as Google likes to take over everything so that you don't have to think about it. But you do have to deliberately think about how to search databases that aren't Google.

Basic Tool No. 1: Boolean Logic

Let's start out with a very basic tool most of us already take for granted: AND, OR, and NOT. To make things clear, throughout this book, when I refer to these three Boolean operators, I will use all uppercase letters. Actually, it is not a bad idea to capitalize these operators when searching, as there are a few (granted, very few) online databases that require Boolean operators to be capitalized. Among the databases that require capitalization

63

are *HeinOnline*, *PubMed*, and the *Primo* discovery tool that we use at the University of Denver. In addition, the EBSCOhost interface has an option to require caps, if the local library administrator so desires. When teaching Boolean logic, I consider capitalizing regardless of the database being taught. That way, users are more likely to get the expected results in the few databases that require it. This practice also serves as a teaching tool to emphasize the search strategy.

This notion of language having mathematical precision was developed in the mid-1800s by the mathematician George Boole (1815–1864). Boole was an English mathematician and philosopher. In his works, he did not have in mind database searching, but rather the logical processes that are the foundation of modern mathematical logic (Boole 2016).

It's not that Boole invented AND, it's that his logical and algebraic representation of the concepts of AND, OR, and NOT earned him the name association. Now we refer to *Boolean logic* and *Boolean operators*. (We can be thankful that his name was so simple and short!)

AND—The Narrowing Boolean Operator

Even though in real language AND can be used to add things to a conversation, in Boolean logic, and in the context of online databases, AND is used for narrowing results.

Language is fascinating. If you ask a child in a candy store which candy she wants, she is likely to say, "I want this, and this, and this, and that one too." All of these "ands" strung together function to broaden the scope of what the little girl wants as a snack. Yet, when "ands" are used in a search query, the result is quite the opposite. In a database search context, AND is a narrowing concept.

In the old days—the days of card catalogs and print indexes—people didn't have to think about logical operators because access to information was simpler and less powerful. If you wanted to find materials about cats and dogs, you would approach a card catalog drawer and look for the subject cards starting with the term *cats* and then look through all those cards just to see if any of them also happened to mention something about *dogs*. We might characterize this kind of access to information as "stage 1" access: access to information linearly, through direct searches of subjects (or authors, or titles), but without the ability to combine concepts. This stage 1 access predominated through the 1980s.

The power of computing has been with us for some time, but it really affected users in a major way in the 1980s with the desktop computer revolution. CD-ROMs accessed via computers and library catalogs accessed on computer terminals and later through desktop computers changed culture and information access in major ways. But it was the onset of the World Wide Web in the early 1990s that made online databases ubiquitous and, with it "stage 2," the era of keyword searching.

With keywords came the Boolean search capability. We could now search for cats AND dogs at the same time, saving time and creating an information access revolution. In this stage, we hadn't yet begun to consider

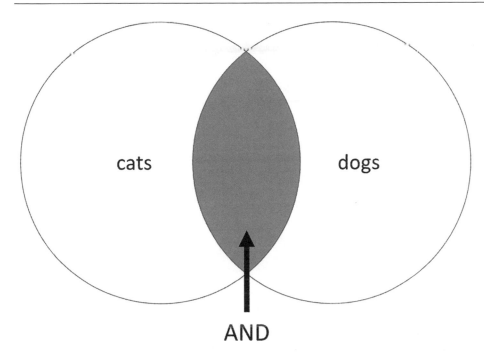

AND

Figure 4.1. Showing overlap of concepts with Boolean operator AND: "cats AND dogs."

that full texts of books or articles could be searched, just that the information formerly contained on catalog cards or indexed in print indexes could be searched. This can be represented by a simple Venn diagram, as shown in figure 4.1.

Some records may contain only cats, with no references to dogs; other records will contain dogs, with no references to cats. The records in the overlapping section in figure 4.1 contain references to both cats AND dogs. Think about the unique characteristics of cats and then of dogs. What characteristics would be in this shared area that are shared by both cats and dogs? Here are some simple ideas:

Cats Only

- catnip
- plays with feather toy
- purring
- meowing
- litter box
- sleeps a lot
- likes alone time
- most do not like playing in water

Dogs Only

- chews on bones
- fetching things
- barking
- perform tricks
- ability to work
- likes socializing
- most like playing in water

Cats AND Dogs

- veterinarians
- leashes
- rolling over
- popular family pets
- adoptable
- show affection

OR—The Broadening Boolean Operator

OR is the broadening operator. It is useful when you want to capture several synonyms in a single search. This is one of several broadening tools; truncation and wildcards are others.

OR is useful in a couple of contexts: when there are several words for the same concept (synonyms) and when you want to link closely related concepts that aren't necessarily synonyms. Concepts that are closely related might include searches for parts of the whole or individual members of a set. Some examples of synonyms and closely related concepts linked with OR are the following:

Synonym Examples

- cats OR felines
- dogs OR canines
- cows OR cattle OR bovine
- Bill Clinton OR William Jefferson Clinton OR President Clinton
- PTSD OR posttraumatic stress disorder
- morning star OR evening star OR Venus

Closely Related Concepts

- Rocky Mountain states OR Colorado OR New Mexico OR Arizona OR Wyoming OR Idaho OR Montana

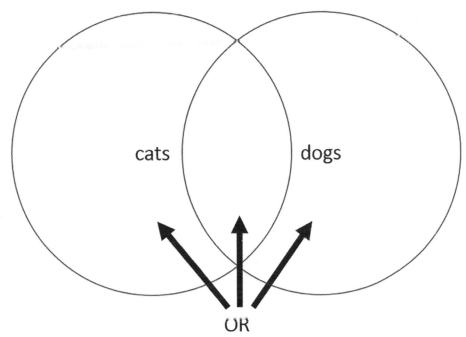

Figure 4.2. Boolean OR operator includes unique and overlapping concepts: "cats OR dogs."

- Chevy OR Chevrolet OR Impala OR Malibu OR Cruze OR Camaro OR Caprice
- Rome OR London OR Paris OR Oslo OR Berlin
- human trafficking OR forced labor OR forced labour OR sex trafficking (Note: We might want to use a wildcard here for labor; see Basic Tool No. 5).

OR is a broadening operator, as illustrated by the Venn diagram in figure 4.2.

The OR operator is sometimes not properly understood. If you are too generous in including terms in your OR statements, you will get too many results and not understand why. If this is the case, it would be best to build up OR statements gradually so that you can understand which terms are more useful for research and which are not.

NOT—The Negating Boolean Operator

There are rare moments when the negating operator needs to be employed. The reason those moments are rare is that NOT is overly powerful, knocking out results you don't want and often results you should be seeing.

Let's suppose that you were searching for materials about Mercury cars. Let's further imagine that one of the articles contained the following in the article abstract:

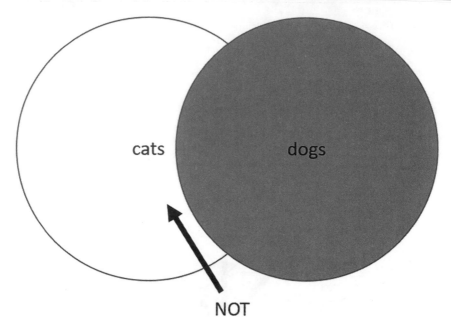

Figure 4.3. NOT Boolean operator represented in Venn diagram: "dogs NOT cats."

"This article is all about Mercury cars, not about the planet Mercury"

Now, if you framed your keyword search as "Mercury NOT planet," you would not retrieve the article with the above abstract, even though its stated purpose was to discuss Mercury automobiles. This may have been the most relevant article for your purposes, but because you used the NOT operator, the article was knocked out of your search results. You will not see the article because the term "planet Mercury" is mentioned in the abstract, and your search phrase excluded it. Because the NOT operator occasionally rules out results in unexpected ways, it really should only be used on rare occasions. Figure 4.3 illustrates the NOT operator.

You need to be aware that some databases have variations in the way the NOT operator is implemented. Occasionally, the negative statement is formed as AND NOT. This is another case of needing to read the vendor-supplied database help screens.

Combining Boolean Operators in Practice

What happens when you want to use more than one Boolean operator in a search string? This turns out to be an important question when you get unexpected results from searches. Let's look at this search:

Mercury OR Ford OR Lincoln AND wholesale OR retail

When we explain this search to another person, we pretty much know what the intended question is: anything about wholesale or retail [sales]

Table 4.1. Processing order of Boolean operators.

Operator	Processing Order	Comments
NOT	1	The exclusionary operator. Use it rarely.
AND	2	The narrowing operator. The most commonly used operator.
OR	3	The broadening operator. When combining with AND, enclose OR statements in parentheses.

of three Ford Motor Company brands. But is that how a computer is going to understand this? No, it is not, and the reason for the difference in interpretation is the way computers handle the processing of Boolean operators. When there is more than one operator in a search statement, they are generally processed in this order:

1. NOT operations are performed first.

2. Then AND operations are performed.

3. Finally, OR operations are performed.

Because it is so important to be mindful of the usual order in which Boolean operators are performed (when you use more than one of them), I have repeated this information in table 4.1.

Of course, the best way to control the order of operations is to use parentheses to disambiguate your search statements.

Nesting and Parentheses

Nesting is not just for the birds, it's for the precision searcher as well. Because computers search the operators AND, OR, and NOT in differing orders, you need mechanisms to tell computers in what order you want to search the terms. You can force the ordering of Boolean operators by placing them within parentheses. This takes away all ambiguity in search strings and allows the searcher to group terms together.

Let's illustrate how different computing systems handle operators.

Academic Search Complete (EBSCO)

cats = 72,365

dogs = 95,976

cats AND dogs = 9,863

cats Or dogs = 158,478

cats NOT dogs = 62,502

dogs NOT cats = 86,113

cats OR kittens OR felines = 75,809

dogs OR puppies OR canines = 107,774

(cats OR kittens OR felines) AND (dogs OR puppies OR canines) = 10,829

cats OR kittens OR felines AND dogs OR puppies OR canines = 101,097

cats OR kittens OR (felines AND dogs) OR puppies OR canines = 101,097

Conclusion: The EBSCOhost interface is processing the AND operator before the OR operator.

ProQuest Central (changing the search to be "Anywhere except full text")

(cats OR kittens OR felines) AND (dogs OR puppies OR canines) = 243,404

cats OR kittens OR felines AND dogs OR puppies OR canines = 1,685,721

(cats OR kittens OR (felines AND dogs) OR puppies OR canines) = 1,685,721

Conclusion: ProQuest is processing the AND first as well.

Academic OneFile (Gale)

(cats OR kittens OR felines) AND (dogs OR puppies OR canines) = 32,352

cats OR kittens OR felines AND dogs OR puppies OR canines = 232,087

(cats OR kittens OR (felines AND dogs) OR puppies OR canines) = 232,087

Conclusion: Gale is processing AND first as well.

U.S. Congressional Serial Set (Readex)

(cats OR kittens OR felines) AND (dogs OR puppies OR canines) = 8

cats OR kittens OR felines AND dogs OR puppies OR canines = 8

cats OR kittens OR (felines AND dogs) OR puppies OR canines = 8

cats OR kittens OR (felines AND dogs) OR puppies OR canines = 8

cats OR kittens OR felines OR dogs OR puppies OR canines = 8

cats AND kittens AND felines AND dogs AND puppies AND canines = 0

Conclusion: For Readex, it's AND first, then OR.

Access World News (NewsBank; Note: These are "all text" searches, which is why the results are significantly higher than the previous databases tested. This is the typical default for searching current news databases.)

(cats OR kittens OR felines) AND (dogs OR puppies OR canines) = 1,343,731

cats OR kittens OR felines AND dogs OR puppies OR canines
= 4,254,999

cats OR kittens OR (felines AND dogs) OR puppies OR canines
= 4,254,999

Conclusion: NewsBank processes AND before OR.

As can be seen in each of the above examples, search engines process AND statements before OR statements. This means that it is essential to place OR statements within parentheses to avoid any kind of ambiguity. Failure to do so will result in unintended result sets.

The order of operations is fairly easy to understand, and you now know how to control it using parentheses. Writing successful search statements in a single search box should then be pretty straightforward. But when we get into advanced search mode, some vendor interfaces are confusing. Look at the advanced search interface for EBSCO's *Academic Search* in figure 4.4.

Suppose you wanted to search for "alligators OR crocodiles AND Florida OR Louisiana." You might logically fill out the search form like this (after adding another row).

When I ran this search, I got 78,023 results, a surprisingly large result set. What I really intended to search was this:

(alligators OR crocodiles) AND (Florida OR Louisiana)

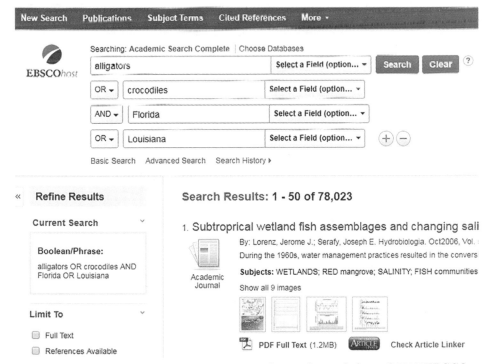

Figure 4.4. Mixing Boolean operators on an advanced search form. ©2017 EBSCO Industries, Inc. All rights reserved.

When I search *Academic Search* like this—with parentheses on a single line—I get 771 results. So how did *Academic Search* really treat our search statement? To find out, we need to lay out all possibilities. By performing a few tests, we should be able to see in which order the search engine processed the Boolean operators.

Let's test to see whether the AND operator was processed before the OR operator. Using parentheses to force the search logic, our logic would then look like this:

alligators OR (crocodiles AND Florida) OR Louisiana

Testing this out I get 78,023 results, the same result as our advanced search form. This demonstrates that this is how the search engine interpreted the information as input into the EBSCOhost search form.

If, on the other hand, OR statements had been processed first, followed by AND statements, then our logic would look like this:

(alligators OR crocodiles) AND (Florida OR Louisiana)

By testing this, we get 771 results. Thus, we can say that vendor forms can be misleading (referring back to figure 4.4) because we cannot tell what is happening unless we do the kind of diagnostic test just demonstrated.

Best Practice: Never mix Boolean operators without using parentheses. Always enclose OR or NOT statements within parentheses to keep them separate from AND statements.

Best Practice: If possible, form Boolean search phrases on a single line with parentheses and avoid using the vendor search form when using multiple operators.

As another possible source of confusion, some databases build Boolean capabilities into their search interface without telling you that they are doing so. *Nexis Uni*'s advanced search is illustrated in figure 4.5.

The phrase "all of these terms" is, of course, the Boolean AND operator; "any of these terms" is OR; and "exclude these terms" is NOT. "This exact phrase" is equivalent to enclosing words within quotes.

It is always helpful to read what vendors say about the way they implement Boolean operators within their search engines. Table 4.2 shows some Boolean idiosyncrasies by selected vendor interface.

Human Language vs. Boolean Operators

Sometimes human language doesn't match the language of Boolean operators. Suppose we encounter this reference question. A student asks, "How can I find research on birds in Idaho, and Colorado, and Montana, and Wyoming—all the Rocky Mountain states?" Our first reaction might be to map out a search string like this:

bird* AND Idaho AND Colorado AND Montana AND Wyoming AND New Mexico AND Arizona AND Rocky Mountain*

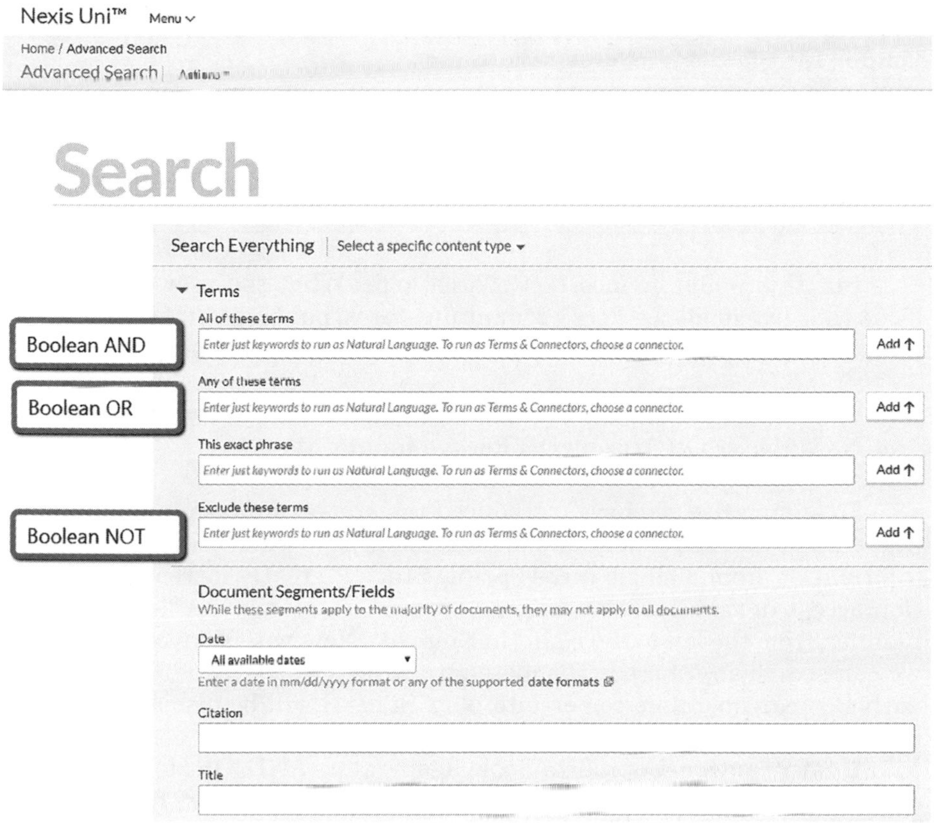

Nexis Uni™   Menu ˅

Home / Advanced Search
Advanced Search | Actions ™

Search

Search Everything | Select a specific content type ▾

▾ Terms

All of these terms

[Enter just keywords to run as Natural Language. To run as Terms & Connectors, choose a connector.]   [Add ↑]

Any of these terms

[Enter just keywords to run as Natural Language. To run as Terms & Connectors, choose a connector.]   [Add ↑]

This exact phrase

[Enter just keywords to run as Natural Language. To run as Terms & Connectors, choose a connector.]   [Add ↑]

Exclude these terms

[Enter just keywords to run as Natural Language. To run as Terms & Connectors, choose a connector.]   [Add ↑]

Boolean AND · **Boolean OR** · **Boolean NOT**

Document Segments/Fields
While these segments apply to the majority of documents, they may not apply to all documents.

Date

[All available dates   ▾]

Enter a date in mm/dd/yyyy format or any of the supported **date formats** ⓘ

Citation

[   ]

Title

[   ]

Figure 4.5. *Nexis Uni* inserts Boolean operators automatically. Reprinted with the permission of LexisNexis.

Table 4.2. Boolean operator idiosyncrasies from selected vendor interfaces.

Vendor Interface	Notes
Alexander Street	AND is default operator. Boolean searches using OR and NOT will not return appropriate results. Case doesn't matter.
EBSCOhost	AND takes precedence over OR. Case doesn't matter. "When Boolean operators are contained within a phrase that is enclosed in quotation marks, the operator is treated as a stop word. When this is the case, any single word will be searched for in its place."
ProQuest	Case doesn't matter. Proximity operators are processed first, then Boolean operators. Order of precedence among Boolean and proximity operators is (1) PRE, (2) NEAR, (3) AND, (4) OR, (5) NOT.
IEEE Explore	Case doesn't matter. Default AND operator.
ACM Digital Library	AND, OR, NOT capitalization required. Default OR operator.

(Continued)

Table 4.2. (*Continued*)

Vendor Interface	Notes
LexisNexis Academic	Case doesn't matter.
HeinOnline	AND, OR, NOT must be capitalized.
Entrez Interface (PubMed, etc.)	AND, OR, NOT must be capitalized. AND is the default operator.

But this would be incorrect search logic. What the user wants is not birds that live in all the Rocky Mountain states, but birds that live in any of the states. The proper search string in this case would be this:

bird* AND (Idaho OR Colorado OR Montana OR Wyoming OR New Mexico OR Arizona OR Rocky Mountain*)

To summarize, we have introduced the states of access to information. Stage 1 was the card catalog and printed index days when users had to access information from a single access point. Stage 2 greatly increased information access in that it was no longer necessary to search in a "left anchored" manner, from the left to the right (in English). Now, with keyword searching, we can search anywhere in the metadata. That's where the ability to search with Boolean operators comes into play. Stage 3 will be discussed later, in the context of proximity searching (Basic Tool No. 4).

Best Practice: Capitalize Boolean operators AND, OR, and NOT when searching because some databases require it, although others do not. This is a best practice to follow when teaching how to search.

Basic Tool No. 2: Controlled Vocabularies

We already discussed controlled vocabularies in chapter 3. Not every database product comes equipped with controlled vocabulary, but it can be useful when it is present. When it is not present, carefully selected keywords can be used.

When Do We Need Controlled Vocabulary?

When do you need to use controlled vocabulary searching? Let me suggest some contexts.

When you need to find "all and only" on a topic. If someone is doing their doctoral dissertation, they are responsible for turning up all relevant information on their topic. They first need to know whether anyone else has already done a dissertation on the same topic. If they have, and if it is from the exact same perspective, then our PhD student is in trouble. But they need to know that. Then, once they have arrived at a topic, they don't want to be embarrassed at their defense, having missed a seminal article on the subject. Undergrads, on the other hand, don't need "all and only"; they just need something on the topic.

When you need extreme precision for a topic. When attorneys want to find similar cases to assist you in a legal matter, and you are paying them expensive billing rates, they need vocabulary that will focus on the precise kind of law being researched.

When you need a unified approach to differing author voices. When topics are new within a field, the vocabulary around the topic has not settled. This is true across many fields. In medicine, new diseases are discovered and may not be fully understood. It is controlled vocabulary that can pull these discoveries together and make them discoverable to other researchers and avoid ambiguity.

Cautions When Using Controlled Vocabulary

You need to be very intentional when you use controlled vocabulary in searching. If you take the time to look up exact thesaurus terms, you had better also use the appropriate field tags when searching. Too many researchers spend time researching subject descriptors, only to lose much of the value of that time by executing mere keyword searches in the end, thus missing the point of discovering the relevant "all and only" records.

There are a couple of cautions about relying on controlled vocabularies. You need to ask yourself the following questions:

- Have controlled vocabulary terms been applied to every record in the database? If not, then a controlled-vocabulary search will only retrieve records that have the terms applied. Another kind of search, such as a keyword search, would need to be done to retrieve these other records. Examples of this situation include *PubMed*, which includes *Medline* records where MeSH subject headings have been applied, but it also includes newly added records where no MeSH heading have been applied. Also, older *PubMed* records will not have MeSH headings. Some aggregator databases, such as *Academic Search*, have back-generated vocabulary applied to some records, but not consistently to all records.

- How were the controlled vocabulary terms applied? Were they applied by professionals considering each record carefully, or were they applied en masse by a computer program without regard to the actual content?

- Consider the quality of the controlled vocabulary being applied. Is it created by an official association in the field, or is it merely a computer back-generated project?

- Has the controlled vocabulary changed over time? Some databases with thesauri explicitly state when terminology has changed. For example, in *PsycINFO*, the term *stigma* was introduced in 1991. That means that for items before that date, you would need to consider alternate search strategies.

- Consider the qualifications of the indexers applying the controlled vocabulary. Do they have sufficient background and training to understand the scholarly article content well enough to be able to knowledgeably apply the correct descriptors?

Not All Controlled Vocabulary Is Created Equal

You need to "consider the source" when deciding on the value of a controlled vocabulary and whether to rely on it. For example, when you read the qualifications necessary to index *Medline* articles, you will find that they must have at least a bachelor's degree in a biomedical science, with an ever-increasing number of indexers having advanced degrees. A reading knowledge of certain modern foreign languages is desired, and they receive extensive training in application of MeSH headings (U.S. National Library of Medicine 2017).

Patents are complex documents that require technical expertise and an extensive legal background to understand. They are carefully reviewed by patent examiners who ensure that the correct classifications have been assigned (U.S. Patent and Trademark Office 2012).

In the highly competitive legal profession, where quality of indexing is crucial to the credibility of the company's reputation, indexers of the highest quality and training are employed. Databases such as *Westlaw* and *Lexis* stand or fall on the quality of their controlled vocabulary. At the other end of the spectrum are pseudo-controlled vocabularies like those that are back-generated by aggregators.

Indexing is not an objective process, like descriptive cataloging; it is subjective. Traditionally, indexing is done by humans who have varying degrees of training, may differ in the way they apply descriptors from other indexers, and may even differ in the way they apply terms themselves from one article to another. Lancaster (2003) has identified several possible factors that can affect consistency in indexing:

- number of terms assigned
- controlled vocabulary versus free text indexing
- size and specificity of vocabulary
- characteristics of subject matter and its terminology
- indexer factors (background and experience of indexer)
- tools available to the indexer
- length of item to be indexed

Best Practice: Study the history and background of databases to the extent possible. This way, you can know whether to place much confidence in the subject terms or just consider them as nonauthoritative suggestions.

Basic Tool No. 3: Field Searching

Database fields were introduced in chapter 2. There are two ways databases generally handle field searching: (1) use of a form to select desired fields to search and (2) use of a command search interface to do it yourself.

The former is easier to use for the beginner; the latter is more complicated, varies for each interface, is generally used by experts, and can make searching very fast and efficient.

Some databases allow libraries to decide whether to present users with a basic search interface or with an advanced search interface. Arguments can be made for either decision. If the decision is made to present a basic search interface, users are presented with a single search box, much like they are accustomed to when searching a Web search engine, such as Google. The argument is that this is familiar, inviting, and encourages users to enter keywords.

Other libraries opt to present users with an advanced search form. Although the screen is busier, with several rows of search boxes visible and pull-down menu selections available, the argument here is that users know up-front the options available to them and can decide at the outset whether they want to just enter keywords, as in a basic search, or if they want to go beyond that and specify fields to search.

In most cases, the result screen will contain limiters to further constrain the search results. There is more on this later with Basic Tool No. 6 in chapter 5. For now, let's focus on how to leverage field searching to get the best results.

Default Fields

By default, most databases preselect for you which fields will be searched. This is by design. These are generally groupings of fields, but not all fields. The power searcher must be fully aware of what a default search does and does not search. This involves studying both the structure of the metadata in the database records as well as the fields, field labels, and field groupings within the search interface.

When performing field searching, pay special attention to field labels and what they mean. This often means taking the time to read the vendor's help pages. In OCLC *WorldCat*, field labels show a hierarchy. For example, "keyword"—we don't know what that means yet because we haven't tested it. In the *WorldCat* search form, we see the following entries indented under the more general "Author" heading:

- Author Phrase

- Corporate and Conference Name

- Corporate and Conference Name Phrase

- Personal Name

- Personal Name Phrase

Field Searching Strategies

Examine the structure of metadata. Check for field consistency. Publisher databases (e.g., Elsevier, Wiley, Sage) tend to have great consistency from record to record in terms of field consistency. Aggregator databases (e.g., Gale, EBSCO, ProQuest), because they often merge metadata from different sources, will have a variety of fields. In EBSCO's *Business Source* database, some records about Microsoft have fields with a DUNS number, and some do not.

Leverage the available fields. Change it up. Don't stop with your first search strategy. Find the three most relevant records in your initial search result. Are there synonyms that you didn't consider the first time? Are there fields that can be used as "hooks" to retrieve a more precise result set? Take these observations and frame another search, a better one, to come closer to "all and only."

Build up searches gradually. If you put in all the values at the same time, you have no idea which search terms worked and which ones did not.

Combining Field Searching with Controlled Vocabulary Searching

Let's say you want to search *ABI/Inform* (ProQuest) to find companies involved in bankruptcy. You might start with a subject heading search. In the ProQuest interface you can select the "Subject Heading – MAINSUBJECT" field tag, then select the "Look up subject headings (all)" link. From there, you can enter the term *bankruptcy*, and, sure enough, it is a valid subject heading with over 28,000 records so tagged in the database. Adding that term to the search takes you back to the advanced search form, where you see the search already entered for you: "Exact("bankruptcy")." You can now use additional fields to limit the search to a particular company (e.g., Toys "R" Us); location (state names work well in this database); or person's name (e.g., Buffett, Warren). You could also do the controlled-vocabulary search first in this case and use the limiters to restrict by these same features.

Subject descriptors aren't always capable of capturing the exact "aboutness" of items. As already mentioned, sometimes indexers don't add enough descriptors, sometimes the article is not fully understood, and sometimes computer processes were used to add subjects. The expert searcher should always play with a variety of search strategies, and mixing it up is an excellent one.

Read the Documentation

Reading the documentation sounds obvious, right? Most publisher and aggregator databases have some kind of help materials available that can be discovered with just a bit of poking around. If that fails, you might try a Google search for the documentation. For example, if you were looking for an in-depth discussion of searchable fields in *ProQuest Dissertations & Theses Global*, you would first go to the help portion of the database, in this case the question mark in the upper righthand corner of the search interface. But after searching through there, you discover that there is not specific information about each of the fields, what information is contained in them, or what the "shape" of the information is.

I recommend a Google search at this point: "site:proquest.com dissertations fields." This is a domain-specific search within Google. You are directing Google to search only within the proquest.com Internet domain. One of the search results is from ProQuest Libguides: http://proquest. libguides.com/pqdt. This is the page you really need. Whereas the help embedded within the database assisted with generalities, it took a Google search to discover exactly what you were looking for: how to frame a search for dissertation adviser, school name, supplementary files, and all other searchable fields.

Exercises

1. Consider these sets of statements:

   a. ducks OR geese NOT migration

   (ducks OR geese) NOT migration

   b. (ducks AND geese) OR loons

   ducks AND (geese OR loons)

   c. (ducks OR geese) AND migration

   ducks OR (geese AND migration)

   (ducks OR (geese NOT migration)) AND lakes

   Try drawing Venn diagrams for the search statements in each of the sets above to see how (or if) they differ. Then try describing in words what the context of the documents retrieved by these statements would be. Test out the statements in the basic search mode of any of these databases that you have access to: *ProQuest Central*; *Academic Search* (whatever version you have access to: *Elite, Premier, Complete,* or *Ultimate*); *Academic OneFile* or *General OneFile*; or *LexisNexis Academic*.

2. You receive a chat question: "What is a good sentence to put into the search bar besides "Why is Keystone XL so controversial."" Using what you know of framing searches, how would you suggest this student construct a search?

3. Using *ABI/Inform*, suggest a search strategy for finding results on Christmas tree farms. Suggest a strategy using the Boolean operators AND and OR. Then suggest another search strategy combining Boolean searching with controlled vocabulary.

References

"Boole, George (1815–1864)." 2016. In *The Hutchinson Dictionary of Scientific Biography*, edited by Helicon. Helicon. Accessed via *Credo Reference* database.

Lancaster, F. Wilfred. 2003. *Indexing and Abstracting in Theory and Practice*. 3rd ed. Champaign: University of Illinois.

U.S. National Library of Medicine. 2017. "Frequently Asked Questions about Indexing for MEDLINE." Accessed November 20, 2017. https://www.nlm.nih.gov/bsd/indexfaq.html.

U.S. Patent and Trademark Office. 2012. *Examiner Handbook to the U.S. Patent Classification System.* Accessed November 20, 2017. https://www.uspto.gov/patent/laws-and-regulations/examiner-handbook-us-patent-classification-system.

Beyond the Textbook

Carrying on the tradition of the fourth edition, additional exercises, search tips, and tutorials will be available on the publisher's Web site at http://www.abc-clio.com/books.librariesunlimited.com/Librarians-Guide-to-Online-Searching. This will be updated periodically with the inevitable database changes.

5

The Searcher's Toolkit: Part 2

Basic Tool No. 4: Proximity Searching

In the previous chapter, you were introduced to the stages in the evolution of searching for information. What I referred to as stage 1 was the time when information could only be accessed one concept at a time: think of the card catalog lookup procedure. Stage 2 referred to the onset of computers and the ability to search multiple concepts within machine-readable records. Things have now further evolved in terms of technology to the point that you are, more often than not, able to search across entire texts of articles, books, and other textual items—what I refer to as stage 3. For these kinds of searches, you need more powerful tools in your toolbox: proximity searching tools.

Why We Need Proximity Searching

Boolean operators work extremely well for short spans of text. For example, when databases search metadata in bibliographic records, AND, OR, and NOT work very well. But when the span of text is long, as in a full-text book, a long journal article, or a newspaper article, you will not be as well served by this kind of search strategy.

Think about the reason you even need proximity searching. You need it because you are trying to search large spans of text as opposed to brief texts, especially texts where the metadata does not have sufficient depth when compared to the length of the text. Newspapers typically have a title, a byline (author), and maybe a brief annotation or abstract. There may not be any subject terms associated with the articles. For this reason, the default search option for many newspaper databases is full text. But in these cases, Boolean operators are often not sufficient. For example, the article may have the term "Japan" in the initial paragraph and the word "Olympics" 20 paragraphs later. It is likely that this article is not really about the 2020 Olympics in Tokyo, but it merely mentions the word in some other context. However, terms that are near each other usually have greater relevance to each other, and by employing proximity operators, we can find the records where this is the case.

The same holds true for book searching. When searching e-book databases (which we deal with more in chapter 9), we are attempting to search large spans of text. We need more power than Boolean operators can offer. Searching for term x in close relation to term y, and not just in the same 400-page work, increases the usefulness of the search results.

In years past, searching *LexisNexis Academic* was quite a challenge. Any search that returned 1,000 or more results would be unsorted, and you could not be certain that the search was even complete. To get accurate results, it was necessary to apply sufficient limits in advance so that the results would be fewer than 1,000. This often proved to be quite a challenge. But with the new *Nexis Uni* interface, just released in the fall of 2017, users get an experience closer to what we get when we search other major databases. The ceiling of 1,000 records retrieved no longer applies.

Let's see what happens in *Nexis Uni* if we just use Boolean operators when searching for newspaper content. The topic is hiking on Colorado trails. If I search the common Boolean way—"colorado AND hiking AND trails"—we get too many irrelevant results (10,000+).

Proximity Operators

At this point, we need to think about how to achieve better relevancy in our results. Think about it: we are searching newspapers in their full text, not just metadata. We want newspaper articles where the term *colorado* is very near the terms *hiking* and *trails*. We need proximity searching here, not Boolean searching. We don't want *colorado* to be in the first paragraph and *hiking* to be far away 15 paragraphs later. *Nexis Uni* uses proximity operators pretty much the same way as *LexisNexis Academic* did, but with just a few minor adjustments. (If you are really concerned about these differences, just look at the *Nexis Uni* help if you subscribe). See table 5.1.

By applying proximity operators to our newspaper search in *Nexis Uni*, we retrieve under 10,000 records and can now be confident that we are seeing all the records we should be. We can now limit results by location, publication type, or other limits (see figure 5.1).

In this example, we searched within the same paragraph, but we could have alternatively specified a proximity of an arbitrary number of words. In the *Nexis Uni* search language, *colorado w/5 hiking w/5 trails* means that *colorado* must be within five words (not counting stop words) of *hiking* and that *hiking* must be within five of *trails* (again, not considering stop words).

Now let's do proximity searching in a different newspaper database, NewsBank's *Access World News*. Looking at the help screen, you'll notice that there are two kinds of proximity operators: *ADJn* (for adjacency, or up to a specified number of words between terms in the order entered) and *NEARn* (for when the terms are not in a specific adjacency order,

Table 5.1. Proximity Operators under Nexis Uni.

Nexis Uni Connector	Meaning and Usage
/p or w/para	Within the same paragraph.
pre/p	*X pre/p y* means that term *x* precedes term *y* by approximately 75 words.
/s or w/sent	Within the same sentence.
pre/s	*X pre/s y* means that term *x* precedes term *y* be approximately 25 words.
w/n (where *n* is a number)	*Feral w/3 cat* finds documents where *feral* is within 3 words either side of *cat*. *W/3– w/5* means in approximately the same phrase; *w/25* means in approximately the same sentence; and *w/75* means in approximately the same paragraph.
pre/n (where *n* is a number)	The *w/n* connector finds terms on either side of the other term. But *pre/n* only finds words in a particular order, where the first term precedes the second term. *Summary pre/2 judgment* would find *summary judgment* but not *judgment summary*, a significantly different term.

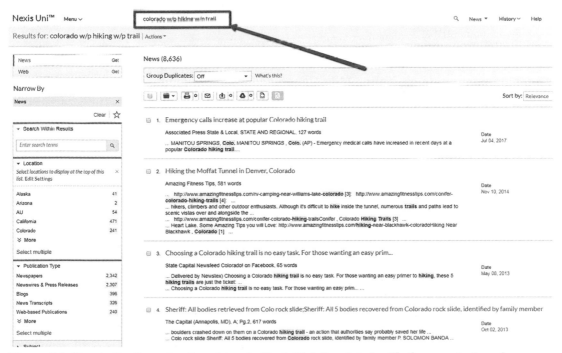

Figure 5.1. Proximity Operator Searching in *Nexis Uni*. Reprinted with the permission of LexisNexis.

Figure 5.2. Proximity searching in Newsbank's *Access World News. Source:* Newsbank, Inc. Used with permission.

but in any order). The *n* in these examples stands for a number. I need the *NEARn* proximity operator. For the example here, I searched "colorado NEAR8 hiking NEAR8 trails." Note that I specified an arbitrary eight-word distance between terms. I could have chosen any number. See figure 5.2. The same search with Boolean AND retrieved nearly 14,000 results.

Unlike Boolean operators, which are nearly universally used in much the same manner (with the occasional exception of databases that force users to capitalize AND, OR, and NOT), there is little uniformity with proximity operators. Nearly all databases that employ these operators use different syntax. The following table of proximity operators in selected databases highlights some of these differences (table 5.2).

Best Practice: Always read the help pages when attempting proximity searches. Never assume the way searches are formed.

Phrase Searching

Phrase searching is closely related to proximity searching. Users became so accustomed to using quotation marks when searching for phrases in Google and other search engines that database vendors had to incorporate searching with quotation marks into their products. Now most databases have this feature, and users find it very intuitive.

Google, as well as other search engines, have forced library databases to change their ways. Through the 1990s, phrase searching was handled in varied ways, depending on the databases. Sometimes terms could be enclosed in quotation marks, but other times proximity operators, such as ADJ (for

Table 5.2. Proximity Operators in Selected Databases.

Database	Proximity Operators (*n* is a number value)
Adam Matthew Interface	*w/n*, within regardless of order
EBSCOhost Interface	*Wn* Within operator; order entered in search *Nn*, Near operator; regardless of order *Exact phrase*; use quotation marks (Note: This is the same as doing *N0* or *W0*.)
HeinOnline	"term1 term2"~n; ordered proximity Example: "Sotomayor hearing"~10
IEEE Xplore	*NEAR/n*; unordered proximity *ONEAR/n*; ordered proximity
Nexis Uni	*w/n, w/p, w/s, pre/n* Example: business profit w/10 tax deduction
NewsBank *Access World News*	*ADJn* *NEARn* Example: Michael ADJ2 Fox (born Michael Andrew Fox, professionally known as Michael J. Fox)
ProQuest Interface	*NEAR/n OR N/n* *PRE/n OR P/n*
Readex Interface (including AllSearch)	*ADJn*; order entered *NEARn*; regardless of order Ex: Verizon ADJ sues (no number same as ADJ1)

adjacency), would need to be used. Now, however, the quotation mark convention is nearly universal.

Quotation marks are most useful with frozen phrases, that is, terms that do not change in the way they are used or referenced. For example, we always say "United States" when referring to the country; we never say "the States that are United." We say "global warming," but not "warming that is global." These have become lexically frozen terminology in our language. Academic literature is replete with accepted terminology that can be easily isolated with phrase searches.

There will be times that you want to find exact terminology, especially when searching full texts such as newspapers, e-book content, or Web pages. The notion of "right of first refusal" is sometimes incorrectly called "first right of refusal." You may want, for some reason, to locate those instances. The phrase search allows for searching an exact phrase as if it were a single term.

Although very powerful, phrase searches should not be used exclusively. There will be instances where alternative turns of the phrase are used. As in all search strategies, you shouldn't get locked into a single way to search for things, but you should always seek to adjust your search tactics based on the search at hand.

Basic Tool No. 5: Truncation and Wildcards

Truncation

To truncate something is to cut it off. This is one of the most useful and used features of databases. Truncation allows searchers to find variations of words, such as plural forms or word suffixes (e.g., the English past tense "ed"). For example, say you want to search for various forms of the word *environment*. These forms include *environments, environmental, environmentalist, environmentalists,* and *environmentalism.* Perhaps the most common truncation symbol is the asterisk (*). By searching "environment*," you can retrieve records containing any and all of the forms of the word *environment* just listed. Think of it as any characters to the right of the truncation symbol but before a space.

Truncation can be very helpful, but it can also backfire and produce too many or irrelevant results. If, for example, you truncated it as "environ*," in addition to all the terms we noted above, you would also retrieve the word *environs*, which doesn't necessarily have anything to do with the topic. Searching "e*" would be ridiculous. First, because, if it worked at all, it would retrieve all words beginning with *e*, and, second, most search systems wouldn't even allow this search to work, as truncation is generally allowed only for words of three or more characters.

As noted above, the nearly universal truncation symbol is the asterisk (*). Search interfaces such as EBSCOhost, the general ProQuest interface, and Gale's databases all use the asterisk as the truncation symbol. Most databases use the asterisk, and it is generally safe to assume it to be the truncation symbol, unless you observe unexpected results.

For many years, *LexisNexis Academic* has used the exclamation mark (!) as the truncation symbol. But now, *Nexis Uni* uses the asterisk as a truncation symbol as well as the exclamation mark. Both symbols work in the same way in *Nexis Uni*. Users should always read the available help information. I know, users rarely read the help. But for librarians and other who want to truly be expert searchers, this is very important to do.

Truncation used to be a more well-known feature among databases. But then Web search engines happened. Search engines like Google do not use truncation. Instead, they tend to do automatic stemming and background synonymy. The problem is that you can't always rely on a search engine to perform for you because they don't tell us how they really work. You just have to play around with different searches until you get the desired results.

Some databases have a stemming feature. This means an automatic truncation. Overt truncation requires a symbol to tell the search function you want all possible characters to the right (in English). In stemming, no symbol is necessary. When you search the term environment, the system automatically assumes that you also want all the other possible forms (*environments, environmental,* etc.). Adam Matthew has a limited stemming feature. A search for *book* will retrieve *book, books,* and *booked,* but it will not return *bookseller. Compendex* (Engineering Village), by default, has an auto-stemming feature that can be disabled if desired.

Wildcards

The idea of wildcards is closely related to truncation. In fact, some vendors use the terms interchangeably. But here we make the distinctions that are most often made: truncation is a character (symbol) that stands in place of any number of characters to the right (but would be to the left in Arabic, Hebrew, etc.). A wildcard stands in the place of a single character or, in many cases, no characters at all. If you were searching for *woman* but also wanted to retrieve *women* in the result set, truncation wouldn't make much sense: *wom**. You can imagine the unintended consequences with that search. Using the nearly universal wildcard character, the question mark (?), we should instead frame our search like this: *wom?n*.

Wildcards may also stand in the place of zero-to-one characters. Rather than explain this, we'll illustrate it. The American spelling is *color*, but the British spelling of the same word is *colour*. A wildcard can be used to account for both instances. If you search "colo?r," you will retrieve both "color" and "colour." Think of all the other common differences in British spellings where this strategy might be useful: saviour, honour, labour, humour, flavour, and neighbour. Then there are other differences, such as organization/organisation, apologize/apologise, and recognize/recognise.

How would you do a search that could account for the British spelling *theatre* (which is also commonly used here in the United States)? Would you search like this: "theat??"? Would you search like this: "theat*"? The problem with the truncation strategy is that it makes the search too broad, as you would also retrieve *theatrical*. Or would you resort to Boolean OR and search "theater OR theatre"?

We can test this out in a few databases. Starting with *Academic Search* (default search fields), we are met with a surprise: the search for "theater" gives us the same number of results as "theatre." It is obvious that EBSCO is doing work behind the scenes for us, giving us a merged result set with either spelling. It should be noted that *ProQuest Central* does the same thing, but Gale's *Academic OneFile* does not.

In recent years, vendors seem to be striving to use similar truncation symbols so as not to be the exception to the rule. The older *LexisNexis Academic* used the exclamation mark as its truncation symbol. But the newer *Nexis Uni* uses the asterisk.

There seem to be more exceptions to the ways that wildcards are used across databases. In the case of EBSCO, the wildcard is represented by a question mark. The pound sign/hashtag (#) in EBSCO is also called a wildcard, but it does not have the same function as the question mark:

- ? stands for one additional character, but not for 0 characters.

- # stands for zero or one instances of a character.

As you can see, rules for wildcards are very precise, persnickety, and even annoying, as rules differ from one vendor interface to another. Unlike Boolean operators where there is a great degree of predictability, wildcards sometimes take careful study to ensure expected results.

The bottom line is that, when in doubt, you should always carefully read the help screens.

Review of Tools 4 and 5

Proximity searching goes beyond what Boolean searching can do in that it gives you greater control of the closeness of words to each other. Phrase searching allows for turning words into longer, more distinctive strings of characters to be able to focus in on discipline-specific terminology. Proximity and phrase searches have the effect of narrowing a search.

Truncation is a broadening strategy that accounts for any number of characters (or no other characters) at the end of a word. Wildcards are internal to words, substituting for alternations in spellings.

Basic Tool No. 6:
Limits to Constrain Your Search

Databases have greatly improved in speed and functionality over the past 30 years. One of the great improvements in this evolution has been the increase in the use of limiters, or facets. What used to require a lot of careful decision making and choices before searching can now be done after the fact. A good example of this is *ProQuest Congressional*. Not so long ago, if you didn't select your search scope at the outset (whether searching for congressional hearings, reports, etc.), searches would take too long. Now, however, even though users can select search scope before hitting the submit button, they don't have to. There is no time penalty for using the side limiters on the results page to focus the search results. This functionality seems to generally be the case across most vendor database products.

Silos and Limits

Some databases limit search results at the outset by "siloing" the information. *LexisNexis Academic* was an example of this. It was not possible to search across all *LexisNexis Academic* content with an initial search. At the outset, users had to preselect whether they wanted to search news, legal cases, statutes or regulations, law review articles, or company information. The new *Nexis Uni* interface changes that; searching is now performed across all content, with facets to allow users to focus on news, cases, statutes, or regulations after the initial search is entered.

American FactFinder also has some information silos going on. Data from the *American Community Survey* is of such a different nature from the Economic Census data, that users must preselect which data set they wish to search (but more on that in chapter 8).

Limits before Submitting Searches

It is common for databases to allow users to limit search results at the same time they submit search requests, including limited to scholarly publications and limiting to full text availability.

Limit to scholarly publications. Perhaps no limit is more important to the undergraduate student learning how to do research. They may not know or care how this limit works, but they view it as essential to their academic success.

Differences between Scholarly and Nonscholarly Journal Articles

One of the skills most important to college students is the ability to identify peer-reviewed journal articles. Also called *academic articles* or *scholarly articles,* these are often one of the most important criteria for inclusion in research papers, and the ability to select them accurately affects a student's grades.

Many databases provide ways to limit to scholarly publications before the search is initiated. But so we are clear on what these publications are, the differences between scholarly and nonscholarly articles are highlighted here:

Scholarly Articles

• Authored by experts in the field with advanced degrees behind their names

• Replete with bibliography or references cited

• Deals with previous literature on the topic

• Often published in a publication with an uninteresting but very descriptive title

Nonscholarly Articles

• Authored by professional writers who are not usually experts in the academic field
• Sources usually not well cited
• Stands alone, with little reference to previous scholarship
• Often published in a publication with a memorable title and slick paper with graphics

---

Most databases do not tell you how to determine whether a journal is scholarly or nonscholarly, although most titles are easy for anyone to guess. A tool that will help with this determination is *Ulrich's Periodicals Directory.* Published by Bowker, a ProQuest company, the directory has an online version known as *Ulrichsweb,* which was mentioned in chapter 1. Reasons for consulting the database include the following:

• Verifying that a journal is indeed scholarly and academic in nature

• Checking on the scholarly nature of journals listed in Google Scholar, as questionable journal content does, on occasion, show up in results there

- Building confidence in one's ability to discern peer-reviewed content from other content

The Summon discovery tool (discussed later in chapter 13) incorporates *Ulrichsweb* into its search results. When users select the "peer-reviewed" limit in Summon, it is *Ulrichsweb* that is used to supply the peer-reviewed determination (Scardilli 2014).

Just because an article shows up tagged as "scholarly" in a database does not mean that you should throw all your evaluative skills out the door. Not every article published in academic journals is itself academic. Let's try a little experiment to test this out.

Go to EBSCO's *Academic Search* database (whichever version you have). Do a keyword search for *engineering*. Next, click the facet for "Scholarly (Peer Reviewed) Journals." Notice that it says "Journals," not "Articles." EBSCO is careful to note that a journal may generally be scholarly while not all content is necessarily scholarly. Now look at the *Academic Search* result set. You will notice that you can further limit with the "Book Review" facet. Do that and examine four or five of the results. You will see that although the database says that the journal is scholarly, the book reviews have the specific purpose of reviewing book titles and not of presenting full scholarly, academic article content. This serves as a lesson that databases can lead you down a path, but they cannot know about every pothole on that path.

Limit to full text. In an aggregator database, a limit to full text generally means a limit to full text that is available in the aggregator database. But this is not as transparent as it may seem. Your library may well subscribe to other sources of full text, but the aggregator database will not know about this and will not be able to search the full text. If you are really concerned about this and need to search a wider swath of scholarly full-text content, then my recommendation is Google Scholar. No, really. Google Scholar, with all its flaws, does an excellent job of searching the full text of a very high percentage of scholarly publications (Brown 2017).

Limits after Results Are Presented

Users have different searching styles. Some prefer constructing all the constraints and limits before hitting the search button, but others like to wait until after results are delivered. Several decades ago, when search engines were much slower, it was almost always necessary to predetermine all the search limits, given the slow processing time of databases. But now, with newer technologies, online databases return more results in faster time, with facets or limiters, usually on the left- or righthand side of the results. These limiter enhancements, which can be turned on or off in an instant, make focusing searches a breeze.

Basic Tool No. 7: Learning from Your Results

This tool is so basic that it's easy to overlook. We do it all the time, but it's important that you do it intentionally, thinking about what you are doing and being systematic about it.

Research is a process, and so is database searching. Searching is a lot like asking a question at a library reference desk. You ask the question because you don't already know the answer. If you knew what the answer was going to be, you could ask a more intelligent and properly framed question. The same is true in searching. You don't really know what resources you are going to uncover. You do your best to use the best keywords or, if taking more time, the best controlled-vocabulary terms.

Tool 7 is simply this: *you start somewhere, examine your initial result set, and then reframe your search.* The result set may have items that are close to what you are looking for, but the wording is different. You learn from that and either throw out your initial ideas or add to them from what you have learned. How exactly do you "learn from" your initial results? You learn by observing what worked and what didn't work and acting on that information. Write down keywords that worked. Look up synonyms to the keywords you found. If the database has a controlled vocabulary, find the subject terms that match your keywords. As you will learn in chapter 10, once you have found your best articles, another learn-from-your-results strategy is to use *Web of Science*, *Scopus*, and Google Scholar to see who cites your best articles.

Terms in the Searching Lexicon

False Drops

We're not talking about rain, here; we're talking about results that are not what you are looking for, or noise. False drops, or false hits, can occur for a number of reasons. Perhaps the most common reason is synonymy: words in a language can have many meanings. Searchers often don't put in sufficient mechanisms to prevent retrieval of irrelevant items. In this section, you will learn some methods for minimizing false drops and retrieving a greater degree of relevance.

Select words that are not prone to ambiguity. If a term is ambiguous, try pairing it with a concept that disambiguates things. The term *mercury* has many meanings. It may mean the Roman god, the make of an automobile, a metal, the temperature, or the planet. ANDing another search term will help clarify the results: Mercury AND automobile, planet AND Mercury, mercury AND thermometer, Mercury AND god AND Rome.

Try searching for a phrase instead of a term with a single word. Use this only if relevant. Phrase searching is often incorrectly used and should only be employed when the phrase is proven to be frozen in the literature. As previously mentioned, *United States* is such a frozen phrase. Nobody would ever say *States that are United*. While *United States of America* is certainly correct, it is not used nearly as often as the shorter *United States* and should generally be avoided. Systematic reviews are an established literature type in the social sciences, so searching the phrase *systematic review* makes sense.

While *United States Congressional Serial Set* is certainly the proper way to refer to the massive set of publications issued by Congress from 1817 to present, many reference in literature refer to it as the *Congressional Serial Set* or simply the *Serial Set*. So it would be ill-advised to search the longest term above.

To summarize, your goal is to get as many true hits as possible and to avoid searches that retrieve false results (dropped into the result set).

Stop Words

Not all words are created equal. Some words carry a lot of meaning, whereas others seem to have no meaning; but we wouldn't communicate very well without them. Function words are words like the articles *a*, *an*, and *the*. Prepositions have functions, but not a naming (noun) function or action (verbal) function. Regular prepositions are very short and simple: *in*, *of*, *at*, *by*. But other prepositions are longer or compound: *under*, *between*, *without*, *within*, *into*, *beneath*, *behind*, *below*. To save processing resources, most databases ignore (or "stop") words that are short or are likely to carry no significant meaning. It can be tricky when the words you are looking for have been declared "stop words" by the database you are searching, as these tend to be the most common words in the language.

It is easy to find stop word lists for various vendors. Rather than providing lengthy URLs to these lists, the easiest way to find them is to search Google. Here are some example searches:

PubMed stop words

EBSCO stop words

ProQuest stop words

Just follow the same pattern for other databases.

A classic example is the phrase from Shakespeare "To be or not to be," where every word is a stop word. Google ignores stop words if the phrase is enclosed in quotes. However, not all databases behave this way. EBSCO, for example, does not search stop words, even if enclosed in quotes. The only way to know how a database deals with stop words is (1) to read the help pages and (2) to test things out.

Recall vs. Precision

When you search a database, the results list returned is called *recall*. But the number of relevant results returned is called *precision*. When you build a search query, you want to retrieve all the desired results (called *true positives*) and none of the undesirable ones (*true negatives*). But it's not that easy. What about the results that were retrieved that you didn't want but that technically met the search criteria as entered? These are called *false positives*. That leaves all the possible results that you are not interested in and that your query didn't find at all: *true negatives*.

We can summarize like this:

True positives are the search results you intended to retrieve. These are relevant for you.

False positives are search results that were retrieved in your result set, but they are not at all relevant.

True negatives are items that were not found in your search, but you don't care about them because they have nothing to do with what you are seeking.

False negatives are search failures. These are items you would have wanted to see, but they were not retrieved. One way to look at this is in table 5.3.

We can also illustrate retrieved items in the context of relevance this way (figure 5.3).

Table 5.3. Retrieval vs. relevance.

	Retrieved	**Not Retrieved**
Relevant	True positives	False negatives
Not Relevant	False positives	True negatives

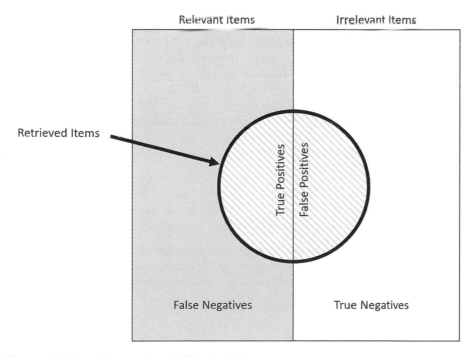

Figure 5.3. Precision and recall illustrated.

Now that we have set up the possible kinds of results, we are ready to define *recall* and *precision*.

Recall: the number of relevant items found divided by the number of relevant items out there (N):

Recall = (True positives)/[(True positives) + (False negatives)]

Precision: the number of relevant items found divided by the number of items found (relevant and irrelevant):

Precision = (True positives)/[(True positives) + (False positives)]

If you have good recall, you don't wind up with a lot of missed but relevant items, but your results could be diluted by a lot of false positives or items that are wrongly retrieved as being relevant when they are not.

If you have good precision, on the other hand, you can be more confident that your results are relevant, but you may be missing a lot of other relevant items in your search (you could have a large number of false negatives). Error rate is just the proportion of both types of errors to the total number of relevant items you ideally would like to retrieve.

Testing a Database

We have covered many concepts to this point. The best way to put these into practice is to do a series of tests in a specific database. This exercise is a good one to do when your library is trialing a new database product. Of course, you could start by reading all the help pages before doing anything. But who does that? I'm sure there is a small subset of librarians that start by reading all the help pages first (I know a librarian who does so!). But for the rest of us, these tests will tell us very quickly how the database works and will simultaneously give us experience and competence with searching.

Field Test: What fields are available, and which fields are searched by default?

Full-Text Test: Does the database search full text by default, or does it just search the metadata only by default? If the database does search full text by default, do all records contain full text, or only selected records?

Boolean Test: Are Boolean operators searched by default? When keywords are entered, are they in an adjacency relationship? Are they ANDed or are they ORed? Do Boolean operators need to be capitalized?

Phrase Test: Does enclosing a series of words in quotation marks force a phrase search?

In addition to the above tests, you should also ask: What are the stop words? What are the truncation and wildcard symbols? Is there implicit truncation or overt truncation?

Exercises

1. A user is looking for information about controlling feral cat populations in city parks. Try searching for results in a favorite database using Boolean operators. Now use the same database, but search the topic with proximity operators. How did you construct your proximity search? How do the results from the Boolean search compare to the results from the proximity search?

2. Why would you want a database to search some words but not others?

3. Someone is looking for information about online library catalogs in public or academic libraries in Japan, South Korea, and China. First, break this question down, analyzing one concept at a time. Online catalogs are sometimes called OPACs. We can break out these concepts like this:

   Concept 1: online catalogs

   > Online catalog* OR OPAC*

   Concept 2: libraries

   > Academic librar* OR public librar*

   > Alternatively, we might put the search together like this:

   > (academic OR public) librar*

   Concept 3: countries

   > Japan OR "South Korea" OR China

   Now, come up with one or more well-constructed search statements (remember to use parentheses!) and test them in one or more multidisciplinary databases (e.g., *Academic OneFile*, *Academic Search*, *ProQuest Central*).

References

Brown, Christopher C. 2017. *Harnessing the Power of Google: What Every Researcher Should Know.* Santa Barbara, CA: Libraries Unlimited.

Scardilli, Brandi. 2014. "Getting the Most Out of Discovery Service." *Information Today*, June 3. Accessed August 31, 2014. http://newsbreaks.infotoday.com/NewsBreaks/Getting-the-Most-Out-of-Discovery-Service-97380.asp.

Beyond the Textbook

Carrying on the tradition of the fourth edition, additional exercises, search tips, and tutorials will be available on the publisher's Web site at http://www.abc-clio.com/books.librariesunlimited.com/Librarians-Guide-to-Online-Searching. This will be updated periodically with the inevitable database changes.

6
Database Interfaces: Vendor Features and Variations

To the uninitiated database user, it may appear on the surface that all databases are pretty much the same. But there are great differences in database types, user interfaces, features, interactions with external content, access to full text, limiters and facets, and personalization features. This chapter looks at many of these features, some of which are nearly universal across databases, while others are unique to particular databases.

Publisher vs. Aggregator Databases

It is important to make a distinction between publisher and aggregator databases. Publisher databases come directly from sources such as vendors, university presses, scholarly societies, or governments. Aggregator databases feature content from multiple publishers in a single interface.

Examples of publisher databases fall into many categories:

Vendor Databases (from commercial for-profit publishers)

- Elsevier's *Science Direct*
- *Emerald Insight*
- *IEEE Xplore*
- *Sage Journals*
- *SpringerLink*
- *Wiley Online Library*

University Press Databases

- *Oxford Scholarship Online*
- Cambridge University Press products (e.g., *Cambridge Core*)

Society Databases

- *American Chemical Society Journals*
- *American Mathematical Society Publications*
- *Royal Society of Chemistry Journals*

Government Databases

- Govinfo.gov (Government Publishing Office)
- National Technical Information Service (NTIS) Database
- *ERIC* database via U.S. Department of Education
- *PubMed*

Publisher database content is generally the most desirable, as the article content is nearly always in PDF format, is the most up to date, and may have additional features, such as recommended additional readings, citing articles, related book content, and various kinds of metrics.

At the other end of the spectrum are aggregator databases. An aggregator is a company that provides access to digitized content from a variety of sources, sometimes to complete issues, other times to selected content (CONSER 2016). Aggregator content is often in PDF format, although for older issues, the PDF may be a scan of a print version. Also, aggregators sometimes only provide the HTML version of content, lacking the original page layout and occasionally the charts, tables, and graphics in their originally published formats.

An advantage of aggregators is that they bring together content from multiple sources, providing a kind of one-stop shopping for content. This can save time over having to visit multiple silos of publisher content. Discovery tools, discussed in a later chapter, are a further development over even the aggregator database in that users can discover content from publishers' sites as well as aggregated content within a single interface.

Examples of aggregator databases include the following:

- *Academic Search* (EBSCO)
- *Business Source* (EBSCO)
- *ProQuest Central*
- *Academic OneFile* (Gale)

- *Project Muse*

- *Hein Online*

Now that you understand the differences between publishers and aggregators, let's step back and think about these differences from the perspective of online searching. Every publisher is rightfully proud of their content, the journals they publish, and their books as well. They also provide a search portal for searching across all the journals and e-books they publish. But this creates an awkward model for the searcher. Do we really expect researchers to search every publisher portal, one after another, in search of relevant information? Under this model, we should create checklists for students to search Elsevier's *Science Direct*, *Wiley Online Library*, *Sage Journals*, *SpringerLink*, *HeinOnline*, *Emerald Insight*, *Taylor & Francis Online*, Wolters Kluwer's *Cheetah* interface, Clarivate Analytics' *Web of Science*, and so forth. There is a time and place for these interfaces, but let's be clear about when that is necessary.

Use the *publisher* interface for the following scenarios:

- You only want to search within a specific journal.

- You need to search the full text of a specific journal.

- You want the special features provided by the publisher interface (as in the citation features provided by *Web of Science*).

- You want the subject-specific features of the portal (as in such legal databases as *HeinOnline* and *Cheetah*).

- You want to search all content from a specific publisher.

Here are the times you would want to use an *aggregator* product to search for content:

- You want to search in a cross-disciplinary fashion for your topic.

- You just want to find information, but you don't care who publishes it.

- You want to search across many document types, such as books, book chapters, book reviews, newspaper articles, dissertations and theses, magazine articles, scholarly journal articles, and image and multimedia content.

- You want the special features offered by an aggregator, such as saving searches or creating alerts to new content.

Even with aggregators, you still need to search many of them to get any kind of completeness of coverage. In business research, you would need to search EBSCO's *Business Source*, ProQuest's *ABI/Inform*, and Gale's *Business Collection* to ensure broad coverage of a topic.

Luckily, there are yet more tools for those occasions when you need to move beyond publisher and aggregator silo searching. The two types of resources for more comprehensive searching across publishers and aggregators are discovery tools (see chapter 13) and Google Scholar.

Databases Available from Multiple Sources

Have you ever noticed that some databases can be licensed through multiple vendors? For example, the *ERIC* database is available from EBSCO, ProQuest, and Ovid, and it is also available for free directly from the U.S. Department of Education. Numerous databases are available through various vendor platforms, either because the metadata was created by your U.S. taxpayer dollars or because the creator was an association that has less interest in providing a platform than in disseminating their records far and wide. Table 6.1 provides a selected list of database content available through more than one source.

Generally, libraries prefer to offer databases through vendor platforms that are already familiar to their user population. This makes the database cross-searchable with other databases and keeps as many databases as possible under a familiar interface. If a library generally prefers

Table 6.1. Database Content from Multiple Sources.

Database	Creator	Vendors
Agricola	U.S. National Library of Medicine	EBSCO Ovid ProQuest ProQuest *Dialog* USDA
Biological Abstracts	Clarivate Analytics	Clarivate Analytics via *Web of Science* interface EBSCO Ovid
BIOSIS	Clarivate Analytics	Clarivate Analytics via *Web of Science* interface EBSCO (Previews) Ovid (Previews) ProQuest *Dialog*
CAS Databases (including *SciFinder*)	Chemical Abstracts Services, division of American Chemical Society (ACS)	CAS ProQuest *Dialog* STN
Catalog of Government Publications	U.S. Government Publishing Office	GPO OCLC FirstSearch
Compendex	Elsevier (Engineering Information)	Elsevier via *Engineering Village* Ovid ProQuest *Dialog* STN
EconLit	American Economic Association	EBSCO Ovid ProQuest

Database	Creator	Vendors
ERIC	U.S. Department of Education	EBSCO Ovid ProQuest ProQuest *Dialog* U.S. Department of Education
GeoRef	American Geosciences Institute	American Geosciences Institute EBSCO *GeoRef Preview* Database *GeoScienceWorld* Database and *OpenGeoSci* Ovid ProQuest ProQuest *Dialog* STN
INSPEC	Institution of Engineering and Technology (IET)	EBSCO Elsevier via *Engineering Village* Clarivate Analytics via *Web of Science* Interface FIZ Karlsruhe (Germany) Ovid ProQuest ProQuest *Dialog* STN International
L'Annee Philologique	Société Internationale de Bibliographie Classique, in collaboration with the Society for Classical Studies	Société Internationale de Bibliographie Classique EBSCO
Medline	National Library of Medicine (US)	EBSCO OCLC FirstSearch Ovid ProQuest ProQuest *Dialog* *PubMed* STN
MLA International Bibliography	Modern Language Association (MLA)	EBSCO Gale (via Traditional Gale Interface) Gale (via *Artemis*) ProQuest (LION Interface)
NTIS Bibliographic Database	National Technical Information Service (U.S. Department of Commerce)	EBSCO Elsevier (*Engineering Village*) NTIS Ovid ProQuest ProQuest *Dialog* STN

(Continued)

Table 6.1. (*Continued*)

Database	Creator	Vendors
Philosopher's Index	Philosopher's Information Center	EBSCO Ovid ProQuest
PsycINFO	American Psychological Association (APA)	APA PsycNET EBSCO Ovid ProQuest ProQuest *Dialog*
Social Work Abstracts	National Association of Social Workers	EBSCO Ovid
Zoological Record	Clarivate Analytics	Clarivate Analytics via *Web of Science* interface EBSCO Ovid ProQuest

EBSCO database products, it is likely that they subscribe to *ERIC*, *PsycINFO*, and the *MLA International Bibliography* through that interface. In some cases, libraries may elect to offer the same database on multiple platforms.

Aggregator Interfaces

A vendor is not the same as a vendor's interface. ProQuest, for example, uses several interfaces for its many databases. When a vendor purchases another company and their databases, they typically don't change the database interface immediately. For example, when Cambridge Scientific Abstracts was purchased by ProQuest several years ago, their original interface was retained for several years. Eventually, all the CSA databases were merged into the new generic ProQuest search interface. As of this date, ProQuest still has some databases that have not been folded into this interface. ProQuest *Literature Online* was previously available under the Chadwyck-Healey interface, but it is now offered under the general ProQuest interface.

NewsBank, along with its subordinate company Readex, has several interfaces for its databases. *Access World News* has an interface that is both searchable and intuitively browsable from the interface. *AccessUN* is an old interface that hasn't been updated in years. The *Archive of Americana* interface from Readex incorporates all the historical periodical and newspaper content covering the breadth of U.S. history as well as the historical government documents contained in the *United States Congressional Serial Set* and

American State Papers. More examples can be given, but suffice it to say that most vendors have multiple interfaces and keeping up with them all can be a challenge.

The interface issue is forever complicated when one vendor buys out another. In recent years, ProQuest has bought out Congressional Information Service (CIS), Cambridge Scientific Abstracts, Alexander Street Press, CSA Illumina, Dialog, Chadwyck-Healey, eLibrary, Ebook Library (EBL), and ExLibris (ProQuest 2017).

EBSCO has acquired NetLibrary, the rights to the H. W. Wilson Company database content, and YBP (formerly known as Yankee Book Peddler).

Like it or not, mergers and acquisitions in the information sector are here to stay. What typically happens is that the acquiring company keeps the older branding and interface and merely adds new ownership information to the search interface. Eventually, the old vendor interface is done away with, and the databases are incorporated into the new vendor's interface. As searchers, we need to be able to deal with continual changes to interfaces.

This book cannot possibly provide support for all the varied functions and features of every vendor interface. But I can suggest two strategies to research the documentation of the various features.

> **Strategy 1:** From within a database, see if any context-sensitive help is available. Sometimes help will be available specific to the database you are searching; other times, it will be more generalized information.

> **Strategy 2:** Use Google to find documentation. I did a Google search on *ebscohost databases* and quickly found documentation beyond what is offered from within EBSCOhost databases (https://help.ebsco.com /interfaces/EBSCOhost).

Interfaces are important. Not only do they present the distinctive features of individual databases, but they make clear the capabilities of what is possible and not possible. In the next few pages, we will look at the major interfaces of the "big three" database aggregators. This will give us a feel for the scope of coverage and the ever-changing features and enhancements that exist today.

EBSCOhost Interface

EBSCO has numerous interfaces, as reflected on their site (http:// search.ebscohost.com) and in figure 6.1.

The most familiar interface to database searchers is the one branded as EBSCOhost. There are several hundred databases available through the EBSCOhost interface (as the primary interface for EBSCO, not surprisingly they try to fold most of their database content into it). I have attempted to group them into meaningful categories here. These lists are not complete, but they are representative of the wide breadth of topics and content available.

Figure 6.1. EBSCO's Multiple Interfaces. *Source:* ©2017 EBSCO Industries, Inc. All rights reserved.

Comprehensive database lists can be found on their Web site (https://www.ebsco.com).

Some of the EBSCOhost databases are marketed to schools and public libraries. These include *MAS Ultra—School Edition*; *Middle Search Plus*; *Primary Search*; *Explora*; *NoveList*, *Consumer Health Complete*; and *Flipster*. Many academic libraries feature some of these databases as well.

The list of available databases through the EBSCOhost interface for academic libraries is quite substantial, including *Academic Search (Elite, Premier, Complete, Ultimate)*; *Alternative Press Index*; *Alternative Press Index*; *America: History & Life* and *Historical Abstracts*; all the H. W. Wilson databases; and many others too numerous to mention here.

Even though presented under the same interface, search fields and limiters differ from database to database. Databases such as *Academic Search* and *Business Source* have fields for searching people, products and reviews, DUNS numbers, NAICS codes, and ticker symbols. For *PsycINFO*, EBSCO had to adapt the interface so that age groups, supplemental materials, population groups, methodologies, and the psychology classification codes could be searched. The *MLA International Bibliography* adds limits for period discussed within indexed works (broken down by century), genre, and a distinction between language of publication and subject language, all of which EBSCO had to find a way to accommodate through the EBSCOhost interface. Although cross-database searching sounds exciting, you lose the database-specific limiting functions when doing so. For power searching, it is never recommended to do cross-database searches.

Image Searching. One of the more stunning features of the EBSCOhost interface is the ability to search metadata for images. This feature is available in selected databases, including *Academic Search*, *Business Source*, *America: History and Life*; *Historical Abstracts*; *The Nation Archive*; *Library, Information Science & Technology Abstracts*; *MASTERfile; Art and Architecture*; *Associated Press Images*; *International Bibliography of Theatre & Dance*; and *Newspaper Source Plus*.

SmartText Searching. SmartText searching is available in nearly all EBSCOhost databases. "You can copy and paste large chunks of text to search for results. SmartText Searching leverages a technology that summarizes text entered to the most relevant search terms then conducts search. This search mode is not available for all databases" (EBSCO 2017). The system then attempts to discern the most relevant search terms in various fields within the database, including abstract, title, and subjects. Of course, I hope that you will become an expert searcher and will not need this feature.

Search History. The search history feature is useful in several ways. It allows users to keep track of past searches to see what worked well and what did not. This feature can also be used to build up a search. For example, an initial search might be *native americans AND poverty* (designated in the EBSCOhost search history as S1 with 353 results), and a second search might be *american indians AND poverty* (designated as S2 with 292 results). After observing that both searches have sizeable result sets, you can use the search history shorthand and do an OR Boolean search, like this: S1 OR S2 (439 results). Can you make a guess as to why the number of results is less than 353 + 292?

Index Browsing and Searching. Vendors like to leverage their online content by creating back-generated indexing of all content contained within the various fields. This is not to be confused with controlled vocabulary, as it was not constructed from a thesaurus authority. As discussed in chapter 3, these indexes are computer-generated logging of all instances of terms within a given field, with attempts to de-duplicate and clean up the data. As most databases have fields that differ from others, I will give only an example of indexes available from *Business Source* here: Author; Author-Supplied Keywords; Company Entity; Document Type; DUNS Number; Entry Date; Geographic Terms; Headings; ISBN; ISSN; Language; NAICS Code or Description; People; Publication Type; Reviews & Products; Thesaurus Term; Ticker Symbol; and Year of Publication.

Saving/Exporting Options. Rather than checking a box, as is done is many interfaces, EBSCOhost wants you to click the folder with a plus sign to temporarily save items. If you don't want the item only temporarily saved, you can create a personalized account, a popular feature across interfaces. After you have saved some items, you can view the content of your folder by clicking the folder icon at the top right of the screen. There are several options available, although the labels tend to confound users. The function of the e-mail link is obvious: users can e-mail the brief citation and abstract, a detailed citation and abstract, or a formatted citation. There is also the option to attach a PDF of the file (in cases where a PDF is available). If desired, a customized field output is available.

Users often get confused between the "save as file" and the "export" options. Saving a file really means saving a link to the file. There are special instructions for saving a PDF, which involves first opening it up in the Adobe Acrobat Reader application and then saving it from there. The export feature may seem cryptic to some as well. What EBSCO means is exporting the citation either directly to citation management software or indirectly to a file in a tagged format that is saved on a local computer (for later importing into citation management software).

Database aggregators have been tripping over each other to provide access to e-books and archival collections. EBSCO's e-book projects include the *Ebook Collection* and the *Ebook Comprehensive Academic Collection*. These collections include the e-books acquired by EBSCO when they acquired *NetLibrary* from OCLC in 2010. EBSCO also acquired YBP from Baker & Taylor in 2015, giving it control of the *GOBI* database for ordering print and e-books for library collection managers.

ProQuest Interface

ProQuest Central includes over 40 databases. Dozens of additional databases under the same interface, but not part of ProQuest Central, include *American Periodicals (1740–1940)*; *PsycINFO* (1806–current); *Periodicals Archive Online*; and *ProQuest Dissertations & Theses Global*, to name just a few. This list goes on.

EBSCO has clearly branded their EBSCOhost product, but ProQuest has not. We will just call their general search interface a "ProQuest" interface.

Clustering of Databases. ProQuest Central is a good example of database clustering. It contains over 40 databases combined in the ProQuest Central collection. In addition, outside of ProQuest Central, there are hundreds of other databases, all searchable through the same ProQuest interface. This includes whatever *ProQuest Historical Newspapers* an institution subscribes to as well as clusters of databases by discipline, such as the SciTech Premium Collection and the Social Science Premium Collection. The *Literature Online* (LION) database and *ProQuest Congressional* are not searchable through this interface.

Let's look at some of the features of the ProQuest interface. One of the first things to point out about the ProQuest interface is that you shouldn't use the back button on your browser. If you want to change your search, use the "modify search" button at the top of the screen. This will save you the frustration of losing your initial search string when navigating the databases.

Default Searching. By default, the ProQuest interface searches anywhere within the metadata as well as within the full text. This is the opposite default from EBSCOhost databases. However, libraries can override this and set up their ProQuest interface defaults to not search full text by default. Searchers should pay special attention to this when searching a ProQuest database, as that may explain why so many results are being returned.

The "autocomplete" feature can assist in framing an on-point search. This can also be turned off if desired.

"On-the-fly machine translation" is the capability of translating an article from its original language to other popular languages, as popularized by Google Translate.

The "cite" feature on every search results page makes for easy citation of one or all results on the page. Over 30 citation formats are listed, and local libraries can adjust the default styles to suit their audiences.

As search results are displayed, "limits" are also clearly displayed at the top of the search screen, just under the search terms. This makes it easy for researchers to see what limits have been applied and remove them if desired.

Alerts can easily be created using the "save search/alert" pull-down option. If you like the way you searched and want to be notified when other results matching your search criteria are added to the database, you can use the "save search/alert" button to set this up. Of course, you will need to set up your personalized account first. You will then be notified when items are added that match your search criteria.

Generating Citations. For quick citations (that is, without having to export citations to bibliographic citation management software first), ProQuest provides a "Cite" link at the top of the results. This is a nice feature to keep in mind. Just select the desired style and pop it into your research paper.

Less clear is how to export citations to bibliographic management software. For this, users must click the "save" pull-down option. A mouseover reveals that this is really the "export/save" option. ProQuest was apparently saving screen space at the expense of clarity.

Saving/Exporting. Selecting items places them in a folder. The folder icon is in the top far right of the results page, but many of the folder options can be executed from the results page without even having to visit your folder, such as e-mailing, printing, and saving items. The "Save" feature is intended both for saving the PDF, HTML, or text content and for exporting citation information to citation software (described above).

ProQuest's experience with e-books is also vast. They have *E-Book Central* (formerly known as *E-Book Library*, the combined *ebrary* and *EBL* acquisitions), which as of summer 2017 contained 850,000 titles, and *Safari Books Online*.

Gale Interface

Formerly clearly branded as the InfoTrac interface, Gale now seems to display the InfoTrac brand name, although sales literature says that it is a "newly reimagined InfoTrac platform." Databases are broken down into two categories: cross-searchable databases and "additional products." Gale has developed a much-improved interface with its Primary Sources interface.

Through their general interface, Gale's numerous cross-searchable databases include EBSCO and ProQuest, including *Expanded Academic ASAP*; *General OneFile*; and *Gale Virtual Reference Library*.

In addition, a typical public library might have these Gale databases: *Biography in Context*; *Educator's Reference Complete*; *Global Issues in Context*; *InfoTrac Newsstand*; *Opposing Viewpoints in Context*; *Science in Context*; *Scribner Writer Series*; *Student Resources in Context*; and *Twayne's Authors Series*.

Other Gale products that are cross-searchable in the Gale Primary Sources interface include *The Times Digital Archive*; *Eighteenth Century Collections Online*; *The Making of the Modern World*; *Nineteenth Century U.S. Newspapers*; *Sabin Americana, 1500–1926*; *British Library Newspapers*; *19th Century UK Periodicals*; *The Making of Modern Law: Trials, 1600–1926*; *The Economist Historical Archive, 1843–2013*; *Archives Unbound*; *Early Arabic Printed Books from the British Library*; *Smithsonian Collections Online*; and *U.S. Declassified Documents Online*.

Gale Literary Sources, also cross-searchable, includes *Contemporary Authors Online*; *Dictionary of Literary Biography Online*; *Literature Criticism Online*; and *Something about the Author Online*.

Public libraries may also have *Opposing Viewpoints Resource Center*; *GREENR* (Global Reference on the Environment, Energy, and Natural Resources); *Health and Wellness Resource Center and Alternative Health Module*; *Kids InfoBits*; *Literature Resource Center*; *LitFinder*; *National Geographic Kids*; *Research in Context*; and *Testing & Education Reference Center*.

Gale's interface encourages browsing by subject more than the other aggregators. Major disciplines are featured on the initial search screen: Biology, Chemistry, Criminal Justice, Economics, Environmental Science, History, Marketing, Political Science, and Psychology are the major categories. Clicking any one of these topics produces an alphabetic list of subtopics. Clicking a subtopic executes a search based on that topic. Because metadata are not visible from this interface, it is difficult to tell whether the search was based on subject descriptors or just terms in the title or abstract.

The machine translation feature in the righthand margin enables users to translate text into any one of 40 languages. The "listen" feature allows users to hear the article being read as they follow along, with highlighting showing the text being read.

Publisher Interfaces

There are too many excellent publisher interfaces to mention here, so I will only make some overarching statements about publisher interfaces.

Publisher interfaces generally do a spectacular job of featuring their content. Publishers with portals include Springer, with their *SpringerLink* portal; *ScienceDirect* from Elsevier, and the *Wiley Online Library*. These major publishers generally have journals numbering in the thousands and are now incorporating their e-book content into the portals as well. Unfortunately, users often only encounter these interfaces when they land on journal content from articles discovered via an aggregator search engine, a Web-scale discovery tool, or Google Scholar.

Publisher portals have advantages and disadvantages. The advantages of using publisher portals are that they tend to be well engineered, are well focused, and have a uniformity to the metadata. The disadvantages are that they are insular, keeping you within the realm of a single publisher to the exclusion of any others. This is not as much of a disadvantage with such society publishers as IEEE and CAS, which feature a wide breadth of materials from society conferences, journals, and other publications. But can you really do science with only Elsevier journal titles?

Common (or Sometimes Not-So-Common) Database Features

In this section we cover some of the features in databases. Many of the features are nearly universal, while others are nearly unique. Some are obvious, while others you may never have considered. These features are presented in alphabetical order.

Backlinking

Have you ever noticed the underlined (or perhaps colored or bolded) hyperlinks in online database records? Sure, you have; they're everywhere: underlined author names, subjects, author-supplied keywords, and many other types of field data, depending on the database. These are intended to help you by executing an exact search for you, without your having to type anything in the search box. For example, if you were to click on a subject in a database record, the database would serve up to you "all and only" the results indexed under that particular subject within the database. You might likely have executed a keyword search rather than an exact subject search, but the backlink is careful to give you only the results from that exact field. Good thing, right?

Well, maybe; but maybe not. When you click on one of those backlinks, you lose the search thread you were currently pursuing and are taken in a different direction. Sometimes getting back to your original train of thought is as simple as using the "back" button. But some databases do not always perform well when using the back button. One way around this is to see whether a database stores a search history and to use that to return to previous searches.

Cross-Searching Databases

One of the advantages of a vendor having many database products to offer is that often they can be cross-searched. There is a time to cross-search and a time to not do it. Cross-searching is useful when doing keyword searching for relatively obscure topics when very few results can be found in individual databases. For example, a patron is looking for resources on the geology of Red Rocks Park near Denver, Colorado. Searches of several individual databases did not turn up many results. Using EBSCO's cross-searching capabilities, more articles were retrieved. Starting with any EBSCOhost database (I started with *Academic Search*), we select the "Choose Databases" link at the top left of the screen. I click the check box for "select/deselect all," and all subscribed EBSCOhost databases will be searched (figure 6.2). In my case, I am cross-searching 94 databases.

When results are returned, I see 31 results (figure 6.3).

If I still feel that 31 results are too few, I can "flip" the search away from the default (metadata only) search over to a full-text search. But because I set up the search in two separate fields, I need to be careful to flip both fields to a full-text search (figure 6.4).

With my search flipped to "TX All Text," I get 71 results, more than double my original search. To be clear, I did two things to expand my search: (1) I did a cross-database search, and (2) I flipped my search to full text.

Other vendors have similar cross-database features, but they all function a bit differently. In the case of ProQuest, the default is to search "Anywhere," that is, full text. Users need to deliberately flip to "Anywhere Except Full Text" to search only metadata.

Figure 6.5 illustrates ProQuest's selecting process for setting up cross-searching of databases by discipline.

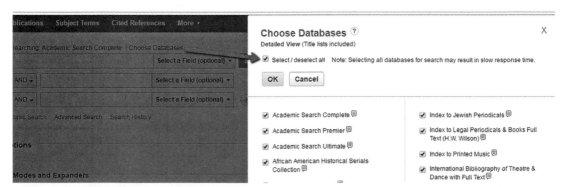

Figure 6.2. Cross-Database Searching in EBSCOhost. *Source:* ©2017 EBSCO Industries, Inc. All rights reserved.

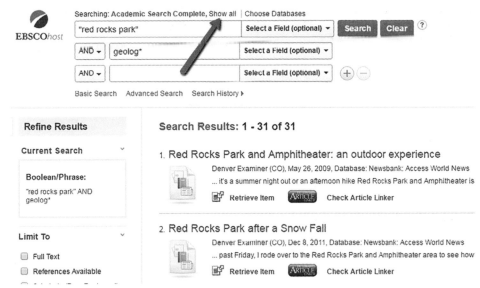

Figure 6.3. Results of Cross-Database Searching in EBSCOhost In EBSCOhost, the "Show all" link means that not all databases being searched are displayed at the top. *Source:* ©2017 EBSCO Industries, Inc. All rights reserved.

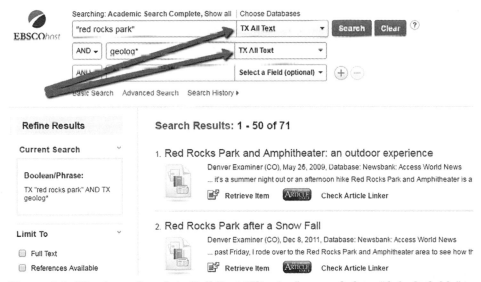

Figure 6.4. Flipping a Search to Full Text "Flipping" a search from "default fields" to "full text" will increase results returned. *Source:* ©2017 EBSCO Industries, Inc. All rights reserved.

Readex recently devised an elegant cross-search feature that covers an impressive array of primary source materials, including *America's Historical Imprints* and *America's Historical Newspapers*. This is quite a different scope than the ProQuest and EBSCO cross-searches.

Gale's Artemis interface is a cross-search system and can be used for both primary sources and literary sources.

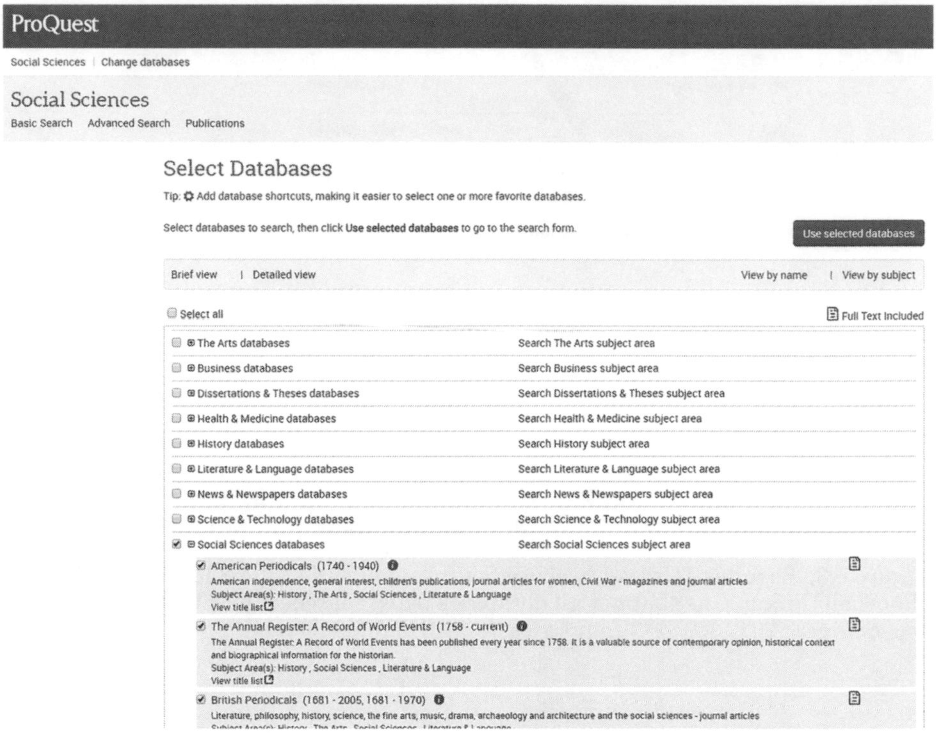

Figure 6.5. Cross-Database Searching under ProQuest Interface. *Source:* The screenshots and their contents are published with permission of ProQuest LLC. Further reproduction is prohibited without permission.

Adam Matthew has AM Explorer as their cross-search platform. Searches can be performed across products held at a local institution or across all products. Results can be filtered by collection, with result totals showing how many result hits are retrieved within each collection.

If cross-database searching is possible under a vendor's interface, then why not just always search this way? There are good reasons why you wouldn't want to do this:

- Retrieving too many results (recall) restricts your ability to find relevant articles (precision).

- Many databases have special features, such as customized limiters and controlled vocabularies, all of which are masked and lost when buried in a cross-search platform where the lowest common denominator rules.

Best Practice: Use cross-database searching as a last resort. Using it as a first resort minimizes the individual strengths and limiters, and you lose the strength of controlled vocabularies. Use this feature when you are not finding sufficient results by other means.

Table 6.2. Citation Generation and Citation Export in Various Databases.

Database/ Interface	Cite Generation	Cite Export
EBSCOhost	Chicago/Turabian Author/ Date; Chicago/Turabian Humanities; APA; MLA; and five other styles.	RIS format; RefWorks; Endnote Web; EasyBib; Generic tagged format; BibTeX; MARC21.
ProQuest	Over 30 styles.	RefWorks, EasyBib, and RIS use "Save" to export. Distinguishes Turabian from Chicago styles.
Readex AllSearch		Just gives general citation advice, but not specific citations.
Readex Individual databases	Presents citation metadata, but it's not formatted for citation styles. Users must do this for themselves.	RIS export only. Not correctly formatted enough to be usable. Best to record citations manually.
Web of Science	N/A	EndNote Web; EndNote Desktop; RefWorks; BibTeX.
Credo Reference	APA, Chicago (humanities); Harvard, MLA.	EasyBib, RefWorks, Zotero.
Adam Matthew	Generic citation	EndNote, RefWorks, Zotero.
Cambridge University Press	Dozens of styles available	CiteULike, EasyBib, Mendeley, RefWorks.
Alexander Street Press	APA, Chicago B, MLA6, MLA7.	EasyBib, EndNote, EndNote Web, Mendeley, Reference Manager, Refworks, Zotero.
Brill	Exports to a text file: MLA, Chicago B.	Refworks.

Citation Generation and Exporting

Many of the larger vendors and some smaller vendors allow for generating citations for bibliographies or exporting citations to citation management software such as RefWorks or EndNote. By citation generation, I mean creating a citation on the screen in one or more selected formats. This does not involve data export but simply a display on the screen and sometimes the ability to e-mail the citations. Computer-generated citations are not always perfect, but they are a big help to the writing process and are always appreciated by students.

Table 6.2 shows some interfaces and their various citation features. Some interfaces perform a direct export, meaning they attempt to open an application on the client computer, or push the data to a Web service. Table 6.2 delineates some of these features in selected databases.

Workaround for Databases without Citation Features

For databases that do not provide instant citation generation, copy the article title and paste it into Google Scholar (presuming the article is academic/scholarly and can be discovered in Google Scholar). This will give you citations in MLA, APA, Chicago (humanities), Harvard, and Vancouver styles. Regrettably, Scholar does not give Chicago author/date style or either of the Turabian styles.

If you want a more normalized experience for exporting citations, I again recommend Google Scholar. Again, copy and paste your article title into Google Scholar; if your article is found, Google Scholar will offer various options for exporting the citation. This will generally work for scholarly peer-reviewed publications, but not for magazines, newspapers, primary sources, encyclopedia entries, or government documents. It may work for book chapters, but I don't recommend it. Too often Google Scholar formats book chapters as if they were the entire book. But if your citation is a scholarly article, chances are that Google Scholar will do the trick.

Citation Tracking

By *citation tracking*, we mean databases that have features similar to *Web of Science*: they either track citations to subsequent articles ("times cited") or they track references within the source articles, or both (see chapter 10 for more about citation databases). This ability to track citations is growing in popularity, as we see vendors and aggregators folding these features into their interfaces. Through various vendors, *PsycINFO* incorporates citations to articles that are within the database. *MLA International Bibliography* follows the same practice.

Command Search

Some interfaces have a command search feature that allows for greater control over searching. *IEEE Xplore* is one such interface. ProQuest has a command line search. Command searching employs field tags and precise syntax in framing searches, and it is extremely idiosyncratic to the search interface. Help must be carefully studied before searching. Users typically won't have much patience for this kind of search, but it is useful in cases where you need it.

OCLC *WorldCat* has an elaborate "Expert Search" mode. All the tools are there, as if you were searching a full-text database and needed powerful proximity operators. Of course, the *WorldCat* database does not allow searching of any full text, so it is difficult to envision a time when this kind of power is needed. But, nevertheless, it's there.

Many databases have an advanced field search, sometimes called "command line" or "expert" searching. This is the kind of searching that was often employed in the early days of online databases, such as *Dialog*. There is great power in this kind of searching, so let's examine it a bit.

The EBSCOhost interface doesn't have a place where is says "command search," but that is what you are doing when you search with tags like the following: DE "online databases" and DE "reference librarians." You can teach yourself to do this by simply paying attention to the field tags from within an EBSCOhost interface. Suppose you want to run a search in *Business Source Complete* on litigation that has been taking place for various companies. Assuming you have a list of stock ticker symbols for the companies you want to search, a time-saving way to do this is to use the following field tags:

TK "MSFT" AND (lawsuit* OR litigation)

TK "GOOG" AND (lawsuit* OR litigation)

TK "AMZN" AND (lawsuit* OR litigation)

You can likely guess from the ticker symbols what companies the symbols represent.

The ProQuest interface has a "Command Line" button on the "Advanced Search" screen that allows you to build up a command line search by using a series of pull-down menus. For example, by using the *ABI/Inform Collection* database and going to the "Advanced Search" page, you see about 23 different field options. But going to the "Command Line" page, you see more search fields available for use: I counted 244 different field options. There aren't that many fields in the *ABI/Inform Collection* database. This is obviously a conglomeration of all possible fields searchable in all databases vended by ProQuest under their general interface. The field "MeSH subject – MESH" is obviously coming from *Medline* or a similar medical database. "Literary technique – LT" and "Literary theme – GLT" are likely from a literature database. So, while it initially seems impressive to see so many available fields under the "Command Search" mode, these options prove less than helpful. However, when you know the exact fields that exist, you can use the "Command Line" feature to your advantage.

E-Mail Alerts

By *e-mail alerts*, we're not just talking about having the ability to e-mail articles or citations to yourself; we're talking about an alerting service. When new articles matching your specified search criteria are added to the database, many vendors now offer the service of e-mailing you notifications that new records matching your criteria have been added. This is a very popular trend, as publisher portals such as Elsevier's *ScienceDirect*, *SpringerLink*, *SciFinder*, *Web of Science*, Sage Journals, and *Wiley Online Library* offer the service as well as aggregators such as ProQuest, EBSCO, Gale, and News-Bank. Even the freely available *PubMed* database offers e-mail alerts after a free registration process. Of course, e-mail alerts are for databases where content is being added. Historical databases where the content is closed will not have this feature.

Full-Text Searching

When searching aggregator databases, care should be taken as to what is being searched and what is not being searched. If you search "all fields except full text," then the scope of the search is metadata only. But if you elect to search "full text," you are only searching the full text within articles that contain full text; the articles that have no full text at all will not be searched, thus somewhat skewing results and possibly omitting results you would normally expect to see.

Let's put this to the test. Using EBSCO's *Academic Search Complete*, we see this article that has a full-text PDF within EBSCOhost:

Segniagbeto, Gabriel H., Koen Van Waerebeek, Joseph E. Bowessidjaou, Koffivi Ketoh, Takouda K. Kpatcha, Kotchikpa Okoumassou, and Kossi Ahoedo. "Annotated checklist and fisheries interactions of cetaceans in Togo, with evidence of Antarctic minke whale in the Gulf of Guinea." *Integrative zoology* 9, no. 1 (2014): 1–13.

We then look for a unique text string that does not cross lines and does not contain strange (gremlin) characters that could potentially mess up searches. Here is such a string:

"lips were dark grey. Two light pigment swirls"

Using this as our control, search for this string with "TX All Text" selected from the search pull-down menu. As predicted, you retrieve just one record, the one in our control set.

We now look for a record from the same result set that has no associated full text. The following is such a record:

Afriyie, John Kwasi, Hobina Rajakaruna, Marouan AA Nazha, and F. K. Forson. "Simulation and optimisation of the ventilation in a chimney-dependent solar crop dryer." *Solar Energy* 85, no. 7 (2011): 1560–1573.

Using our link resolver, we note that the library does have access to this journal through Elsevier *ScienceDirect*. Here is the text string we will use to test:

"wall which was constructed of wood with the inner surface"

When we run this search in the "TX All Text" field, we do not find anything. This shows us that we should use the TX field carefully. It will *only* search text to which the vendor has access, even though your library may have full text through other databases.

I always like to do a cross-check with Google Scholar when I run these searches. Searching that same text string in Scholar brings us only the article we are looking for. This shows us the value of using Google Scholar alongside our licensed databases.

Searching for Plagiarism

Do you suspect a student is guilty of plagiarism? You can use your search skills to uncover it.

A distinguished humanities professor approached me at the reference desk and asked for my assistance. He suspected a student of plagiarizing in a paper about Saint Augustine. As I looked over the paper, one sentence stood out to me: "Thenceforth the combat was conducted in writing against Julian of Eclanum, who assumed the leadership of the party and violently attacked Augustine." How many times have you heard today's students utter the word "thenceforth." I'm guessing never. I searched Google for this sentence (I could also have found the same content using Google Books or Google Scholar) and was able to turn up this exact sentence from the *Catholic Encyclopedia* (1907 imprint). It turned out that a majority of the student's paper was lifted directly from the *Catholic Encyclopedia*, the main divergences being the introduction and the conclusion to the paper.

There is a trade-off when opting to search the full text contained in databases. You will get more results (greater recall) but less relevance (lower precision). My recommendation is to search just the metadata first, either by using the controlled vocabulary or simple keywords, and see how well those results serve you. If these results are not satisfactory, you should then search the full text contained in the database. Remember, the two kinds of searching require two kinds of thinking: searching metadata means you need to think like an indexer (broad thinking, "aboutness" of the content from a high level, and controlled vocabulary), and searching full text means you need to think like an author (author's terminology within the field).

Fuzzy Searches

Fuzzy searching is an approximate string-matching technology that is found in a few search engines. This is the same kind of technology used in automated spell-checking systems. *HeinOnline* has a fuzzy search feature.

EBSCO uses fuzzy matching in result sets to account for possible optical character recognition (OCR) errors in the scans of full texts, archaic spellings, and dialectic variations (such as British versus American variants). In EBSCO databases, it's a feature that is done in the background. An example of an EBSCO database where this is evident is the *Historical Digital Archives*. It is also used in databases such as the *American Antiquarian Society Historical Periodicals* and *Gateway to North America*. EBSCO applies fuzzy matching to words of five characters or more. This helps with cases of imperfect OCR. It is not uncommon for letters to be misidentified, and fuzzy matching is an attempt to correct for that. In addition, it was common in older English-language texts for lowercase "s" to be rendered with a "long s" that looks more like today's letter "f." Fuzzy matching also accounts for this.

Handwriting Recognition

Adam Matthew has recently begun using artificial intelligence (AI) to bring full-text searching to historical texts with OCR that can be trained to recognize handwriting. There is more about this with e-books in chapter 9.

HTML vs. PDF Files

Some databases, especially aggregators, often have full text available as HTML or PDF, but sometimes only as HTML format. The reason for this is quite simple: they are not always able to acquire PDF files from publishers. Not all PDFs are created equal. Publisher database portals generally have source code-generated versions of articles. These are versions created directly from submitted and processed files and will be the smallest in size. Aggregators often do not have these files, but they generate them on their own, sometimes from scans of print journals. These may be significantly larger is size than the publisher versions.

Limit Articles by Length

The feature of limiting by length is especially handy when a student says he or she needs an article that is at least 300 words for an assignment. Searching aggregator interfaces like those from the big three often yields too many short articles, and you just wish that there was a way to weed these out. Well, there is in some interfaces.

The following EBSCO databases all offer a length limit: *Academic Search*; *Business Source*; *Environment Complete*; *Science Reference Center*; *SocINDEX*; *GreenFILE*; *Art & Architecture Complete*; *Communication & Mass Media Complete*; *Peace Research Abstracts*; *LISTA* (*Library, Information Science & Technology Abstracts*); *LISA* (*Library, Information Science & Technology Abstracts*); and *International Bibliography of Theatre & Dance*.

The basic Gale interface, the one that contains Gale's *Academic OneFile*, *Agriculture Collection*, *Business Collection*, *Communications and Mass Media Collection*, *Computer Database*, *Criminal Justice Collection*, *Culinary Arts Collection*, *Diversity Studies Collection*, *Expanded Academic ASAP*, *Fine Arts and Music Collection*, and all others under the same interface have a "Word Count" field tag where you can intuitively enter numbers with a greater than (>) or a less than (<) sign before the number.

Limiters/Facets

There are two philosophies when searching. One is to perform all the restrictions, limits, and search syntax before hitting the search button.

This harkens back to the early days of searching, the days of *Dialog*, when searching cost serious money. Searchers needed to think things through very clearly so as not to waste money when executing a search. The second approach involves simply entering terms into a search box (keywords at least, but possibly also field searching or controlled-vocabulary searching) and then doing the limiting later. This second approach is possible thanks to newer Internet technologies, such as Apache Lucene (which makes searching incredibly fast) and Apache SOLR (which is one of the early technologies that made facets possible in displayed records).

Vendor interfaces are faster than ever before, and they are using limiters and facets in the results displays. Notice in figure 6.6 that users are not only provided with search suggestions as they type, but they can also apply presearch limits by source type, document type, and language.

If, however, a user chooses not to do a presearch limit, those same options will be available in the form of facets on the results screen (figure 6.7).

ProQuest Congressional has a very different presearch limit function, as it contains so many unique primary source materials. It makes no difference, however, whether the limits are done before or after submitting the search, as the database works very fast in either case. This is a significant improvement over older versions of the database.

NewsBank's *Access World News* allows users to either select limits before submitting a search or to navigate facets after results are returned. The advantage of waiting until a search is executed is that you can see how many results would have been returned for other limits, as shown in figure 6.8.

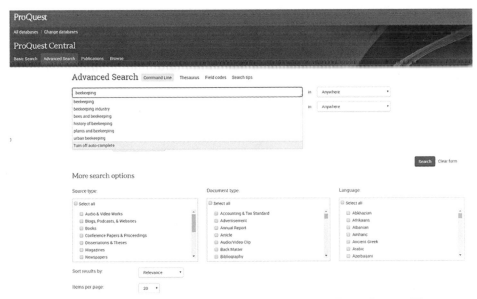

Figure 6.6. ProQuest Search Suggestions Appear as Users Type. *Source:* The screenshots and their contents are published with permission of ProQuest LLC. Further reproduction is prohibited without permission.

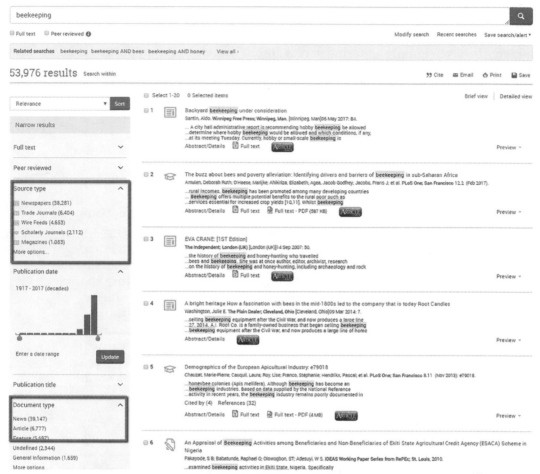

Figure 6.7. Limiters and Facets Focus Complex Results. *Source:* The screenshots and their contents are published with permission of ProQuest LLC. Further reproduction is prohibited without permission.

Gale's newer interface for *Academic OneFile* seems to even discourage selecting limits before submitting searches. From the results screen, it is easy to see the consequences of selecting alternative content types, document types, and other limits (figure 6.9).

The Gale interface offers very clear presearch limiters and post-search facets, although users will need to get used to the fact that they are on the right side rather than on the left, as is popular in other interfaces.

Natural-Language Searching

Nexis Uni allows for natural-language searching. This is designed more for the novice searcher than for the expert, but it can't do any harm to play

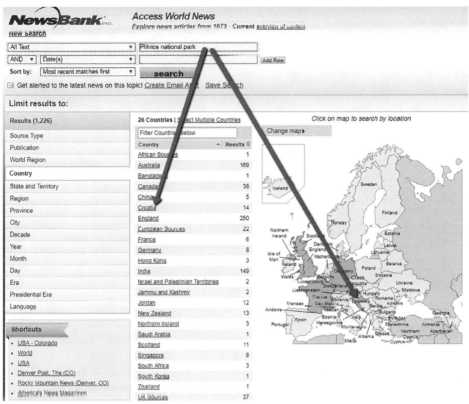

Figure 6.8. Limiters within NewsBank's Access World News Interface. *Source:* NewsBank, Inc. Used with permission.

around with the feature. After all, searching is all about discovery, and discovery often comes in unexpected ways.

Natural-language searching allows users to simply ask such questions as the following: What regulations exist for the grading of raisins? The search engine does not understand sentences like the human brain does. Rather, it is taking key terms out of the question and searching those terms. Notions of causation, subordination, and other relationships are not understood. Perhaps we will see those features in search engines of the future, but not today. Although you do retrieve results, it may take longer to sift through them.

Personal Accounts

When users create a log-in identity with a vendor, they establish a personal account (or user profile) with that vendor. This allows searchers to save search terms and articles for consultation at a later time. This is useful when running the same search repeatedly over time, for example, in monitoring news content. Most major vendors now have this feature, often with "My" as

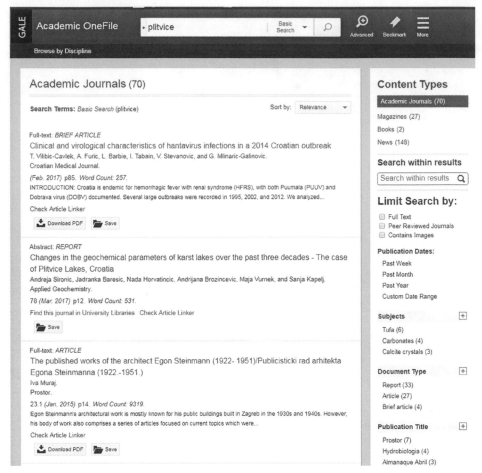

Figure 6.9. Gale Search Interface Emphasizing Postsearch Limits. *Source:* Gale. Screenshot from ACADEMIC ONEFILE. ©Gale, a part of Cengage, Inc. Reproduced by permission: www.cengage.com/permissions.

the first word of the link (My Research, My Archive), and occasionally just a "Sign In" link.

Phrase Searching

In an apparent nod to the success of search engines and user expectations with searching the Web, most vendors have implemented phrase searching with quotation marks into search interfaces. Up until the mid-1990s, phrase searching was a special kind of proximity searching, with adjacency operators needing to be employed to get phrases searched properly. Search engines like Google popularized phrase searching with the use of quotation marks to indicate "search these words as phrases" that forced many search engines to change the way searches were done. This is a clear case of user preferences forcing vendors to change the way they do things.

Something to keep in mind is that many computer programs, such as Microsoft Word, "smarten" quotation marks by turning straight or dumb quotation symbols (") into curly or smart symbols (" "). When copying and pasting searches into some databases, these "smart" quotation marks are not always well received.

RSS Feeds

RSS feeds were one of the innovations in the early days of the World Wide Web. The Web itself came into use in 1993, and RSS (which stands for either Rich Site Summary or Really Simple Syndication, take your pick) was making its way into Web sites beginning around 2000. News aggregator services or software was used to load and read the feeds. In the database world, some researchers would track new issues of journals and new database entries with these feed services. Although some researchers still use RSS feeds, which continue to be offered by some vendors, most of the scholars I talk to grew tired of having to go to different places to track the many journals and databases they wanted to follow. The browsing service called BrowZine, from Third Iron (see discussion below), is used by many to replace the RSS feed model.

Search History

It is good to be systematic and careful when doing research. Documenting searches you have done and strategies implemented saves time and prevents overlooking untried search strategies. The search history features available in many databases can not only help with remembering what you have already searched but can also be used to combine previous searches.

Running searches on the individual concepts in your search topic and then combining them in the search history can be a powerful shorthand method to doing fast searches. Let's say you were using EBSCO's *Business Source*, and you wanted to create a table of how many articles there were for selected countries for a specific topic: the hospitality industry. You run a search just for

DE "HOSPITALITY industry"

Then you do a search for

GE China

From your search history, you combine the first two searches to arrive at 503 results. At this point, you could one of the following:

Run a series of searches, ANDing search 1 with each of the other country terms.

Do a search for GE Japan OR GE Korea OR GE Thailand OR GE Vietnam OR GE Philippines and then combine that set with search 1 in the search history.

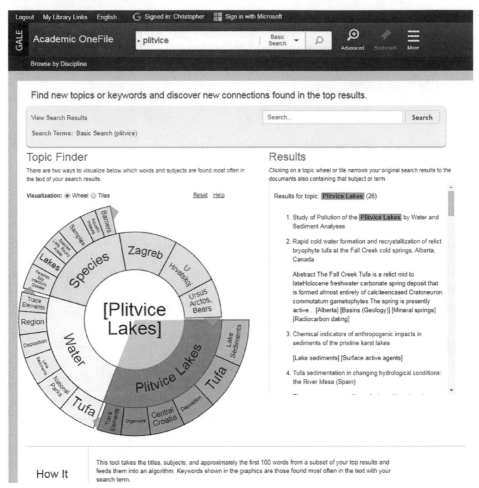

Figure 6.10. Gale's Topic Finder Assists Concept Visualization. *Source:* Gale. Screenshot from ACADEMIC ONEFILE. ©Gale, a part of Cengage, Inc. Reproduced by permission: www.cengage.com/permissions.

Best Practice: Use the "Search History" feature (when available) to make exhaustive searching of topics less exhausting.

A record of search histories is useful when it is necessary to carefully document searches performed and search results, which is often required by medical librarians doing research for medical personnel. Search histories are also useful to document changes in your topic over time, to describe searches performed for academic articles, and to keep track of descriptor or keyword combinations used so that you don't needlessly duplicate research. The search history is also useful simply for decoding your results, should they seem to be mysterious.

In the search example from *PsycINFO* below, both the EBSCOhost and ProQuest interfaces retrieved the same 14 articles, but the same search history reveals that that search syntax differs slightly between them:

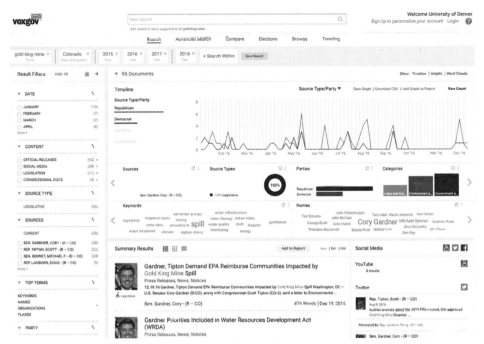

Figure 6.11. *Voxgov* Search of Primary Source Government Publications with Social Media Sources. *Source:* ©2017 Voxgov. All rights reserved.

EBSCOhost *PsycINFO* interface:

(DE "Posttraumatic Stress Disorder") AND (DE "Curriculum")

ProQuest interface:

MAINSUBJECT.EXACT("Posttraumatic Stress Disorder") AND MAINSUBJECT.EXACT("Curriculum")

Visualization

Gale's Topic Finder is a creative way for users to explore and limit topics through visualizations (figure 6.10).

A rather unusual approach to visualization has been undertaken in the *voxgov* database, vended by East View Information Services (figure 6.11). This database attempts to unite primary source materials (governmental press releases, official agency issuances, the *Congressional Record*, the *Federal Register*, and other government agency publications) with social media utterances from government officials (the president or presidential candidates, members of Congress, cabinet members). In this case, YouTube, Facebook, and Twitter are tracked on a real-time basis. The interface is visual, with breakdown by party affiliation and demographic characteristics of members of Congress. The weakness of this database is that it seems to the novice user that demographic information from the public at large is presented, when in fact it is just the makeup of House and Senate members. It remains to be seen whether this visualization will offer any research value.

Another example of visualization can be found in a freely available U.S. government resource, the *Foreign Aid Explorer* (https://explorer.usaid.gov). Aid given to foreign countries can be viewed by country, agency, and type of aid over time.

Now that we have covered selected features among various databases, we need to look at an entirely different tool, one that is all about browsing, and not searching.

Browsing for Content

The assumption in this book so far has been that we will be searching for things—articles, images, books, whatever. Most vendor interfaces present us with an empty search box, and it is up to us to know what we should be typing in the box. But that is not the only possible way to approach the information quest. When Yahoo! first came out in the mid-1990s, it was primarily a browsable directory—a hierarchy (Notess 2009). Although browsing didn't last in the case of search engines, there is still a place for it. Just think how helpful it is to be able to look up and down shelves of books arranged in

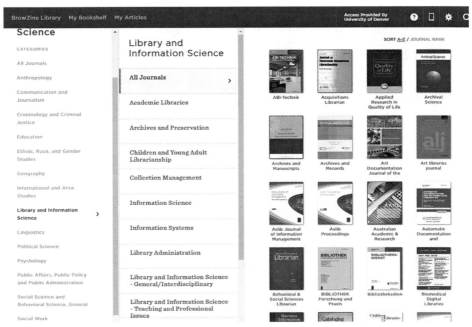

Figure 6.12. Browzine's Personal Bookshelf. *Source:* ©Third Iron, LLC. All rights reserved.

a classified order, whether the Library of Congress, Dewey, Superintendent of Documents, or some other classification system.

One of the disadvantages of our online world of content is that journals are no longer in front of us. Researchers who have been around for several years had habits of visiting libraries to peruse their favorite print journals. Whether those current journals were arranged in call number order or alphabetical order, users of days past would go to the shelves just to see what new article content had been published so they could keep current in their fields. I often have researchers approach the reference desk asking how they can browse for journals the way they used to do with print journals. They may have tried RSS feeds as a notification service with a limited degree of success, but that method only works for certain publishers.

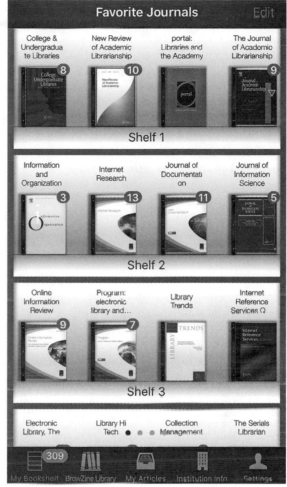

Figure 6.13. BrowZine Provides Notifications of New Content.

In this age of "search" and online databases, researchers have been forced to either go to a database with an empty search box and enter some terms, or to go to a journal publisher or aggregator page that allows for browsing of individual journal issues. This is a very tedious, nonintuitive process, and one that ultimately does not replicate the print experience very well.

For this reason, one product, BrowZine (from ThirdIron), has created a market niche for itself. BrowZine functions as an online journal notification service. It is superior to previous methods of notification that included subscribing to individual journal notifications from vendors and RSS feeds from vendors or aggregators. It has solved the problem of new journal content notification by creating an app for smartphones and tablets and a Web interface that customizes journal monitoring preferences. BrowZine has built-in synchronization between the smartphone, tablet, and Web versions, allowing you to access favorite journals and saved articles no matter which device you are using at the time.

Searching for articles is not what BrowZine is about; it is expressly designed for browsing journals within one's field of interest (figure 6.12). Preferred journal titles can be saved to a "bookshelf," and individual articles can be saved within the interface for later offline reading (for smartphones and tables only).

The system can also be set to send regular notifications about new articles that have not yet been read (figure 6.13).

Another browsing tool, for popular magazines rather than for peer-reviewed journals, is *Flipster*, from EBSCO. *Flipster* is also gaining popularity. Entire magazine content in a page-turning environment mimics the experience of having the actual print magazine in your hands. Graphics and page layout are fully replicated, so users get the full experience intended by the publisher.

Exercises

1. Select a Gale database under the Gale interface. Depending on your institutional subscriptions, you may have access to *Infotrac Newsstand*, *U.S. History in Context*, *World History in Context*, *Gender Studies Collection*, *Academic OneFile*, *Popular Magazines*, *General OneFile*, or a host of other Gale products. Enter one of these Gale databases. On the top of the Web page, you should see "My Library [name of your library]" followed by "Gale Databases." Click the "Gale Databases" link, and you will then see all the Gale databases to which your library subscribes. The first part of the list is cross-searchable databases, followed by additional products from Gale that are not cross-searchable.

   Use this interface to piece together several databases on a topic. For example, you might group together *U.S. History in Context*, *Academic OneFile*, *Military and Intelligence Database*, *U.S. History Collection*, and the *War and Terrorism Collection*. Now click "Continue" to see a search box that allow cross-searching of all the databases you selected. In the search results, note which databases are giving the most relevant search results.

2. Find documentation on all the features available within the Readex AllSearch interface. Could more training information be found using Google Searching or from within the interface itself?

3. Do the same exercise as in number 2 above, but this time with the ProQuest interface.

4. Go to any EBSCOhost database and perform any search that retrieves records. Now save some of these records into a folder. Go into the folder and save a PDF file to your local computer. You can either use the save feature or the e-mail feature to do this. Now

export the bibliographic citations to these same records to whatever citation management software you have access to, such as RefWorks or EndNote. If you don't have access to those, you can use the "Generic bibliographic management software" option, which will push the citation information to an HTML screen on your computer that you can save to your computer as a text file or simply look at to appreciate the tagged fields.

5. Search for the word *dirigibles* in EBSCO's *Academic Search* with default settings (that is, not searching within the full text of articles). Note how many results you retrieve. Now, change the pulldown menu so that you are searching "TX All Text." Note how many results you get this time. Which search strategy gave the best results? Can the search results be improved by searching with controlled vocabulary? What is the controlled vocabulary term for *dirigibles* in this database?

References

CONSER. 2016. *CONSER Cataloging Manual*. Module 31. Remote Access Electronic Serials (Online Serials). Washington, D.C.: Library of Congress. Accessed August 7, 2017. http://www.loc.gov/aba/pcc/conser/more-documentation.html.

EBSCO. 2017. "Applying Search Modes in EBSCOhost and EBSCO Discovery Service." Accessed December 17, 2017. https://help.ebsco.com/interfaces/EBSCO_Guides /EBSCO_Interfaces_User_Guide/Applying_Search_Modes.

Notess, Greg R. 2009. "Yahoo!'s Long Strange Journey." *Online*, Nov./Dec. 33, no. 6: 42–44.

ProQuest. 2017. "History & Milestones: ProQuest, Libraries and the Evolution of Research." Accessed December 29, 2017. http://www.proquest.com/about /history-milestones.

Beyond the Textbook

Carrying on the tradition of the fourth edition, additional exercises, search tips, and tutorials will be available on the publisher's Web site at http:// www.abc-clio.com/books.librariesunlimited.com/Librarians-Guide-to-Online -Searching. This will be updated periodically with the inevitable database changes.

7
Social Science Databases

As you have seen so far in this book, vendors have a wide variety of database offerings on every academic and nonacademic topic. We have focused on popular vendor interfaces, such as the ProQuest interface, Gale interface, and the EBSCOhost interface. We have also looked at several general go-to databases, such as Gale's *Academic OneSearch*, *ProQuest Central*, and EBSCO's *Academic Search*. These databases are all multidisciplinary in nature; they all contain articles on virtually every topic because they collect index records and full text from many sources. There is definitely a time and place for these mega one-size-fits-all products, but there is also a place for specialized discipline specific databases.

With this chapter, we begin a survey of discipline-specific databases within many disciplines, beginning with the social sciences. But why do you even need these databases, given the broad nature of the mega-aggregated products? Several reasons come to mind. The huge databases on all topics don't have the discipline-specific controlled vocabulary necessary to really do in-depth research as often required for academic purposes. Nomenclature specific to psychology will differ slightly from that of sociology, and because of that, you need to pay attention to the designation and application of the controlled-vocabulary terms. Another reason is that in many fields, long before there were databases, indexes had been developed over the decades documenting the rich history of publication within a field. *Psychological Abstracts* and its antecedent titles were the groundwork for the *PsycINFO* database. Before the *Sociological Abstracts* online, there was *Sociological Abstracts* in print. Practitioners of the field have been accustomed to searching those tools and still rely on them for current information within their fields.

The social sciences cover a broad swath of fields, including anthropology, sociology, psychology, law, political science, and education. Applied social science disciplines, such as library and information science and social work, are also members of this set. The field of linguistics has a strong social science component, but it also can branch into humanities when applied to texts and into science when considering sound waves and brain theories. But we'll cover linguistics here under social science.

The reality is that some disciplines have developed strong "official" bibliographies of record, where other disciplines are lacking these. Without a doubt, the *PsycINFO* database, vended by many but published by the American Psychological Association, is the strongest example in the social sciences of an official record of the field. At the other end of the spectrum, we find political science and international studies. These fields are so broad that no one database can lay claim to having all of the official body of work.

This chapter examines several disciplines in greater depth, with attention to search examples.

Library and Information Science

Let's start with library and information science, as most readers of this book are likely either students or practitioners of the field. Library science can branch out into humanities interests such as literature and archives as well as engineering and technology (e.g., computer programming, library systems, user interfaces, and information sciences).

The closest thing to an official index in the field is the historic H. W. Wilson index, *Library Literature & Information Science*. But there are several other sources for library and information science content. Table 7.1 shows the scope and coverage of the core library science content.

Other databases that have strong holdings in library and information science include *ERIC* (various vendors), *ACM Digital Library* (Association for Computing Machinery), *Computer & Information Systems Abstracts* (ProQuest), and *IEEE Xplore* (Institute of Electrical and Electronics Engineers) as well as general interdisciplinary databases such as *Academic Search* (EBSCO), *Academic OneFile* (Gale), and *ProQuest Central*.

Table 7.1. Scope and Coverage of Selected Library Science Databases.

Database	Vendor	Dates Covered	Content Scope
Library Literature & Information Science	EBSCO (data from H. W. Wilson)	1984 onward	Over 400 journals
Library Literature & Information Science Retrospective	EBSCO (data from H. W. Wilson)	190–51983	Over 1,500 journals
Library Science Database	ProQuest	1970 onward	About 269 journals
Library and Information Science Abstracts (LISA)	ProQuest	1970 onward	Over 440 journals
Library Information Science & Technology Abstracts (LISTA)	EBSCO (open access)	1960s onward	Over 560 journals

Table 7.2. Comparison of EBSCOhost Databases in Library Science.

Search Term: Controlled Vocabulary (Default Search)	
Library Literature & Information Science Full Text (H. W. Wilson)	1,453
Library Literature & Information Science Retrospective: 1905–1983 (H. W. Wilson)	13
Library, Information Science & Technology Abstracts	1,793
Library, Information Science & Technology Abstracts with Full Text	1,799
All 4 databases	**5,058**

Let's look at some of the features of the *Library Literature & Information Science* database. As previously mentioned, one of the advantages of having aggregator databases is their ability to cross-search other related databases at the same time. From within the EBSCO interface of the *Library Literature* database, select the "Choose Databases" button at the top of the screen. From there, you can see and select other databases related to the field. In this case, you can select *Library Literature & Information Science Full Text* (H. W. Wilson); *Library Literature & Information Science Retrospective: 1905–1983* (H. W. Wilson); *Library, Information Science & Technology Abstracts*; or *Library, Information Science & Technology Abstracts with Full Text* by clicking the check boxes next to each of these four databases to ensure the broadest search scope.

You get more search results in this combined context than for each database individually, as table 7.2 shows.

Although the individual database totals in table 7.2 add up to 5,058, I suspect that there is significant overlap and duplication between *LISTA* and *LISTA with Full Text*. When smaller searches are performed, EBSCO provides this information: "Note: Exact duplicates removed from the results." Apparently, this process is not performed with larger result sets.

Library Literature Thesaurus

Looking at the online thesaurus to EBSCO's *Library Literature & Information Science Retrospective*, it is interesting to see that the vendor has recently been converting the older H. W. Wilson subject headings into more modern subject descriptors (figure 7.1).

Notice in figure 7.1 that most of the subject headings (designated by the two dashes between different semantic notions) are now unauthorized, with users being directed to use the newer subject descriptors containing a single semantic notion. It appears that EBSCO is attempting, at least in part, to get out of a messy mixture of subject headings (originally used by H. W. Wilson) and subject descriptors (preferred by most modern online databases).

EBSCO has been making changes to the underlying subjects within this thesaurus. As previously discussed, *Library Literature* is an H. W. Wilson

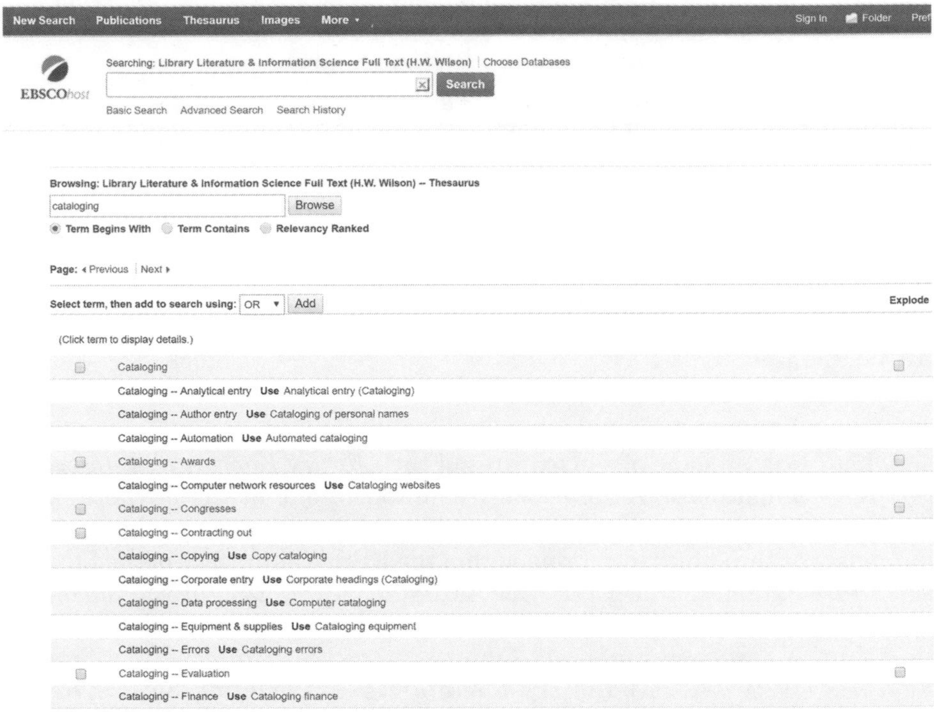

Figure 7.1. EBSCO's Shift from Subject Headings to Subject Descriptors in
H. W. Wilson Databases. *Source:* ©2017 EBSCO Industries, Inc. All rights reserved.

product that goes way back to 1905. In those days, saving space was the
important thing. The 1923 publication of *Search List of Subject Headings*
by H. W. Wilson apparently influenced subjects within the Wilson indexes—
subject headings that were pre-coordinated with multiple semantic notions
stacked together in a single entry (EBSCO 2015).

In recent years, after the acquisition of the H. W. Wilson databases by
EBSCO, the subject schema has been changing. In 2014, subject headings
were used, as shown below. In 2017, many of these headings have been converted to descriptors, as illustrated by selected changes in table 7.3.

As you can see, EBSCO has been hard at work converting subject headings into subject descriptors. Whether this will continue is not known. All
that can be said is that headings and descriptors currently coexist in the
thesaurus, and you must consider that when searching.

A word of caution: if your library subscribes to both the online *Library
Literature & Information Science* as well as *Library Literature & Information Science Retrospective*, the thesauri are different! Table 7.4 shows terms
beginning with "Online searching" in each of the respective thesauri.

As you can see, the term *online searching* is not even used in the current thesaurus. The preferred terms seem rather awkward. Imagine if this
book's title were to follow that rule: *Librarian's Guide to Electronic Information Resource Searching*. Not very memorable! You can immediately observe
that the older thesaurus is still employing subject headings with no attempt
to change these to subject descriptors. The current thesaurus has changed

Table 7.3. EBSCO's Changes to H. W. Wilson Subjects.

Subject Headings in 2014	Subject Descriptors in 2017
Archives – Conservation & restoration	Preservation of archival materials
Bibliographic instruction – Handicapped	Library orientation for people with disabilities
Cataloging – Automation	Automated cataloging
Electronic records – Law & legislation	Electronic record laws
Fiction – Collections	Fiction collections
Information science – Government policy	Information policy
Library schools – Curricula	Library school curriculum
Publishers & publishing – Serial publications	Serial publications
Young adults' libraries – Book selection	Book selection in young adults' libraries

Table 7.4. Difference in Thesaurus Terms between LL&IT Current and Retrospective.

LL&IT Retrospective Thesaurus	LL&IT Current Thesaurus
Online searching Online searching – Aims and objectives Online searching Bibliography Online searching – Evaluation Online searching – Finance Online searching – Humor, satire, etc. Online searching – Humor, satire, etc. Online searching – Standards Online searching – Statistics Online searching – Terminology **Use** Information science – Terminology Online searching – Time and cost studies	• Online searching **Use** Electronic information resource searching • Online searching – Teaching **Use** Study & teaching of Internet searching

these terms to single semantic notions, at least in these cases, although we might want to quibble with their choices. The reason I bring this up is that if you were interested in finding "all and only" relevant records within the field of library science over a long time period using controlled vocabulary, it will be necessary to do two completely separate thesaurus searches because there is a disconnect between the two.

Search Example 1: Identifying Terms Using the *Library Literature* Thesaurus

Let's assume that you want to find articles on how library school curriculum is changing in response to advances in information technology (IT). There are two ways you could go about this: (1) you could first search the thesaurus to try to locate relevant terms, or (2) you could just do a keyword search as best you can, then observe what subject terms are used in the best records, and re-execute a search using the controlled vocabulary you observed in the records.

In the previous (fourth) edition of this text, the answer to this search example looked quite different. The suggested search statement at that time was the following:

(DE "ibrary schools—Curricula" OR DE "Information science—Study & teaching") AND "information technology"

But now things have changed. Specifically, EBSCO has been hard at work in updating its thesaurus to change selected Wilson-style subject headings into single-notion subject descriptors. The descriptor regarding curricula is now "Library school curriculum," and the heading for information science study and teaching is now "Information science education," a single semantic notion containing three words.

With these things in mind, your search statement would now look like this:

(DE "ibrary school curriculum" OR DE "Information science education") AND "information technology"

Alternatively, you could opt to search like this:

(DE "ibrary school curriculum" OR DE "Information science education") AND (DE "information technology")

The second alternative searches information technology as a subject descriptor, a more restrictive search, thus we expect fewer results. The former search, with information technology searched as a phrase across any unspecified field in the default set of search fields, would retrieve more search results.

Now that you have search results, which journal has the most articles on this topic? (Hint: Look for the publication facet on the left.)

Search Example 2: A Lesson in Problem Solving

You want to find some information on *chat services* as part of *reference*. You start by looking up *reference chat* in the thesaurus (hint: use the "Relevancy Ranked" option). The first two results you get should be the following (with scope notes included): *online chat* and *electronic reference services (Libraries)*. It should be noted that this thesaurus has relied heavily on the *Library of Congress Subject Headings* for their scope notes:

Online chat. This result includes works on services that allow a person using a computer to engage in conversation by typing messages to people in real time. Works on services, commonly called *newsgroups* and *LISTSERV lists*, that allow a computer user to post messages to and read messages from a group of people who have a common interest, usually by means of the Internet, a commercial online service, or electronic mail, are entered under "electronic discussion groups." Works on services that allow a computer user to post messages to and read messages from a group of people who have a common interest via a dedicated telephone line established for the purpose are entered under "Computer bulletin boards."

Electronic reference services (Libraries). This result includes works on reference services in which users can ask questions through e-mail, instant messaging, or forms on Web sites and receive answers from librarians.

Now let's play with different ways to use what we have just learned:

DE "Online chat" AND DE "Electronic reference services (Libraries)"

I get 5 results. All records do, in fact, contain those subject descriptors. But this seems to be too constraining:

DE "Online chat"

I get 36 results by not including that additional subject terms.

"Online chat" – No field specified

I now get 88 results. But these results are not necessarily pertaining to electronic reference services.

DE "Online chat" AND reference services

This received 14 results. It seems that the subject term "Online chat" was very helpful, but "Electronic reference services (Libraries)" was not so helpful. By simply doing a default search on "reference services," I was able to sufficiently narrow results to a good degree of relevancy.

Now that we have some relevant results, I encourage you to become comfortable with dealing with the results. Each of the major vendors has its own way of managing results. The EBSCOhost interface uses a folder paradigm. Try the following tasks with the results you have from your online chat search.

Task 1: Save at least three results to a folder. (Hint: Clicking on the folder icon in the far right adds the item to the folder.)

Task 2: Click the folder icon at the top right of the results page. This should show you just the three (or more) items you selected. Now "select all" and e-mail all the records to your e-mail address. You can decide whether you want PDFs attached and whether you want brief citation format, brief citation and abstracts, or detailed citation and abstract. You may also choose to include a citation format of your preference.

Task 3: Back at the folder view select all records and use the "export" function to save the citations in a format usable to bibliographic management software, as we discussed in chapter 6. But for now, just save the records in "Generic bibliographic management software" format. I know that these results aren't usable in the format presented, but it illustrates that results can be output with field tags that bibliographic management software will be able to parse and import.

By the way, if you just want a simple citation to quickly use in a paper, the EBSCOhost interface provides an easy way to do this one record at a time. From the results page, click on the title of the record you want to cite. This takes you to the detailed metadata view. On that page, you will see a "Cite" button or link. Clicking this gives you about nine different citation formats. It is likely that the most useful formats will be APA (American Psychological Association), Chicago/Turabian Author-Date, Chicago/Turabian Humanities, or MLA (Modern Language Association) style.

Education

One of the outstanding databases in education is the *ERIC* database. The *ERIC* index itself is a project of the U.S. government, having been founded in 1966 under the Office of Education (when it was organized under the Federal Security Agency), and what eventually became the Department of Education. The index consists of two parts: the index to journals and the index to other publications. As it originated as a print publication, the *Current Index to Journals in Education* (CIJE) covered journal articles and designated each of these entries with an "EJ" prefix to the entry number. These articles are generally peer-reviewed, commercial publications requiring subscription access via the publisher or an aggregator. The second component of *ERIC* is *Resources in Education* (RIE). This is a hodge-podge of "other" content, including books, book chapters, conference papers, *ERIC Digests* (freely available government content distributed through depository libraries), doctoral dissertations and theses, and reports of various types. Each of these entries was designated with an "ED" prefix to the entry number.

A massive *ERIC* fiche collection exists in many college and university libraries, although some have recently been discarding *ERIC* fiche because a high percentage of content is available online through the *ERIC* site. Other institutions realize the value of keeping *ERIC* fiche collections for cases where content is not online. Even if a library holds the fiche collection, not all RIE publications are represented in fiche because of copyright restrictions. Generally, books and dissertations are not included. However, a check of a local library catalog or dissertation database can locate these materials in many cases.

ERIC Thesaurus

ERIC also has a well-developed thesaurus. For years, this thesaurus was issued in print as the *Thesaurus of ERIC Descriptors*. As previously noted, *ERIC* is one of the most available databases to vendors, and each of them incorporate the *ERIC* thesaurus into their online interface. It is not necessary to purchase *ERIC*, as the entire database, thesaurus and all, is available for free from the Department of Education (https://eric.ed.gov). However, most vendors include *ERIC* for free, or for a nominal fee, in addition to other subscribed content. The advantages to searching ERIC via a vendor is that the database can be cross-searched with other databases.

To become familiar with the *ERIC* database, let's look at the thesaurus, first from the free *ERIC* interface and then from one of the vendor interfaces. The easiest way to access the free *ERIC* databases is simply to search Google for "eric database."

Thesaurus Search 1: In the free *ERIC* database, select the "Thesaurus" tab and type "eating." You will see that there are three descriptors, one of them completely irrelevant. *Cheating* is obviously a false drop, likely because the search finds the letters e-a-t-i-n-g anywhere in a term, so *cheating* is ruled in, even though it shouldn't be. Now click the check box for "include synonyms" and hit "Search." Subject descriptors that are synonyms appear in italics, and there is one relevant descriptor (*binge eating*, term introduced in 2004), and three false drops containing the word *heating*. When you search with the "dead terms" check box selected, you'll see that there are no relevant terms. Clicking on the descriptor "eating disorders" gives you the full thesaurus entry, including the scope note, broader terms, narrower terms, related terms, and "used for" terms—descriptors that are not authorized but which point to the authorized term, in this case *eating disorders*.

Thesaurus Search 2: Again using the free *ERIC* thesaurus, type "high school" into the *ERIC* thesaurus tool. You see 10 authorized results. Notice that when *high school* is used as a noun, it is pluralized because it is a count noun. Adjectival usages are without the "s," as in *high school freshmen*. Clicking both the "include synonyms" and the "include dead terms" boxes reveals that there are 25 related synonym terms in addition to the original 10. Click on a term of your choosing to relationships within the *ERIC* thesaurus.

Now let's compare the thesaurus work you just did in the free version with one of the vendor implementations. As my library subscribes to *ERIC* under the ProQuest interface, that's what I will use here. But you should use whichever version you have available at your library.

Searching the ProQuest *ERIC* thesaurus (with the "contains words" option selected), we see the same kinds of results we saw with the Department of Education's free *ERIC*. The false drops containing the terms *cheating* and *heating* are included among the results. As long as you understand that this is how this feature works, you can deal with this strangeness.

The one major difference with this vendor interface is the option to "explode" descriptor terms. Don't worry, nobody gets injured. Exploding here just means maximizing the underlying thesaurus structures. Not only is the term itself searched, but also all subordinate narrower terms as well.

Let's take the term we were working with in Thesaurus Search 2: *high school*. When you do a "begins with" search for *high school*, you see in this thesaurus, as in the free version, that the authorized term is *high schools*. You also notice that there is an icon seemingly showing multiple documents. This is meant to signify that there is additional information underlying the descriptor. In this case, there is a narrower term, *vocational high schools*. From within the thesaurus interface, we can click "Add to search" to have the thesaurus term searched. Remember, if you take all the time to look up controlled vocabulary, it really makes sense to search the descriptor fields rather than just the default indexed fields. In this case, I get 62,598 results. If I had searched the default keyword fields, I would have retrieved over 90,000 results.

Command line search: SU.EXACT("High Schools")

Command line search of exploded search: SU.EXACT.EXPLODE ("High Schools")

Now let's explode our search. In the case of the descriptor high schools, exploding retrieved 39,666.

subject("High Schools") = 83,154 results

How can we explain these differences in search results? The answer centers on the fact that exploding a subject includes narrower terms mixed in with the search results. In this case, results for *vocational high schools* was included in the exploded results. The general subject search retrieved more results because we did not specify exact subjects but the term *high school* in any subject, for example, *junior high schools*.

ERIC Results

The free *ERIC* database does an amazing job of packaging results. Facets on the left allow users to further limit by publication date; [subject] descriptor; source (source journal or publishing source); author (allowing users to see the most prolific authors on the topic); publication type; education level (school or grade level of intended audience); audience (whether practitioners, teachers, parents, community members, students, etc.); (geographic) location; laws and policies referenced; and reference to assessments and surveys. Most vendor products allow limits to peer-reviewed content, and this free interface has that feature as well.

The check box "full text available on ERIC" is clear to those familiar with the historical development of the database, but this will not include most people. As all the EJ records point to licensed content that is not available from ERIC, clicking the full-text check box is not going to make that content magically appear. Rather, the results will be limited to only the ED materials for which ERIC has full text. This is a very high percentage, but not all. Results not available will include full-length books, dissertations, and other works under copyright.

The various vendor interfaces are able to accomplish what the free interface cannot: it can link out to EJ articles that your library subscribes to with OpenURL technology and proxy authentication. This is one of the tremendous advantages of using one of the vendor interfaces. These versions of *ERIC* are also able to link to the ED full text; they simply link to the content on the Department of Education *ERIC* project site.

In addition, the vendor platforms have citation tools that the free ERIC does not have, which is another huge advantage.

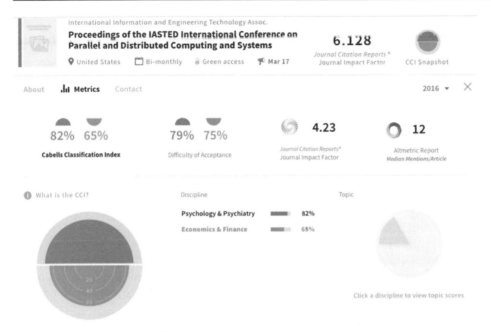

Figure 7.2. Cabell's Home Page Showing Selected Features. *Source:* Used with permission.

Other Education Databases

The H. W. Wilson databases, now under the umbrella of EBSCO, cover education historically. *Education Abstracts*, *Education Full Text*, and *Education Index Retrospective (1929–1983)* provide broader coverage than *ERIC* of the scholarly literature in education.

But article indexes aren't the only databases for education. *Cabell's Directory*, which originally could be licensed as the "Educational Set," now called *Cabell's Scholarly Analytics*, provides information about publishing opportunities by means of scholarly analytics data on several fields, including education. Libraries have the option of subscribing to information for journals in education, business, health/nursing, math/science, and psychology/psychiatry. I bring this up here in the education discussion because it can be an excellent way to discover top journals in education as well as publishing opportunities, as it gives information about journal acceptance rates and mentions in the social media (see figure 7.2).

Psychology

Without question, the most important database to psychology students is *PsycINFO*. With data produced by the American Psychological Association and offered out to multiple competing vendors in addition to their own platform, the *PsycINFO* database contains a full breadth of psychological scholarship from the 1880s to present. Multiple publication types are indexed and abstracted in the database, from books and book chapters to dissertations and journal articles.

Physical Analogs to Database

This database actually has a long history of physical analog indexes that preceded it and which are incorporated into it. Included in the database are records from the following resources:

- *Psychological Abstracts* from 1927 to 2006
- *Psychological Bulletin* 1921–1926
- *American Journal of Psychology* 1887–1966
- *Psychological Index* (1894–1935), citations to English-language journals only
- Important books in psychology from 1840 onward

These older records are in the database, but subject descriptors are not controlled and fixed fields such as age group and form/content are not present. This is a very important fact to keep in mind when searching for these older materials.

In addition to the older records, recent records include psychology journal articles, books with relevance to psychology, and doctoral dissertations selected from *Dissertation Abstracts International* (A and B). The print publication, *Psychological Abstracts*, ceased print publication in 2006, so there is no physical analog to most of the entries after that time (American Psychological Association 2017).

Age Groups

PsycINFO has several features that are extremely powerful and possibly unique. First, age groups are not encoded in the controlled vocabulary. If, for example, you wanted to find research on teens, you would not find the terms *teenagers* or *adolescents* in the thesaurus (table 7.5).

What you will find in the *PsycINFO* thesaurus are entries with these terms used as *adjectives* rather than nouns:

Children of Alcoholics

Teenage Fathers Use Adolescent Fathers

Teenage Mothers Use Adolescent Mothers

Teenage Pregnancy Use Adolescent Pregnancy

Adult Attitudes

Adult Children Use Adult Offspring

Adult Children of Alcoholics Use Children of Alcoholics

As you can see, age group terms are not incorporated into the *PsycINFO* thesaurus. So how can you search for age groups? This was not an omission; it was intentional. *PsycINFO* incorporates age group information into fixed

Table 7.5. Age Groups Not Encoded in *PsycINFO* Thesaurus.

Term Begins With	Message from Thesaurus
Teenagers	The term(s) you entered could not be found
Adolescents	The term(s) you entered could not be found
Adults	The term(s) you entered could not be found
Children	The term(s) you entered could not be found

fields. By doing this, they increase the power of the database. You can more easily discover fixed field age groupings played against variable-length field subject descriptors. Here is the way the *PsycINFO* database breaks down age groups and makes them searchable as fixed fields:

Childhood (birth–12 years)

Neonatal (birth–1 month)

Infancy (2–23 months)

Preschool Age (2–5 years)

School Age (6–12 years)

Adolescence (13–17 years)

Adulthood (18 years and older)

Young Adulthood (18–29 years)

Thirties (30–39 years)

Middle Age (40–64 years)

Aged (65 years and older)

Very Old (85 years and older)

Note that you can search by broader groupings, like *childhood, adolescence*, or *adulthood*, or by more narrow groupings. Also note that records in the database may be tagged with multiple instances of age groupings, as appropriate. The *PsycINFO* record for the title "Representations of self and parents, and relationship themes, in adolescents with Post Traumatic Stress Disorder (PTSD)" gives the following age group values within the record, shown with the subject descriptors as well.

Subjects

Adolescent Development

Parents

Posttraumatic Stress Disorder

> Self-Perception
>
> Interpersonal Relationships
>
> Age Groups
>
>> Childhood (birth–12 yrs)
>>
>> School Age (6–12 yrs)
>>
>> Adolescence (13–17 yrs)
>>
>> Adulthood (18 yrs & older)
>>
>> Young Adulthood (18–29 yrs)

Some databases encode certain types of information outside a thesaurus, in a separate controlled-vocabulary listing. It is very common, for example, for databases to not include geographic locations in the thesaurus, but to have an alternate controlled vocabulary or to just encode it with fixed field data. You always need to ask yourself when using a thesaurus whether notions of geography, age groups, personal names, corporate names, or other items are handled within the thesaurus or someplace else within the database.

To effectively do a search for age groups or population groups in *PsycINFO*, you must rely on the advanced search features (figure 7.3).

Buried down on the EBSCOhost advanced search screen are some fixed field limiters, one of which is "Age Groups." It is here that you would limit to "Adolescence (13–17 yrs)" to limit research to articles about teens. The same features are available in the ProQuest interface as well (figure 7.4).

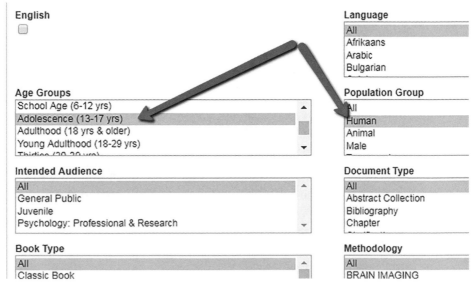

Figure 7.3. Age Group Limits under the EBSCOhost Interface of *PsycINFO.*
Source: ©2017 EBSCO Industries, Inc. All rights reserved.

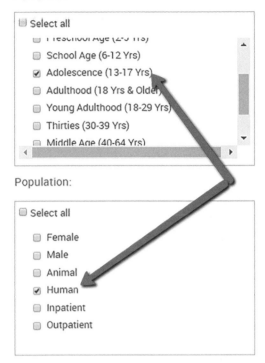

Age group:

Figure 7.4. Age Group Limits under the ProQuest Interface of *PsycINFO. Source:* The screenshots and their contents are published with permission of ProQuest LLC. Further reproduction is prohibited without permission.

Other Special Search Fields

Notice that other fixed field limiters include the ability to limit to human or animal research; intended audience (e.g., juvenile, research); presence of supplemental materials; and, very importantly, methodology. A complete description of all fields is provided by the American Psychological Association (http://www.apa.org/pubs/databases/training/field-guide.aspx).There are very few databases that contains fields for limiting by research methods (*PubMed* has some capabilities for limiting to certain kinds research methods). Possible limiting fields given in the database include the following:

Brain Imaging

Clinical Case Study

Clinical Trial

Empirical Study

Experimental Replication

Follow-Up Study

Longitudinal Study

Prospective Study

Retrospective Study

Field Study

Interview

    Focus Group

Literature Review

Systematic Review

Mathematical Modeling

Meta-Analysis

Metasynthesis

Nonclinical Case Study

Qualitative Study

Quantitative Study

Scientific Simulation

Treatment Outcome

Twin Study

(*Source:* American Psychological Association 2016.)

Each of the fixed fields featured in the *PsycINFO* database can be leveraged against the subject descriptors from the thesaurus to create some very specific and powerful search results. If only this much care and attention could go into all major databases across all disciplines.

Search Examples

Search Example 1: "I am looking for scholarly articles that are empirical studies on listening."

First, you need to do your thesaurus work. When you go into the *PsycINFO* online thesaurus and type "listening" (with the "Term Contains" radio button selected), you see the following results (figure 7.5):

It seems that the closest descriptor here would be "Listening (Interpersonal)." You may also notice that this descriptor has an explode option, meaning that there is at least one narrower term (in this case that term is "Active Listening"). To capture both descriptors, select the "Explode" box and then hit "Add." You can now execute the search, realizing that you have not yet applied the fixed field limit for empirical studies. After you get your initial results, go to the "Advanced Search" screen (the database will hold on to my terms—(DE "Listening (Interpersonal)" OR DE "Active Listening")—and select "empirical study" under the "methodology" section (figure 7.6).

It's difficult to tell from figure 7.6, but "Empirical Study" has several research types subordinate to it, as we noted above. We initially retrieve 706 results. Now you can execute your search and get 301 results, eliminating all the items that are not empirical studies.

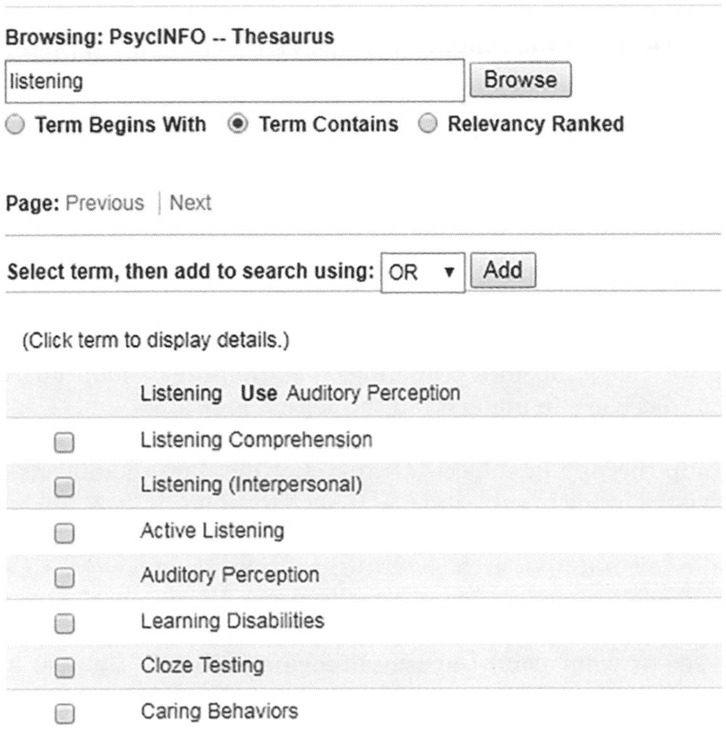

Browsing: PsycINFO -- Thesaurus

| listening | | Browse |

○ Term Begins With   ◉ Term Contains   ○ Relevancy Ranked

Page: Previous | Next

Select term, then add to search using: | OR ▾ | Add |

(Click term to display details.)

	Listening **Use** Auditory Perception
☐	Listening Comprehension
☐	Listening (Interpersonal)
☐	Active Listening
☐	Auditory Perception
☐	Learning Disabilities
☐	Cloze Testing
☐	Caring Behaviors

Figure 7.5. Thesaurus Search in EBSCOhost *PsycINFO* for Term Contains *Listening. Source:* ©2017 EBSCO Industries, Inc. All rights reserved.

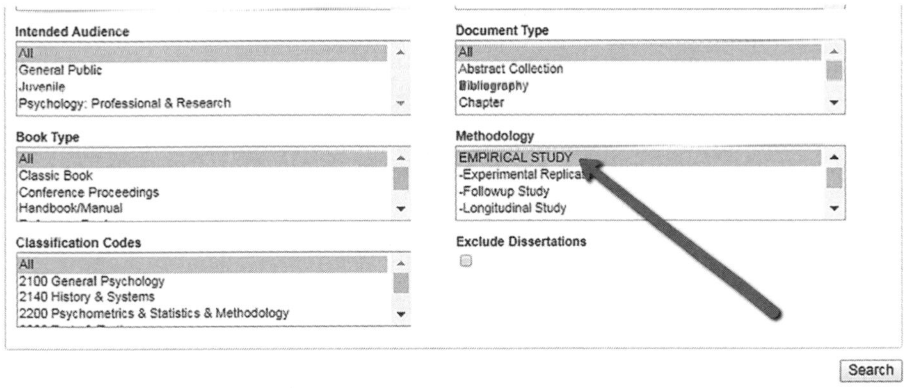

Figure 7.6. *PsycINFO's* Limit by Methodology under EBSCOhost Interface. *Source:* ©2017 EBSCO Industries, Inc. All rights reserved.

Search Example 2: A patron asks this question: "I'm having trouble finding articles on how group therapy/psychoeducation could be beneficial to elderly adults in assisted living." Let's see if we can help this patron.

First, observe the separate concepts that you need to deal with: *group therapy* or *psychoeducation, elderly adults,* and *assisted living.*

Group therapy or psychoeducation. If you go to the thesaurus and type in "Group Therapy," the thesaurus returns this: "Group Therapy **Use** Group Psychotherapy." This means that "Group Therapy" is not a valid heading, and you should use "Group Psychotherapy" instead. Then look up "Psychoeducation" and discover that it is a valid term. You determine that an OR statement would be in order in this case for these two descriptors.

Elderly adults. You now know that this thesaurus does not encode age groups in the thesaurus itself, but that the *PsycINFO* database deals with age as a separate limiter (facet). Consider this when framing your search.

Assisted living. If you look up this term in the thesaurus, you'll discover that it is a valid subject descriptor.

Before you jump into searching, it is helpful to map out the search string so that you can understand the search logic:

(group therapy in subjects OR psychoeducation in subjects) AND
(assisted living in subjects) AND (Aged limiter OR Very Old limiter)

I like to build up searches a little at a time to ensure that I am getting results. If I fail to get sufficient results, I need to know this so that I can reassess my strategy. By building up my search a little bit at a time, it is easy to see at what point the search begins to fail. If I put in a complete, finely crafted search statement all at once that produces no results, I will have no idea which terms were the culprits.

Start out by going to the *PsycINFO* "Advanced Search" screen and entering ""group therapy" OR psychoeducation" and selecting "DE Subjects" from the pull-down menu. This gives you 3,949 results and tells you that you are likely on the right track. Now enter ""assisted living"" on the line below with "DU subjects" selected from the pull-down menu. The default Boolean operator AND is the connector at the beginning of the line, as shown in figure 7.7.

But when you run the search, you only get one result. What if you flip your selection so that you search default fields (changing the pull-down menu option in the EBSCOhost interface to "Select a Field")? You now get two records. This is still not what you were hoping for. It seems that you need to consider another strategy. What if you run two separate searches:

Search 1: (group therapy in subjects OR psychoeducation in subjects) AND (Aged limiter OR Very Old limiter). This produces 319 results.

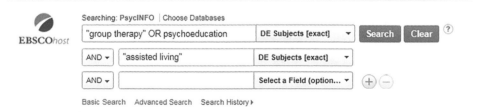

Figure 7.7. Searching *PsycINFO* with Subject Fields after Thesaurus Work. *Source:* ©2017 EBSCO Industries, Inc. All rights reserved.

Search 2: (assisted living in subjects) AND (Aged limiter OR Very Old limiter). This gives you 378 results.

Perhaps this tells you that your area of inquiry has not been adequately dealt with in the academic literature; you can forge ahead with new research. You might consider searching within the full text of articles contained in the EBSCOhost interface, realizing the weaknesses of doing this (that it will only search full-text articles available with this interface and will miss potentially relevant articles that are not available). Yet, even with this strategy, you still only retrieve 3 articles. At least now you understand why your patron started out by saying he was having trouble.

Maybe you can consider other tools that may help, such as Google Scholar. There is more on Google Scholar in chapter 14, but as I brought it up here, we can frame a Google Scholar search like this:

"assisted living" elderly "group therapy" psychoeducation

From this, you retrieve 235 articles, most of which are from superb journals within the field.

Combining Search History Sets

Shortcuts are always a good thing to have in your toolbox of search skills. When building up complex searches, it is helpful to have a shorthand way to reuse what you have already done. Let's look at an example of using EBSCOhost's search history feature and a shorthand way to reuse past searches.

Let's assume we are looking for empirical studies on test interpretation in the context of reading. We can start with a search using the thesaurus descriptor "test interpretation." Once we get these results, let's apply the *PsycINFO* methodology facet for "empirical study." Now let's clear all previous results and do an exact subject search (DE tag) for "reading."

Now we can hit the "Search History" link and see a running history of what we have been doing so far. Notice that new searches are added to the top of the table, so table 7.6 should be read from the bottom up.

Table 7.6. *PsycINFO* Search History for Our Search Strategy.

Search ID#	Search Terms	Search Options	Actions
S3	DE reading	Search modes: Boolean/ phrase	View results (26,642)
S2	DE "Test Interpretation"	Narrow by methodology: - empirical study Search modes: Boolean/ phrase	View results (574)
S1	DE "Test Interpretation"	Search modes: Boolean/ phrase	View results (2,045)

What we would really like to see here is the intersection (AND Boolean operator) of search S2 and search S3. We can use a shorthand method to make this happen. We can simply type this in the search box (default search, just keep "Select a field" selected): S2 AND S3. We get three focused results using this method.

The advantage of using search histories in this way is to gradually build up searches, ensuring at each step that there will be results from the database and that you did not make a logical or typing error someplace. It also allows you to use a quick shorthand way to refer to previous searches.

As you have seen, the strengths of the *PsycINFO* thesaurus, together with the available fixed fields and the vendor's search capabilities, combine to make searching *PsycINFO* in an online environment an extremely powerful and time-saving experience.

Sociology

Sociological Abstracts is the go-to database for sociology. Originating as a print abstracting source, its online presence, now owned by ProQuest, indexes scholarly journal articles, dissertations and theses, books, and conference papers and proceedings. Vocabulary is controlled by the *Thesaurus of Sociological Indexing Terms*, with many print editions and now fully incorporated into the online interface. Unlike *ERIC*, which is produced by the U.S. Department of Education and made available freely from a government Web site as well as through three major vendors, and unlike *PsycINFO*, which is produced by the American Psychological Association and licensed by various vendors, *Sociological Abstracts* is only available through a single vendor, ProQuest. This is because ProQuest purchased Cambridge Scientific Abstracts a number of years ago and thus has exclusive rights to the content.

This database makes use of search histories, and a shorthand method can also be used to refer to previous searches. In the ProQuest interface, the search history is called "Recent Searches." Notice that the information and layout are very close to the EBSCO *PsycINFO* database (table 7.7).

We can use a shorthand method from this search history to expand our search results. S1 refers to our first search, and S2 to the second one. Rather than retyping each of the terms in a complex search statement, we can simply do this search: "S1 OR S2."

Table 7.7. ProQuest's *Sociological Abstract*'s Search History Similar to EBSCOhost Interface.

Set	Search	Databases	Results
S2	SU.EXACT("Group Norms")	*Sociological Abstracts*	308
S1	SU.EXACT("Norms") AND SU.EXACT("Taboos")	*Sociological Abstracts*	10

When I do this, I get 317 results, not the 318 I expected. Any guesses as to why this would be the case? You may have guessed the answer already: duplicated records have been removed. Apparently, there was one record in both the S1 and S2 sets.

A Cross-Discipline
Controlled-Vocabulary Exercise

At this point, it would be informative to put your research skills to the test to solve a reference question. A patron wants to find scholarly articles about how use of e-mail affects face-to-face communication. This question may have been addressed in several social science disciplines, including education, psychology, and sociology. For this exercise, let's research the three respective controlled vocabularies from the three major databases in each of these fields: the thesauri from *ERIC*, *PsycINFO*, and *Sociological Abstracts*. Then we will construct searches based on what we find.

ERIC Thesaurus

A search for *email* in the thesaurus yielded no results. When the thesaurus query was changed to *electronic mail*, it turns out that electronic mail is the authorized descriptor. The broader term is *computer mediated communication*.

There was also an entry in the *ERIC* thesaurus for *face to face communication*—an unauthorized term. It referred us to *synchronous communication* as the authorized term (broader term *communication (thought transfer)*.

PsycINFO Thesaurus

A search for *email* immediately pointed us to *computer mediated communication* as the authorized entry. Note that in the *ERIC* thesaurus this was the broader term for *email*.

Face to face did not yield any results, so we need to use a different strategy. In this case, let's search the full *PsycINFO* database (rather than the thesaurus) to see how indexers may have treated items with the notion of face-to-face communication. Searching the full database this way, with the default sort by descending date, we discover articles on the topic with no official descriptors having yet been assigned. This is common in databases that strive to make content public but where there is a lag time in indexing. Looking through several of the recent items where subject descriptors have been assigned, we see several candidates for descriptors: *oral communication*, *interpersonal interaction*, and *communication* among them. This exercise is an excellent lesson in how thesaurus terms may be variously applied by different indexers (or even the same indexer) at different times. Indexing is an imprecise art.

Going back to the thesaurus, let's see which of these come closest to capturing our topic. The scope note for *oral communication* says that this is "Expression of information in oral form." But that is overly broad, as it does not necessarily entail an in-person or face-to-face experience. *Interpersonal interaction* is a very broad term with 20 narrower terms listed, many of them subdividing with even narrower terms. Among those 20 terms, *interpersonal communication* seems to come closest to the idea.

Sociological Abstracts Thesaurus

A search in the thesaurus for *Sociological Abstracts* found nothing for either *email* or *electronic mail*. As *computer mediated communication* had been used by *PsycINFO* and as a broader term for *email* by *ERIC*, we tried that. There is an entry in the *Sociological Abstracts* thesaurus for *Computer Mediated Communication*. There are no narrower terms, but many related terms: *Computer Assisted Instruction, Computer Assisted Research, Computers, Distance Education, Human Technology Relationship, Internet, Interpersonal Communication, Microcomputers,* and *Social Interaction*. It seems that this descriptor is possibly the closest one, but far from perfect.

As for the *face to face* aspect, if you search that in the thesaurus, you'll get this: "Face to Face (1963–1985)." This tells you that the term was an authorized term from 1963 through 1985, but it no longer is. Clicking on the term tells us that the current authorized term is *Social Interaction.*

So, now let's try to put all of this together by framing searches in each of the three social science databases based on what we have learned from the controlled-vocabulary study.

ERIC Search

You have some pretty good descriptors for *ERIC*, so you can do a search like this: "DE "electronic mail" AND DE "synchronous communication"." However, you only get a single result. When you examine the record, you see that it does indeed contain the two descriptors. To expand search results, do some ORing: "(DE "electronic mail" OR "email") AND (DE "synchronous communication" OR "face to face")." You are allowing for the fact that index terms may have not been consistently applied or that broader or narrower terms may be necessary. You are searching for the same descriptors but also allowing for default keyword fields to be searched (which would include abstracts and author-supplied keywords). You now retrieve 121 results.

PsycINFO Search

Starting with the thesaurus, you find the term *interpersonal interaction* and then click the "explode" button to add it to the search criteria. This fills the search box with the broad descriptor *interpersonal interaction* and also DE searches for each of the narrower terms. Things are starting to get complicated, and your query now looks like this:

DE "Interpersonal Interaction" OR DE "Assistance (Social Behavior)" OR DE "Charitable Behavior" OR DE "Collaboration" OR DE "Collective Behavior" OR DE "Conflict" OR DE "Cooperation" OR DE "Employee Interaction" OR DE "Group Participation" OR DE "Group Performance" OR DE "Interpersonal Attraction" OR DE "Interpersonal Communication" OR DE "Interpersonal Compatibility" OR DE "Interpersonal Influences" OR DE "Male Female Relations" OR DE "Participation" OR DE "Peer Relations" OR DE "Persecution" OR DE "Rivalry" OR DE "Social Dating" OR DE "Stranger Reactions"

You now need to add the *email* part of the search using an AND Boolean operator. When you add the AND criteria, you need to make sure to enclose the OR statements in parentheses to avoid a logic disaster:

(DE "Interpersonal Interaction" OR DE "Collaboration" OR DE "Cooperation" OR DE "Interpersonal Attraction" OR DE "Interpersonal Communication" OR DE "Interpersonal Influences") AND DE "Computer Mediated Communication"

From this search, you get 714 results, but that is likely because many parts of the OR statement (a result of the explode command) are not relevant to your topic. You need to remove some of these less relevant terms, like *employee interaction*, which has nothing to do with the user's question. Now you are left with a search like this:

(DE "Interpersonal Interaction" OR DE "Collaboration" OR DE "Cooperation" OR DE "Interpersonal Attraction" OR DE "Interpersonal Communication" OR DE "Interpersonal Influences") AND DE "Computer Mediated Communication"

This still seems very broad, but you run the search anyway and get 521 results.

It seems that our descriptors for *face to face communication* are not serving us well, so we need to consider amending the search. We then frame this search string:

DE "Computer Mediated Communication" AND "face to face"

We intentionally did not use *face to face communication* so as to broaden the search a bit. We get more results (632 this time), but the relevancy seems closer.

Sociological Abstracts Search

Now for the final database. We initially enter this search:

DE "Computer Mediated Communication" AND DE "Social Interaction"

Many of these 112 results seem too broad or not relevant. We then play around with ANDing and ORing descriptors and keywords in the search terms and finally land on this:

(DE "Computer Mediated Communication" AND (email OR electronic mail)) AND (DE "Social Interaction" OR "face to face")

As you can see, thesaurus searching is not as precise as we would like it to be, but it can be very helpful. Sometimes controlled vocabulary can exactly capture the desired search so that you can arrive at the "all and only" of search results. More often than not, however, the terms may be behind the times (as in the case of descriptors across the three thesauri for electronic mail) or not exactly capture the essence of what researchers are trying to discover.

This took a lot of work. Each of the three disciplines had differences in the ways they used controlled vocabulary, even though they are closely allied fields. In fact, we couldn't really get many results at all without resorting to augmenting our search strings with keywords in addition to subject descriptors.

Another Approach: Google Scholar

A completely different approach, and one that might seem heretical to some, is to use Google Scholar in a case like this. Google Scholar knows nothing of controlled vocabularies; instead, it searches the full text of a very high percentage of scholarly publications. For a search topic like this one, terms like *email* and *face to face communication* would be searched within the full text across all academic disciplines, with Google doing its synonymy magic in the background (for example, finding articles with *e-mail* or *electronic mail*, in addition to *email*).

Performing the Scholar search "email "face to face communication"" yielded 34,300 results (realizing that Google tries ANDing terms first and then ORing terms, which accounts for the massively higher number of results). Because Scholar positions the most relevant results first, we shouldn't need to worry about the massive number of results. The most relevant results in the first few pages, and the links to our related articles, should suffice in moving us forward in our research. But there will be more on Google Scholar later.

Business

The study of business is often considered a social science discipline, but the database resources used by business students are so specialized that the topic could take up a chapter of its own. What is covered here are just the most important general business databases.

General Business Databases

Each of the big three vendors have their own version of a "mega" business database, with slightly differing emphases. EBSCO has their *Business Source* database, which comes in a variety of sizes/prices: *Elite*, *Premier*, *Complete*, and *Ultimate*. ProQuest has *ABI/Inform*, and Gale has their *Business Collection*, which incorporates *PROMT*, *European Business ASAP*, *Business Index ASAP*, *Business & Company ASAP*, *General Business File*, and *Business International & Company Profiles*.

Business Directories

Hoovers (Dunn & Bradstreet) provides company and industry information for both public and private companies. There are fewer databases that provide financial information for private companies than for public companies, and this is understandable. Private companies are, by definition, private! They no more have to provide their financial information to the public than you or I have to make our IRS Form 1040s public. So how is it that *Hoovers* has this information? It's a well-honed guestimate, as you will note by the generous categories of answers. Take Dell as an example. Annual sales are "estimated" to be $42.57 billion. If they were a public company, there would be no estimating; it would be actual numbers filed by the company. Other databases that specialize in private company information are *PrivCo* and *CB Insights*.

ReferenceUSA is both a residential and a business phone directory. It is particularly useful for locating local businesses, such as all the Starbucks locations in a given area. For private entities, it gives broad revenue estimates that are very useful.

One of the most useful features for business research is the DUNS number. This is a kind of authority control for business entities. It is extremely important when trying to distinguish between headquarters and subsidiaries. Databases that use DUNS numbers include *Hoovers*, *Business Source*, *ABI/Inform*, *ReferenceUSA*, and Standard & Poor's *NetAdvantage*.

Industry Databases

Companies exist within industries, and thus databases that provide overall industry statistics, trends, and scholarly articles are important. *IBISWorld*, *Plunkett Research Online*, and *First Research* (Mergent) can provide those insights.

Several databases specialize in data that show how companies are performing with an industry by providing industry ratios. Standard & Poor's *NetAdvantage* provides ratios by industry and for individual companies. Both public and selected private companies are included, but ratios are only available for public companies. Dunn & Bradstreet's *Key Business Ratios* is another database in this area. *Bizminer*, from the Brandow Company, shows financial ratios based on industry grouping or specific NAICS code.

Market Research Data

Students often discover market research reports they want by using Web search engines such as Google. They then appear at library reference desks asking for research reports that cost many thousands of dollars and expect that the library should have it in their collection or be willing to pay for it. It's at this point that market research databases come into play.

To some extent, market research is built into some of the aggregator databases, such as *Business Source* (with its SWOT analyses and market research reports facets), *ABI/Inform* (market reports), and Gale's *Business Collection*. Libraries often subscribe to market research reports through such databases as *MarketResearch.com Academic*, *Mintel Academic*, or *Passport GMID*. *Statista* is a new contender in the business statistical database world. We will discuss this database in chapter 12.

Additional Resources for Social Science

Table 7.8 provides selected additional social science database resources.

Table 7.8. Selected Additional Databases for the Social Sciences by Discipline.

Discipline	Database (Vendor)
Social Sciences Generally	*Humanities & Social Science Index Retrospective: 1907–1984* (H. W. Wilson (EBSCOhost)) *International Bibliography of the Social Sciences* (*IBSS*) (ProQuest) *SAGE Research Methods* (SAGE) *Social Science Database* (ProQuest) *Social Sciences Citation Index* (part of *Web of Science* (Clarivate Analytics))
Anthropology	*AnthroSource* (American Anthropological Association (Wiley)) *Anthropological Literature* (EBSCO) *eHRAF World Cultures* (Human Relations Area Files) *Bibliographia Mesoamericana* (Foundation for the Advancement of Mesoamerican Studies (Open Access))
Economics	*EconLit* (EBSCO) *NBER Working Papers* (National Bureau of Economic Research) *World Development Indicators* (World Bank)
Law	*Campus Research on Westlaw* (Thomson Reuters) *Criminal Justice Abstracts* (EBSCO) *HeinOnline* (William S. Hein & Co., Inc.) *Index to Legal Periodicals & Books* (EBSCO) *Nexis Uni* (formerly *LexisNexis Academic*) *ProQuest Congressional* (ProQuest) *ProQuest Legislative Insight* (ProQuest) *ProQuest Regulatory Insight* (ProQuest) *ProQuest Supreme Court Insight* (ProQuest)

Discipline	Database (Vendor)
Linguistics	*ABELL: Annual Bibliography of English Language and Literature* (ProQuest, LION interface)
	Linguistics & Language Behavior Abstracts (*LLBA*) (ProQuest)
	Modern Language Association International Bibliography (ProQuest, LION Interface; EBSCO; Gale (via Artemis))
Political Science	*Columbia International Affairs Online* (*CIAO*) (Columbia University Press)
	CQ Researcher (CQ Press, an imprint of SAGE)
	PAIS International (ProQuest)
	Public Affairs Index (EBSCO)
	ROPER Center Public Opinion Archives (Roper Center for Public Opinion Research)
	Worldwide Political Science Abstracts (ProQuest)
Psychology	*APA Style Central* (American Psychological Association)
	PsycTESTS (American Psychological Assn. (EBSCO))
	PubMed (National Library of Medicine; contains a lot of psychiatry and mental health information)
Social Work	*Social Services Abstracts* (ProQuest)
	Social Work Abstracts (EBSCO, Ovid)
Sociology	*SocIndex* (EBSCO)
	Sociological Abstracts (ProQuest)

Table 7.9. Brainstorming Free vs. Fee Business Resources.

Free (No Charge Business Information)	Fee (Subscription-Only Business Information)
SEC EDGAR public company filings	Value-added company ratios
County Business Patterns (US Census Bureau)	Directories of private companies
Historical banking statistics from the Federal Research Board	Banking statistics for Eastern European banks
Consumer price index for past 20 years for the United States	Top 25 businesses in the hospitality sector for Houston, Texas
. . . keep on adding	. . . keep on adding

Exercises

1. Let's compare the freely available *ERIC* interface and a vendor interface. First, go to the free *ERIC* interface (https://eric.ed.gov) and use the thesaurus to find the controlled-vocabulary term for the notion of library school. Once you find the authorized term, use the "Search collection using this descriptor" link to execute a search. Note the number of results (1,293).

Now, let's use the vendor-based *ERIC* interface to which your college has access (this might be via Gage, EBSCO, or ProQuest). Use the built-in thesaurus to do the same thing as you did with the free *ERIC*. Be sure to not search by keyword but by the *exact subject*.

How might you explain the difference in the number of results?

2. Use the thesaurus feature within the EBSCOhost database *Library Literature* and see how many articles there are about online searching. Now do the same strategy using EBSCOhost's *Library, Information Science & Technology Abstracts* database. Which database had more items? Provide an analysis by type of journal (academic journals, magazines, trade publications, etc.). If your library subscribes to ProQuest's *Library Science Database*, see what the controlled vocabulary is in that database. Which works better in this database, the controlled vocabulary or a keyword search strategy?

3. Have a brainstorming session with yourself. On a piece of paper (or a whiteboard), draw two columns: one for business information that is freely available and the other for business information that is fee-based (that is, only available from subscription databases). I'll get things started. The information in each column does not need to relate to the other column (table 7.9).

4. A student is asking for some scholarly research on the history of social welfare. Make some recommendations on some general or interdisciplinary databases for her to search. Also make a recommendation for a subject-specific database to search. Recommend some search strategies to search the databases you recommended. Suggest both subject terms as well as keywords to search.

5. You are helping an undergraduate student with research on the "outdoor education industry." You first need to find out what this industry is all about. Use some interdisciplinary databases for this. Explore relevant databases to see whether there are any market research reports surrounding this topic. See if there are any scholarly articles in appropriate databases on the topic as well. As you search, try to refine the keyword and subject terms you use. Of course, you will not have the benefit of a back-and-forth reference interview with the student, but do the best you can by yourself.

References

American Psychological Association. 2016. "Guide to the Fields in APA Database Records." Accessed July 19, 2017. http://www.apa.org/pubs/databases/training /field-guide.aspx.

American Psychological Association. 2017. "*PsycINFO* Highlights: Quick Facts." Accessed December 29, 2017. http://www.apa.org/pubs/databases/psycinfo/?tab=3.

EBSCO. 2015. "Everything You Wanted to Know about *Sears List of Subject Headings* but Were Afraid to Ask." Accessed July 11, 2017. https://www.ebsco.com /blog-archives/article/everything-you-wanted-to-know-about-sears-list-of -subject-headings-but-were.

Beyond the Textbook

Carrying on the tradition of the fourth edition, additional exercises, search tips, and tutorials will be available on the publisher's Web site at http://www.abc-clio.com/books.librariesunlimited.com/Librarians-Guide -to-Online-Searching. This will be updated periodically with the inevitable database changes.

8

Government Information Databases

Searching for government information is a specialty all its own. It could be argued that it should be featured in the social sciences chapter, as indeed many of the publications of the three branches of the U.S. government concern social science and public policy topics. But they also touch upon science, engineering, and to a limited extent the humanities. There are also so many databases with which competent reference librarians should be familiar. Given that too many reference librarians have that "deer in the headlights" approach to questions relating to these materials, I have decided to have a stand-alone chapter on searching databases for government information.

The interesting thing here is that, unlike the other disciplines covered by this book, government information has many more *free* databases that contain the information. That ethic of keeping Americans informed by means of free access to information about their government has been documented back to the Colonial era (U.S. Government Printing Office 2016). In 1813, a resolution was passed by Congress providing for the distribution of documents, including those of future congresses, to state legislatures, governors, colleges and universities in each state, as well as historical societies. It was deemed so important to collect and distribute the workings of Congress that, beginning in 1817, what became known as the *United States Congressional Serial Set* was created to collect and disseminate documents created by Congress, and occasionally of the executive branch, not only for those in the nation's capital but to each of the states as well.

Through the creation of the Government Printing Office (GPO), in 1861, the federal government took over printing what had often been delegated to local private printers and newspapers. The Printing Act of 1895 relocated the superintendent position within the Government Printing Office from the Interior Department, renaming the position Superintendent of Documents, and further strides were made at creating bibliographic control of documents and distributing those documents systematically to the states (U.S. Government Printing Office 2010). This act is considered the beginning of a distribution system that would eventually become the current Federal Depository Library Program (U.S. Government Printing Office 2016).

Because of this strong commitment to free access to government information, most government databases have no licensing fees. There are a few exceptions, generally under the Commerce Department. That department is allowed to charge fees for the National Technology Information Service (NTIS) technical reports database (15 U.S.C. 1151-1157).

The Federal Depository Library Program is a robust program administered through the Government Publishing Office. In the past, libraries considered it prestigious to belong to the program and to be able to receive documents in a tangible (physical) format, mostly paper but sometimes microfiche or computer disks. Beginning in the mid-1990s, government agencies began issuing documents in electronic format in addition to print—and often instead of print. The GPO has done a masterful job of navigating the difficult issues surrounding the popularity of electronic formats, including developing and implementing authentication protocols for official documents so that they can be acceptable in the nation's courts, cataloging electronic publications with permanent URLs (PURLs), and, at the same time, archiving Web content as a backup. They have also been creating online information portals for ease of public access; providing digital content for mass downloading for institutions wishing to host government content themselves; digitizing legacy print content, such as the historic *Congressional Record*; and providing quality training and education conferences and webinars.

Today, there are about 1,200 government information librarians across the 50 states and the District of Columbia, as well as in American Samoa, the Federated States of Micronesia, Guam, Northern Mariana Islands, Puerto Rico, and the Virgin Islands. Many of them are in academic libraries, but you will also find them in public libraries, law libraries, federal agencies, court libraries, and tribal libraries. They are eager to assist members of the general public in their quest for government information of all types. Full disclosure—I am one of these librarians. And now you know why the fifth edition of this book contains an entire chapter devoted to government information.

Freely Available U.S. Government Information Portals

In general, the U.S. government databases are freely available. The Government Printing Office (since 2014 known as the Government Publishing Office) has taken the lead in disseminating government information to the public through what is now known as the Federal Depository Library Program. The federal government, in both the print and electronic publishing eras, is among the most prolific publishers in the world. Generally, this content is free of copyright. Because of this, commercial vendors are able to appropriate this content, add value to it, and sell it through their own platforms. Before looking at value-added vendor content, let's take a look at what is freely available.

Govinfo.gov: The GPO's Portal

Govinfo.gov is the third generation of information portals from the GPO (Vance-Cooks 2017). The first was *GPO Access*, which many librarians will remember (1995–2010). While *GPO Access* was free, the technology quickly became outmoded and needed to be replaced. The launch of *FDsys* in 2010 marked a significant update in the quality of indexing and ease of use in the new portal (https://www.gpo.gov/fdsys is the official URL, but fdsys.gov conveniently flips over to that URL). In 2016, *Govinfo.gov* was launched, and things have become even easier to use. All content from *FDsys* has been migrated over to it. Table 8.1 shows the breakdown, by government branch, of available content.

Notice that *Govinfo.gov* is strongest in its representation of congressional publications. This is because the GPO is a congressional agency rather than

Table 8.1. *Govinfo.gov* Content Coverage for Three Branches of Government.

Legislative Branch

Congressional Record	Bound edition	1873–2010
	Daily edition	1994–present
Congressional bills	103rd Congress–present	1993–present
Public and private laws	104th Congress–present	1995–present
Statutes at Large	82nd Congress–present	1951–present
Congressional legislative calendars	111th Congress–present	2009–present
Congressional reports	104th Congress–present	1995 present
Congressional documents	104th Congress–present	1995–present
Congressional hearings	104th Congress–present	1995–present (selected)
Constitution of the U.S.: Analysis & Interpretation	Current and selected historical editions	1992–present
Economic Indicators	Council of Economic Advisers for the Joint Economic Committee	1995–present (monthly)
Miscellaneous publications	Independent council investigations, Green Book, Plum Book	various dates
Government Accountability Office (GAO) reports		1989–2008 (selected)
Congressional rules and procedures	House Rules, House Practice, Precedents of the U.S. House, Riddick's Senate Procedure, Senate Manual	various dates
U.S. Code		1994–present

(Continued)

Table 8.1. (*Continued*)

Executive Branch

Federal Register (FR)	Vol. 1–present	1936–present
Code of Federal Regulations (CFR)		1997–present
LSA; List of CFR sections affected from the FR		1997–present
Budget of the U.S. Government	Budget, analytical perspectives, historical tables, etc.	FY 1996–present
Economic Report of the President		1995–present
Compilation of Presidential Documents	Known as the *Daily Compilation of Presidential Documents* until the Obama administration	1992–present
Public Papers of the President	George H. W. Bush (1991–1992); Clinton (all years); George W. Bush (all years); Obama (2009– (not yet complete)	1991–recent

Judicial Branch

United States court opinions	Select courts District courts; courts of appeal; bankruptcy court	2004–present
Independent council investigations	Clinton impeachment; Madison Guaranty Savings & Loan; several others	1998–present, selected docs
Selected federal judicial publications	*Clinton v. City of New York* (history of line-item veto notices); *State of New York, ex rel. Eliot Spitzer, et al., v. Microsoft Corporation*	1998; 2000

an executive one. Executive publications are strong for presidential issuances and regulations, but not at all strong for executive agency publications. Court opinions are available for U.S. appellate courts, but our Supreme Court opinions are not among them. These decisions are freely available at https://www.supremecourt.gov. Users needing court decisions should make their way to *Nexis Uni* (formerly *LexisNexis Academic*) or *Westlaw Campus* for these opinions.

Not only can *Govinfo.gov* be searched, but it can also be browsed. A browsing feature is a relatively rare feature in online databases these days, but it is extremely helpful when it comes to certain kinds of government information. For example, being able to browse the *Compilation of Presidential Documents* to see what our chief executive is doing and saying on a daily basis is highly informative. Perusing public laws in consecutive order aids in contexts where exact public law numbers are not known and when date browsing would be helpful. Browsing the *Federal Register* by date and then by agency allows for access to information that is often more helpful than trying to wade through search results, especially when selecting the proper search terms is difficult.

Another helpful feature is the ability to search by citation. In this age when many libraries have placed valuable reference resources, including legal resources, in remote storage, being able to search the United States Code (like the citation used above, 15 U.S.C. 1151-1157); the Code of Federal Regulations (for example, 42 CFR Part 483); or the *Federal Register* (for example, 77 FR 4334) by citation makes legal lookups easy.

Search Example 1: You are writing a paper about President Trump and his references to CNN as "fake news." Your professor demands that all resources be cited. You know that presidential speeches are transcribed, and you are hoping to find some of these references for your paper. Go to *Govinfo. gov* and search this way:

"fake news" AND CNN

By putting fake news in quotes, you are forcing a phrase search and increasing relevancy in your recall. You have a lot of results, but use the "Collection" facet on the left to limit results to *Compilation of Presidential Documents* (figure 8.1). Clicking the PDF under each result will retrieve the official PDF version of the presidential remarks.

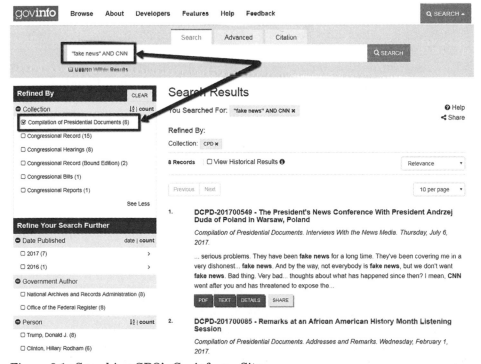

Figure 8.1. Searching GPO's Govinfo.gov Site.

Figure 8.2. Advanced Search from *Govinfo.gov*

Unfortunately, *Govinfo.gov* will not help you with how to cite what you have found. But the GPO provides citation advice: https://www.gpo.gov/help /about_compilation_of_presidential_documents.htm.

Search Example 2: You want to find out what the federal budget amount is for space exploration for fiscal year 2018. Begin by going to *Govinfo.gov*. To be most efficient, you will need to use the "Advanced Search" tab. Don't worry about the date limit for now. In the middle column, select only the check box for "Budget of the United States Government." Search in full-text for *space exploration* (figure 8.2).

Next you will see date facets (limiters) in the left margin. These are not sorted by date (which would make sense), but by number of hits in decreasing order of hits. As the FY18 budget comes out the year before, in 2017, be sure to select only that facet. The first result is titled *Budget FY 2018—National Aeronautics and Space Administration*. You can click on the PDF link and see the page from the budget in its official, authenticated format. Use the "search" command to find the phrase *space exploration* within this subsection of the budget. Notice the entire section of the document with the heading "Exploration." You can also examine the second item on the result list: *Budget FY 2018—America First: A Budget Blueprint to Make America Great Again*. This will provide additional textual background.

Congress.gov: The Library of Congress's Portal

For years, researchers have been familiar with the *Thomas* legislative database, which started in 1995. It closed down mid-2016 and was replaced by *Congress.gov*. *Congress.gov* is an excellent example of good programming and an intuitive user interface. It functions much better than any of the commercial databases for finding legislation sponsored by House and Senate members and tracking votes. It links to bill versions and congressional reports, but it does not contain congressional hearings, as *ProQuest Congressional* or *ProQuest Legislative Insight* are able to do.

Not only does *Congress.gov* cover the current Congress, with updated information generally posted the following government business day, it also has complete records and full text from previous Congresses back to the 104th Congress in 1995, with bill tracking back to the 93rd Congress in 1973.

Try this in *Congress.gov*. Select the name of a favorite (or not-so-favorite) representative or senator from your state. You can easily use form at the bottom of the Web site to do this if you cannot remember the names. Once you have one selected, click the "Sponsored Legislation" link in the lefthand margin. Under "Status of Legislation" (also on the left), select "Became Law." This will quickly show you how many pieces of legislation, sponsored by your selected representative/senator, have been passed into law. None of the commercial databases can do this task as quickly.

Search Example 1: Let's start off with a relatively simple legislative history example. Fred Thompson was an actor on the TV program *Law and Order*, but he was also a U.S. senator from Tennessee. He died in 2015, and an act of Congress designating a building in Nashville, Tennessee, the Fred D. Thompson Federal Building and United States Courthouse (Public Law 115-39) was passed to honor him. Let's find the legislative intent behind this act of Congress.

You can generally find this in congressional reports. To do this, start out with the *Congress.gov* database. First, set the pull-down menu to "All Legislation" so that you search all available years, not just the current year. Search *Fred Thompson* and notice that there are several resolutions, but one of the early results clearly states that H.R. 375 (115th Congress, 2017-2018) became law. This is the law you are looking for.

Also on that result screen is a congressional report, H. Rept. 115-23. Clicking on that takes you to the ugly text version of the report. But by clicking the PDF link, you see a PDF with the GPO authentication seal in the upper left corner of the screen. You are looking for the part of the report that says something about purpose of legislation, need for legislation, background, or the like. You see in the contents that there is a section titled "Purpose of Legislation" and also "Background and Need for Legislation." Here you can read a very nice brief biography of the senator.

This is a simple search example, but it can serve as a pattern for more complex search examples that you may encounter.

Search Example 2: You want to see which members of Congress have sponsored effectual legislation on issues of health. By "effectual," we mean legislation that went on to become law. To find this out, go to *Congress.gov* and select the "advanced search" tab. About halfway down the advanced search page, you will see subjects and two ways to select specific subjects to search. The first way is by major policy area, and the second way is to use a controlled vocabulary: "Legislative Subject Terms." This vocabulary, developed by the Library of Congress, is built into *Congress.gov*. You can familiarize yourself with this terminology here: https://www.congress.gov /help/field-values/legislative-subject-terms.

Let's use the term *comprehensive health care* for the search. Select the check box and "apply" it to the search criteria. Now you are taken back to the advanced search form. You need to click, under "legislative types," the "only legislation that can become law" box. This will clean up the search results a

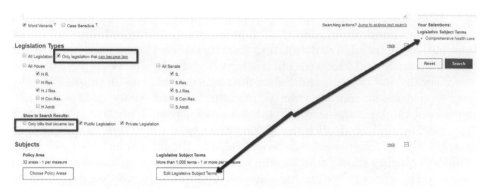

Figure 8.3. Part of the *Congress.gov* Advanced Search Form.

bit by ruling out resolution actions that express the sentiment of Congress but will not go on to become law. Check the box "only bills that became law" now or later from the limiters (figure 8.3).

Now select multiple Congresses, so that you can see actions over time. For this example, select the 111th through the 115th Congress (2009–2018). Now you are ready to execute the search. In late 2017, 470 results were returned. You now need to use the limiters on the left to show only legislation that became law. You can find this option under "Status of Legislation." By expanding the "Sponsor" facet, you see the names of congress members who were sponsors of major pieces of health legislation.

Catalog of Government Publications (CGP): The GPO's Online Catalog

The *Catalog of Government Publications* (https://catalog.gpo.gov) is the OPAC for the GPO. As the GPO doesn't have a physical library (it never has kept copies of the publications it catalogs), records in the CGP are for items distributed to depository libraries and not an inventory of what is on shelves at the GPO headquarters in Washington, D.C. It is an invaluable record of distribution of paper, fiche, and other tangible formats as well as an access point to government-issued permanent URLs (known as PURLS). It functions like a local library catalog in that it does not allow for full-text searching of any content, only searching of metadata.

The GPO started creating MARC records in July 1976, and all these records are in the CGP. In 1995/96 URLs started to be incorporated for selected congressional publications. This URL-adding initiative has grown, and now 97 percent of what the GPO distributes to depository libraries is also online. Because agency publications sometimes disappear (we don't expect government agencies to post PDFs online and keep them at the same Internet location forever—that's what libraries are for), the GPO takes steps to help in providing permanent access to publications. When the GPO creates a PURL, it also archives the documents, if it is at all possible to do so, so that in the event of a document disappearing, the archived version can be made live and active.

The CGP is continually being improved and updated. For years, the GPO maintained shelf list cards of items distributed through the Federal Depository Library Program. These cards are being converted into catalog records in the CGP, creating a historical access point for items that had only previously been found in the print *Monthly Catalog of United States Government Publications*.

Search Example 1: You want to look for information about social security benefits from other countries. Go to CGP and type "social security" world." The results screen will show records for both print and online, but we want to focus on online access. Note: Don't be thrown off by the dates that are over a decade old. These are serial publications, and the dates refer to when the serial began, not to all the available dates. From this result set on the first two screens, you see the following relevant records:

Social security programs throughout the world. Americas (Online)

Social security programs throughout the world. Africa (Online)

Social security programs throughout the world. Asia and the Pacific (Online)

Social security programs throughout the world. Europe (Online)

Without even going into the full bibliographic records, from the browse screen you are given PURLS for Internet access.

Search Example 2: From time to time, some agencies publish comic books. In 1994, the Consumer Product Safety Commission published *Sprocket Man*, a comic book about bicycle safety. Searching for this title in the CGP brings up three records for this title: the first record is for the electronic version, the second record for the print version, and the third was created from the shelf list conversion project. From the results screen, you can easily see the PURL so that you can read the comic book online. But let's say that you really want to get your hands on a physical copy of this book.

From the second record, the record for the print version, click the title. This brings up the full MARC record. Now use the" Locate in a Library" link, fill out the form (I recommend just filling in your state; you will see all the libraries in the state that should have received this item based on item selection criteria). Keep in mind that this is an approximation and not the same as looking up the title in a library's local online catalog. Don't drive 100 miles across your state without first at least checking the local catalog record for the library you intend to visit, as these estimated holdings often do not reflect reality.

Search Example 3: A patron wants to read about what his father experienced in World War II in the Signal Corps. What government publications can help him read about this? Let's search in the CGP to see what we can find. Searching "signal corps" retrieves 72 records. A promising book is *Getting the Message Through: A Branch History of the U.S. Army Signal Corps*. The CGP record contains a PURL for the online version (http://purl.access.gpo.gov/GPO/LPS76128), but as you read it, you discover that several of the images (pp. 21, 167, and 269) are not loading at all. You would like to consult a physical copy of the book. You can use the "Locate in a Library" feature from within the full MARC record to see which libraries in your state are likely to have the physical volumes. Another option, often available, is to see whether government content is available in either the HathiTrust (https://www.hathitrust.org) or the Internet Archive eBooks and Texts (https://archive.org/details/texts). In this case, this book is freely viewable via the HathiTrust (https://catalog .hathitrust.org/Record/003092628). There is more about the HathiTrust below.

Census.gov and *American FactFinder*: Tools of the Census Bureau

The U.S. Census Bureau Web site has long been famous as a helpful source for statistics and census data. *American FactFinder* is the primary resource for accessing data from the decennial censuses of the United States (the past two decennial censuses), the American Community Survey, and recently the Economic Census. *American FactFinder* is examined in greater depth with search examples in chapter 11.

The Census Bureau Web site is famously informative. If you type "births" in the search box at *Census.gov*, the first search result tells you, "The U.S. Census Bureau is not the primary source on births. The primary source is Centers for Disease Control (CDC) National Center for Health Statistics (NCHS)." Then it gives you the URL. What helpfulness! When was the last time a company told you that they were not the best place for a service, but that you should go to a different company? The Census Bureau Web site is full of referrals to other agencies when it is not the proper information source.

Other Full-Text Sources for Government Information

It is clear that not all older government publications have been digitized, but that is quickly changing. Copyright laws generally prohibit items published after 1922 from being made available without fear of lawsuits. That is the reason you often see databases stopping their coverage at 1922. For example, outside the realm of government information, *Afro-American Imprints* from the Library Company of Philadelphia (a NewsBank database) has coverage dates from 1535 to 1922. *The Arizona Republic* newspaper (ProQuest) has coverage from 1890 to 1922. Databases wanting to provide access to resources from 1923 onward must go to great lengths to secure rights and be safe from lawsuits. However, these extra steps are not necessary in the case of U.S. federal documents because they are free of copyright and are in the public domain.

Unfortunately, initiatives such as Google Books often do not take the time to curate these publications, and the result is that government documents that should be freely available are locked down in Google Books. The good news is that HathiTrust, the consortial endeavor that

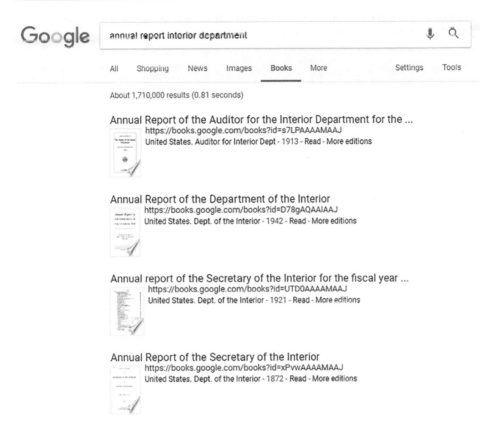

Figure 8.4. Government Document Serials in Google Books. *Source*: Google and the Google logo are registered trademarks of Google Inc. Used with permission.

has partnered with Google Books from the beginning, has many of these publications freely available for reading. So, while Google Books may be the place one discovers government publications, it may well be that HathiTrust is the place of ultimate fulfillment, that is, the full-text target.

Another strong feature of HathiTrust is the way that it treats serial publications. Google Books treats an annual report of a government entity as a separate publication, and it is difficult to find the relationship between issues. If you do a Google Books search for "annual report interior department," you get results as seen in figure 8.4.

But if you do the same search within the HathiTrust database (catalog search, not full-text search), you can easily land on a serial record with "full view" versions organized by year of publication (figure 8.5).

HathiTrust also has full text for post-1922 government documents more carefully curated than you will find in Google Books.

The disadvantage of HathiTrust is that you will not be able to download entire full texts unless you are in a library that is a member of

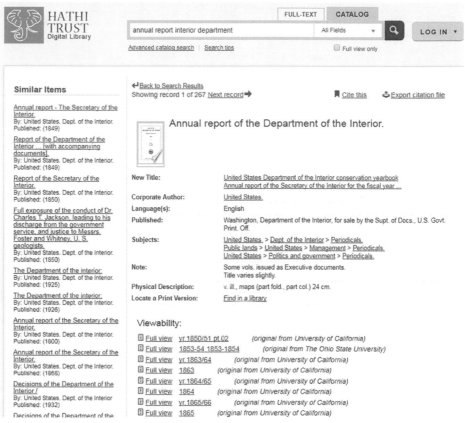

Figure 8.5. Government document serials in HathiTrust. Government document serials in HathiTrust. *Source*: HathiTrust. Used with permission.

HathiTrust—generally a larger academic library. You will be able to download one page at a time, but this can be time-consuming.

Another option for full downloading of government documents is in the texts area of the Internet Archive (archive.org). Figure 8.6 shows a government publication from 1957 that is fully viewable and downloadable in multiple formats.

Only a small percentage of government publications are in the Internet Archive, as compared to HathiTrust. But when they are, the user experience is stunning.

Search Example: Remember the search for Signal Corps publications a few pages ago? None of the following publications had online versions according to the *Catalog of Government Publications*. But they could all be located as PDFs in the HathiTrust project. Here are those seven titles with no URL in the CGP, but with content available online via HathiTrust (table 8.2).

Not all U.S. government publications are online, but a very high percentage of them are. The HathiTrust is a major reason for that and is a source to become familiar with.

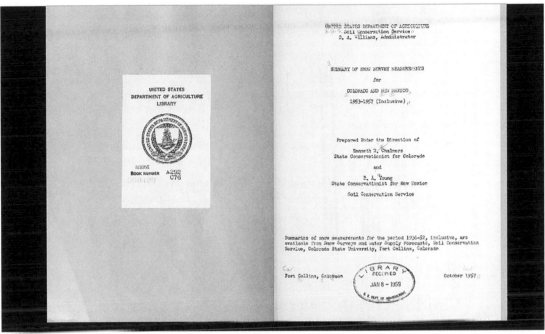

Figure 8.6. Internet Archive Book with Multiple Download Options.
Source: https://archive.org/details/CAT10682755.

Table 8.2. Finding Full Text in HathiTrust.

Title from the CGP	Location within HathiTrust
The Signal Corps: the outcome (mid-1943 through 1945)	https://catalog.hathitrust.org /Record/102120263
The United States Army and World War II. Set 4, The Technical Services, Part I (Chemical, Ordnance, Transportation, and Signal)	(This is a CD-ROM with many titles contained within; each of the titles within the contents can be found within the HathiTrust.)

(Continued)

Table 8.2. (*Continued*)

Title from the CGP	Location within HathiTrust
The Signal Corps: the test (December 1941 to July 1943)	https://catalog.hathitrust.org /Record/003903960
Breaking codes, breaking barriers: the WACs of the Signal Security Agency, World War II	https://catalog.hathitrust.org /Record/011417743
The Signal Corps: the emergency (to December 1941)	https://catalog.hathitrust.org /Record/000815537
The Signal Corps, the emergency (to December 1941). Technical services	(Same as above, just cataloged a bit differently.)
U.S. Army in World War II the technical services: the signal corps: the emergency	https://catalog.hathitrust.org/Reco rd /010741493

Vendor Databases for U.S. Government Information

U.S. Congressional Publications

ProQuest has taken the lead in providing access to congressional publications, including the *Congressional Record*, hearings, reports and documents, and committee prints and Congressional Research Service reports. In 2010, ProQuest purchased the Congressional database from LexisNexis, which had originally been produced by the Congressional Information Service (CIS). Libraries have the option of just subscribing to the index, but they may also purchase or subscribe to the full text, including the *U.S. Congressional Serial Set*. Libraries have the option of subscribing just to the indexing of *ProQuest Congressional*, or they may opt to subscribe to digital content or to purchase it.

The search portal allows for searching by the usual access points of title, subject, and all keywords either across metadata fields or within the full text. Other searchable fields include names on maps, bill numbers, Public Law numbers, *Statutes at Large* citation, Superintendent of Documents (SuDocs) numbers, and congressional hearings witness name and affiliation. This makes it easy, for example, to locate the times Michael D. Brown, the former undersecretary of emergency preparedness and response, testified before Congress about the Katrina disaster.

Readex published the entire digital *Serial Set* before ProQuest, and these two competing products to the *Serial Set* provide access never before possible. It should be emphasized that Readex only digitized the *Congressional Serial Set* and not the other congressional content, like the hearings, committee prints, CRS reports, and *Congressional Record*. Figure 8.7 shows the Readex interface.

There are pros and cons to each digital *Serial Set* version. The Readex *Serial Set* has superior cataloging and indexing for its collection. Not only does Readex employ extensive controlled vocabulary for subject terms, it also has a names authority control system for every name (not just author) mentioned

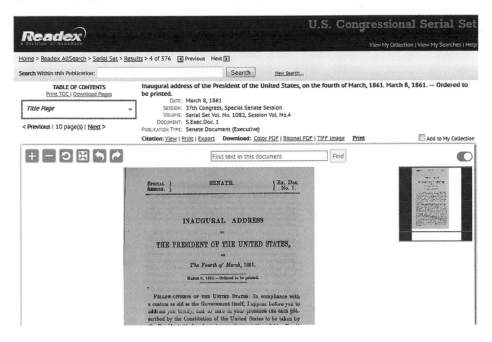

Figure 8.7. Readex Serial Set Contains Stunning Color and Bitonal Images.
Source: ©Readex, a Division of NewsBank, Inc. Used with permission.

within the 16,000 volumes. In addition, it has a geography control for places and physical features. These features allow for browsing of the massive collection.

Most users have no idea how to approach the huge collection of primary source materials that are contained in the *Serial Set*. Being able to browse by geographic location brings the collection close to home. Genealogists will find that browsing by personal name can open up previously unknown research avenues. This is an unparalleled research achievement. But it comes at a significant price. The ProQuest *Serial Set* has undergone significant improvements since it was purchased from LexisNexis. The brief catalog titles that had not been based on examining the original materials have now been corrected. The ProQuest product integrates best with other ProQuest modules, making it a favorite of law schools and many other researchers. Also, the PDFs from ProQuest are easier to deal with and to search within.

ProQuest also has *Legislative Insight*, which presents legislative histories for most public laws of the United States. Growing out of the legislative histories originally done in their *ProQuest Congressional* database, this database is a major enhancement in that it includes full text for every document (reports, hearings, *Congressional Record* references, etc.) in PDFs within the database itself, without needing to link out to other modules. When the project is complete, most Public Laws from the 1st Congress in 1789 to the present will be fully represented in the database.

U.S. Executive Branch Publications

Current executive branch publications are well tracked in the *Catalog of Government Publications* (CGP), along with PURLS for online access.

However, older executive branch materials are not so easy to find, as the GPO has only been cataloging materials in the CGP since 1976 and has only recently begun adding older documents. The HathiTrust has many older government publications in full text, and because they are in the public domain, they are fully searchable and somewhat accessible in that database. There is no cutoff for materials published after the 1922 copyright cutoff date because they are not copyrighted. But as good as HathiTrust is for these materials, it is far from complete in its coverage.

For a fee, libraries can purchase, through *ProQuest Congressional*, the *Executive Branch Documents* materials. Initially issued only in microfiche format and covering the documents listed in the *Checklist of United States Public Documents 1789–1909* (U.S. Government Printing Office 1911), ProQuest has digitized the entire series, and is even continuing beyond the initial fiche series to dates well into the 1940s. Although some of these documents are available through the HathiTrust and Internet Archive, the *Executive Branch Documents* are by far the most complete one-stop place to find these older documents.

So here is a question for you: why does ProQuest include the Executive Branch Module under the *ProQuest Congressional* interface? Doesn't that sound like they are making the executive branch subordinate to the legislative branch? That's a great question: glad you are paying attention. The reason is that many executive branch annual reports were issued in the *Serial Set*, and sometimes outside the *Serial Set*. For example, if a researcher wants to find all the annual reports of the War Department, he or she would need to do two separate searches, one for the reports within the *Serial Set* and another search for reports outside the *Serial Set* but contained in the Executive Branch Documents collection. By placing both databases under the same interface, users are able to see combined results without having to figure out all these complexities.

U.S. Judicial Branch Publications

When people think of the judicial branch, they most commonly think of court cases. Because of the various court rules, the Government Publishing Office has not historically distributed these cases, with the exception of the U.S. Supreme Court cases. The databases most relied on within the legal community are Lexis, Westlaw, and Bloomberg Law. Those outside of the legal profession don't have access to these expensive databases, but rather to academic versions. The newly styled *Nexis Uni* is the replacement for *LexisNexis Academic*. *Westlaw Campus Research* is the competing Thomson Reuters product. These provide basic access to appellate case law, state and federal statutes and regulations, and much more—just not as much as the full *Lexis* and *Westlaw*.

A Note about the Federal Depository Library Program

In this chapter, we have discussed not only freely available government databases, but also several commercial databases, some of them quite pricey. If you are not fortunate enough to have access to these wonderful databases, all you need to do is contact a federal depository library (FDL) in your state. The Federal Depository Library Program is composed of "regional" depository libraries (receiving all items distributed to the GPO) and "selective" depository libraries. Regionals are especially tasked with providing government information to the citizens of their states. These libraries can often run searches for you in commercial databases that contain government information, and in some cases, they may be able to e-mail you PDF results under special contract provisions they have with vendors.

To locate a FDL library near you, use the directory of FDLs at https://www.fdlp.gov/about-the-fdlp/federal-depository-libraries.

International Publications

Now, we will briefly discuss some selected international information. The United Nations has some excellent databases that are easy to access.

Official Document System (ODS)

The *Official Document System* (ODS), available at https://documents.un.org, is a database that contains the full text, usually in the six official languages of the United Nations, from 1993 onward, of selected documents going back to 1946. You can search by UN symbol number, words in the title, words in the full text, or a controlled subject list (the system won't even allow you to enter unauthorized subjects). This database is the place to go for anyone assisting Model UN students. (The Model UN program is an authentic simulation of the UN General Assembly; Google it!)

UNBISnet (United Nations Bibliographic Information System)

While ODS focuses on documents, UNBISnet (http://unbisnet.un.org) is the online catalog of the UN Dag Hammarskjöld Library in New York and the Library of the UN Office at Geneva. Coverage is from 1979 onward, with selected earlier documents. The database interface also provides access to voting records of the General Assembly and Security Council, as well as an index to speeches from 1983 onward.

United Nations iLibrary

The UN iLibrary is intended to be a comprehensive information portal targeting students, scholars, and policy makers. It includes complete e-books and important series, such as the *Yearbook of the United Nations*, the *Human Development Report*, and the *United Nations Statistical Yearbook*, just to name a few. It is the easiest way for high school and college students to experience UN publications without being overwhelmed with symbol numbers and other technical database issues. Citation help is provided as well as export features to bibliographic management software.

United Nations Treaty Collection

Official treaty texts for both bilateral and multilateral treaties can be found in the *United Nations Treaty Collection* (https://treaties.un.org). Of importance to international scholars is the status of multilateral treaties—dates of signing, ratification, and accession—and any reservations that are appended. The *United Nations Treaty Series* (*UNTS*), contained within the *UN Treaty Collection*, is the official source of digital copies of treaties.

Other International Databases

Besides the United Nations, other international organizations with databases include the following:

- European Union (*Eurostat: Your Key to European Statistics*; *AMECO* (macroeconomic database); *Eurobarometer* (public opinion))
- World Health Organization (statistics and publications databases)
- UNESCO (*UNESDOC* database of publications)
- UNESCO (also has an online thesaurus)
- ASEAN (statistics database)
- Organization of American States (*OAS Observatory on Citizen Security*)
- United Nations Development Programme (UNDP) (*Human Development Reports* database)
- World Bank (*World Development Report* and statistical databases)

Table 8.3 provides some additional information.

Table 8.3. Selected Additional International Databases.

Database Name	Database Description
ASEANstats	Association of South East Asian Nations (ASEAN). Portal to several databases on trade, investment, tourism, population, and other indicators. http://www.aseanstats.org.
Human Development Reports	United Nations Development Programme (UNDP). Includes the well-known Human Development Index (HDI), country reports, Gender Development Index, Gender Inequality Index, and more. http://hdr.undp.org.
OAS Observatory on Citizen Security	Organization of American States (OAS). Database of indicators for crime, police personnel, criminal justice system, prison system, victimization, and demography data. http://www.oas.org/dsp/observatorio/database/indicators .aspx?lang=en

Database Name	Database Description
UNESDOC	United Nations Educational, Scientific and Cultural Organization (UNESCO). All UNESCO documents and publications since 1945, plus library acquisitions. Uses UNESCO Thesaurus. http://unesdoc.unesco.org.
World Development Report and World Development Indicators	World Bank. Indicators are related to the *World Development Report*. Indicators include the Gini Coefficient, a measure of income inequality. http://www.worldbank.org/en/publication/wdr /wdr-archive. http://databank.worldbank.org.

Foreign Government Publications

Researchers need to keep in mind the difference between publications from international organizations (e.g., United Nations, European Union, ASEAN) and publications from foreign governments (e.g., Mexico, the United Kingdom, Japan). Foreign government information is most easily accessed via Google. Yes, Google is the primary finding aid for official documents for countries outside the United States. To do this effectively, we need to learn a bit about Google power searching.

Top-Level Domains (TLDs)

Each country of the world is assigned a top-level Internet domain, or TLD. As the Internet was begun in the United States, there is no single TLD for the United States, but many. You are already familiar with the commercial domain (.com) and likely also the educational domain (.edu). But in the United States, there are also .net, .gov, .mil, and many others. The .us domain was intended to be used by states and local jurisdictions, but this never caught on.

To find all the TLDs of the world, you need to search Google for "tld." Look for the result that says "List of Internet top-level domains," from *Wikipedia*. On that page, you will see the TLD for every country and for places that aren't even countries but have been assigned a top-level domain. For example, from that list you will see that Belarus is .by, and Laos is .la.

Now that you know how to find country domains, you need to be able to locate the government subdomains for the country. This is sometimes very easy; other times it is not. Let's say you are looking for government publications from Colombia. Looking at our TLD list from *Wikipedia*, you see that .co is the TLD for Colombia. We start with a Google for "site:co."

Notice that we do not search for "site:.co." You certainly could do the search like this, and you would get the same results. But I purposely leave out the "dot" when I am teaching this skill because some people don't see the dot and search with a space. But placing a space there breaks the search syntax and returns incorrect results. So, as a best practice, always omit the period before a TLD search.

Best Practice: Search Google for top-level domains without the period and be sure there is no space after *site:*.

Foreign Government Subdomains

Now you need to find out the government subdomain (if there is one). Subdomains are assigned by countries, not by the Internet Assigned Numbers Authority division of ICANN. There are a couple of strategies you could use for figuring this out:

1. You could use the site search combined with a word for government. For Colombia, you could search "site:co government." That didn't work well in this case. Let's try this again. The word for *government* in Spanish is *gobierno*. So now let's try "gobierno site:co." You now clearly see from the Google search results that Colombia uses gov.co for government sites.

2. Another way you could approach this is by guessing the government subdomain. Common subdomains to test are the following (where xx stands for a country TLD):

   .gov.xx (examples: Syria, gov.sy; Papua New Guinea, gov.pg; China (mainland), gov.cn; Russia, gov.ru)

   .go.xx (examples: Tanzania, go.tz; Japan. go.jp)

   .gob.xx (*gobierno* in Spanish)

   .gouv.xx (*gouvernement* in French)

   .government.xx (example: Netherlands, government.nl)

Some countries seem to have multiple patterns. Norway uses government.no for English-language pages, but regjeringen.no for Norwegian-language pages. Ecuador uses gob.ec for Spanish and gov.ec for English. Canada often uses gc.ca for government sites, but many government sites are migrating to canada.ca. This is a very fluid situation, so researchers should not make any assumptions. Always test before relying on results.

The use of English varies on foreign government Web sites. Don't expect much English from France or some Latin American countries. However, there is a surprising number of English-language documents to be found on Japanese and Chinese government sites. If you can read a foreign language, it is always advisable to search in that language, combining your foreign-language skills with the domain searching illustrated here.

Substantive Foreign Government Publications

What file type is often used for substantive publications? That's right, PDF format, or .pdf. Just as you used the Google search syntax to specify the domain and subdomain you wanted to search within Google's index, so too you can specify the file type you want to search. The Google search syntax for this would be "filetype:pdf." Just as in site-specific searching, the best practice is to not place a period before PDF, even though it will work. By restricting search results to PDF files, you can more easily hone in on relevant materials and steer clear of nonsubstantive Web sites.

Search Example 1: Japan and China have been fighting for years about rights to disputed islands in the Pacific Ocean. You want to find arguments on both sides of this issue from government Web sites. You also know that each country has a different name for the islands: China calls them the Diaoyu Islands, but Japan calls them Senkaku Islands. Let's start with China, with the government subdomain being gov.cn. Search Google like this: "site:gov.cn diaoyu filetype:pdf." The first document retrieved is *The Question of Diaoyu Island*, and in five pages, it presents the position of mainland China. Now let's find Japan's position by searching this way: "site:go.jp senkaku filetype:pdf." The first result is a 24-page PDF, *The Senkaku Islands*, and is a presentation of Japan's position.

Search Example 2: You want to find official documents from both Ukraine and Russia about the Crimean Peninsula occupation. The TLD for Ukraine is .ua, and after playing around a bit, you discover that the government subdomain is gov.ua. A search for "site:gov.ua crimea russia filetype:pdf" turns up many relevant PDF documents in English. Now search for the Russian perspective. Searching "site:gov.ru crimea ukraine filetype:pdf" likewise turns up many relevant results in English, but from the opposing viewpoint.

Exercises

Because not all readers of this book will have access to the proprietary databases mentioned in this chapter, these exercises are restricted to the freely available U.S. government databases.

1. Pick a favorite hot topic. It may be gun control, school choice, marijuana, abortion, climate change, or another topic that you select. Perform a search for that topic in *Govinfo.gov*. Which "collection" has the most results for that topic? Which collection, or type of document, did you find most interesting? Now find the most recent results on the topic. Compare the results for the oldest results for that topic. Has the rhetoric changed over the years?

   (Note: The GPO has digitized the *Congressional Record* back to the early years, but they have not digitized other congressional materials, such as reports, documents, and hearings, that far. When you search for congressional materials for items before 1995 or so, you will see *Congressional Record* in the results, but not other congressional materials. For those items, you will need to search *ProQuest Congressional*.)

2. What was the exact quote from George W. Bush about the difference between a squirrel and a bomb? (Hint: Using *Govinfo.gov*, you should be able to find this in two places: *Public Papers of the Presidents* and *Compilation of Presidential Documents*.)

3. You are doing research on Title IX (of the Education Act of 1972), the federal civil rights law that prohibits sex discrimination in education. You want to read the law as amended (as it stands today) in the United States Code. You have a citation (20 U.S.C. 1681-1688) and want to read it for yourself (in the official version). Find the full text of the law using *Govinfo.gov*. (Hint: You cannot search for a range of sections, such as 1681–1688; you need to search for a specific section, such as 1681.)

4. Using *Congress.gov*, select your congressional representative from the "Current Members of Congress" section at the bottom of the page. Find her/his sponsored legislation and then, using the status of legislation facets, find out how many sponsored bills actually became law.

References

U.S. Government Printing Office. 1911. *Checklist of United States Public Documents 1789–1909.* 3rd ed., revised and enlarged. Washington, D.C.: Government Printing Office.

U.S. Government Printing Office. 2010. *100 GPO Years, 1861–1961: A History of United States Public Printing.* Sesquicentennial ed. Washington, D.C.: U.S. Government Publishing Office. Accessed December 29, 2017. https://permanent .access.gpo.gov/lps126616/GPO_100Years.pdf.

U.S. Government Publishing Office. 2016. *Keeping America Informed: The U.S. Government Publishing Office: A Legacy of Service to the Nation.* Revised ed. Washington, D.C.: U.S. Government Publishing Office.

Vance-Cooks, Davita. 2017. "Prepared Statement before the Committee on House Administration, U.S. House of Representatives: On Transforming GPO for the 21st Century and Beyond." Wednesday, May 17, 2017. Accessed December 29, 2017. http://docs.house.gov/meetings/HA/HA00/20170517/105962/HHRG-115 -HA00-Wstate-Vance-CooksD-20170517.pdf.

Suggested Readings

Hartnett, Cassandra J., Andrea L. Sevetson, and Eric J. Forte. 2016. *Fundamentals of Government Information: Mining, Finding, Evaluating, and Using Government Resources.* 2nd ed. Chicago: Neal-Schuman.

Beyond the Textbook

Carrying on the tradition of the fourth edition, additional exercises, search tips, and tutorials will be available on the publisher's Web site at http:// www.abc-clio.com/books.librariesunlimited.com/Librarians-Guide-to-Online -Searching. This will be updated periodically with the inevitable database changes.

9
Humanities Databases

The *humanities* is a very broad term that encompasses many disciplines, including art (all kinds of art, from painting, to sculpture, to video art); architecture; archaeology; film; history; literature; music; philosophy; religion; and theater. Each of these disciplines is extremely broad and extends across all cultures and all time periods. Primary sources of study take into consideration literary texts, sacred texts, archival papers of people and groups, visual materials, scores, historical newspapers, legal documents, and anything else of historical, literary, or religious interest. Humanist may interact with texts or productions, or they may create them

Databases of interest to humanities students and scholars include historic e-book texts (which may previously have been purchased by libraries in microfilm or microfiche formats); sound recordings of music, from the well-known composers and performing artists to not-so-well-known music from diverse and foreign cultures; images of paintings, pottery, and sculptures; dictionaries of customary language usage, dialects and regional accents; and graphical representations of costumes used in staging plays. Humanists are not only interested in scholarly secondary sources on their topics, but also the primary sources, some of which can only be found in archives and museums spread far and wide. Vendors are making humanities research more accessible these days by providing digital access to archival resources, unique films, rare books, and other texts that would have required travel budgets to access in previous generations of scholarly endeavors.

As Suzanne Bell notes in the previous edition to this work (Bell 2015), a high percentage of people attracted to library school come from humanities backgrounds with previous majors in English, history, or related fields. For that reason, this chapter focuses on just two areas of the humanities, literature and history. We will also discuss newspaper databases, the ever-growing e-books databases, and archival databases, as vendors are producing some interesting offerings in those areas.

Literature Databases: MLA International Bibliography

The Modern Language Association (MLA) produces what is arguably the closest product to the database of record for language and literature. Produced by the Modern Language Association of America, the *MLA International Bibliography* (*MLAIB*) is the online version of a print index that began in 1921. It not only covers literature, but also the broader topics of human communication and related topics of formal linguistics (e.g., phonology, phonetics, syntax, semantics, pragmatics, discourse analysis); folklore (including music and art); dramatic arts; and language teaching. It includes journal articles, books, book chapters, dissertations, working papers, conference papers and proceedings, and selected book reviews. Because it is a language and linguistics database, it contains records for hundreds of languages—both materials in various languages as well as languages as subject of study.

The *MLA Thesaurus*, accessible via a link at the top of the EBSCOhost interface, uses "See" and "Used For" references. It also has relational features, such as "Broader Terms," "Narrower Terms," and "Related Terms," but not for every entry. Because the terms are consistently applied by the MLA, users should be able to rely on them with a higher degree of consistency than EBSCO's subject index terms. For a fuller discussion of EBSCO's index terms, see the discussion in chapter 3.

Another feature is the *MLA Directory of Periodicals*, a separate module within the *MLAIB* interface, which provides detailed information on the journals and book series covered within the database.

The MLA does not have an interface of its own, but it does provide index records to each of the three large database publishers: Gale, EBSCO, and ProQuest. The three big aggregators each have their own way of featuring literature databases. *Gale Literary Sources* integrates several databases together under the Artemis interface. Included in the cross-searchable platform (if a library subscribes) are *Literature Criticism Index*, *Literature Resources Center*, *MLA International Bibliography*, *LitFinder*, *Dictionary of Literary Biography*, *Something about the Author*, and *Contemporary Authors*. ProQuest offers the *MLAIB* as a premium module under their LION platform. EBSCO offers the *MLA International Bibliography* and the *MLA Directory of Periodicals* as separate databases, and both are cross-searchable with other EBSCOhost platform databases, such as *Academic Search*. Table 9.1 shows details of the database. Note the number of searchable fields.

MLAIB Distinctive Features

Several features of the *MLA International Bibliography* set it apart from other databases and are worthy of note. While most databases allow users to limit by date, in literature, it is important to be able to limit by date of content under discussion, as that is how research topics are most often approached in literature, not just date of publication. Each of the vendor interfaces of the *MLAIB* have a "Period" limiter by which materials can be limited to 100-year slices of time:

B.C.

0–99 A.D.

100–199 A.D.

. . .

1700–1799 A.D.

1800–1899 A.D.

1900–1999 A.D.

2000–2099 A.D.

Even though these time breakdowns are very artificial in terms of relating to literary eras, they do help to provide a more refined relevance in retrieval, which is always the goal.

Since the Modern Language Association is all about language, language limiters are prolific in this database. Eighty language limiters are shown in the EBSCOhost interface, many of them with just one item in the database. Search results reveal that there are items in at least 138 languages. But it is informative to see the distribution of items by language for the more prolific languages.

Table 9.2 shows the top 30 languages represented in the *MLAIB* database as of mid-2017.

Although 61 percent of the database contains English-language articles, there is strong representation of international scholarship the world over.

Searching *MLAIB*

As with many databases, one can search using the basic/standard interface or the advanced search interface. As this book is likely being used by librarians and library students, I recommend the *advanced search interface* so that you can more easily view all the search refinement options available to you. With the advanced search, you can easily see how to limit time period and genre at the outset.

The pull-down menu for searching the *MLAIB* is so long that it is easy to overlook the searching power available. Of course, there are the usual fields for searching the various title fields: article title, collection title, and journal title. There are also special kinds of fields that deserve special attention (table 9.3).

Even though the database includes these specialized fields, the recommended strategy is to browse the respective indexes to get a feel of what is contained in the fields and then to search "Subjects – All," as that searches across all the specialized subject fields (see figure 9.1).

Search Example: Looking for Peer-Reviewed Articles Analyzing Death in Chinese Literature

To search for peer-reviewed articles that analyze death in Chinese literature, start by making sure that the *MLA Thesaurus* uses *death* and *Chinese*

Table 9.1. Database Spec Sheet for MLA International Bibliography.

Database Name	MLA International Bibliography
Creator	Modern Language Association
Vendor/Interface	ProQuest/LION EBSCO/EBSCOhost Gale/Artemis
Scope	Over 2.8 million citations. Over 4,400 journals going back to the 1920s.
Physical Analog	*MLA international bibliography of books and articles on the modern languages and literatures* [title varies]. 1969–present
Searchable Fields	TX All Text AU Author SU Subject Terms AB Abstract BT Collection Title DT Date DS Dissertation Info ED Editors FK Folklore Topic GD Genre GC Genre/Classification IB ISBN IS ISSN IP Issue SO Journal Title LA Language of Publication LN Linguistics Topic TQ Literary Technique GT Literature Topic GE Location MD Media NT Notes PG Pages TM Period SA Primary Subject Author SK Primary Subject Work PB Publication Info RX Review Excerpt BR Reviewed By CP Scholarly Theme or Discipline SE Series SP Start Page SL Subject Language LT Subject Literature TC Table of Contents TI Title VI Volume

Database Name	MLA International Bibliography
Limiters	Document Type
	Image Types
	Historical Era
	Publication Type
	Language

Table 9.2. Top Languages in the *MLA International Bibliography*.

Language	Number/Items	Percent/Items
English	1,726,257	61.23%
French	239,075	8.48%
German	216,617	7.68%
Spanish	166,538	5.91%
Italian	88,190	3.13%
Russian	73,245	2.60%
Portuguese	28,272	1.00%
Ukrainian	24,544	0.87%
Chinese	22,458	0.80%
Dutch	20,867	0.74%
Romanian	19,507	0.69%
Polish	17,868	0.63%
Turkish	16,690	0.59%
Serbo-Croatian	14,256	0.51%
Swedish	13,412	0.48%
Japanese	13,271	0.47%
Lithuanian	9,689	0.34%
Esperanto	9,483	0.34%
Slovenian	8,845	0.31%
Danish	8,689	0.31%
Czech	8,493	0.30%
Latvian	8,146	0.29%
Norwegian	7,527	0.27%
Hungarian	6,872	0.24%
Bulgarian	5,355	0.19%
Slovak	4,858	0.17%
Hebrew	4,135	0.15%
Estonian	3,400	0.12%
Catalan	2,974	0.11%
Greek	2,949	0.10%

Table 9.3. Examples of Selected Specialized Subject Fields in *MLAIB*.

Pull-Down Selection (Browse via Index)	Examples
Folklore Topic	Afro-Ecuadoran women, death rites, faith healing, harvest rites, Jainism, jazz music, magic, masks (costume), obscene jokes, rap music, sword dance, tall tale
Genre (also available as a fixed field selection from Advanced Search)	autobiography, biography, drama, fiction, letters, novel, periodicals, poetry, prose, saga, short story
Linguistics Topic	accusative case, Brazilian linguistics, comparative linguistics, dialectology, grammatical categories, initial consonants, lexicography, morphology, paralinguistics, sign languages
Literary Technique	abstraction, ballad, baroque style, falsehood, fantasy, irony, parable, satire, truth
Literature Topic	aging, allegory, animals, lesbianism, madness, outsider, racism, science, trauma, zombie
Location	Adirondack Mountains, Babylonia, Cuzco (city), East Asia, East Cleveland, Gabon, Jablanica Region (Serbia), Labrador, Oaxaca, Quebec City, Ruhr Region, Tahiti, York (England)
Scholarly Theory or Discipline	action theory, factor analysis, game theory, iconography, information theory, paleography, Sapir-Whorf hypothesis
Subject Literature	Afghan literature, Belorussian literature, East German literature, Flemish literature, Honduran literature, Icelandic literature, Japanese literature

literature as authorized terms. Searching for *death* in the thesaurus, you find that it is an authorized term and that the broader term is *mortality*, and there are three narrower terms not related to the topic at hand. There are some related terms that might be relevant, such as *burial*, *demise*, *dying*, and *execution*. You might consider adding these terms to your search in addition to *death*.

    Chinese literature is also an authorized term, with possible related terms being *Classical Chinese literature* and *Taiwanese literature*. When framing your search, it will be important to use the proper search tags, rather than just entering terms as general keywords. You can do this by using the check boxes to add terms to the search or by entering terms into the boxes with the appropriate pull-down selections made. Here are examples of each of these two ways of framing this search. These search strings were recovered using the EBSCOhost "Search History" feature.

    Search entered via check boxes within the thesaurus:
    (DE "death" OR DE "burial" OR DE "demise" OR DE "dying" OR DE "execution") AND (DE "Chinese literature" OR DE "Classical Chinese literature" OR DE "Taiwanese literature") (104 results)

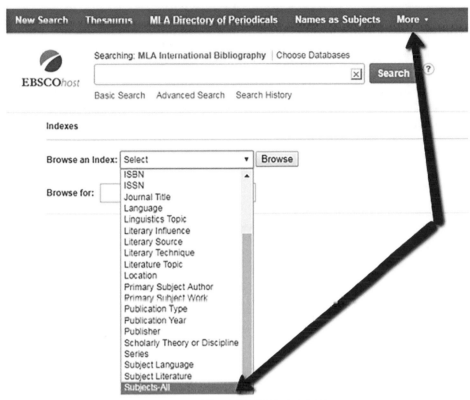

Figure 9.1. Searching "Subjects – All" in EBSCO's *MLAIB* Interface.
Source: ©2017 EBSCO Industries, Inc. All rights reserved.

Search entered from the search boxes and pull-down menus:
SU (death OR burial OR demise OR execution) AND SU (chinese
literature OR classical chinese literature OR taiwanese literature)
(133 results)

So why the difference in results here? This is easily explained by the
fact that the thesaurus entry method uses the DE search tag, a more specific
tag that refers to only authorized search terms in the subject field. The DE
search tag is not available from the pull-down menu selection; only the SU
tag is. The SU tag searches not just the subject descriptor field but other
subject fields as well.

Dissertations in *MLAIB*

Dissertations from *Dissertation Abstracts International* that fall within
the appropriate scope appear as records in the *MLAIB* database. This is often
a great source of confusion to library users. Many times, users click the OpenURL links to get to the full text. When this fails, they often place interlibrary
loan requests. This is a rare case of one index (*MLAIB*) pointing to another
index rather than to the actual full text that the user ultimately desires.

For example, the entry in *MLAIB* for the title *The Jeweled Broom and the Dust of the World: Keichu, Motoori Norinaga, and Kokugaku in Early Modern Japan* gives the "source" as "Dissertation Abstracts International (DAI) 2017 July; 78 (1) U of California, Los Angeles, 2016 Abstract no: DA10158427." To the experienced librarian, it is obvious that one index is citing an entry in another index, but students often miss this fact.

Perhaps, in the future, better linkages will provide deep links to the actual dissertations, whether from *ProQuest Dissertations & Theses Global* or to copies held in institutional repositories (as many of them are). I noticed recently that the EBSCO version of *MLAIB* includes a link to the ProQuest database, so libraries that subscribe to the full content will, in fact, be linked directly to the digital dissertation.

MLA Thesaurus and Names as Subjects Index

There are two sets of controlled vocabulary in *MLAIB*: the subject thesaurus and the names as subject index. To show that this database's thesaurus incorporates "Broader Terms," "Narrower Terms," "Related Terms," and "Used For" references, we will examine the subject descriptor "television and video," as represented through the EBSCOhost interface (figure 9.2).

Figure 9.2. EBSCOhost *MLAIB* Thesaurus Structure Example. *Source:* ©2017 EBSCO Industries, Inc. All rights reserved.

The first thing to note is at the very end of the thesaurus entry: the terms *television* and *video* are not authorized terms. You can tell this because there are no check boxes to the left of them. Instead of these two unauthorized terms, the single term *television and video* is used in their place. Two broader terms are in the hierarchy, *dramatic arts* and *mass media*. There are numerous narrower terms. Related terms include names of companies within the industry and terms closely related to the topic. The check boxes to the left of the terms indicate that the terms are authorized in the thesaurus. The boxes can be checked if users desire to add selected terms to their database search criteria.

Students often take the time to look up authorized subject descriptors, but then they only execute keyword searches. As they have taken the time to research the exact descriptors, they should follow through by searching these descriptors with the proper search tags. By clicking the search boxes to the left of the terms, the interface automatically adds the terms with proper field tags to the search query. This can also be done manually, using the proper field tags—in this case, either "DE Descriptor," which retrieves only items from the thesaurus, or "SU Subjects –All," which will also include author-supplied subject keywords.

Notice, however, that at least under the EBSCOhost interface, "DE Descriptors" is not listed from the pull-down menu. In the search box, the system pasted in the subject term using the "DE" field tag with the term enclosed in quotation marks. You can use this syntax pattern to manually search the database, even if the interface doesn't explicitly offer you that option (figure 9.3).

Not only does the *MLA Thesaurus* contain subject terms, it also has names of characters. Names of fictional characters from stage and literature are designated with "(character)" after the name. So if you search "character" with the "term contains" button selected, you will see many examples of characters contained in the vocabulary. Examples include Falstaff, Sir John (character); Finn, Huckleberry (character); Baggins, Frodo (character); Rochester, Edward (character); March, Jo (character); and Prynne, Hester (character). There are also thesaurus entries for "figure" representations. Examples are Godiva, Lady (figure); Tom Thumb (figure); Rapunzel (figure); Lancelot (figure); Death (figure); Big Bad Wolf (figure); Atlas (figure); and Tamar (figure in Genesis). MLA does not tell us what the differences are between characters and figures.

MLA keeps names as subjects in a separate controlled-vocabulary listing. These are not names of characters, but names of authors and creators. In figure 9.3 above, you can access this feature via the "Names as Subjects" link within the EBSCOhost interface. When you enter this controlled-vocabulary section, you immediately notice that many entries to works beginning with "A" are themselves not authorized entries but instead point to the author of the work. When you click on an author's name, you see a brief entry that may contain birth and death dates, the national literature the author influenced, the language(s) the author used, and the literary period by century.

The "Names as Subjects" feature is very important and necessary for discovering and navigating records in the *MLAIB* database. Think of it as a parallel feature to the subject thesaurus. There are five subject-related

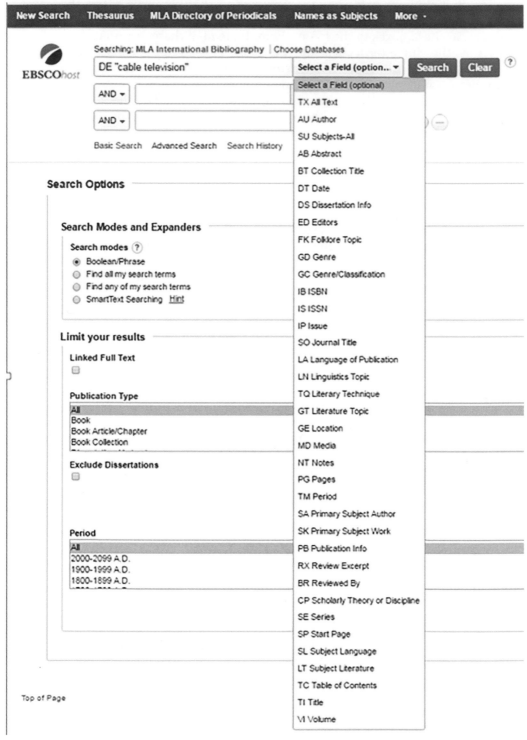

Figure 9.3. *MLAIB* under EBSCOhost Interface Offers More Than the Usual Number of Fields to Search. *Source:* ©2017 EBSCO Industries, Inc. All rights reserved.

fields, as illustrated in figure 9.4. These fields work together to identify and disambiguate records under the category "General Subject Areas." Having the "Names as Subjects" helps distinguish between "Morrison, Toni," name as subject (searched with the "SA Primary Subject Author" field (2,086 hits)) and Morrison, Toni, as author (searched with the "AU Author" field (25 hits). Once you have used the "Names as Subjects" feature, you can use the "SA Primary Subject Author" field on the search form to find the results.

Records in *MLAIB* have several subject fields grouped together under the "General Subject Areas." Those five fields, together with their field tags, are

LT Subject Literature

TM Period

SA Primary Subject Author

SK Primary Subject Work

GD Genre

These fields can all be searched at the same time with the "Subjects – All" field tag in the advanced search form, as can be seen in figure 9.3.

Injury, Pain, and Change in **War** And **Peace**: The Cases Of Nikolai Rostov and Prince Andrei Bolkonsky

Authors:	Rosenshield, Gary
Source:	Russian Review (RusR) 2015 Oct; 74 (4) 642-664 [Journal Detail]
Peer Reviewed:	Yes
ISSN:	0036-0341 1467-9434 (electronic)
General Subject Areas:	*Subject Literature*: Russian literature *Period*: 1800-1899 *Primary Subject Author*: Tolstoĭ, Lev Nikolaevich (1828-1910) *Primary Subject Work*: Voĭna i mir (1865-1869); War and Peace *Genre*: novel
Subject Terms:	treatment of pain; of Rostov, Nikolaĭ (character); Bolkonskiĭ, Andreĭ (character); relationship to revelation; truth
Document Information:	*Publication Type*: journal article *Language of Publication*: English *Update Code*: 201508 *Sequence Numbers*: 2015-1-49180
Electronic Access:	*DOI*: 10.1111/russ.12052
Abstract:	Physical pain plays an important but unusual role in the War and Peace. In the pre-twentieth century literary landmarks in which physical pain figures prominently, pain is closely linked to the idea of justice. In Dante, it is condign justice; in Aeschylus, Sophocles, and Dostoevsky, injustice that threatens the national or world order. In Tolstoy, by contrast, pain is much more closely associated with revelation, transformation, and truth. We can see this plainly in the changes that take place, through pain, in the lives of two of the male protagonists, Nikolai Rostov and Andrei Bolkonsky. Pain of course also plays a significant role in The Death of Ivan Ilyich, but I have chosen to focus, at least here, on War and Peace, because War and Peace presents the relation between pain, revelation, and truth in greater detail, over a much longer period of time, and in radically dissimilar characters. What at first Nikolai and Andrei seem to have in common is that their physical pain stems directly from their battle injuries. Nikolai is injured at Schöngrabern in 1805; and Andrei at Austerlitz in 1805 and again at Borodino in 1812. But there are also surprising similarities regarding the effects of pain in their lives, similarities that need to be examined-as well, of course, as dramatic differences-if we are to achieve a better understanding of Tolstoy's use of physical pain as a transformative catalyst. By analyzing Nikolai's and especially Andrei's traumatic injuries and both their short and long-term effects, I hope to show how Tolstoy employs the shock of excruciating physical pain as a means of leading two of his male protagonists toward spiritual transformation and the revelation of truth.
Accession Number:	2015832664

Figure 9.4. Careful Control of Subjects under the *MLAIB*. *Source:* ©2017 EBSCO Industries, Inc. All rights reserved.

In figure 9.4, you can see the fields groups together as "General Subject Areas" displayed.

Think about the information organization factors that make these kinds of distinctions necessary. It wouldn't be feasible to encode subject literature (in this case Russian literature), the time period (19th century), the author of the work, the subject of the work, and the genre all in a single thesaurus. Of these five fields, two of them are encoded in the *MLA Thesaurus*: "Subject Literature" and "Genre." "Primary Subject Author" is in the "Subject Names" index. In this case, the entry for Tolstoi is "Tolstoĭ, Lev Nikolaevich (1828–1910)." The popular way Americans refer to him is Leo Tolstoy, but the name's entry states, "This entry is used for Tolstoy, Leo."

Browsing Indexes

We have examined two controlled-vocabulary systems (the subject thesaurus and the names as subjects thesaurus) employed by *MLAIB*. These are produced by the MLA and incorporated into each of the three vendor interfaces. In the EBSCOhost interface, under the "More" button, you will notice the "Indexes" link. This is another example of vendor-supplied back-generated indexes, as mentioned in chapter 3. These index features have nothing to do with the MLA but are features of the EBSCOhost interface and are specific to individual databases. The browsable and searchable indexes for the *MLAIB* database under EBSCOhost are shown in table 9.4.

You can see several of the above indexes at work in the record in figure 9.5.

Table 9.4. Browsable and Searchable Indexes for EBSCOhost's *MLAIB*.

Index Type	Notes
Accession Number	Control number from database. Sorry, I don't see the usefulness of this index.
Author	Useful in bringing together items by a single author.
Book Source	Titles of books and conference proceedings.
Dissertation Source	Colleges and universities issuing dissertations.
Editors	Editors.
Folklore Topic	Topics include baby bottle nipple, cacao growing, Easter eggs, game boards, ice cream, Japanese Americans, magic spell, and paper cutting.
ISBN	International Standard Book Numbers.
ISSN	International Standard Serial Numbers.
Journal Title	An easy way to see all items from a single journal.
Language	Retrieve articles in over 100 foreign languages.
Linguistics Topic	Broad topics like philology and syntax, and narrow topics like temporal adverb, affricate consonants, and military slang.

Index Type	Notes
Literary Influence	Influence *on* an author, rather than influence *of* an author. Influence by personal name, genre, and literary movement.
Literary Source	References to history, culture, and titles.
Literary Technique	Examples: abolitionist movement, fable, failure, naming, paganism, and tall tale.
Literature Topic	Differs from subject of article; these are topics of the literature under discussion.
Location	Locations within articles or literature. Includes countries, places, and geographic features.
Primary Subject Author	Preferred form of a name. For example, for the author W.E.B. DuBois, the authorized form of the name in this database is: Primary Subject Author: Du Bois, W. E. B. (1868–1963).
Primary Subject Work	Example: Primary Subject Work: The Color Purple (1982).
Publication Type	Only eight possibilities exist for this field: book, book article, book collection, dissertation abstract, edition, journal article, translation, and Web site.
Publication Year	Year in the form of four integers; no date ranges.
Publisher	Publisher. Publisher names are not normalized or controlled.
Scholarly Theory or Discipline	Includes terms like act theory, game analysis, the Holocaust, modernity, sector analysis, and Yuan dynasty period.
Series	Series titles grouped together.
Subject Language	Language under discussion in work, not language of work being indexed.
Subject Literature	Subject of literature under discussion.
Subjects – All	Combined subject indexes.

The record in figure 9.5 shows fields coming from several controlled vocabularies. Each of these vocabularies work together as control mechanisms to ensure that users can locate materials with greater precision.

By now you can see two things going on. The true controlled vocabulary coming from MLA in the subject thesaurus and names listing is a more principled kind of control. The vendor, in an attempt to add to the control mechanisms, has added a series of back-generated indexes through the smoke and mirrors magic of computers, but these indexes are not curated and contain errors and anomalies.

You can see this as you browse the series index for *MLAIB*. In the EBSCO-host interface, select the "More" button to see the "Indexes" link (figure 9.6).

Poetics in Motion: Appropriating C. K. Williams's Poetics in Film-The Case of Tar

Authors:	Zauderer, Elizabeth Faye
Source:	Interdisciplinary Literary Studies: A Journal of Criticism and Theory (ILS) 2017; 19 (1): 102-124. [Journal Detail]
Notes:	English summary.
Peer Reviewed:	Yes
ISSN:	1524-8429
General Subject Areas:	*Subject Literature:* American literature *Period:* 1900-1999 *Primary Subject Author:* Williams, C. K. (1936-2015) *Primary Subject Work:* Tar (1983) *Genre:* poetry
Subject Terms:	treatment in The Color of Time (2012)
General Subject Areas:	*Genre:* film genres *Literature Topic:* dramatic arts *Media:* film
Subject Terms:	biographical film; The Color of Time (2012)
Document Information:	*Publication Type:* journal article *Language of Publication:* English *Update Code:* 201702 *Sequence Numbers:* 2017-1-6058; 2017-8-1317
Electronic Access:	https://muse-jhu-edu.du.idm.oclc.org/article/650304
Accession Number:	2017392152

Figure 9.5. *MLAIB*: Many Control Mechanisms at Work. *Source:* ©2017 EBSCO Industries, Inc. All rights reserved.

Notice that in figure 9.6 you are browsing the "Series" index. There is clear evidence that these series titles have been back generated by computers from existing records. The series entry "abhandlungen der akademie der wissenschaften in gottingen. philologisch-historische klasse" has 2 records, but "abhandlungen der akademie der wissenschaften in gottingen: philologisch-historische klasse" has 137 entries. Obviously, these are the same series, the only difference being the punctuation (a period versus a colon) in the middle of the series titles. Even though these entries have not been normalized, they are nevertheless helpful in trying to locate complete runs of obscure series.

Similar evidence of back generation and lack of authority control appears in the author index. Given the uniqueness of the name, it's quite possible that each of the entries in table 9.5 refers to the same person.

Also, under the "More" button in the EBSCOhost interface, you will notice the "Cited References" feature. This feature will appear if you are searching a single EBSCOhost database, but multiple databases. Cited references are discussed more in chapter 10's "Web of Science" section.

MLA Directory of Periodicals

Unlike other databases, the MLA produces a separate *MLA Directory of Periodicals* that accompanies the *MLAIB*. The directory not only includes a list of journals indexed, but it also provides requirements for the publication in the various journals, subscription information, and editorial details. Depending on the vendor, the directory may be integrated with the *MLAIB* interface or featured as a separate database.

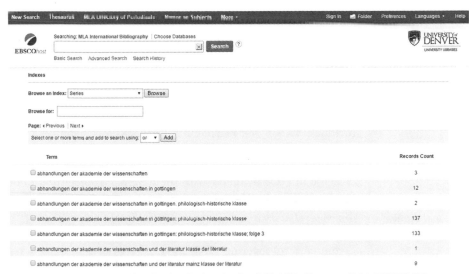

Figure 9.6. Browsing the Series Index in the *MLAIB*. *Source:* ©2017 EBSCO Industries, Inc. All rights reserved.

Table 9.5. Variations of Author Names in the EBSCO Author Index in *MLAIB*.

Names from Author Index	Record Count
shakh-azizova, t.	1
shakh-azizova, t. k.	1
shakh-azizova, tat'iana	1
shakh-azizova, tat'iana k.	1
shakh-azizova, tatiana	2

History Databases—*America: History and Life* and *Historical Abstracts*

We now transition from literature to the realm of history. For many years, ABC-CLIO published the two central databases for history: *Historical Abstracts* and *America: History and Life*. We will abbreviate these as *HA* and *AHL*, respectively, in this section for ease of reference. Both titles existed as print indexes for many years. In 2007, both products were acquired by EBSCO, which is the sole provider of both databases today.

Notice that the title is not *United States: History and Life* but *America: History and Life*. This is because Canada is also fully covered in the scope of the product. The rest of the world is covered in the *Historical Abstracts* database. After these two products were acquired by EBSCO, EBSCO added full-text options to each database. Your library may subscribe to *Historical Abstracts* or to *Historical Abstracts with Full Text*. The same holds true for *AHL*. Many of the full-text titles are not available through any of the other EBSCOhost databases, such as *Academic Search*.

Table 9.6 shows the database background for *America: History and Life*.

Table 9.6. Spec Sheet for the *America: History and Life* Database.

Database Name	*America: History and Life.*
Creator	ABC-CLIO.
Vendor/Interface	Available from EBSCO via EBSCOhost platform.
Scope	United States and Canada history; selective indexing of 1,700 journals.
	Includes indexing for journal articles, books, book chapters, book reviews, and dissertations. Covers publications 1955 to present.
	Selected full text available with the *America: History and Life with Full Text* subscription.
Physical Analog	*America: History and Life.*
	Published 1964–present, with retrospective v.0 (that's right, volume zero) covering 1955–1964.
Searchable Fields	TX All Text
	AU Author
	TI Title
	SU Subject Terms
	AB Abstract
	KW Author-Supplied Keywords
	GE Geographic Terms
	PE People
	PS Reviews & Products
	CO Company Entity
	SO Publication Name
	IS ISSN (no dashes)
	IB ISBN
	AN Accession Number
Limiters	Document Type
	Image Types
	Historical Era
	Publication Type
	Language

Table 9.7 shows the background information for the *Historical Abstracts* database.

Distinctive Features of *AHL* and *HA*

The interface to *AHL* and *HA* should be very familiar to you by now. It is the EBSCOhost interface. But there are some significant differences from other EBSCOhost databases.

1. CLIO Notes. The link to CLIO Notes appears at the top left of both *AHL* and *HA*. This feature presents historical periods in outline form and broken down by significant events, social movements, and people. Each subheading links to a concise description of the topic and provides research

Table 0.7. Spec Sheet for *Historical Abstracts* Database.

Database Name	*Historical Abstracts.*
Creator	ABC-CLIO.
Vendor/Interface	Available from EBSCO via EBSCOhost platform.
Scope	World history, excluding United States and Canada, from 1450 to present; selective indexing of over 2,300 journals.
	Includes indexing for journal articles, books, book chapters, book reviews, and dissertations; covers publications 1955 to present.
	Selected full text available with the *Historical Abstracts with Full Text* subscription.
Physical Analog	*Historical Abstracts.*
	Published 1955–present.
	In 1975, it was split into Historical Abstracts. Part A, Modern History Abstracts, 1775–1914, and Historical Abstracts. Part B, Twentieth Century Abstracts, 1914–.
Searchable Fields	TX All Text
	AU Author
	TI Title
	SU Subject Terms
	AB Abstract
	KW Author-Supplied Keywords
	GE Geographic Terms
	PE People
	PS Reviews & Products
	CO Company Entity
	SO Publication Name
	IS ISSN (no dashes)
	IB ISBN
	AN Accession Number
Limiters	Document Type
	Image Types
	Historical Era
	Publication Type
	Language

questions for further study. CLIO Notes provides excellent background information for high school and undergraduate college students. As an example, here is the outline of "[1960–1969] The Sixties" from *AHL*:

Chronology of Events

Civil Rights

Chronology of Events

Civil Rights and Other Movements

Key Civil Rights Organizations

Protest Tactics

Rulings and Legislation

Counterculture

Chronology of Events

Countering the Establishment

Counterculture Activism and Events

Alternative Lifestyles

Presidents Kennedy and Johnson

Chronology of Events

JFK's Domestic Visions

JFK's New Frontier Abroad

LBJ's Great Society

LBJ's Foreign Policy

The Vietnam War

Chronology of Events

The Origins of US Involvement

Americanization and "Johnson's War"

Opposition to the War

Nixon and the Vietnamization of the War

Social and Political Movements

Chronology of Events

The New Left

Neoconservative Movements

Feminist and Minority Movements

The Antiwar Movement

The Environmental Movement

Bibliography

2. Limit to Time Periods. The advanced search pages have some different limit options that are extremely important. Time periods are especially important to historians. We are not talking here about publication dates (the date an article or book was published), but the historical era under discussion. You will notice two kinds of date limits on the advanced search interface: the usual publication date limiter and the "historical period" limit, with the ability to specify a range of years. The interesting thing about this feature is that you don't need to know ahead of time how the years have been "sliced and diced" within the database. As an example of this, let's search *AHL* like this:

(all text boxes blank)
Under Limit Your Results → Historical Period → Year 1864 [Select Era: c.e. (AD)] to Year 1864 [Select Era: c.e. (AD)]

This form entry is illustrated in figure 9.7.

Now hit the "Search button." I get over 202,000 results. Here are some of the historical period breakdowns that this search retrieved:

Historical Period: ca 1750 to ca 2017

Historical Period: 1864

Historical Period: 1861 to 1865; 1865 to ca 1877

Historical Period: 1801 to 2017

Historical Period: ca 500 BCE to ca 2017

Historical Period: 1775 to 2017

Every one of these historical periods contains the year 1864. What a powerful feature for anyone doing historical research! Of course, you can include a much broader range of years as well.

3. Subject Terms. Although there is no formal thesaurus available, as there is in *ERIC*, *PsycINFO*, or *Sociological Abstracts*, there is a series of compiled indexes, with subjects being one of the indexes. To get to this rather hidden feature within the EBSCOhost interface, click the "More" button at the top of the page, select "Indexes," and then select "Subject Terms." Browsing the subject terms index by the term *telegraph* reveals that this database uses a subject headings approach, as evidenced by the

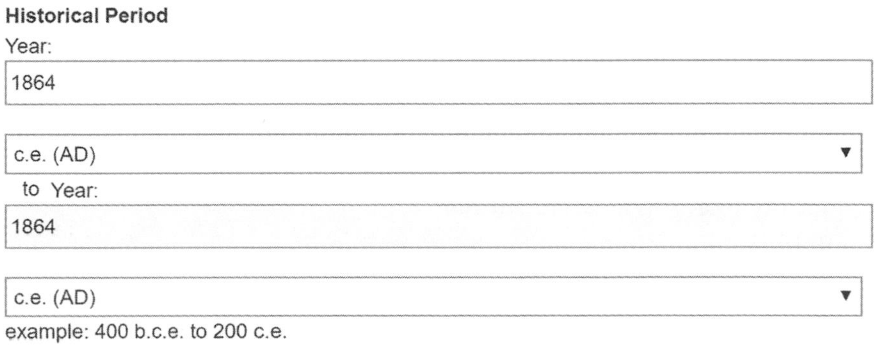

Historical Period

Year:

1864

c.e. (AD)	▼

to Year:

1864

c.e. (AD)	▼

example: 400 b.c.e. to 200 c.e.

Figure 9.7. Searching Historical Periods in *America: History and Life*.
Source: ©2017 EBSCO Industries, Inc. All rights reserved.

use of hyphens to distinguish multiple semantic notions within the same subject term:

telegraph & telegraphy	259
telegraph & telegraphy -- law & legislation	2
telegraph & telegraphy -- printing system	1
telegraph & telegraphy -- social aspects	3
telegraph & telegraphy -- united states	5
telegraph & telegraphy -- united states -- history	12
telegraph & telegraphy employees	4
telegraph & texas register (periodical)	1
telegraph cables	3
telegraph cables -- history -- 19th century	1
telegraph chess -- history -- 19th century	1

4. Images. As with other EBSCOhost databases, images within articles can be searched. This can be important when doing historical research. Although this feature is found within the EBSCO interface to *AHL* and *HA*, you are actually searching the EBSCO "Image Quick View Collection." Go to the "More" tab at the top of the search page and select "Images." You will now see a form where you can enter terms and limit them to black-and-white photograph, color photograph, graph, map, chart, diagram, or illustration.

Let's type "Gettysburg" into the search box. As you begin to type, the smart index suggests entries that already exist in the database. Let's just use "Gettysburg" by itself and select the "map" option from the limits section of the form. Results include a map of the National Cemetery of Gettysburg, a map of the Gettysburg Campaign, and other interesting results. This feature alone takes the traditional print versions of these indexes to an entirely new level.

Search Example 1: Finding Book Reviews

Not every database indexes book reviews, but these history databases do. Suppose you want to find a review for a book authored by David McCullough about the Wright Brothers. You might think that we would search *America: History and Life* like this:

McCullough, David → AU Author
AND
Wright Brothers → TI Title

In a way, this search works, but it succeeds in retrieving the book itself, not reviews of the book. In this database, to retrieve book reviews, you must place the author of the book in the "PE People" field and the book title in the "PS Reviews & Products" field. A bit unintuitive, isn't it? This search will bring up the book reviews you are expecting:

McCullough, David → PE People
AND
Wright Brothers → PS Reviews & Products

It is informative to look at selected fields from a full record for one of these results:

Title: The Wright Brothers.
Authors: Giffard, Hermione
Source: History Today. Dec2015, Vol. 65 Issue 12, p64–65. 2p.
Document Type: Book Review
Reviews & Products: Wright Brothers, The (Book)
People: McCullough, David G., 1933–
Wright, Orville, 1871–1948
Wright, Wilbur, 1867-1912

Notice that the author (McCullough) is in the same field grouping as the two Wright brothers (the "People" field).

You could also have searched for "Wright brothers" as a default keyword search and then, from the "Advanced Search" screen, limit by "Document Type: Book Review." Indeed, there are several paths to accomplishing this task, but the advanced searcher needs to be aware of how fields are used in the case of book reviews. This is the way these two history databases work and is not transferrable to other database products.

Search Example 2: Finding Material about a Topic in a Particular Period

Let's do our second search example in the sister product, *Historical Abstracts*. Suppose you want to know about the situation in Croatia during the Second World War. You could frame an initial search like this:

Croatia → Select a Field (in other words, just a general keyword
    search initially)
AND
Second World War → Select a Field (again, a general keyword
    search, as we have no idea what the subject terms look like in
    this database)
LIMIT TO (from the Basic or Advanced Search screen)
Historical Period
Year: 1939
Era: c.e. (AD)
To Year: 1945

Now, take a look at several of these results and note the patterns. It appears that *Historical Abstracts* does not use *Second World War* as a subject. Rather, it uses *World War II*. *World War II* shows up in the subject terms field both as a subject descriptor (a single semantic notion) and as a subject heading (one or more semantic notions, as evidenced by the terms that have dashes within them, such as *World War II – Propaganda*).

Also note the presence of the "Geographic Terms" field in some of the records. Many of these records contain *Croatia*. Now we can reframe our search for greater precision.

Croatia → GE Geographic Terms
World War II → SU Subject Terms
LIMIT TO (from the Basic or Advanced Search screen)
Historical Period
Year: 1939
Era: c.e. (AD)
To Year: 1945

With these search parameters, you get 234 results. You can now limit your results to peer-reviewed (175 results) or to additional subjects as necessary.

Search Example 3: Searching Cited References

Following cited references is usually, and rightly, associated with *Web of Science*, the name of the database that contains *Science Citation Index*, *Social Sciences Citation Index*, and *Arts and Humanities Citation Index*. Even though these indexes, originally produced by the Institute for Scientific Information (ISI) and now owned by Clarivate Analytics, are what most scholars look to for scholarly citations, there are many other databases that track citations. *AHL* and *HA* are among those databases.

For historians, book publishing is especially important as well as citations to scholarly books. Let's search for citations to Dee Brown's book *Bury My Heart at Wounded Knee*. To do this, you need to go to the "Cited References" link at the top of the *AHL* search interface (figure 9.8).

After clicking "Search" you get 44 citing articles. But only a subset of these have check boxes to the left. These are the articles for which records are available in *AHL*. By selecting each of these check boxes and then hitting "Find Citing Articles," you are able to retrieve the records for articles that cite Brown's book (figure 9.9).

This cited reference search can be used in conjunction with results from *Web of Science* and Google Scholar, both of which have much broader scopes.

Historical Newspaper Databases

Newspaper databases are covered in this edition because of the tremendous growth in the digitized content of papers from before 1923. We will

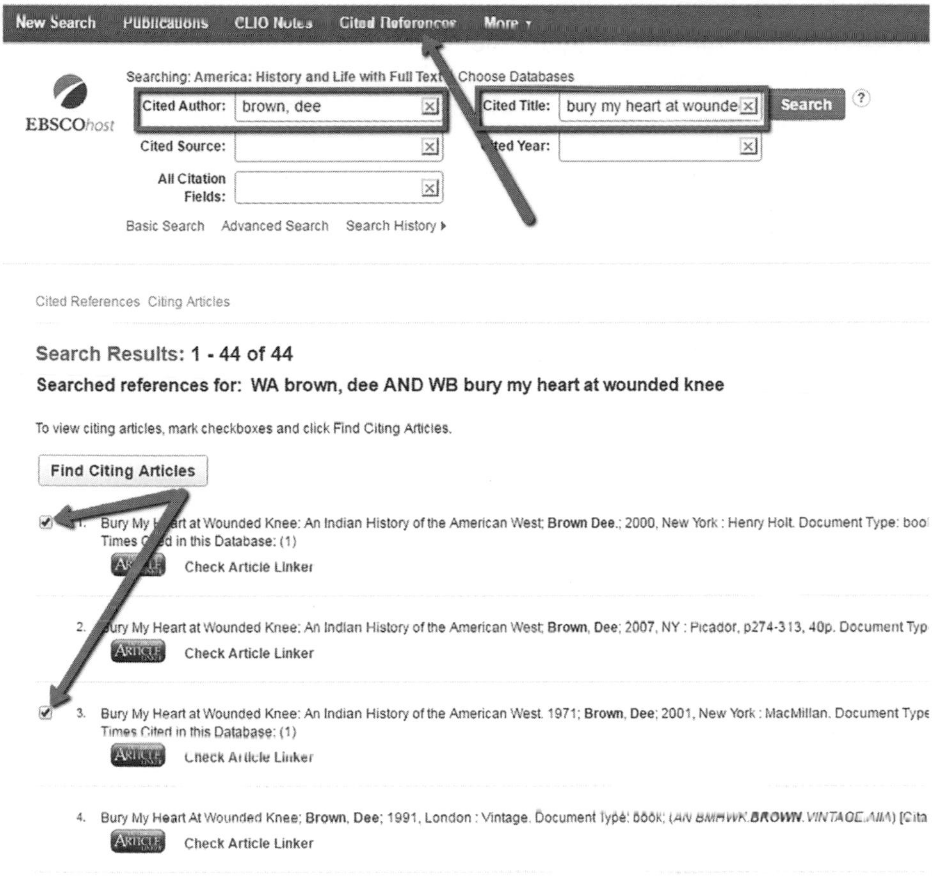

Figure 9.8. Cited References Searching in *America: History and Life. Source:* ©2017 EBSCO Industries, Inc. All rights reserved.

endeavor to survey selected offerings of papers from a variety of vendors. This section specifically focuses on historical newspaper content as opposed to current newspapers because there is such a difference in these two content types. Historical papers are nearly always scans of entire pages, including advertisements and page layout. Current newspaper content is very often text only and out of context. Researchers accessing current news are primarily interested in the news text itself. However, historical humanities research views the news in its historical and cultural contexts, and placement on the page can be an important aspect of understanding and interpretation.

One of the characteristics of most newspaper databases is that the default search is full text rather than metadata only. For magazine and journal article searching, there is generally sufficient metadata to enable searching by default of just the metadata, thus restricting the recall to more relevant material. But newspaper content is so prolific that it would be a nearly impossible task to create metadata for each article in the same way it is done for journal content. Thus, the searching generally defaults to full-text searching. For this reason, special care should be taken to learn and use proximity operators to enhance relevance of the recall.

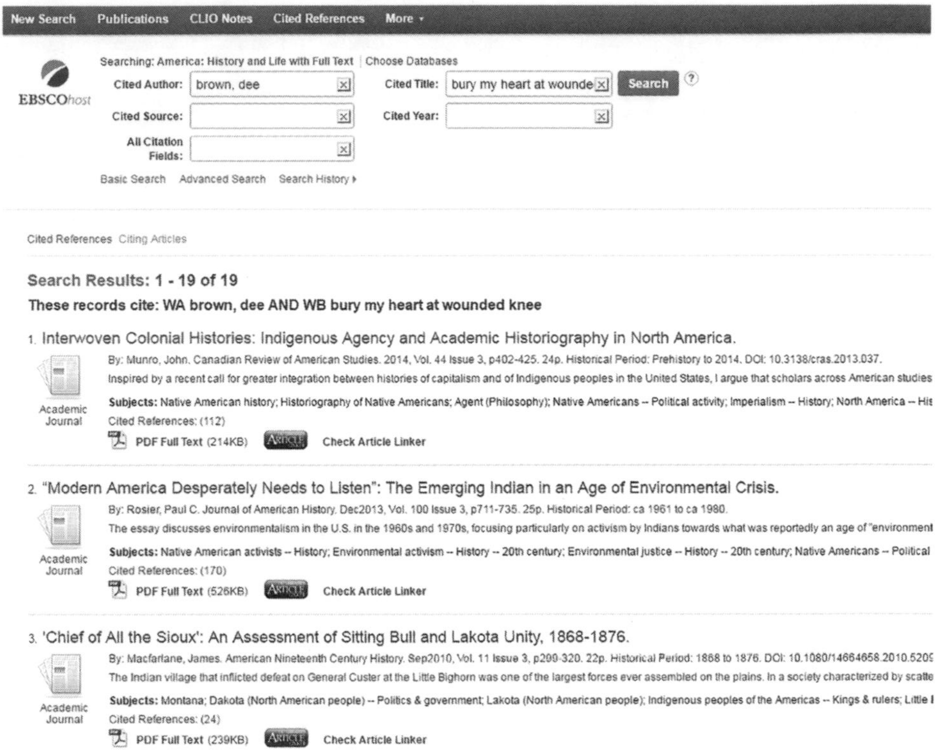

Figure 9.9. *America: History and Life:* "These Records Cite" Clearly Marked.
Source: ©2017 EBSCO Industries, Inc. All rights reserved.

Searching Newspaper Content

Searching newspaper databases is challenging for several reasons:

- Newspaper titles, unlike titles for scholarly articles, are usually not very descriptive of the underlying content.

- Metadata for newspaper articles is usually very scant. Subject terms may be minimal, and the title and lead paragraphs may be the only metadata. Thus full-text searching will need to be done.

- You many need to use proximity operators rather than Boolean operators to search effectively.

- The optical character recognition (OCR) for some newspaper content may not have been checked by a human and can contain errors that render the text unfindable.

It is essential to consider the time period you are researching when searching. Don't fall into the trap of using current terminology in your full-text searches. It is a good idea to browse several issues of the newspaper in the same year to get a feel for the times before you start searching.

If searching for the despicable experiences African Americans endured under slavery in the 1800s, as documented in contemporary newspapers, a search like "slavery AND narrative*" would not work. Searching in Readex's *America's Historical Newspapers* entails doing a full-text search of the newspaper content of the day in the language of the day. The only available metadata will be the headline, the article type, the title of the newspaper source, and the date and page numbers. There will be no subject analysis and no abstract in these cases. Suggestions for finding slave experiences when you can't search with today's nomenclature include the following strategies:

- Browse several of the newspaper titles from the time period and location you are interested in. Get a feel for how articles were written, the topics covered, and word selection used.

- Isolate some newspaper titles that tend to have the materials you want, and limit searching to within these titles.

- If you are searching for material around the time of an event, be sure that you have the event dates and then search around that time period.

- Search very broadly and generally. For the search illustrated above, you may just want to search "slave*" at first, then only add terms to the search when you feel comfortable with what the search will uncover.

Search Example 1: Japanese Americans during World War II

We want to find newspaper accounts of attitudes among the general public toward Japanese Americans during World War II. As we are searching the full text of newspapers, proximity operators would likely serve us better than Boolean operators. I went to the Readex "Help" button to learn about their proximity search syntax. I initially searched with NEAR10 and NEAR20, but I ended up using NEAR30 because it seemed to tease out better results. Here is the search syntax I used:

Japanese NEAR30 discriminat* (with a date limit of 1941–1945)

Notice that I didn't search Japanese Americans, as that terminology was not used in those years. See figure 9.10.

Paying attention to the search results informs us of other ways we could search. The phrase *Japanese extraction* is one that could be used next time.

Google offers a tool that, while not very authoritative, can nevertheless assist in word selection when searching full-text newspaper and e-book databases. The Google Books Ngram Viewer (https://books.google.com/ngrams) searches the words of books digitized through the Google Books project and can graphically show when terminology was in use over the decades. For example, figure 9.11 shows the Google Ngram for the terms *American Indians* and *Native Americans*.

Now it's time for a few newspaper search examples.

Search Example 2: Sand Creek Massacre

Let's search for newspaper accounts of the infamous Sand Creek Massacre. We need some hooks to assist us in our search. By simply searching Google

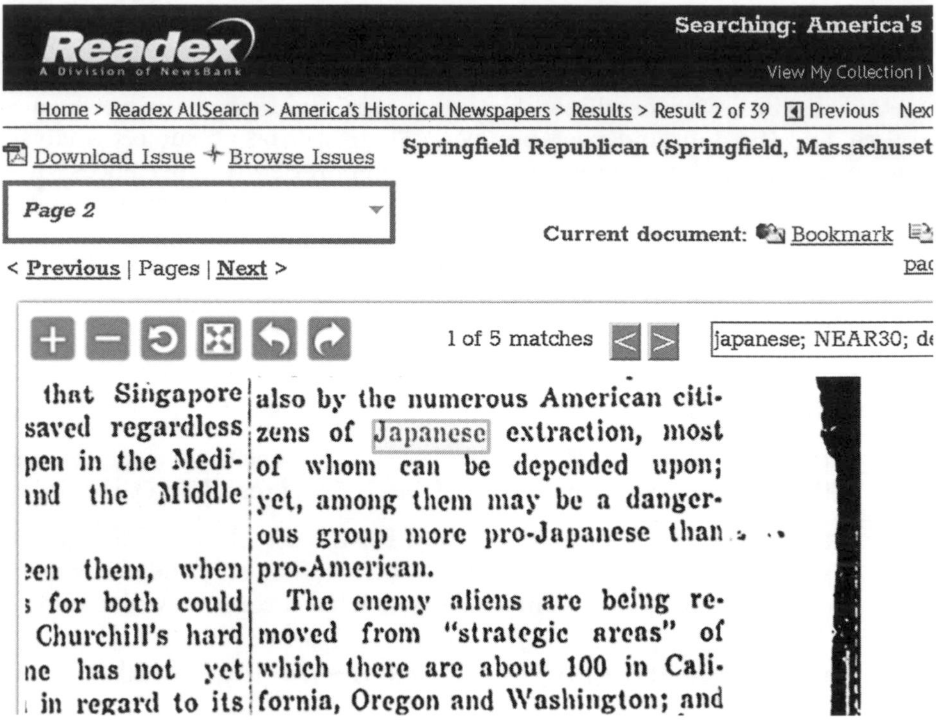

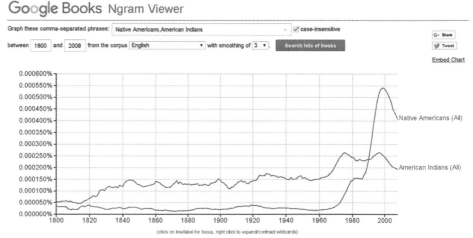

Figure 9.10. Search Result from Readex's *America's Historical Newspapers.*
Source: ©Readex, a Division of NewsBank, Inc. Used with permission.

Figure 9.11. Google Books Ngram Viewer Example Graph. *Source:* Google and the
Google logo are registered trademarks of Google Inc. Used with permission.

(yes, it's okay to search Google as long as your information comes from a rep-
utable source or the information can be cross-referenced with other resources
as a confirmation), we need a date hook: when did the Sand Creek Massacre
occur? We quickly discover that it was November 29, 1864; that it took place in
Colorado; and that U.S. Army colonel John Chivington led the attack.

Now that we have some hooks, we need to consider search terminology. Keep in mind that the term *massacre* was not used immediately after the event. We can do a Google Books search for "Sand Creek Massacre" and then use the "Tools" button and limit to the 19th Century. We then discover an 1867 Senate document titled "Sand Creek Massacre." Still, let's stay away from searching the term *massacre* when looking for accounts immediately after the event.

The first task is to find databases that contain newspapers that existed around the date in question. In this case, appropriate databases include *America's Historical Newspapers* (Readex), *Gale Newsvault*, and *ProQuest Historical Newspapers*. In *America's Historical Newspapers*, I searched

> chivington AND "sand creek" with limit of 11/29/1864 to 12/31/1865 (26 results)

In *Gale Newsvault*, I searched

> chivington AND "sand creek" with dates between 11/29/1864 to 12/31/1865 (49 results)

And in *ProQuest Historical Newspapers*, I searched

> chivington AND "sand creek" with dates between 11/29/1864 to 12/31/1865 (12 results)

Search Example 3: Psychiatric Hospitals in 18th-Century England

To find 18th-century psychiatric hospitals in England, I poked around in Google Books a bit and discovered that the term *lunatic asylum* was likely used in England at that time. Then I accessed a database that covered that historical period. But I was able to do so using two different interfaces from the same vendor.

In *17th–18th Century Burney Collection Newspapers* (Gale, via traditional Gale interface), I searched

> lunatic asylum* in Entire document (with no date limits, as it is already restricted to the 17th and 18th centuries]; limit to news (21 results)

And in *17th–18th Century Burney Collection Newspapers* (Gale, via Artemis Primary Sources interface), I searched

> lunatic asylum* AND England in Entire document with limit to News section in the Burney Collection (34 results)

What's going on here? To be honest, I don't know. We are searching the same database through different interfaces and getting different results. Of course, we could list all 34 results from the Artemis interface and compare

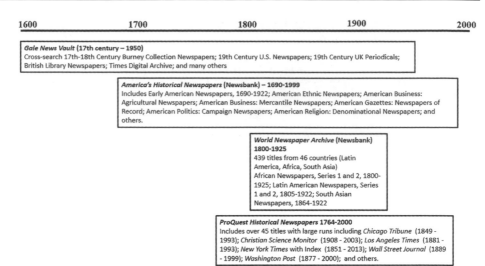

Figure 9.12. Historical Newspapers in Timeline View.

them with the 21 results from the traditional interface if we really cared to come up with a theory. But simply accepting and acknowledging that different engines operate on the same data in differing ways and can produce different results is just as important. This is a valuable lesson for you to keep in mind.

Vendor Database Coverage Dates

The date coverage of vendor-supplied content for online newspapers can be quite confusing. There is a lot of coverage for older newspapers that are in the public domain (that is, before 1923). Because of the complexities of purchasing publishing rights, there is much less coverage for papers after 1922, but selected coverage does exist and is ever increasing. In an attempt to navigate coverage dates for historical newspapers, figure 9.12 provides general dates of coverage. Keep in mind that this is subject to change, as vendors continually add content to enhance their database packages.

Free Newspaper Databases

It should be noted that there are many freely available newspaper databases, especially for papers before 1923. Among the larger freely available newspaper databases are the following:

- *Chronicling America*, Library of Congress: http://chroniclingamerica
  .loc.gov

  Chronicling America includes over 2,300 newspapers from most of the 50 states, the District of Columbia, and Puerto Rico. Some titles have only a few issues, but others have extensive coverage. This is a useful resource for local history and for augmenting the commercial newspaper databases.

- *Elephind.com:* https://elephind.com

  Elephind.com is a metadata harvesting project with links to historic digital newspaper sites hosting the digitized versions. They have harvested content from English-language newspapers from the United States and Australia.

- *Colorado Historic Newspaper Collection:* https://www.coloradohis toricnewspapers.org

- *California Digital Newspaper Collection:* https://cdnc.ucr.edu /cgi-bin/cdnc

- *Illinois Digital Newspaper Collection:* https://digital.library.illinois .edu/collections

- *Texas Digital Newspaper Program:* https://texashistory.unt.edu /explore/collections/TDNP

- *Hoosier State Chronicles: Indiana's Digital Historic Newspaper Program:* https://newspapers.library.in.gov

- *Trove* (Australian newspapers): http://trove.nla.gov.au

As they do not collect revenue, free newspapers databases typically do not have the resources to correct the optical character recognition (OCR) that is done to index the full text. As a result, there may be full-text errors.

Here is an example of such an error from the *Colorado Historic Newspaper Collection*. The *Aspen Daily Times*, July 23, 1896, has this sentence buried on the front page: "He spent some time in conference with Secretary Carlisle this morning." But the OCR rendering came out like this: "Ho spout somo tlmo In oonforence with Boorotary Carlisle this morning." In fact, the headline of this article reads as follows: "IS A ROBUST INFANT. The Populist National Party has Wonderfully Grown. ON THE VERGE OF A CRISIS HOWEVER." But the OCR for the last part of the headline comes out as "ON TflBMGB OF A CRISIS HOWEVER." This typo of thing frequently happens when working with old newspapers because the print is often light or blotchy due to the printing practices of the time. Although these tools generally allow full-text searching, users must be especially persistent and not give up on the first attempt.

E-Books and the Humanities

The importance of digital humanities in recent years has opened up new areas of research. Word frequencies, spelling variations, and n-gram studies are now possible with the large corpus of textual materials. Let's take a look at some of these digital advances and their impacts.

From Microform to E-Books

E-books are available for newly published books, but many older books are also being scanned and made available through package subscriptions.

This is nothing new. Bibliographers such as Pollard and Redgrave, followed by Wing, carefully documented early English-language books. Then came the microform publishers that located the books from these bibliographies and produced microform versions of the entire texts. Research libraries purchased these major sets to accompany the print finding aids.

The database that is now *Early English Books Online* (Chadwyck-Healey (ProQuest)) is based on these works by Pollard and Redgrave and Wing:

> Pollard, Alfred W., and G. R. Redgrave. 1976–1991. *A Short-Title Catalogue of Books Printed in England, Scotland, & Ireland and of English Books Printed Abroad, 1475–1640.* 2nd ed. rev. & enl. London: Bibliographical Society.

> Wing, Donald Goddard. 1945–1951. *Short-Title Catalogue of Books Printed in England, Scotland, Ireland, Wales, and British America and of English Books Printed in Other Countries, 1641–1700.* New York: Index Society.

Many libraries have purchased the microform series *Early English Books*, published by University Microfilms International (later purchased by ProQuest) and then purchased them all over again in database format through ProQuest.

Before the database *Early American Imprints*, Series I and Series II, from Readex, the same vendor published and sold micro-opaque cards to libraries with full text of the entries from Charles Evans's bibliography and subsequent works. The microform set called *Early American Imprints*, Series I, and *Early American Imprints*, Series II, is based on these works:

> Bristol, Roger P. 1966. *Supplement to Charles Evans' American Bibliography.* Charlottesville, VA: Alderman Library.

> Evans, Charles. 1903–1959. *American Bibliography: A Chronological Dictionary of All Books, Pamphlets, and Periodical Publications Printed in the United States of America from the Genesis of Printing in 1639 Down To and including the Year 1820.* 14 vols. New York: P. Smith.

> Shaw, Ralph R., and Richard H. Shoemaker. 1958–1966. *American Bibliography, a Preliminary Checklist for 1801–1819.* 22 vols. New York: Scarecrow Press.

> Walters, Willard O., and Charles Evans. 1933. *American Imprints, 1648–1797.* Cambridge, MA: Harvard University Press.

As it can be challenging to keep many of these historic e-books initiatives straight, figure 9.13 is an attempt to sort it out.

Note Gale's *ECCO* and ProQuest's *EEBO* can be cross-searched together. In a rather refreshing bit of vendor cooperation, ProQuest has supplied Gale all the metadata for the *EEBO* books. Thus, scholars are now able to search across records from 1473 through 1800 with the Gale interface, if the library chooses to make these options available.

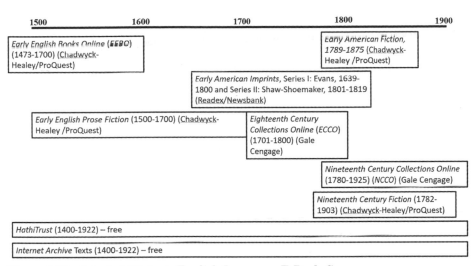

Figure 9.13. Selected Historic English-Language E-Book Coverage.

Searching e-books is similar to searching newspapers. There is more metadata available for e-books in the form of catalog records, but the metadata to full-text ratio—something I call the "information access anomaly"—means that metadata searching is just searching the general "aboutness" of the book and not very deeply inside. Instead, deep searching of the full text is going to be necessary for full discovery.

Handwritten Text Recognition

One of the more exciting developments in humanities research has been text recognition for cursive handwriting. Adam Matthew has developed software that can be trained to recognize handwriting, and it has been applied to all modules of the *Colonial America* database. If you have ever tried to read the handwriting of others, you know what a challenge this can be. Now imagine trying to read the handwriting of people several centuries before us. Without the ability to search across this text, you are merely seeing a digital version of microform without the ability to use the full-text search capabilities you have become so accustomed to doing. It's likely that we will see more of this technology in the future, which will open up manuscripts and enhance research.

Archival Primary Source Databases

As far as primary source databases, we are not discussing primary sources in the sciences but in the social sciences and humanities. A primary source in chemistry might be an original experiment documented in the academic literature. But outside of science, primary sources refer to original manuscripts, handwritten letters and memos, collected papers of individuals, images, objects, documents from government agencies, and speeches—the raw materials of history. They can be anything under study.

Contemporary newspapers (e.g., today's *Denver Post*) would generally not be considered a primary source. But if one were researching the history of early Colorado in the 1870s, then those early Colorado newspapers would be evidence of history and considered as primary sources. But unlike the sciences, where original experiments might be published in peer-reviewed journals, materials published in scholarly academic journals would generally not be primary sources (unless, of course, they were the object of a study).

Although this section has been placed in the humanities chapter, it could well have been covered in social sciences, as many primary sources are of importance for those fields as well. But given that this edition includes a separate chapter for government publications, which is largely social sciences, primary sources will be covered here.

The past several years have seen vendors tripping over themselves to sell access to unique archival holdings, early printed books that have been digitized, and early runs of newspapers. In some cases, book and newspaper content that had been available for years in microform collections are now available digitally.

Unlike books, archival sources are unique, as they are held by only one library. True, there may be different versions of primary sources, such as the five extant versions of Lincoln's Gettysburg Address, but even those have distinctive differences. Individual libraries continually endeavor to provide access through institutional repositories and other digitization efforts. Those initiatives can usually be uncovered through skillful search engine queries. The focus in this book is on database content provided by vendors. Vendor archival content is becoming ever-more extensive, as table 9.8 shows.

The *Gale Primary Sources* database, within the Artemis platform, has a term-frequency visualization feature that allows users to see how words and terms have varied over time within the same corpus. This is similar in function to the Google Ngram Viewer. Figure 9.14 shows term frequencies of *tyrant**, *despot**, and *dictator** from 1700 to 2016 within 34 databases of the *Gale Primary Sources* database.

Gale's *Early Arabic Printed Books* database also has this feature.

Nontextual Databases: Images, Sounds, and Video

Let's take a brief look at two image databases: *AP Images*, from the Associated Press, and *Artstor*, from Ithaka, the people who created *JSTOR*.

Image Databases

AP Images contains historic photographs from the photojournalists of the Associated Press. While previously offered under the AP's own interface, EBSCO has purchased exclusive rights to the database and offers it under its EBSCOhost interface. The database contains over 12 million photographs dating back to 1826 as well as audio sound bites and professionally produced graphics. EBSCO has back-generated indexes that allow browsing by document type (audio, photo, print graphics, text archive, and video); event (any event you can think of); geographic terms; subject person; subject terms; and others. As this is generally nontextual, browsing may be just as

Table 9.8. Selected Vendor-Hosted Archival Databases.

Vendor	Archival Project and Description
Accessible Archives	*Accessible Archives*. African-American Newspapers, American Military Camp Newspapers, American County Histories, Civil War, Women's Suffrage Collection, and various older periodicals and newspapers.
Adam Matthew	Selected list includes *African American Communities*; *American History*; *American Indian Histories and Cultures*; *American West*; *Apartheid South Africa, 1948–1980*; *China, America and the Pacific*; *China: Culture and Society*; *China: Trade, Politics and Culture*; *Church Missionary Society*; *Colonial America*; *Defining Gender*; *Eighteenth Century Drama*; *Eighteenth Century Journals*; *Empire Online*; *Everyday Life and Women in America*; *First World War*; *Migration to New Worlds*; *Race Relations in America*; *Romanticism: Life, Literature and Landscape*; *Shakespeare in Performance*; *Slavery, Abolition and Social Justice*; *Socialism on Film: The Cold War*; *Women in the National Archives*; and *World's Fairs*.
Alexander Street Press	Emphasis on audio and video archival materials, including *American History in Video*; *British and Irish Women's Letters and Diaries*; *Meet the Press* [TV show archive]; *North American Immigrant Letters, Diaries, and Oral Histories*; and *Smithsonian Global Sound for Libraries*.
Chadwyck-Healey (ProQuest)	*Archive Finder*. This includes all entries from the *National Union Catalog of Manuscript Collections* (NUCMC), names and subjects from the National Inventory of Documentary Sources in the United States (NIDS), and names and subjects from the National Inventory of Documentary Sources in the United Kingdom and Ireland (NIDS UK/Ireland). Note: This is not a full-text resource, but a digitized version of a large print index of archival collections and indexing of ProQuest archival microform projects. A subset of this is *C19: The Nineteenth Century Index*.
EBSCO	*Arte Público Hispanic Historical Collection*: Series 1 and 2; *Associated Press Images Collection*; *Civil War Primary Source Documents*; *Gateway to North America: People, Places, and Organizations of 19th-Century New York*.
Gale	*Archives Unbound; American Civil Liberties Union Papers, 1912–1990*; *Archives of Sexuality & Gender*; *Associated Press Collections Online*; *Brazilian and Portuguese History and Culture*; *China from Empire to Republic*; *Crime, Punishment, and Popular Culture 1790–1920*; *Indigenous Peoples: North America*; *Smithsonian Collections Online*.
Readex	*American Broadsides and Ephemera*; *American Pamphlets*; *The American Civil War Collection*; *The American Slavery Collection*; *Civil Rights in America*.

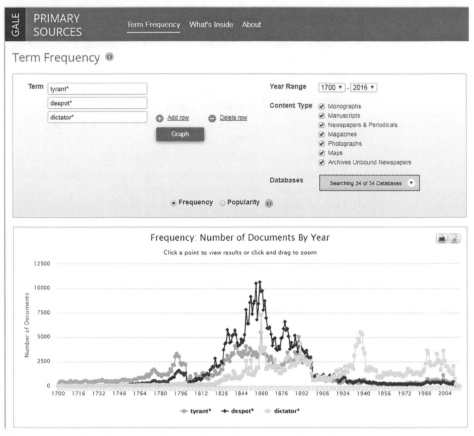

Figure 9.14. *Gale Primary Sources* Term-Frequency Visualization Feature.
Source: Screenshot from *Gale Primary Sources.* ©Gale, a part of Cengage, Inc.
Reproduced by permission: www.cengage.com/permissions.

useful as searching. Each photo is accompanied with sufficient metadata for adequate sourcing: creation date, photographer, location, and image resolution. Because images are challenging to cite, the EBSCOhost cite button in the left margin provides this information in multiple formats.

Artstor contains art and visual representations from a variety of disciplines. As with the *AP Images* database, *Artstor* features several browsing options: browse by collection (institutions represented in the database); classification (by which they mean broad categories, such as architecture and city planning, decorative arts, fashion, performing arts, photographs, prints, and sculpture, to name just a few); or by country. Browsing is the best way to explore this visual database content, especially when you have no idea what the database contains, much less what words to enter in a mysteriously blank search box. Once you discover some objects you find interesting, click on an image and familiarize yourself with the available fields. The fields in the records differ depending on the type of artwork. For example, records for oil paintings and sculptures have fields for "work type" and "style period." In contrast, records for photographs emphasize image source information and location. The advanced search function allows for field searching, but

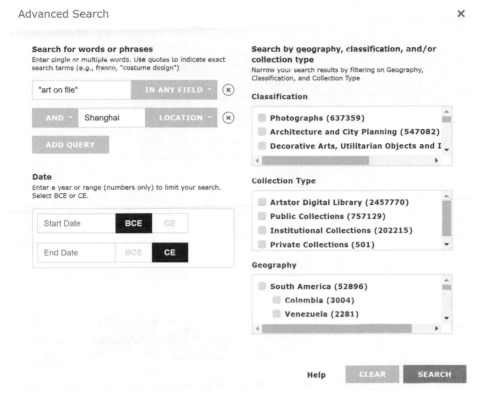

Figure 9.15. *Artstor* Advanced Search. *Source:* Reproduced courtesy of *Artstor*. All rights reserved.

if you are unfamiliar with all the fields, it would be best just to enter keywords "in any field." Figure 9.15 shows the way the advanced search allows for limits.

Notice that you can search with the asterisk as the truncation symbol. In this case, using truncation expanded the result set by 3 items. Results are presented as thumbnails in figure 9.16.

Streaming Audio and Video Databases

You are probably already familiar with such smartphone apps as Shazam that can search by a snippet of recorded music and almost immediately identify the work. In the world of library databases, however, we are not searching audio files directly, but the metadata behind them. There are some excellent databases that can be searched that will retrieve music and audio content.

Although there are many audio and video databases on the market, the increased speed of data transfer over various technologies and the amazing capabilities of smartphones make the streaming market an attractive one for database vendors. Streaming music is already available through *NAXOS Music Library*, audiobooks via Overdrive, and streaming documentaries and instructional videos from numerous vendors. Many vendors now embed

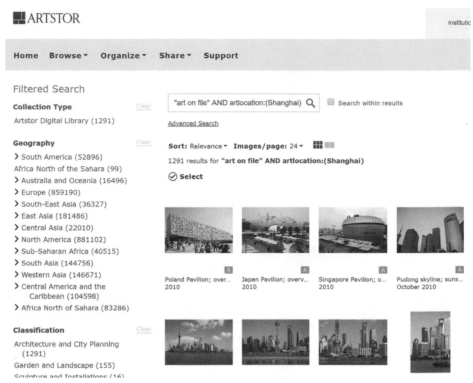

Figure 9.16. *Artstor* Results Display. *Source:* Reproduced courtesy of *Artstor*. All rights reserved.

video content into their more traditional databases. Newsbank's *Access World News* is beginning to index and link to television news coverage from selected sources.

Alexander Street Press (ProQuest) has several streaming music and video offerings available by subscription. The many components of their *Music Online* databases cover opera, classical music, American music, jazz, and popular music, among others. Their video projects include *Theatre in Video*, *Social Work Online*, *American History in Video*, and *Anthropology Online*. The *Docuseek2* subscription provides access to hundreds of documentary films.

A relatively new start-up company, Kanopy, offers a database of streaming films (especially foreign), documentaries, and instructional videos that are popular with both public and academic libraries.

Additional Resources for Humanities

Several databases stand out as all-purpose humanities databases, including *JSTOR*, *Project Muse*, *Humanities Index Retrospective: 1907–1984*, *Humanities Full Text*, and *Humanities International Complete* (these last three databases are H. W. Wilson databases vended by EBSCO).

Table 9.9. Additional Resources for the Humanities.

Discipline	Database (Vendor)
Humanities Generally	*Humanities & Social Science Index Retrospective: 1907–1984* (H. W. Wilson—EBSCOhost)
Art	*Art & Architecture Complete* (EBSCO) *Art Full Text* (EBSCO) *ARTbibliographies Modern* (ProQuest) *Oxford Art Online* (Oxford University Press)
Film Studies	*FIAF International Film Archive* (ProQuest) *Film & Television Literature Index* (EBSCO) *Internet Movie Database* (imdb.com)—free resource that serves as an authoritative source for film and television information
History	*International Medieval Bibliography* (Brepolis) *Iter: Gateway to the Middle Ages & Renaissance* (University of Toronto Libraries)
Linguistics	*Linguistics and Language Behavior Abstracts* (ProQuest)
Music	*International Index to Music Periodicals* (ProQuest) *Music Index* (EBSCO) *Oxford Music Online* (Oxford University Press) *RILM Abstracts of Music Literature* (EBSCO)
Philosophy	*L'Année Philologique* (EBSCO) *Philosopher's Index* (ProQuest) *Stanford Encyclopedia of Philosophy* (plato.stanford.edu)—free
Religion	*ATLA Religion Database* (EBSCO) *Old Testament Abstracts* (EBSCO) *New Testament Abstracts* (EBSCO) *Index to Jewish Periodicals* (EBSCO) *Oxford Islamic Studies Online* (Oxford University Press)

As noted at the beginning of this chapter, Gale has been combining many of its humanities products together under an interface called Gale Artemis. *Gale Artemis: Literary Sources* includes database and e-books on contemporary authors and literary criticism in an interface that includes a topic finder visualization tool that some may find helpful. When a term is entered into the tool, visual results can be displayed as a wheel or as tiles. Clicking on a term drills down further into the database and displays relevant results in a separate panel.

Table 9.9 provides a selective list of other databases available in various fields within the humanities, some simply indexes and others offering abstracts and full text.

Exercises

1. Compare the version of *MLAIB* described in this chapter with the version at your school, if available (and different). What are the advantages and disadvantages of each?

2. In the *MLAIB* subject list (thesaurus), how is the author of *Huckleberry Finn* listed? As Samuel Clemens or under his pseudonym, Mark Twain? Or both? Compare this to your local online catalog; which name is used there?

3. Go to *Gale Literary Resources*, if your library subscribes. Do a search for "Joseph Conrad" and note the number of results. Now do a search for "Conrad, Joseph (British novelist)"—the interface should suggest this subject as you start typing. Note the results from this search. How do you explain the differences between the first search and the second one?

4. Find full-text sources for Belknap, Jeremy. *The Foresters, An American Tale; Being a Sequel to the History of John Bull the Clothier. In a Series of Letters to a Friend.* Boston, Printed by I. Thomas and E. T. Andrews, 1792. Hint: Use free resources as well as subscription sources for this.

5. The Battle of Gettysburg, July 1–3, 1963, was commemorated by Lincoln's Gettysburg Address on November 19 of that year. Use archival sources and newspaper sources from that time period to find the text and commentary on Lincoln's speech.

6. Using the *America: History and Life* database, find book reviews of *1491: New Revelations of the Americas before Columbus* by Charles C. Mann.

7. Using *Historical Abstracts*, how many times has *A Military History of India and South Asia: From the East India Company to the Nuclear Era* by Daniel P. Marston been cited?

Reference

Bell, Suzanne S. 2015. *Librarian's Guide to Online Searching: Cultivating Database Skills for Research and Instruction.* 4th ed. Santa Barbara, CA: Libraries Unlimited, an imprint of ABC-CLIO.

Beyond the Textbook

Carrying on the tradition of the fourth edition, additional exercises, search tips, and tutorials will be available on the publisher's Web site at http://www.abc-clio.com/books.librariesunlimited.com/Librarians -Guide-to-Online-Searching. This will be updated periodically with the inevitable database changes.

10
Science, Engineering, and Medical Databases

The science-related disciplines differ considerably from the social sciences and humanities. We cannot possibly cover all aspects of science and their databases. But what we can do is focus on a few distinctive databases that point out what is important to scientists, engineers, and medical researchers. One of the key ways the databases in these subject areas differ is highlighted by their approach to controlled vocabulary.

We focus in this chapter on three areas that are related, yet are quite different. To the chemist, being able to search by specific chemical substances is very important. In this field, the "controlled vocabulary" is the chemical compound itself, and having a way to uniquely identify them with a classification system is critical.

In the premier database for medical research, *PubMed*, control is exercised through a carefully crafted and applied controlled vocabulary, the Medical Subject Headings (MeSH). These subjects, applied by medical professionals, help searchers examine materials with extreme precision and accuracy, exactly what you need and expect when dealing with such an important topic, our health and well-being.

Databases for the engineer focus on technology, from patents, to presentations about technology at conferences, to technical reports. Terminology is often beyond the reach of lay understanding. One of the most challenging of vocabularies is found underlying patents and how they are classified.

The *Web of Science* database illustrates yet a different emphasis, not that of subject terms, but of bibliographic citations. Being cited is not just a way to get tenure at a university, it is a way of finding scholarly impact and how scientific discovery is shared. *Web of Science* is much broader than just the scientific disciplines, as the database also contains modules for social sciences and humanities. It was such a hit in the fields of science that it spread to other disciplines, and it remains the gold standard today for tracking what other scholars say about scholarship.

Primary sources in the sciences tend to differ from primary sources in the humanities and social sciences. Rather than looking to old newspapers, old texts, or government publications for primary research, scientists look for reports on original research, experiments, data sets, and "primary studies." To a scientist, a primary source is more likely to be a write-up of an experiment as found in a peer-reviewed journal. The very resources that social scientists and humanists use for secondary research is the kind of resource a scientist might use to look for primary research.

SciFinder

There are many science- and engineering-related databases that could be introduced at this point, but they tend to have many of the same features that have been demonstrated in other databases. For that reason, we will turn our attention to the features of a database produced by the American Chemical Society (ACS), *SciFinder*.

I bring up this amazing database because it's unusual among databases and because of the varieties of searching methods available. *SciFinder* is not merely an article database. It contains a merging of several key ACS reference resources: *Chemical Abstract Service (CAS) Registry*, *Chemical Abstracts Service Source Index (CASSI)*, and *Chemical Abstracts*. Each of these titles represents a massive amount of research, having occupied many shelves of book space in reference departments over many decades.

The *CAS Registry* is the official assigning authority for chemical structures old and new. More than 135 million organic and inorganic substances are uniquely identified through the *Registry*. The *CASSI* search tool is freely available and can be used to provide background information for chemistry publications (http://cassi.cas.org). But the centerpiece of all these CAS publications is *Chemical Abstracts* itself, the definitive bibliography for the field. The print versions of *Chemical Abstracts* occupy considerable space in academic libraries. But when libraries subscribe to *SciFinder*, libraries may opt for remote storage for these volumes.

Not only can the *SciFinder* database be searched by author, title, and subject, but because it contains references to patents, it can be searched by patent number, patent assignee name (may be a person or a company), inventor name (always a personal name), and, most importantly, by chemical structure, molecular formula (like H_2SO_4, entered as H2SO4 for sulfuric acid), or chemical property (boiling point, density, electrical conductivity, melting point, and refractive index, to mention just a few).

SciFinder also contains relevant records from *Medline* (Gamble 2017) (see more about *Medline* later in this chapter). You can even enter a search by *drawing* a compound! As this is not a chemistry textbook, we will not assume that you would want to draw chemical compounds the way that a chemist would do. But showing these features to chemists for whom drawing structures is as natural and likely easier than writing out their names is very beneficial. Librarians should know how to use the controlled-vocabulary language of chemistry, in this case not subject terms like we usually see, but the CAS chemical compound number as found in the *CAS Registry*, which is embedded within *SciFinder*.

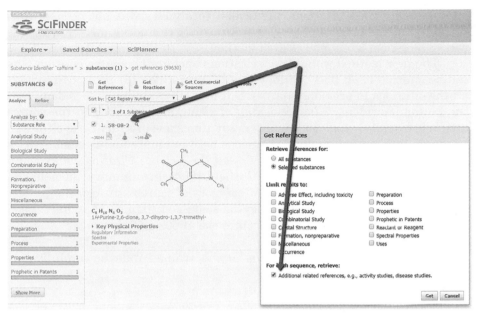

Figure 10.1. *SciFinder* Substance Identifier for Caffeine. *Source:* ©Chemical Abstracts Service. Used with permission.

Suppose you wanted to do a search for caffeine. Using the online "substance identifier," we find that the *CAS Registry* number for caffeine is 58 08-2. We can now get references from *SciFinder* with a variety of limits, including disease studies, as illustrated in figure 10.1.

This powerful database contains many other features. The best place to discuss these is not here, but to search Google like this: "scifinder tutorial." This search will turn up official videos from the American Chemical Society and library guides from various science librarians.

Web of Science and Other Citation Indexes

Think about what you have learned thus far in this book about search strategies in relation to databases. What was once only possible with physical volumes has now been largely replaced by online versions. Print indexing tools are either placed in remote storage or discarded entirely. You can search with the exactness of controlled-vocabulary terms that capture the concepts in an attempt to get to the "all and only" relevant records, or you can use keyword searching to hopefully retrieve concepts either within the metadata or in the full text of the works themselves. These are two very logical methodologies for locating relevant resources. But Eugene Garfield envisioned another way, one not fraught with the limitations of indexers' comprehension (or lack of comprehension) of articles, or with the searcher's limitations in terms of selecting keywords with which to search. This method would be a more formal one, tracking articles cited within articles and tracking later articles that cite the article in question. Garfield, the "father" of citation searching (Jacsó 2010), founded the Institute for Scientific Information (ISI) (Garfield 1964) and used computational power in the 1960s to automatically track citations. Controlled vocabulary was not needed, thus speeding up the process of getting from article to finding mechanism; this was to be a completely new search method.

The new method would track citations back to the source citation. The source citation itself had citations to its sources. The ISI project would list all the citations to previous sources. But it is when the reverse is done that the power is evident. When indexing of citing articles back to the source article is compiled, you can see how many times a source article is cited and by whom, and you can make distinctions between more highly cited articles and those not so highly cited. He viewed the *Science Citation Index* as an international inventory of science (Garfield 1964). In summary, Garfield and ISI had created a revolutionary new category of search strategies.

You might think of a typology of search strategies that have been spawned by computer technologies since the 1960s as follows:

Strategy 1. *Controlled vocabulary*. A trained indexer carefully assigned terms to articles.

Strategy 1A. *Pseudo-controlled vocabulary*. A database of back-generated terms provides automated indexing. The quality of the controlled vocabulary itself, the method of extracting index terms, and the inconsistencies in the application of index terms should be considered when using products with pseudo-controlled vocabulary.

Strategy 2. The searcher selects what she thinks are relevant keywords, trying her best to work with synonyms and modifications to get the desired results.

Strategy 3. *Automatically track citations*. By scanning bibliographies, articles used and cited in the course of research can be tracked. One problem with this method is that there is no way to automatically know whether articles are cited positively, negatively, or neutrally.

The Scope of ISI's Citation Indexes

Originally, it was just *Science Citation Index*. But the value of this methodology quickly became apparent, and *Social Sciences Citation Index* was born. A bit later, *Arts & Humanities Citation Index* came into being, although it has never risen to the prominence of the other two resources. Each of these resources has a title list of the journals covered. As of mid-2017, there are 8,895 journals tracked in *Science Citation Index*, 3,262 in *Social Sciences Citation Index*, and 1,785 in *Arts & Humanities Citation Index*. Although the journal coverage is impressive, it is not all-inclusive. Selection criteria govern which journals are included and which are not (Clarivate Analytics 2016). It should be noted that Clarivate Analytics purchased the *Web of Science* suite from Thomson Reuters in 2016.

Source Document

To understand how a citation index works, you need an illustration (figure 10.2). At the center of everything is a source document. Think of this as the object of study, the article under consideration. Usually at the end of the source document is a bibliography or list of references cited. Papers that include this source document in their bibliographies are tracked. Generally, the more times a work is cited, the more important the work is. It is possible, of course, that a work gets cited many times because it is noteworthy for being bad research.

Cited References: Tracing Research Back in Time

While traditional indexes are busy creating metadata from tables of contents of journals, citation indexes focus on the bibliographies, the articles cited in scholarly articles. By creating an index of all articles that subsequently cite the source document, you can follow interaction with a scholar's thoughts. From the perspective of the source author, the more times that author is cited, the better it looks in terms of promotion and tenure possibilities, as it demonstrates greater impact in the academic community. The source document itself cites previous research, which, in turn, continues the scholarly chain of interacting with previous research. The idea here is to keep straight the two parts of this endeavor: the author's citations and citations to the author.

Let's take an article from *Web of Science* as an illustration. Let's look for Eugene Garfield's 1964 article about *Science Citation Index*. The full title is *"Science Citation Index—A New Dimension in Indexing,"* and it is from the journal *Science*. When you enter this title into SCI (that is, *Web of*

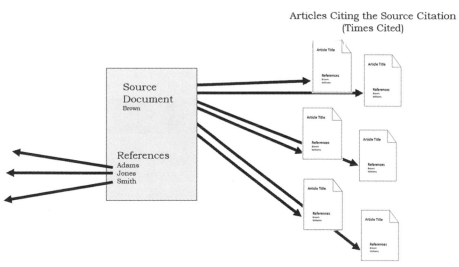

Figure 10.2. Illustrated Model of a Citation Index from Perspective of the Source Document.

Science) you get no results. You had entered both the title and the subtitle. But when you enter the title without the subtitle, you get the intended article (figure 10.3).

Notice the difference: the article "A" is missing from the subtitle in *Web of Science*. In other words, because of this slight difference, the indexing is different than we would expect. This kind of anomaly occurs all the time in database searching, and searchers need to be aware of this possibility.

Best Practice: If a search initially fails, try using fewer search terms to see if you can retrieve what you are looking for.

You need to view the full record to see all the relevant elements (figure 10.4).

Notice that Garfield's article itself contains 54 cited references (i.e., references that the author cites in his article) and that since its publication in 1964 it has been cited 185 times (at least in the journals tracked by *Web of Science*). In figure 10.5, the lefthand side shows an excerpt from *Web of Science* of cited items from Garfield's article in alphabetical order. The righthand side shows an excerpt from the actual article with citations in order of use within the article.

Citations to an Author: Tracing Research Forward in Time

After the 1964 appearance of Garfield's article, it was cited 185 times. By clicking the "185 results" link, you are taken to the citation report showing 169 articles. Why did the results screen claim that there were 185 citing articles, but when we click through we now only see 169 articles? It all comes down to scope. Not all the 185 articles in which Garfield was cited are from journals that are covered in the database. In other words, *Web of Science* accurately lists all citations from Garfield's bibliographic citations, but not all of these are from journals tracked within the database. From the citing articles screen, you will see a link to "Create Citation Report." Clicking this gives you some interesting analysis (figure 10.6).

Looking at the total publications box in figure 10.6, you will see a graph of usage over time. This shows us much recent interest in Garfield's article.

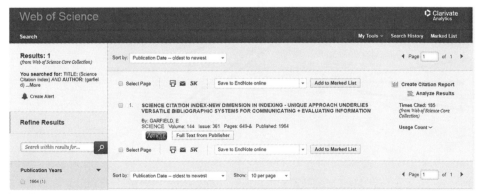

Figure 10.3. *Web of Science* Display Showing Brief Title in Browse View Screen. *Source:* Certain data included herein are derived from the *Web of Science*® prepared by Clarivate Analytics, Philadelphia, PA. All rights reserved.

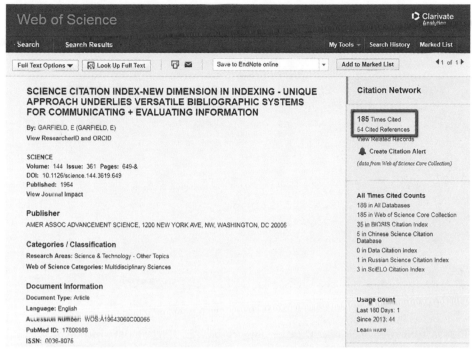

Figure 10.4. *Web of Science* Display Showing Cited References and Subsequent Citations. *Source:* Certain data included herein are derived from the *Web of Science*® prepared by Clarivate Analytics, Philadelphia, PA. All rights reserved.

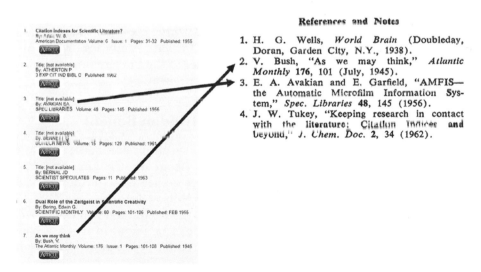

Figure 10.5. *Web of Science* Cited Articles Compared with References from Print Publication. *Source:* Certain data included herein are derived from the *Web of Science*® prepared by Clarivate Analytics, Philadelphia, PA. All rights reserved.

The "h-index" is an attempt to provide a fair weighting to articles so that articles that are very highly cited and those that have not yet been cited do not skew the weighting. Here is how it works: "An index of h means that there are h papers that have each been cited h times." Got it? It's kind of dense, but if you think about it for some time, it will begin to make sense.

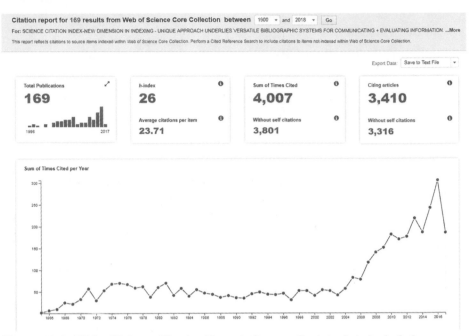

Figure 10.6. *Web of Science* Citation Report. *Source:* Certain data included herein are derived from the *Web of Science*® prepared by Clarivate Analytics, Philadelphia, PA, USA. All rights reserved.

Web of Science was at one time living under the "Web of Knowledge" interface. This interface branding was apparently so named to accommodate other products, such as *Biological Abstracts, Medline, Zoological Record*, and several other databases. Apparently, under Clarivate Analytics ownership, the *Web of Science* branding is now used to refer to the overarching interface as well as the core collection covering 1900 to present.

Book Reviews to Academic Books: A Hidden Benefit

Book reviews can often be found in aggregator databases such as EBSCO's *Academic Search Complete*, Gale's *Academic OneFile*, and *Pro-Quest Central*. In addition, there are databases dedicated to academic book reviews, such as *Book Review Digest* (an H. W. Wilson database via EBSCO) and *Book Review Index Online* (Gale). But a rather hidden benefit to *Web of Science* is that reviews to academic books can be found in it. As a book review is, by definition, a cited reference, search for book reviews in *Web of Science* using a cited reference search.

Other Citation Databases

Scopus

Although *Science Citation Index, Social Sciences Citation Index*, and *Arts and Humanities Citation Index* eventually evolved into the massive

Web of Science database, it is not the only product of its kind. *Scopus*, produced by Elsevior, provides serious competition.

There is a fierce rivalry between *Web of Science* and *Scopus*, with large corporate entities behind each. *Scopus* likely covers more journals, but *Web of Science* goes back further in time. There have been several articles comparing the coverage and efficacy of *Web of Science*, *Scopus*, and Google Scholar (Adriaanse and Rensleigh 2013; Harzing and Alakangas 2016).

Google Scholar

While both *Web of Science* and *Scopus* are very expensive citation-tracking databases, Google Scholar does it for no charge. Those skeptical about Google Scholar's citations need only read some of the academic literature comparing Scholar to the two fee-based databases (see citations mentioned above). Very often, Google Scholar presents more citations for the following reasons:

- Some citations are to what I call "Google Books bleed-through" into Google Scholar. This means that book content often shows up in Google Scholar, where you are generally expecting scholarly article content. There is no limiter or facet to turn the books off or on; they just show up.

- Scholar sometimes includes citations from nonscholarly sources— e.g., conference papers, doctoral dissertations, master's theses, and even academic curriculum vitae (CVs) can be found in Scholar.

- Scholar harvests materials posted in institutional and digital repositories from universities and associations.

- Scholar harvests selected materials from federal and state Web sites.

These and other factors go toward upping the citations to source articles.

While *Scopus* and *Web of Science* are bidirectional (you can see the references cited by an article as well as the later articles that cite that article), Google Scholar citations are unidirectional. You can only see subsequent citations to the source article.

Citation Tracking in Other Databases

Many other fee-based databases are now incorporating citation linkages within their interfaces. *PsycINFO* (with information provided by the American Psychological Association) contains bi-directional citations, that is, both the citations contained within an article and subsequent citations to that article are indexed and searchable (figure 10.7).

Note, however, that the subsequent citations to the articles are to "times cited in this database," meaning that articles from journals that cite an article that is not covered by the *PsycINFO* database (in other words, out of scope) will not be counted. For example, if an article in a sociology journal not covered in *PsycINFO* (not within its scope) happens to cite an article in *PsycINFO*, the citation to that sociology article would not be counted because the *PsycINFO* database has no way of knowing about the existence of articles outside of its scope. This is just something to keep in mind with researching citations.

Some databases under the ProQuest interface include cited and citing references for academic article content. Generally, this feature works for databases containing scholarly, peer-reviewed journal content and not for trade journal literature, primary source materials such as archival materials or government publications, or e-book content. Although this feature doesn't work for all databases, it does work in databases for which ProQuest has been provided the data (peer-reviewed content only). Rather than giving you a long list of databases that have this feature, why don't you see how many ProQuest databases you can find through your library that have these features.

EBSCOhost databases have cited and citing references for selected articles only. Now, do the same exercise for EBSCO databases: how many can you find that have cited articles?

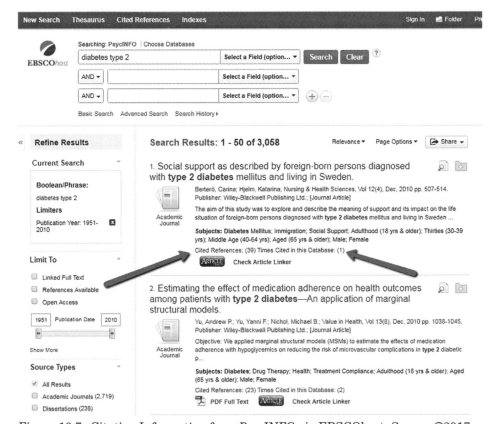

Figure 10.7. Citation Information from *PsycINFO* via EBSCOhost. *Source:* ©2017 EBSCO Industries, Inc. All rights reserved.

There are few other databases that deserve comment. *Engineering Village* notes times cited in *Scopus*. *ACM Digital Library* has both references within articles and subsequent citations. *Wiley Online Library* includes "literature cited" as well as "citing literature." Look through your library's databases and see if you can find additional databases.

Journal Citation Reports

Now that there is a massive database of citations back to source articles, it is only logical that this data be used to evaluate the relative impact of the journals that contain the articles. This is the mission of *Journal Citation Reports*, a module within *Web of Science* that can also be accessed on its own.

Very often, users come to the reference desk saying that they need to access important journals in their field, but with little guidance otherwise. In these cases, you might consult *Journal Citation Reports* to see which journals have a higher impact factor and are thus more likely to have weightier content. This is also a good strategy when trying to find which journals are good targets to aim for in one's publishing career. Figure 10.8 shows library science journals ranked by impact factor. Keep in mind that these are information and library science journals overall, and they are not broken down by subdiscipline, like public services, technical services, information technology, and so on.

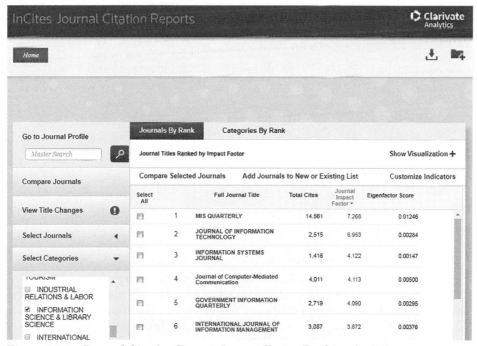

Figure 10.8. *Journal Citation Reports* Impact Factor Ranking for Information Science and Library Science Journals. *Source:* Certain data included herein are derived from the *Web of Science*® prepared by Clarivate Analytics, Philadelphia, PA. All rights reserved.

This chapter does not go into the different metrics other than citation counts used to weigh the relative importance of journal articles—metrics like the journal impact factor or Google Scholar's h-index. For that, please see Bollen, Van de Sompel, Hagberg, and Chute (2009).

Alternative Metrics

The weaknesses of the journal impact factor have been noted by many (Thelwall and Fairclough 2015; Moustafa 2015). What was originally intended to gauge the impact of entire journals has been taken well beyond the original intention and stretched to apply to the impact of individual authors and even countries. Authors have learned how to game the system. Universities often require certain metrics as measures for gaining tenure. The original concept was based on a print-based world, but then along came online publishing and open-access journals. Different methods of measurement become possible in today's online environment. Downloads, tweets, bookmarks in bibliographic citation management systems, and discussions on blogs are all possible additional ways that scholarly content can be measured. This is what alternative metrics are all about.

Some databases are beginning to incorporate these alternative metrics into their records. Here is a representation of a record from *ACM Digital Library* showing downloads of the article over time:

Airplanes aloft as a sensor network for wind forecasting

Ashish Kapoor, Zachary Horvitz, Spencer Laube, Eric Horvitz

April 2014 IPSN '14: Proceedings of the 13th international symposium on Information processing in sensor networks

Publisher: IEEE Press

Bibliometrics:

Citation Count: 2

Downloads (6 Weeks): 2, Downloads (12 Months): 21, Downloads (Overall): 145

Wiley Online Library, Nature Publishing Group, Springer, and *BioMed Central* are among the databases that use the Altmetric Attention Score (Altmetric 2017). This provides numbers of tweets and mentions on blogs, Facebook, Google+, Reddit/Pinterest, YouTube, *Wikipedia*, and government Web sites as well as the number of readers using Mendeley and Cite U Like.

EBSCO Discovery Service (*EDS*) uses alternative style citations from Plum Analytics (an EBSCO company) in its discovery service to gather usage, captures, or downloads; mentions in social media; and citations. Look for these alternative metrics to grow in the near future and for them to be incorporated into database records.

Engineering Databases

What Engineers Do

The Royal Academy of Engineering suggests that engineers are driven by what makes things work or what makes things work better. Their report identifies six engineering "habits of mind" that define and describe the ways engineers act (Royal Academy of Engineering 2014):

1. Systems thinking

2. Adapting

3. Problem-finding

4. Creative problem-solving

5. Visualizing

6. Improving

Engineering literature is replete with papers, articles, and other works showing evidence of these six habits of mind. Pure science endeavors to discover causation in the physical universe, whereas engineering seeks to apply those insights and discoveries and insights to solve problems, create new technologies, and make our lives better (Fosmire 2014). Timeliness of research in critical. Because getting articles published in peer-reviewed journals sometimes takes too much valuable time, engineers often communicate their work through conference papers and proceedings. In addition, they also rely on handbooks and manuals (for things like properties of materials), technical reports, and standards. Table 10.1 shows some important databases covering various document types of interest to engineers.

Analysis of Selected Engineering Databases

Four important engineering databases are *IEEE Xplore*, the *ACM Digital Library*, and two databases that run under the Engineering Village interface, *Compendex* and *INSPEC*.

Table 10.2 below provides some differences in scope and background in the major engineering databases.

Also important to engineering research are e-books, many of which serve as reference works so that engineers can quickly "get the code." Examples of these would be the CRCnetBASE series of e-book collections, as noted in table 10.1

PubMed and *Medline*

We have made a point throughout this book to focus on the premier databases within each field, and in the field of medicine nothing surpasses *PubMed*. A little bit of background is necessary here. Since 1960, there have

Table 10.1. Selected Databases Covering Engineering Research.

Document Type	Database	Notes
Technical reports	*NTIS* Database (under the U.S. Dept. of Commerce) *CiteSeer*X (Pennsylvania State U.	Freely available (https://www.ntis.gov). Freely available (http://citeseerx.ist .psu.edu).
	Technical Report Archive & Image Library (TRAIL) Collaborative effort with Center for Research Libraries, U. of Arizona, U. of Michigan, HathiTrust, U. of North Texas, and U. of Washington	Freely available (http://www .technicalreports.org).
	SciTech Connect	Freely available (https://www.osti.gov /scitech).
Conference papers and proceedings	*Compendex* (Engineering Village interface; owned by Elsevier)	Licensed database.
	IEEE Xplore (Institute of Electrical and Electronics Engineers)	World's largest technical professional organization. Licensed database.
	ACM Digital Library (Association for Computing Machinery)	Licensed database.
	INSPEC (Elsevier)	Licensed database. Can run on the Ei Compendex interface; incorporates *Scopus* citations.
Manuals and handbooks	*CRCnetBASE* (Taylor & Francis)	Handbooks contained in numerous collections that can be subscribed to separately: *CivilENGINEERINGnetBASE* *ElectricalENGINEERINGnetBASE* *GeneralENGINEERINGnetBASE* *IndustrialENGINEERINGnetBASE* *MechanicalENGINEERINGnetBASE* *MiningENGINEERINGnetBASE*
	Knovel	Material property search. Licensed database.
Patents	U.S. Patent Search	Freely available (https://www.uspto .gov/patent).

Document Type	Database	Notes
	Google Patents	Freely available (https://patents.google.com).
Standards	*IHS Markit Standards*	Freely available (https://global.ihs.com).
	American National Standards Institute (ANSI)	Fee-based database (https://www.ansi.org).
	ASTM Compass	Originally *American Society for Testing and Materials*. Now known as *ASTM International*. Licensed database.
	IEEE Xplore	Licensed database.
Articles	*ACM Digital Library*	Licensed database.
	Compendex	Licensed database.
	INSPEC	Licensed database.
	IEEE Xplore	Licensed database.

Table 10.2. Three engineering databases: Scope and background

	Engineering Village (*Compendex* and *INSPEC*)	*IEEE Xplore*	*ACM Digital Library* including *ACM Guide to Computing Literature*
Scholarly articles	Yes; citations and abstracts	Yes	Yes
Conference papers and proceedings	Yes	Yes	Yes
Dissertations	Yes	No	Yes
Physical analog	Engineering Index (1969 onward)	Index to IEEE publications.	ACM guide to computing literature
Controlled vocabulary	EI Thesaurus	INSPEC Thesaurus is used, but not independently accessible.	ACM Computing Classification System & ENCompassLIT Thesaurus (for that section)
Standards	No	IEEE published standards.	No

been monthly print publications published by the National Library of Medicine called *Index Medicus*, covering journals in all areas of medicine. These were cumulated annually into *Cumulated Index Medicus*, again a print publication. These cumulations superseded the monthly indexes, but they still took up a significant amount of shelf space. The online database version, which first appeared as *Medline* has Medical Subject Headings carefully applied to each record by indexing professionals with medical backgrounds.

The entirety of *Medline* is now incorporated into the broader umbrella known as *PubMed* and runs under the Entrez browser interface. This is the same interface that hosts the Human Genome Project, the famous DNA mapping project. In all, 39 literature and molecular databases are searchable under this interface (National Library of Medicine 2006). It is important to note that *PubMed* contains more than the *Cumulated Index Medicus/Medline* content. Because the field of medicine is changing so quickly, researchers and doctors can't wait for indexers to apply Medical Subject Headings to entries before they enter the database. Figure 10.9 shows the relationships between the products as they exist today. A subset of *Medline* records, *PMC* or *PubMed Central*, are freely available records with accompanying full text. There is a separate search pull-down selection from within the Entrez interface that will retrieve *PMC* free full text. This is most useful for people who don't have access to college or university subscriptions to premium journal content.

It is very easy to confuse the many projects related to medical research: *Medline*, *PubMed*, and *PubMed Central*. Figure 10.9 attempts to show the relationships among these projects.

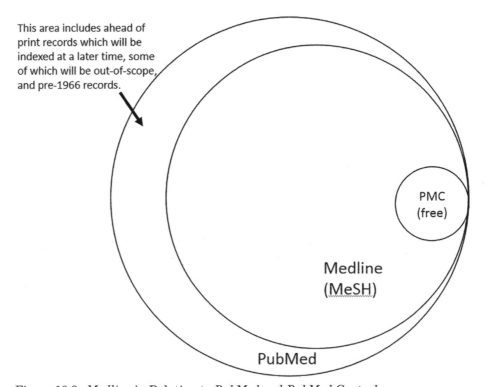

Figure 10.9. *Medline* in Relation to *PubMed* and *PubMed Central*.

As mentioned previously, also contained in *PubMed* are "ahead of print" records that have not yet been fully indexed and have not yet had MeSH headings applied. It is important for medical professionals to be aware of this information ahead of time. There is also a subset of pre-1966 records that have not been indexed for other reasons. These include articles from medical journals that may not be related to medical fields, such as pieces about plate tectonics or astrophysics. The thesaurus to *PubMed* is the Medical Subject Headings, also accessed via the Entrez interface.

MeSH: Medical Subject Headings

We have already mentioned MeSH several times, but we need to go into a bit more depth. Because the MeSH headings are so carefully applied to records prepared for *Medline*, I thought it best to quote directly from the official Web site:

> Each MeSH descriptor appears in at least one place in the trees, and may appear in as many additional places as may be appropriate. Those who index articles or catalog books are instructed to find and use the most specific MeSH descriptor that is available to represent each indexable concept. For example, articles concerning Streptococcus pneumoniae will be found under the descriptor Streptococcus Pneumoniae rather than the broader term Streptococcus, while an article referring to a new streptococcal bacterium which is not yet in the vocabulary will be listed directly under Streptococcus. (National Library of Medicine 2016)

The MeSH headings are accessed via the Entrez browser with a direct URL (https://meshb.nlm.nih.gov) or as a pull-down option from within *PubMed* (figure 10.10).

As an example of a MeSH heading appearing in multiple places in the tree structures, take the term *Diabetes Mellitus* as an example (figure 10.11). Notice that diabetes mellitus lives in two places, as a metabolic disease and as an endocrine system disease.

Figure 10.10. Entrez Browser's Many Databases.

Tree Number(s): C18.452.394.750, C19.246
MeSH Unique ID: D003920
See Also:

- Diabetes Insipidus
- Diet, Diabetic
- Prediabetic State
- Scleredema Adultorum
- Glycosylation End Products, Advanced
- Glucose Intolerance
- Gastroparesis

```
All MeSH Categories
        Diseases Category
                Nutritional and Metabolic Diseases
                        Metabolic Diseases
                                Glucose Metabolism Disorders
                                        Diabetes Mellitus
                                                Diabetes Mellitus, Experimental
                                                Diabetes Mellitus, Type 1
                                                        Wolfram Syndrome
                                                Diabetes Mellitus, Type 2
                                                        Diabetes Mellitus, Lipoatrophic
                                                Diabetes, Gestational
                                                Diabetic Ketoacidosis
                                                Donohue Syndrome
                                                Latent Autoimmune Diabetes in Adults
                                                Prediabetic State

All MeSH Categories
        Diseases Category
                Endocrine System Diseases
                        Diabetes Mellitus
                                Diabetes Complications
                                        Diabetic Angiopathies +
                                        Diabetic Cardiomyopathies
                                        Diabetic Coma +
                                        Diabetic Ketoacidosis
                                        Diabetic Nephropathies
                                        Diabetic Neuropathies +
                                        Fetal Macrosomia
                                Diabetes Mellitus, Experimental
                                Diabetes Mellitus, Type 1
                                        Wolfram Syndrome
                                Diabetes Mellitus, Type 2
                                        Diabetes Mellitus, Lipoatrophic
                                Diabetes, Gestational
                                Donohue Syndrome
                                Latent Autoimmune Diabetes in Adults
                                Prediabetic State
```

Figure 10.11. Example of MeSH Heading Tree Structures in *PubMed*.

This ability for a term to live in multiple places makes the MeSH system different from the *PsycINFO* or the *ERIC* thesauri. Yet, it makes sense that, for example, Type 2 diabetes needs to be categorized as a glucose metabolism disorder as well as an endocrine system disorder. Notice that these tree structures very clearly show broader terms, narrower terms, and related terms. Not shown in figure 10.11 is the scope note.

That the MeSH system is truly subject headings (under my definition) as opposed to subject descriptors is amplified by the subheadings feature within the MeSH interface (figure 10.12). That is, these subheadings are equivalent to writing out "Diabetes Mellitus – analysis or Diabetes Mellitus – congenital."

Diabetes Mellitus

A heterogeneous group of disorders characterized by HYPERGLYCEMIA and GLUCOSE INTOLERANCE.

PubMed search builder options
Subheadings:

☐ analysis	☐ economics	☐ parasitology
☐ anatomy and histology	☐ education	☐ pathology
☐ blood	☐ embryology	☐ physiology
☐ blood supply	☐ enzymology	☐ physiopathology
☐ cerebrospinal fluid	☐ epidemiology	☐ prevention and control
☐ chemical synthesis	☐ ethnology	☐ psychology
☐ chemically induced	☐ etiology	☐ radiotherapy
☐ chemistry	☐ genetics	☐ rehabilitation
☐ classification	☐ history	☐ statistics and numerical data
☐ complications	☐ immunology	☐ surgery
☐ congenital	☐ metabolism	☐ therapy
☐ diagnosis	☐ microbiology	☐ transmission
☐ diagnostic imaging	☐ mortality	☐ urine
☐ diet therapy	☐ nursing	☐ veterinary
☐ drug therapy	☐ organization and administration	☐ virology

☐ Restrict to MeSH Major Topic.
☐ Do not include MeSH terms found below this term in the MeSH hierarchy.

Tree Number(s): C18.452.394.750, C19.246
MeSH Unique ID: D003920

Figure 10.12. MeSH Subheadings.

Searching *PubMed*

The *PubMed* interface has an interesting array of searchable fields. The default is to search all fields. But users can also search various kinds of author fields, including corporate author (an agency or organization), personal author (by entering either first or last name), or a single author field that searches across all author instances. Various MeSH terms can be searched, including MeSH major topics, MeSH subheadings, and MeSH terms. You may want to try a twofold search strategy: (1) search *PubMed* by MeSH terms first; (2) search the same topic without using the MeSH fields. The reason for this is that newer items will not yet have MeSH headings assigned to them, and you would not retrieve these items by searching only MeSH headings. It is extremely crucial to understand this distinction so that you don't miss recent research on your topic.

PubMed has a way to search for articles that contain systematic reviews or meta-analyses. You cannot do this from the initial *PubMed* starting point (https://www.ncbi.nlm.nih.gov/pubmed). Instead, from the starting Web page, you need to click "Clinical Queries" under the *PubMed* "Tools" category. Or you can go directly to this page: https://www.ncbi.nlm.nih.gov/pubmed /clinical. This searches a subset of the *PubMed* database that contain clinical trials and systematic reviews. This is very useful if you are interested in these kinds of studies. Results displayed from searches initiated there are displayed in three columns: Clinical Study Categories, Systematic Reviews, and Medical Genetics.

Here is one more hint about searching in *PubMed*. We have all become accustomed to phrase searching, thanks to Google. We enclose a phrase in quotes, and Google will search for that precise phrase and return results.

This is especially useful when trying to search a full text for an exact quote. Phrase searching also works in *PubMed*, as you would expect it to. It finds the exact phrase as searched. But *PubMed* suggests that you might not want to do that very much, as it has a synonymy feature to help us out with medical terminology. For example, I searched ""kidney failure"" in *PubMed* (November 23, 2017) and retrieved 90,889 results. But if I search without the quotes, that is, just "kidney failure," I get 196,186 results. Any guesses as to what is going on here? PubMed is performing synonym mapping in the background. It finds results not just for kidney failure, but also for renal failure or any combination of the terms.

Search Example 1: Topic Search

Let's say you want to find research on Lyme disease in children. You want to capture the latest research, so for the moment, let's not search MeSH subject terms but do a general keyword search. You can start typing *Lyme*, and the interface suggests *Lyme disease*, exactly what you want. Note that these suggestions are not sanctioned by anyone, they are simply what other people have entered most often.

On the results page, *PubMed* does not, by default, show all the facets that are available. You need to make sure to enable them. For this search, be sure to enable the "Sex," "Subjects," and "Ages" facets, as shown in figure 10.13.

The search for Lyme disease retrieved over 12,000 results. To refine the results, you can select some facets to filter out the irrelevant items. Selecting the "Human" facet rules out the animals. If you wanted research from veterinary science journals on the kind of animals that transmit Lyme disease, you can deselect "Humans" and select "Other Animals" instead. Now that you have selected the "Humans" facet, you need to further restrict to children. The "Ages" facet that you just enabled allows you to select "Child: birth–18 years." This pulls my results down to just over 300.

Search Example 2: Field Code Searching

There are two ways to build up field searches in *PubMed*. One way is to use the advanced search interface and enter terms into various fields. This method is familiar to users of the EBSCOhost, Gale, or ProQuest interfaces. But another way to enter searches is to use field codes directly. Common field codes include the following:

All Fields [ALL]

Author [AU]

Corporate Author [CN]

Grant Number [GR]

ISBN [ISBN]

Journal [TA]

Language [LA]

MeSH Major Topic [MAJR]

MeSH Subheadings [SH]

MeSH Terms [MH]

PMID [PMID]

Text Words [TW]

Title [TI]

Title/Abstract [TIAB]

Using these field codes, you can piece together search statements even more quickly than using the pull-down menu items. Keep in mind that the default Boolean operator is AND (in other words, if you do nothing, AND

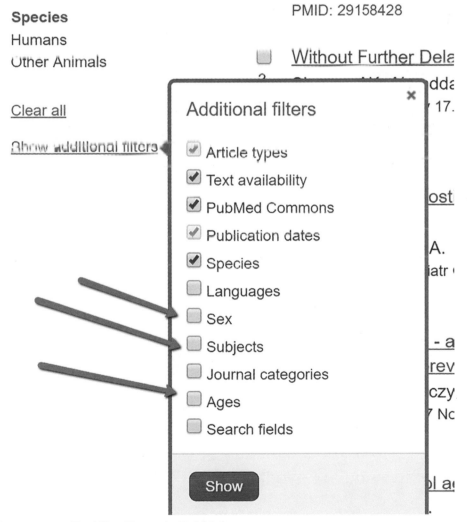

Figure 10.13. Enabling Facets in *PubMed*.

will be understood between search terms). Boolean operators, if used, must be capitalized.

With this in mind, let's assume for this search example that you want to find articles about prevention of burnout in nurses. You could frame a search like this:

nurs*[TI] AND burnout[TI] = 768 results

This retrieves information only from the title field. But you can make this search even better. Notice in the field list above that there is a field tag for "Title/Abstract." You might reframe your search like this:

nurs*[TIAB] AND burnout[TIAB] = 2085 results

Notice that by using a search tag that encompasses both title and abstract fields, you get more results. You may want to focus my search on the prevention aspect by amending the search as below:

nurs*[TIAB] AND burnout[TIAB] AND prevent*

Getting the Full Text

When libraries properly register with *PubMed*, the library's link resolver can be displayed within individual *PubMed* records. (To see these instructions, simply search Google for "PubMed linkout.") This is the most convenient way for users to retrieve full text. For example, the general link for *PubMed* is https://www.ncbi.nlm.nih.gov/pubmed, but the LinkOut link for the University of Denver Library is: http://www.ncbi.nlm.nih.gov/entrez /query.fcgi?otool=coudplib. After the registration is complete, users will be able to click the link, authenticate, and retrieve full text, if available (figure 10.14).

Figure 10.14. Library OpenURL Links Showing up in *PubMed*.

Table 10.3. Additional suggested databases in science, engineering, and medicine.

Discipline	Database (Vendor)
Chemistry	*PubChem* (free) (https://pubchem.ncbi.nlm.nih.gov) *ACS Publications* (American Chemical Society)
Physics	arXiv (free) (https://arxiv.org) NASA Astrophysics Data System (free) (http://ads.harvard.edu) NASA Technical Report Server (free) (https://www.sti.nasa.gov)
Science	*Science and Technology* (ProQuest)
Engineering	*SciTech Connect* (free) (https://www.osti.gov/scitech)
Medical	*Cumulative Index to Nursing and Allied Health Literature* *(CINAHL)* (EBSCO) *EMBASE* (Elsevier)
Biology	*BioMed Central* (free) (https://www.biomedcentral.com) *Biological Abstracts* (licensed from various vendors)

The other way to get full text is to search the title in Google Scholar. Just make sure that your Scholar library settings are properly set up for your local library. As the instructions for setting this up sometimes change over time, the best way to do this is to search Google like this: "google scholar library settings."

MedlinePlus and *PubMed Central*

If you find that *PubMed* results are too academic, difficult to understand, or that you do not have access rights to the full text, here are two suggestions. *MedlinePlus* (https://medlineplus.gov) is specifically designed for patients and their families. It functions like a reference portal for definitions, latest treatments, and drug information, and it contains many videos and illustrations. *PubMed Central* (https://www.ncbi.nlm.nih.gov/pmc) is a free full-text archive of biomedical and life science journal content. Users will not need a subscription because all articles are open access.

Other Science, Engineering, and Medical Databases

Table 10.3 gives suggestions of additional databases in the fields of science, engineering, and medicine.

Exercises

1. If you have access to *SciFinder*, look up the diabetes drug that goes under the commercial name, Glucophage. (Hint: Use the Substance Identifier.) What is the *CAS Registry* number for this drug? What

are some other names for this drug? Based on articles associated with this drug, which of these names is most often used in article titles?

2. Find an academic article of interest to you. Perhaps it is one you wrote yourself or one that you read for one of your classes. Using *Web of Science* or *Scopus*, whichever is available to you, find out how many times this article was cited and how many references are contained in the article.

3. Using your library's database list, see how many databases you can find that incorporate alternative metrics into their records. (Hint: Be sure to look for this feature only for scholarly articles.)

4. Using *PubMed*, find articles on heart failure in young adult women.

5. In *PubMed*, start typing "male pattern baldness" and see how many results you get. You have too many results, and you need to devise a strategy to get a more workable result set. What strategies do you recommend to get a more focused result set?

References

Adriaanse, Leslie S., and Chris Rensleigh. 2013. "*Web of Science*, *Scopus* and Google Scholar: A Content Comprehensiveness Comparison." *Electronic Library* 31, no. 6: 727–744.

Altmetric. 2017. "How Is the Altmetric Attention Score Calculated?" Accessed November 7, 2017. https://help.altmetric.com/support/solutions/articles/6000060969 -how-is-the-altmetric-score-calculated.

Bollen, Johan, Herbert Van de Sompel, Aric Hagberg, and Ryan Chute. 2009. "A Principal Component Analysis of 39 Scientific Impact Measures." *PloS One* 4, no. 6: e6022. https://doi.org/10.1371/journal.pone.0006022.

Clarivate Analytics. 2016. "The *Web of Science* Journal Selection Process." July 18. Accessed August 11, 2017. http://wokinfo.com/essays/journal-selection-process.

Fosmire, Michael. 2014. "Engineering Research." In *Research within the Disciplines: Foundations for Reference and Library Instruction*, edited by Peegy Keeran and Michael Levine-Clark, 2nd ed, 215–236. Lanham, MD: Rowman & Littlefield.

Gamble, Alyson. 2017. "*SciFinder*." CCAdvisor. http://www.ccadvisor.org/review /10.5260/CCA.199265.

Garfield, Eugene. 1964. "Science Citation Index: A New Dimension in Indexing." *Science* 144, no. 3619: 649–654.

Harzing, Anne-Wil, and Satu Alakangas. 2016. "Google Scholar, *Scopus* and the *Web of Science*: A Longitudinal and Cross-Disciplinary Comparison." *Scientometrics* 106, no. 2: 787–804.

Jacsó, Péter. 2010. "The Impact of Eugene Garfield through the Prism of *Web of Science*." *Annals of Library and Information Studies* 57, no. 3 (September): 222.

Moustafa, Khaled. 2015. "The Disaster of the Impact Factor." *Science and Engineering Ethics* 21, no. 1: 139–142.

National Library of Medicine. 2006. "Entrez Help." Updated May 31, 2016. https:// www.ncbi.nlm.nih.gov/books/NBK3837.

National Library of Medicine. 2016. "MeSH Tree Structures." Accessed July 7, 2017. https://www.nlm.nih.gov/mesh/intro_trees.html

Royal Academy of Engineering. 2014. "Thinking Like an Engineer: Implications for the Education System." Accessed October 26, 2017. http://www.raeng.org.uk /thinkinglikeanengineer.

Thelwall, Mike, and Ruth Fairclough. 2015. "Geometric Journal Impact Factors Correcting for Individual Highly Cited Articles." *Journal of Informetrics* 9, no. 2: 263–272.

Beyond the Textbook

Carrying on the tradition of the fourth edition, additional exercises, search tips, and tutorials will be available on the publisher's Web site at http://www.abc-clio.com/books.librariesunlimited.com/Librarians -Guide-to-Online-Searching. This will be updated periodically with the inevitable database changes.

11
Numerical and Statistical Databases

Numerical and statistical databases are more popular than ever, and they present challenges not found in textual databases. That's because they're all about numbers. The metadata is different, and the searching is different. But even more challenging is that we likely don't know the scope of these databases. What years are covered by the Census Bureau's *American Fact-Finder* database? Where do I search for airport statistics? Which database contains data on the number of people diagnosed with Alzheimer's disease? These are just some of the kinds of questions that come up.

Add to this the technology layer that is now possible: integrating mapping along with statistics. This is the ability to take data and geocode it to make meaningful map representations useful in social science research and public policy decision making.

Kinds of Numbers

It would be helpful to do a little brainstorming about numbers. First, let's discuss the kinds of numbers found in statistical and numerical databases. There are statistics that count people and households, including what their occupations are, how much money they make, how long it takes them to commute to work, their educational attainment, whether they have health care, their marital status, their disability status, their race and national origins, their poverty status, and their veteran status. Housing information, including number of bathrooms, building materials, energy efficiency, laundry facilities, and whether their residences have Internet access can be easily discovered. Business statistics include topics such as company assets and expenditures; characteristics of business owners (women-owned, minority owned, etc.); employment; labor costs; and sales. Statistics on every sector of the economy include agriculture statistics, such as how many acres have been planted for each crop type, how much water is used, and crop yield. Transportation statistics cover all modes of commercial and personal transportation, including freight shipments, highway traffic, shipping by sea, and air traffic at every airport. Economic statistics for countries cover national accounts, monetary exchange rates, balance of trade and direction of trade between countries, and national debt.

There are derived statistics, for example, when one number is divided into another to create an index. Examples of this would be the Human Development Index, the Gini coefficient (you can Google it!), the consumer price index, and the producer price index. Business and industry ratios fall into this category. Then there are the many business ratios, like quick ratio, current ratio, price/earnings ratio, and countless others—basically dividing one number into another number to derive benchmarks and points of comparison. Index numbers can be derived to show environmental well-being and to compare one country to other countries (as can be found in the World Development Indicators). If you can think it, it may well exist with some entity out there collecting the data and hopefully making the statistics available. That's not to say that it will be freely available or even reasonably priced. It's amazing how many statistical data sets are free, but this is not always the case. Sometimes statistics need to be purchased from companies who invested money in gathering them in the first place.

Who Collects Numbers?

Next, let's examine who is collecting statistics and numbers. This will offer clues as to where to look for specific types of information. When it comes to big number-gathering endeavors, like censuses, it is only the government that can afford to be comprehensive. Smaller entities, such as businesses or associations, have to do sampling of some form or another. Even governments do sampling because of the massive nature of information gathering that takes place. Sampling is not a bad thing; it's just that there will be a margin of error to consider when a sample number is projected to an entire larger population.

Some statistics are freely available, as those from the U.S. government generally are. Others are locked up in proprietary databases, often at great expense to access. Examples of licensed, proprietary databases that contain statistics are *OECD iLibrary*, *IBISWorld*, *Value Line*, and *Hoover's Online*.

Searching for Numbers as Opposed to Text

Searching for textual information is relatively simple. Just go to a search engine and type in your best guess for relevant keywords. But how do you search for numbers? You can't just search: *405,459* or *59%*. That makes no sense. Rather, you need to have indirect search strategies to be successful in your searching. In what I call a *direct search strategy*, you simply put keywords (or subject terms) into a search system of some sort (an online database like *Academic Search* or *ProQuest Central* or an Internet search engine like Google), and you retrieve results. However, some topics do not lend themselves to a direct search strategy; you must search indirectly. If you wanted to find exports of automobiles from Japan to Italy, for example, rather than doing a direct search, *Japan AND Italy AND automobiles AND exports*, you might do better with this indirect search strategy: *export AND database AND international trade*.

Basic Statistical Starting Strategies

Many librarians feel uneasy working on statistical questions. One reason might be that they don't get good results when attempting direct-style searches. Another common reason is that they get close to the desired answer, but they don't get down to exactly to what they, or their library patron, wants. For example, they may not have the correct geography. Very commonly, the geography they found is too general, maybe down to the state level, but they need statistics down to the zip code or census block level. Another reason some find statistics intimidating is that they don't go through the thought process of considering what agency or group would be interested enough in the type of statistics you're after to collect them. After having collected the data, how might they make that information available? Would they put it on the Web for free, or are they more likely to lock it in a fee-based database?

There are some tools that can make these questions less intimidating.

"Who Cares?" Tool 1: Google Web

That's right, Google Web. I purposely call it Google Web to distinguish it from Google Scholar and Google Books. Searching Google takes a bit of skill for statistical information. That's because you cannot usually search directly for the statistics, as the information is often contained in a database that is opaque to Google's indexing. First, try searching directly. You just might find what you are looking for. But if that doesn't work well, then try an indirect search strategy.

For example, let's say you are looking for the number of housing units in the 80210 zip code that are renter-occupied versus the number that are owner-occupied. Typing that question into Google will help a little bit. Actually, Google often provides direct statistics with links to source information. But in most cases, you will need an authoritative series of statistics. In these cases, you need to perform indirect Google searches. You might search Google for the renter-occupied question like this: *housing statistics*. Google suggests the U.S. Census Bureau and points to a helpful guide page with links to available datasets.

Tips for Searching Google for Statistics

1. Try to find the statistics by asking your statistical question in the Google search box. I call this the "go for the gold" approach. You just might get lucky and turn up the statistics right away.
2. Try an indirect search strategy. Search Google for terms like *statistics maritime interdictions* or a similar search: *data crimes at sea international*. Use your synonym skills to change up the terms you search by.
3. Try using Google advanced search techniques, such as domain-specific searching. Try searching like this: "site:un .org maritime statistics crime" or, again, "international data maritime interdictions site:org."
4. Use Google's "filetype" command to find statistics kept in database formats like Excel. Excel uses the file extensions .xls and .xlsx. You can try this Google search: "pet ownership statistics filetype:xls." As newer Excel files have the .xlsx extension, you can rerun the search with that alternation: "pet ownership statistics filetype:xlsx." Your results will likely be different.

"Who Cares?" Tool 2: *ProQuest Statistical Insight*

If *Statistical Insight* is available to you, it can be very useful for checking the question of "who cares?" from the viewpoint of traditional publications, especially those issued serially over time. The following description of its historical background explains what it contains and its value to us. (This is an example of why it is important to know the physical analog versions of a database). Before the database was with ProQuest, it was owned by LexisNexis, who had bought it from Congressional Information Service (CIS).

CIS issued this reference tool as three print indexes. The first was *American Statistics Index (ASI)*, which covered U.S. statistics. This index featured statistics issued in government publications, and it provided a valuable index to depository collections back when everything was in print. International and foreign statistics were the focus of the *Index to International Statistics (IIS)*. This index covered two categories: statistics emanating from international bodies, such as the United Nations, its organs, and other international bodies, and foreign governments, such as the governments of Germany, Japan, and so on. Their third statistical index, *Statistical Reference Index (SRI)*, covered statistics from sources outside the scope of *ASI* and *IIS*. The *SRI* portion was the most complex, as it covered six categories of statistical-issuing entities. Thinking of them in terms of their pneumonic associations may be a useful way to help remember all six (table 11.1).

When all else fails, this resource provides a helpful pathway. I don't often use *Statistical Insight* to find actual statistics, but I do use it to get a frame of reference and to inform me of "who cares" about the statistics I am looking for (that is, who publishes the statistics). Then I search for the statistics from the Web site of the issuing agency, as the *Statistical Insight* tables are likely too old for what I am looking for.

Table 11.1. Six Categories within the *Statistical Reference Index*.

Abbreviation	*Statistical Reference Index* Category
A	Associations
B	Business
C	Commercial publishers
R	Research institutes
S	State agencies
U	Universities

The six categories found in the *Statistical Reference Index* are still reflected in the database version, *ProQuest Statistical Insight*. The six categories of statistical-issuing agencies can guide you into doing focused Google searching. For example, associations can be a rich source of industry and trade statistics. *Statistical Insight* can provide you with the names of these associations, which is just the hook you need to search for relevant statistics on the Web. Sometimes these statistics are freely available; at other times, they are available only to members or for a fee. But it doesn't hurt to try. *Statistical Insight* itself may contain the association statistics, depending on the kind of subscription your library has. The same strategy should be used for the other five categories within the database.

"Who Cares?" Tool 3: *ProQuest Statistical Abstract of the United States*

Admittedly, this resource is focused primarily (but not exclusively) on U.S. statistics. If you have a foreign or international statistical question, you may want to go directly to "Who Cares" Tool 4. ProQuest has taken over publication of a resource that from 1878 through 2012 was published by the U.S. Census Bureau and was the bible for U.S. statistics. But they have also conveniently folded in all the previous years into the interface, providing cross-searching capability for all years. The ProQuest fee-based version follows the same principles of organization and citation as previous editions. Every table cites to the original table and how users can find more detailed information on the topic.

If you don't have access to the *ProQuest Statistical Abstract*, then you could consult the historic versions of *Stat Abs*, all of which are online through the Census Bureau (simply search Google for "statistical abstract of the united states," and you will see the Census Bureau Web site featuring online versions back to 1878). This strategy involves looking at older volumes of *Stat Abs* to see where the data came from. Every table in *Stat Abs* gives attribution to the source. More recent annual volumes will have URLs in them. The URLs may have changed since publication, but at least you will know the name of the issuing agency. This will give you a clue as to where to look for current data. If you need older statistics from the *Statistical Abstract*, a much better source than the annual version is the *Historical Statistics of the United States* (see below).

One of the greatest features of the old *Stat Abs*, and one which still exists in the ProQuest continuing version, is the inclusion on nongovernmental sources of statistics. For example, the table for summary characteristics of hospitals includes data provided by the American Hospital Association. The Investment Company Institute provides statistics on individual retirement accounts (IRAs). Data on credit card holders is provided by the *Nilson Report*, a respected newsletter of the industry.

"Who Cares?" Tool 4: Identifying the Players: National and International Agencies

National Agencies. There are over 100 U.S. federal agencies that issue data, and we just need a little help figuring out who they are. That's where *Fedstats* (https://fedstats.sites.usa.gov/agencies) can help. The site lists 13 principal statistical agencies, including the Bureau of Economic Analysis, Bureau of Justice Statistics, Bureau of Labor Statistics, and the Census Bureau. But it is the larger list of additional agencies that really assists searchers in getting to the right federal agency. These agencies include the Bureau of Prisons, the Drug Enforcement Administration, the FBI, the National Cancer Institute, and the United States Geological Survey, just to mention a few.

International Agencies. On the international side of things, the United Nations Statistics Division has a helpful site, similar to *Fedstats*, that lists statistical programs of the United Nations as well as other autonomous organizations (https://unstats.un.org/home/international_agencies). The U.S. Census Bureau comes to our aid when trying to locate foreign national statistics with their site (https://www.census.gov/population/international/links/stat_int.html). You can also just Google "united nations programmes agencies" to find out more about the many agencies that exist and may offer international statistics. The common go-to UN agencies that have statistics are the Food and Agriculture Organization (FAO); the International Labour Organization (ILO); the International Telecommunication Union (ITU); the United Nations Educational, Scientific and Cultural Organization (UNESCO); and the World Health Organization (WHO).

But the United Nations isn't the only international organization with statistics. You might also want to consider such entities as the African Development Bank, the Asian Development Bank, Caribbean Community (CARICOM), the European Development Bank, Eurostat (European Union), the International Energy Agency (IEA), the International Monetary Fund (IMF), the Inter-American Development Bank, the Organisation for Economic Co-operation and Development (OECD), the Organization of the Petroleum Exporting Countries (OPEC), the World Bank, and the World Trade Organization (WTO).

As there are over 3,000 international bodies, often referred to as international organizations (IGOs), be sure to search the freely available IGO search feature from the Union of International Organizations (http://www.uia.org/igosearch).

Foreign National Sources. The U.S. Census Bureau comes to your aid when trying to locate foreign national statistics with their site: https://www.census.gov/population/international/links/stat_int.html. Although it is usually a better use of time to get individual country information from one of the UN agencies (because foreign data differs so much from country to country), there are times when you need in-country statistics on the provincial, prefectural, or whatever a country calls is subdivisions level. Please see the section on foreign government publications to see how to search within the Internet top-level domains for each country of the world.

What is the difference between international statistics and foreign statistics? This is a good question and is often a source of great confusion.

International Statistics. By *international*, we mean more than one country, multinational, global, or worldwide. International statistics will be issued by the United Nations. But don't forget about the many subsidiary entities of the United Nations (https://unstats.un.org /home/international_agencies).

Foreign Statistics. Foreign statistics are issued by individual countries. Please see the section on foreign government publications to see how to search within the Internet top-level domains for each country of the world. Most countries have a statistical bureau or agency with publicly available data. Because foreign data differs so much from country to country, it is usually a better use of time to get individual country information from one of the UN agencies. But there are times, for example, when searching for subnational statistics (that is, statistics on the provincial, prefectural, or whatever a country calls is subdivisions level), that in-country statistics will help the most.

"Who Cares?" Tool 5: Do a Literature Search

If you are totally lost, try searching the scholarly literature in the field to see how other researchers approach the topic and what statistical sources they use. You can do this using general aggregator databases such as EBSCO's *Academic Search*, *ProQuest Central*, or Gale's *Academic OneFile*. Another approach is discipline-specific databases (see the relevant chapters within this book). And, finally, you can use Google Scholar.

Putting the Tools to Work

Example Search: Let's say that you want to find statistics on fisheries. You want all available statistics, from government statistics to commercial statistics.

Go to ProQuest *Statistical Insight* and type "fisheries" into the search box. When the results are returned, click the plus sign (+) next to the "Source" facet (figure 11.1).

⊟ Source

  ⊟ International Organizations

    All International Organizations (3,528)

    International Bank for Reconstruction and Development (United Nations: World Bank Group) (751)

    Thailand National Statistics Office (Thailand) (466)

    Statistics Bureau of Japan, Ministry of Internal Affairs and Communications (Japan) (250)

    All China Marketing Research (China, People's Republic) (233)

    Statistics Indonesia-BPS (Indonesia) (106)

    European Union (74)

    Peru National Institute of Statistics and Informatics (Peru) (72)

    Statistical Service of Cyprus (Cyprus) (72)

    Vietnam General Statistics Office (Vietnam) (72)

    Asian Development Bank (69)

  ⊞ Federal Agencies

  ⊞ Commercial Publishers

  ⊞ State Agencies

  ⊞ Associations

  ⊞ Research Organizations

  ⊞ Universities

⊞ Countries & Regions

⊞ Local Area

Figure 11.1. *Statistical Insight* Facets Showing International Agencies for the Search "Fisheries". *Source:* The screenshots and their contents are published with permission of ProQuest LLC. Further reproduction is prohibited without permission.

This will give you the categories that harken back to the origins of this tool, because you get results from international organizations (IIS), federal agencies (ASI), and five of the six categories from SRI (see table 11.2 below). Further drilling down produces copies of the actual documents (if your institution subscribes to this content). You can then search for more current statistics, or you can use the tables within *Statistical Insight*, if they meet your needs.

From your fisheries search in *Statistical Insight*, you see the following organizations that issue statistics:

    International Organizations

      World Bank

      Thailand National Statistics Office

      Statistics Bureau of Japan

      All China Marketing Research

      Statistics Indonesia

      European Union

      And others

    U.S. Federal Agencies

      National Marine Fisheries Service

      Office of management and Budget

      Foreign Agricultural Service

      Department of Agriculture

      Bureau of Census

      And others

Table 11.2. *Statistical Insight* Examples of Agencies in SRI with Statistics Related to the Search "Fisheries".

Statistical Insight Facet	Entity with Fishery Statistics
Commercial publishers	ProQuest
	Bernan Associates
	Commodity Research Bureau
State agencies	Hawaii Dept. of Business, Economic Development, and Tourism
	Alaska Dept. of Labor and Workforce Development
	Florida Dept. of Agriculture and Consumer Services
Associations	Council of Better Business Bureaus
	National Association of State Budget Officers
	Foreign Policy Association
	Regional Airline Association
Research organizations	Center for American Progress
Universities	University of Florida: Bureau of Economic and Business Research

Statistical Insight also has listings for data from commercial publishers, state agencies, associations, research organizations, and universities (as denoted in table 11.2).

Whereas *Statistical Insight* will give you more of the viewpoint of traditional publications, especially those issued serially over time, you might also try using Google to locate fishery statistics. First, you need to locate the entities (organizations, governments, associations) that would likely issue such statistics. To do that, start by searching Google for "fisheries statistics." Looking over these initial search results, you'll see that the interested statistical-issuing organizations include the United Nations Food and Agriculture Organization (fao.org), the U.S. National Oceanic and Atmospheric Administration (noaa.gov), the European Commission (europa.eu), and the Organisation for Economic Co-operation and Development (oecd.org). There are likely other entities as well.

We would want to structure domain-specific Google searches like this:

site:fao.org fisheries statistics

site:noaa.gov fisheries statistics

site:europa.eu fisheries statistics

site:oecd.org fisheries statistics

You should also look up country-specific information, first by finding the top-level domains (TLDs) for relevant countries, finding government subdomains, and then doing site-specific searching. Using the *Wikipedia* page for TLDs   (https://en.wikipedia.org/wiki/List_of_Internet_top-level_domains), you note that the domains of several relevant countries for which fishing is important, the Philippines (.ph), Norway (.no), and Japan (.jp), to get started.

Searching Google for "site:ph government," you discover that gov.ph is the government domain for the Philippines. For Norway, it appears to be dep. no. And Japan is go.jp. There is no uniformity of second-level government domains across countries. It takes a bit of persistence to discover these. You are now prepared to set up searches like this:

site:gov.ph fisheries statistics

site:dep.no fisheries statistics

site:go.jp fisheries statistics

For more insights about searching freely available statistics using Google, I recommend my book about Google searching, *Harnessing the Power of Google: What Every Researcher Should Know* (Brown 2017).

Diving into Statistical Databases

We don't have the luxury within the confines of this text of introducing you to every sophisticated statistical database on the market in addition to the free resources out there. Rather than doing that, let's recall the principles of how to approach learning new databases and their features:

- Determine the database scope. If you don't know the scope, you don't know how to dive in. What data is included? How was the data collected? What are the dates of coverage?

- What is this database all about? Is it about people, companies, countries, cities?

- Who collects the data? What are their methods?

- What are the geographies?

- What are the dates?

- How is the data collected?

With these background considerations in mind, let's dive in to several databases.

Example Search 1: Let's try to find the difference in the cost of living between Denver and San Francisco. We might start by using Google: "cost of living database." We see some nongovernmental databases, but to get authoritative data, let's restrict results to the .gov domain: *cost of living database site:gov*. We see the result for Consumer Price Index from the Bureau of Labor Statistics, and we go there. After poking around in the various CPI databases, we find what we want in the "Average Price Data" section. Although the CPI is not exactly the same as cost of living, it is a close approximation.

Example Search 2: We want to find which cities in Colorado have the highest violent crime rate. There are many possible ways to search for a good database, but we start by searching Google like this: "violent crime database site:gov." We find the *Uniform Crime Reporting Statistics Database* from the FBI here: https://www.ucrdatatool.gov. Looking at the choices in the left margin, it seems that the best selection for this question is "local law enforcement agencies (city and county) – multiple agencies, one variable." We then select all agencies in Colorado and select our one variable, *violent crime rate*, and quickly retrieve a table with crime rates for 57 Colorado agencies from 1985 to the present.

These examples show how you can search for data without having any idea ahead of time what agency is going to have the data you need. Of course, it isn't always so easy. There are times you will need to send an e-mail to a mail distribution list or to ask a statistics librarian about the best data source.

American FactFinder

Now that we have discussed searching generally for statistics, let's look at some specific databases that will assist you for U.S.-based statistics. *American FactFinder* (AFF) is the Census Bureau's primary statistical presentation database. It has several features for the novice user, such as Community Facts and Guided Search. I encourage you to try these features out, but you are seeking to become an expert searcher, right? So, the exercises from AFF in this chapter will encourage you to use the "Advanced Search" features.

To introduce you to AFF, you need to know a bit of Census Bureau background. The decennial census goes all the way back to the U.S. Constitution (Article 1, Section 2), which requires a count every 10 years for congressional apportionment. Thus, the first census was in 1790, and it has occurred every 10 years thereafter.

As you might imagine, the questions asked over the years have changed and evolved: for example, the census no longer collects statistics on slaves, as it did in the early censuses. This means that some longitudinal studies need to consider how to reflect numbers over time. There is a resource that has already done this for you: *Historical Statistics of the United States: Colonial Times to 1970*. That resource is discussed in a later section.

Not only does the Census Bureau collect and disseminate what is now known as the Decennial Census of Population and Housing, it also does so for business and commerce. Known as the Economic Census, the data are collected based on a classification system. The original classification system, the Standard Industrial Classification (SIC), is a hierarchical system first arranged by major divisions, such as agriculture, mining, construction, manufacturing, and so on. Under that are major divisions with 2-digit codes, and under that are individual industries with their four-digit codes (https://www.osha.gov/pls/imis/sic_manual.html). This system prevailed from 1937 until it was replaced by the North American Industry Classification (NAICS) system in 1997.

The only reason for introducing the history lesson here is that SIC didn't totally die. As you may have already discovered in chapter 2, "How Databases Work," many databases still use SIC as a searchable field, even though that system has been dead for over 20 years. Examples of databases that still use SIC codes include *ReferenceUSA*, *Standard & Poor's NetAdvantage*, *Hoover's*

Online, and *First Research* from Mergent. The economic census data looks very different from decennial census data, as you would guess. The focus is on business type, number of employees, and revenue.

Another thing you need to know is that the decennial census is taken every 10 years (on the 0 years), and the economic census is taken every 5 years (on the years ending in 2 and 7). The *American FactFinder* system contains data from the last two decennial censuses as well as the last two economic censuses. In addition to this, AFF contains data from the American Community Survey (ACS). The ACS is important to researchers because most people don't like to wait 10 years for data to be produced from the decennial census. The ACS is a "rolling" census in that it is being taken continuously. It replaces the "short form" and "long form" system used in past decennial censuses, where more detailed questions were asked of a sampling of the population (via a longer form) and then statistically imputed to the entire population. Complete explanations and documentation can be found on the Census Bureau Web site, but to cut to the chase, when looking for the most granular and current data, use the ACS five-year data over the one-year or three-year data sets.

Population estimates and population projections are available from the Census Web site as well. Every state has a demography unit that provides estimates to the Census Bureau for counties and places. This is useful in the years between population censuses and can be a valuable resource. In most cases, you can Google "xx state demography" (where xx is a state name) and find each state's demography agency.

Just as the ACS is the way to keep up to date with population and housing statistics, there are ways to get data for intervening years of the economic census. *Annual Survey of Entrepreneurs*, *Annual Survey of Manufactures*, *Survey of Business Owners*, *County Business Patterns*, and *Zip Code Business Patterns* are some of the annual data that can be accessed via AFF.

Let's jump right in to searching AFF with some examples. I recommend that power users (that's you!) always use the advanced search mode of AFF. You get all the options available to you that way.

Search Example 1: Using the 2016 American Community Survey 5-year estimates for Wichita, Kansas, what is the number of the population 65 years and over with no health insurance?

First go to the AFF Web site at https://factfinder.census.gov. Then select "Advanced Search." Now you are ready to begin constructing your query.

It often doesn't matter the order you begin constructing your query with, but as the AFF site only includes data sets that meet the criteria you have selected, it's often best to start by selecting geography, in this case, Wichita. Cities, towns, and villages are all considered "places" in census terminology, so begin by clicking the "Geography" tab on the left and select your geography type; in this case, you will select State→Place. Next, select Kansas as your state, then add Wichita city, Kansas, to your selections. When you have done this correctly, you will see your selections displayed in the upper left corner of your browser screen. Having finished adding geographies, you can close this modal dialog box. If you desired to add other geographies for comparison, you could do that as well (see figure 11.2).

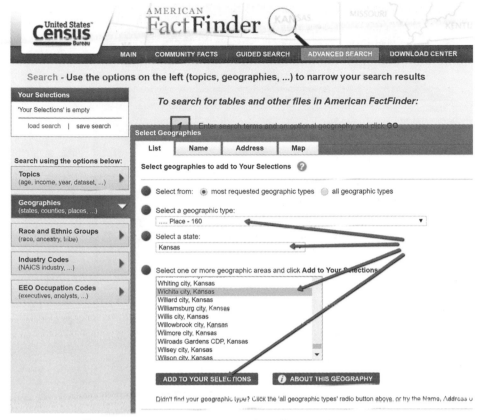

Figure 11.2. Selecting Geographies in *American FactFinder*.

As the example question is asking for data from a specific Census program, let's eliminate all other program data sets and only include data sets from the ACS 5-year estimates. To do this, under "Topics," select the dataset selection. Now, select "2016 ACS 5-year estimates" (figure 11.3). The reason it says "estimates" is that the data is based on a sampling of the population, not like the decennial censuses that attempt to be as close as possible to gathering data from 100 percent of the population. They sacrifice statistical accuracy to gain currency of data.

You can now collapse the dataset selection and expand "People." You will see among the choices there "Insurance Coverage." You only have one choice here, so go ahead and select "Health Insurance" (see figure 11.4).

You can now close your dialog box, and you see a couple dozen tables that meet all the criteria in the upper lefthand corner of the screen. You can immediately rule out all the tables beginning with "Imputation of . . .," as these are matters of importance to statisticians. You want to focus on the most relevant table to answer our question, and that would be "Health Insurance Coverage Status by Sex by Age." Now you can see the answer—at least the parts you need to add together. Pay close attention to the display of information. Males and females are broken out separately, and the ages are as well.

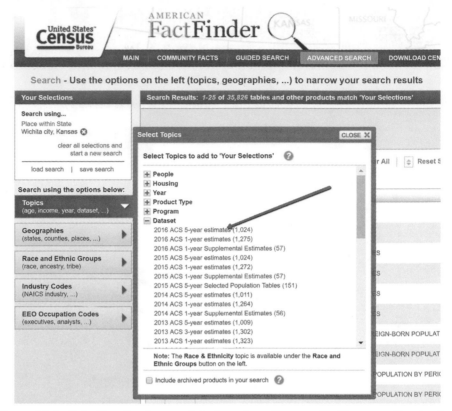

Figure 11.3. Selecting the Appropriate American Community Survey estimates in *American FactFinder.*

Males 65–74	90
Males 75 and over	34
Females 65–74	206
Females 75 and over	19
Total	**349**

Notice that it is easy to view data for previous years from within the result screen.

Search Example 2: You just bought a beachfront rental property in Wilmington, North Carolina, and you are not sure what to charge for rent. Using the 2016 ACS 5-year estimates, which cash rent range has the highest number of renter-occupied units?

Let's go again to the AFF Web site at https://factfinder.census.gov and select "Advanced Search." Select your geography by going to State→Place, selecting North Carolina, and then Wilmington City. Now click as follows: Topics→Housing→Financial Characteristic→Gross Rent. From here you see several possibilities from the ACS 2016 5-year estimates. Clicking on "Gross Rent" from the 2016 5-year database gives you a table, and you can clearly

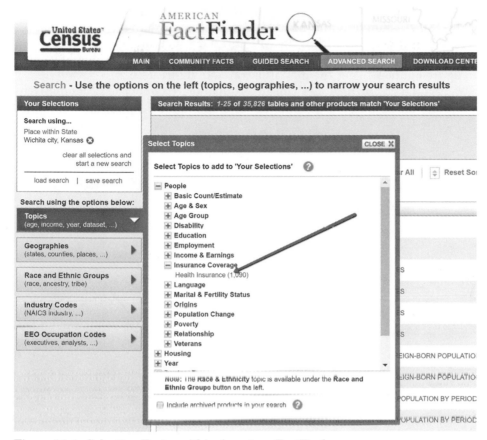

Figure 11.4. Selecting Topics within *American FactFinder.*

see that the rent range with the highest number in the category is $1,000–$1,249 with 4,984 instances. You might also want to select the table that says "Median Gross Rent by Bedrooms" from the 2016 ACS 5-year estimate. This gives you rent ranges by number of bedrooms.

Search Example 3: For your community block development grant, use the 2016 ACS 5-year estimates to identify those Wisconsin counties or county equivalents whose population aged 85 years and over is at or above 3.5 percent.

Go to Topics→Product Type→Geography Comparison Table. When you get to that page, in the "Refine your search results" box at the top of the page, type "Wisconsin" into the box for state, county, or place and then hit "go." Going to the second page of results, you will see a table from the 2016 5-years estimates labeled "Percent of the total population who are 85 years and over – State – County / County Equivalent" (figure 11.5). That's the one you want.

You can now see a row for each of Wisconsin's 72 counties as well as a total percent for the state as a whole. There are three counties where the population aged 85+ is 8.5 percent or greater: Iron County, Door County, and Price County. Note: If you had selected the table with the same title, but from the ACS 1-year estimates, you would only see 23 counties. That's because the sampling is not done all at the same time, but incrementally over several years. Now you understand why we often prefer to use the 5-year estimates.

It is also possible within the AFF interface to create a map to illustrate the data. Now that you already have this Wisconsin data, you should be able to figure out how to get the map illustrated in figure 11.6.

Search Example 4: Let's do an example search from the Economic Census this time. In completing your beauty salon business plan, you need to use

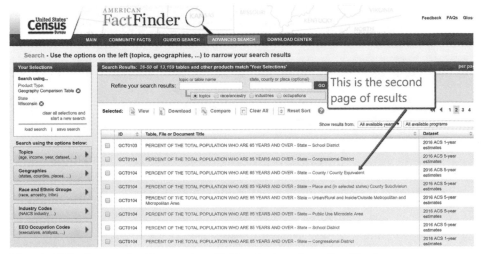

Figure 11.5. Geography Comparison Tables in *American FactFinder*.

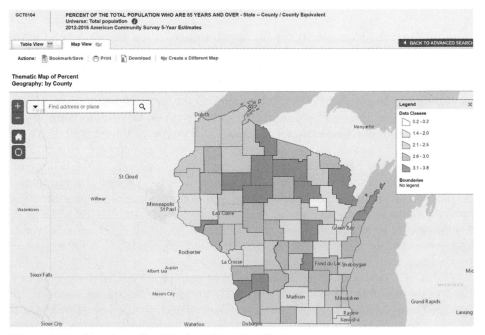

Figure 11.6. *American FactFinder*'s Mapping Feature.

the 2012 Economic Census to document the number of beauty salons already located in Covington city, Washington. What is that number of establishments?

To do this search, you need to look up the NAICS code for beauty salons. That's easy because it is also on the Census Bureau Web site. You can go to the Census home page (census.gov) and type NAICS into the search box. After you arrive at the NAICS Web site, enter "beauty salons" into the keyword search box for the 2017 NAICS search. You will see that the code needed is 812112. Back in AFF, start in Advanced Search, then Topics→Dataset→2012 Economic Census. In the "Refine your results" box for geography, type "Covington city, Washington," and hit "go." Then in the "Refine your search results" box for topic, type the NAICS number, 812112. You should now see a table that tells you there are 11 beauty salons in Covington city, Washington. The economic census provides a snapshot of business every five years, but for more up-to-date information, the *County Business Patterns* data can be accessed through the AFF interface as well.

There is so much more that AFF can do, including mapping of results. To find out about all these features, I encourage you to look for the help button within AFF. Another strategy is to search the Web for "american factfinder tutorial." You will see a lot of videos and library guides that show other features of AFF.

One of the biggest shortcomings of AFF is that it is not an archival resource. In libraries, we are accustomed to keeping materials forever, and we expect that our databases will do the same. But the Census Bureau doesn't see it that way. Although they do provide downloadable data files to the 1990 Census, they no longer provide access to it through their searchable interface. And that's when we need to rely on third-party vendors to fill that gap. That's where *Social Explorer* comes in.

Social Explorer

Social Explorer, now owned by Oxford University Press, not only has the 1990 Census, which cannot presently be searched via AFF, but they have data going back to the first census in 1790. You search Census data through an interface that mimics the original (and very popular) version I of AFF, and you can also create maps to tell a census story. Although the full economic census is not accessible through *Social Explorer*, *County Business Patterns* and *Zip Code Business Patterns* are. In addition, there are many other data series from the U.S. government (data on health, cancer, and crime) as well as often requested religion data with numbers of religious adherents and congregation size. Non-U.S. data includes the U.K. Census, Canadian Census, and World Development Indicators. Table 11.3 provides a more complete listing of data available through the tables in *Social Explorer*.

There are two ways to retrieve data: using the tables view or the maps view. Not all data is viewable through maps, however.

As an example of the power of map visualization, you can see how "gentrification" around the Coors Field baseball park in Denver has brought in wealthier households. Figure 11.7 compares households with incomes of over $75,000 in 2000 with households in 2015.

Table 11.3. Selected Statistical Series Available through *Social Explorer* Tables.

Program	Description
U.S. Decennial Censuses	1790 to latest
American Community Surveys	5-year, 3-year, and 1-year estimates from the beginning (2005) until present
U.S. Decennial Censuses on 2010 Geographies	The 1990, 1980, and 1970 censuses on 2010 geographies provide a powerful visual comparison tool.
U.S. Population Estimates	2010 to present
U.S. Business Patterns	County business patterns; zip code business patterns; nonemployer statistics (recent).
U.S. Religion Data (RCMS)	Not government statistics, but collected by the Religious Congregations and Membership Study. Congregational membership data for 1980, 1990, 2000, and 2010.
U.S. Crime Data (UCR)	Uniform Crime Reporting Program by county annually from 2010.
U.S. Crime Data (FBI)	Additional crime data from 2010.
U.S. Health Data	Collected by the County Health Rankings & Roadmaps program annually from 2010.
U.S. Religion Data (InfoGroup)	
Canadian Census	2011
United Kingdom Census	2011
European Statistics Data	1990, 2000, 2010, 2011, 2012, 2013, 2014, etc.
World Development Indicators	1960, 1970, 1980, 1990, 2000, 2010, 2013, 2014, 2015, etc.

Historical Statistics of the United States

The Government Printing Office (years before it became the Government Publishing Office) published an important statistical work that tabulated and normalized statistics from the United States over time. The original *Historical Statistics of the United States* is available online via the Census Bureau Web site (U.S. Census Bureau 1975). But the Census version is static PDFs that represent the print version. More recently, Cambridge University Press has taken this project to new levels by making the project into a dynamic, online database. While incorporating the original data, Cambridge adds to the data with up-to-date statistical tables that are downloadable in multiple usable formats.

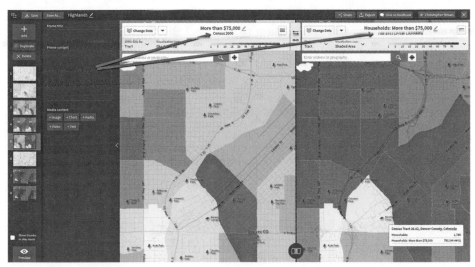

Figure 11.7. *Social Explorer* Side-by-Side Map Comparison. *Source:* ©Oxford University Press (http://www.oup.com). Used with permission.

Census statistics, vital statistics, and economic statistics from various government agencies, previously published in sources such as the annual *Statistical Abstract of the United States*, Vital Statistics, and others are tabulated with a time series view.

Search Example: *Life Expectancy.* After first browsing and not getting very far, I searched "life expectancy." There is a mixture of tables and essays in the results, so clicking the "tables" check box in the left margin eliminates essays and only displays tables. I still didn't find what I was looking for. So, I took out the word *expectancy* and just searched for *life*. This showed me two tables that were titled "Expectation of life," a title I was not expecting. In fact, each of these four tables contained statistics potentially relevant to the question:

Expectation of life at specified ages, by sex and race: 1850–1998

Life table l(x) values at selected ages, by sex and race: 1850–1997

Fertility and mortality, by race: 1800–2000

Expectation of life at birth, by sex and race: 1850–1998

Statista

Largely a business database and rather new on the scene, *Statista* (the company headquartered in Germany) provides some stunning results in terms of business statistics, population and consumer statistics, and infographics. The emphasis on browsing for data encourages discovery beyond the ubiquitous empty search box that so often perplexes searchers with the common "how do I search?" question.

Statista has an option to prioritize results by location. If you are researching a topic relevant to Europe, then turning off this feature is desirable.

Statista aggregates sources from government, commerce, and industry to provide trends and forecasts, marketing data, industry reports, and infographics. It is a goldmine for answering those difficult questions from business students. Examples of tables included in the database are Major League Baseball total attendance at regular season games; flavors of chewing gum/bubble gum used in the United States; hospitals, clinics, and medical centers advertising spending in the United States; U.S. smokers switching to e-cigarettes; number of libraries in the United States, by type of library; and most popular limited-service hamburger restaurants in the United States.

Additional Statistical Mapping Databases

We have just begun to scratch the surface in terms of databases that can map data. Think of how useful this feature could be for public policy classes: finding food deserts in large urban areas, determining areas with cost-burdened homeowners down to the census tract level, being able to see which school districts have the best pupil-to-teacher ratios, or seeing violent crime rates visually across a state. Imagine how mapping these factors could help in developing a research paper or a grant proposal.

Business applications also abound. Determining income level within residential areas can help with identifying business locations or targeted mailings. Unlike *American FactFinder*, which only has government-gathered data, these third-party systems incorporate commercially-gathered data in addition to the freely available government data. Being able to visually integrate these multiple data sources provides a powerful communication tool.

PolicyMap

When I was first introduced to *PolicyMap*, we had it as a trial database at my university. I saw that I had an upcoming reference consultation on the topic of *food desserts*. I was perplexed as to why someone needed help with this kind of delicious research, but I was all prepared for the meeting. When the student told me the topic was *food deserts*, that caught me off guard. That is a totally different concept. It turns out that *PolicyMap* actually has a feature where limited supermarket access (LSA) areas can be mapped along with whatever other variable you want to add in, such as household income. The student was thrilled with the mapping result, and I was left hungry for some dessert.

SimplyAnalytics

SimplyAnalytics lets you map out business locations. For example, you can find the location of all Starbucks coffee shops and which areas have the highest concentration. Or put 812310 (the NAICS code for coin-operated laundries and drycleaners) into the search box and find which areas don't have them nearby. *SimplyAnalytics* has business components that are not present in *PolicyMap*.

UNdata

The United Nations is a huge series of complex organizations, many of which issue their own statistics. Many of these statistical divisions have had their statistics aggregated on the Web site data.un.org:

Food and Agriculture Organization (FAO)

International Labour Organization (ILO)

International Monetary Fund (IMF)

International Telecommunications Union (ITU)

United Nations Children's Fund (UNICEF)

United Nations Development Programme (UNDP)

United Nations Framework Convention on Climate Change (UNFCCC)

United Nations Industrial Development Organization (UNIDO)

United Nations Office on Drugs and Crime (UNODC)

United Nations Population Division (UNPD)

United Nations Statistics Division (UNSD)

World Health Organization (WHO)

World Meteorological Organization (WMO)

World Tourism Organization (UNWTO)

Because the data have been normalized to fit into the aggregated portal, it is often easier to download data from this site than from the original issuing agency.

UN Comtrade Database

Trade statistics are often requested by students studying business and international relations. Although it is easy to find such statistics when the United States is one of the trading countries (import or export), finding these trade statistics by country and by commodity when the United States was not a party has traditionally been a challenge. But the *UN Comtrade* database nicely fills this gap. It is available at https://comtrade.un.org/data. There is a bit of a learning curve, but here is a quick guide to navigating this valuable database.

Step 1: Select type of product and frequency, goods (things, materials), or services. As you select, the subsequent options change. Most users will likely want to select "goods" (things like imported and exported automobiles, wheat, etc.). If you select "services," the only choice for "frequency" is "annual." But if you select "goods" (the default selection), you can choose "annual" or "monthly." Most users will likely want annual data.

Step 2: Select the desired classification system. The classification system is the standards used to slice and dice the information. If you select "services," things are easier, as there is only one classification system available: EBOPS 2002. This stands for the *extended balance of payments classification system*, last updated in 2002. The 2002 is just a reference to the classification schedule update, not the data itself. If you select "goods" in step 1, then things seem confusing and overwhelming. You see three available classification systems: HS, the Harmonized System; SITC, the Standard Industrial Trade Classification; and BEC, Broad Economic Categories.

A rather clear explanation of the HS and SITC systems can be found here: http://legacy.intracen.org/mas/sitchs.htm. BEC stands for Broad Economic Categories classification, and a full explanation can be found here: http://ec.europa.eu/eurostat/ramon/other_documents/bec/BEC_Rev_4.pdf.

After reading all this documentation, you hopefully realize that you can't go wrong with either one. Maybe just accept the default HS selection and keep the "as reported" button selected. That way you will get the most available data.

Step 3: Select the desired data. Just type in the years for which you want data (as far back as 1962). The "Reporters" and "Partners" selection initially seems confusing. *Reporters* simply means the country reporting the data, and it is the reporting country from which the direction of trade derives its meaning—imports to the reporting country and exports from the reporting country. "Partner" is the other country—the trading partner.

Trade flows includes imports and exports as well as re-imports and re-exports. Re-imports are goods imported into the same country as previously exported; re-exports are goods imported into the same country as previously imported. But these statistics are also included in the overall import and export statistics. So, unless you need extra granularity, maybe it is best to just ignore this level of analysis.

In the last box under step 3, the commodity codes, all you need to do is to start typing and the system suggestively brings up available possibilities. For example, I want to find import and export data for cars, and I start typing "automobiles," thinking that this would be the term used. It is not—no results. So, then I start typing "cars." I see that this term works: "8703 – Motor cars and other motor vehicles; principally designed for the transport of persons." This is not so difficult after all! It will take a bit of playing around to get this to work for you, but you will be amazed at how well this database works and the amount of data freely available.

If this advanced search seems too overwhelming, you can use this shortcut query form: https://comtrade.un.org/db. You can also access selected sections of the data through the UNdata Web site (data.un.org).

Additional Statistical Databases, Fee and Free

It is not possible to list every open source or licensed statistical database in this chapter. What you see in table 11.4 is a brief list to showcase the great variety of databases available to the online searcher.

Table 11.4. Selected Free and Fee Statistical Databases.

Free Statistical Databases	
Eurostat – European Statistics	http://ec.europa.eu/eurostat/data/database
National Bureau of Statistics China	http://www.stats.gov.cn/english
OECD Data (tools for comparison and visualization)	https://data.oecd.org
OECD Statistics (data tables)	http://stats.oecd.org
Office of National Statistics (Great Britain)	https://www.ons.gov.uk
Statistics Canada	https://www.statcan.gc.ca/eng/start
U.S. Bureau of Economic Analysis	https://www.bea.gov
U.S. Bureau of Justice Statistics	https://www.bjs.gov
U.S. Bureau of Labor Statistics	https://www.bls.gov/data
U.S. Bureau of Transportation Statistics	https://www.bts.gov/browse-statistical-products -and-data
U.S. *CIA World Factbook*	http://purl.access.gpo.gov/GPO/LPS552
U.S. National Agricultural Statistics Service	https://www.nass.usda.gov
United Nations Development Programme, Human Development Data	http://hdr.undp.org/en/data
United Nations Statistical Databases	https://unstats.un.org/unsd/databases.htm
World Health Organization Statistical Information System (WHOSIS)	http://www.who.int/whosis/en
Fee Statistical Databases	
Cross-National Time-Series Data Archive	Over 200 years of annual data from over 200 countries with 196 variables. https://www .cntsdata.com
Data-Planet	Claims to be "the largest repository of standardized and structured statistical data."
Euromonitor Passport GMID (Global Market Information Database)	Covers the entire world, not only Europe. Covers over 350 markets and over 200 countries.
Hoover's Online	Industry and company statistics, including selected private companies.
IBISWorld	Market intelligence data.

(Continued)

Table 11.4. (*Continued*)

Free Statistical Databases	
ICPSR (Inter-University Consortium for Political and Social Research)	Uploaded data from scholars in social science and political science. Data from many print data resources are available in digital format through ICPSR.
OECD iLibrary	Different presentation from the free content from OECD above.
SAGE Stats	Statistical data gathered from over 400,000 government and nongovernment datasets searchable in a single interface.
Value Line	Public company and industry data and analysis.

Big Data

Universities and their libraries are in a big rush to provide archival and accessible storage for their universities' intellectual output, including big data sets being produced by researchers. Partly to comply with grant funding, these repositories contain all kinds of data.

One of the more popular big data subscription resources is ICPSR—the Inter-University Consortium for Political and Social Research, based in Ann Arbor, Michigan. Researchers have posted past projects into the repository, and it has become a valuable resource for reusing data, in compliance with usage restrictions, of course.

Many of the print data publications of past years have been digitized and made available through ICPSR. For example, nearly all U.S. Census publications that were originally issued in print volumes are now available in digital formats. Other examples of useful categories include election results from all over the world, historic crime statistics, characteristics of school students, cost-of-living indexes, lifespan data, land value data, household surveys, public library data, and salary data. The emphasis is data sets in political and social sciences, not the hard sciences.

Most of the data in ICPSR is not readily viewable in tables or graphs. Unlike such statistical products as *ProQuest Statistical Insight*, *Statistical Abstract of the United States*, or *American FactFinder*, these are raw data sets. They are often available in multiple formats, such as SAS, Stata, and SPSS, and also sometimes as ASCII text or Excel. But the Excel files will require use of a codebook and are not easily read and interpreted without a lot of work. Although many universities have statistical labs with these software packages installed on workstations, individual users would need to purchase these software packages and learn how to use them.

On the federal government level, there is data.gov, the U.S. government's open data initiative. As of mid-2017, there are nearly 200,000 data sets in the fields of agriculture, climate, consumer, ecosystems, education, energy, finance, health, local government, manufacturing, maritime, ocean, public safety, and science and research.

Finding Big Data Sets on the Internet

You can use Google to find large data sets. At first, try searching like this (assuming you want to find data on fracking):

datasets fracking
data sets fracking
data sources fracking

If you want government data on the topic, you might try restricting a Google search to the .gov domain or to the relevant state domain. This tells Google to only give you results from a particular domain and not just any Internet resource. Please note that *site:* is a very particular syntax; *site* must be lowercase, and there must be no space after the colon.

site:gov data sources fracking
data fracking oil gas site:gov

If you were interested in finding big data for the state of Colorado, you would search using both the official Colorado Internet domain of colorado.gov and the original domain of state.co.us:

data fracking oil gas site:colorado.gov
site:state.co.us data fracking oil gas

Most states have multiple Internet domains that contain information not on the other domains. For example, in Colorado, the front-facing server is Colorado.gov. But there is a back server that contains many important documents at state.co.us. Nearly all states have a similar situation, and searchers must know what each of these server domains are and search them to get complete results. The same patterns hold true for county and municipal governments in the United States.

For more about searching state and local domains, see chapter 4 of *Harnessing the Power of Google: What Every Researcher Should Know* (Brown 2017).

And don't forget to search data.gov as well.

Exercises

1. Using *American FactFinder*, do a little research on the zip code where you live. What is the most surprising thing AFF turned up that you hadn't known before? You can explore first languages spoken at home, travel time to work, education attainment, or any area that interests you.

2. Using *American Factfinder*, find how many black or African American–owned businesses there are in the metropolitan statistical area (MSA) that contains Indianapolis, Indiana. (Hint: Topics→Business

and Industry→Business Owner; Use Add/Remove Geographies to limit to a specific MSA.)

3. You want to compare the number of passengers flying out of Chicago's O'Hare Airport with the number of passengers flying out of Chicago's Midway Airport for the most recent available year. You want to find the rankings of these two airports compared with other airports in terms of passenger traffic. You also want to do a time study of the past 10 years of data. (Hint: There are two federal agencies that collect this data, but they do not have the data presented in the same manner; the numbers are slightly different.)

4. You want to do some research on credit card complaints. (Hint: Start with *Fedstats* to identify relevant federal agencies.)

   a. Try to solve this with statistics from federal agencies.

   b. Try to get specific complaints from federal agencies.

   c. Try to download a large data set about this topic.

5. Using the Google search skills noted in this chapter, find a database that provides data on acres of wheat planted, by county, in the state of Illinois.

References

Brown, Christopher C. 2017. *Harnessing the Power of Google: What Every Researcher Should Know.* Santa Barbara, CA: Libraries Unlimited.

U S. Census Bureau. 1975. *Historical Statistics of the United States: Colonial Times to 1970.* Bicentennial edition. Accessed August 10, 2017. https://www.census.gov/library/publications/1975/compendia/hist_stats_colonial-1970.html.

Beyond the Textbook

Carrying on the tradition of the fourth edition, additional exercises, search tips, and tutorials will be available on the publisher's Web site at http://www.abc-clio.com/books.librariesunlimited.com/Librarians-Guide-to-Online-Searching. This will be updated periodically with the inevitable database changes.

12

From Bibliographic Databases to Full-Text E-Books

Much of this book has been focused on databases of articles, such as journal articles and newspaper articles (commonly referred to as A&I, or abstracting and indexing databases). However, it is important to touch on databases that have book content, or bibliographic databases. In fact, it was the introduction of online library catalogs in the 1970s and 1980s, often referred to as OPACs (online public access catalogs) in library literature, that lead the way to online searching, the need to teach Boolean operators, and the transformation of searching for book content.

One of the mainstays of reference work over the years has been the ability to find what other libraries have in their holdings. In addition, we often need to search beyond our own library holdings just to verify the proper citation of a work and at times to place an interlibrary loan request for a user. Consortial library cooperation that began with the *National Union Catalog* (NUC) venture of the mid-1900s is now, for the most part, available online through *WorldCat*, although some would disagree (Beall and Kafadar 2005).

Before the introduction of the Web-based *World Cat* bibliographic catalog in 1998, there was the OCLC bibliographic database. It was a tool for catalogers to create bibliographic records, reference librarians to discover records, and interlibrary lending. The FirstSearch interface to *WorldCat* has now been used for many years by reference librarians as an essential window to the combined cataloging of the world's libraries. *WorldCat* doesn't have everything, but it is the largest single bibliographic database in the world and is indispensable to reference and research.

WorldCat

Libraries cannot exist by themselves. Cooperation and networking is the name of the game. We have referred several times in this book to the old days of libraries, the days of card catalogs and print indexes. In those days, catalogers would handle books one at a time and create descriptive catalog entries following the rules of the day, as well as creating access points for subjects. This was all very time-consuming. The idea of a combined or union catalog stated in 1901 with Librarian of Congress Herbert Putnam, but it was quickly discovered that the holdings of several major libraries, such as Harvard University, Boston Public Library, and New York Public Library, could not be counted on as the complete record of books held by American libraries (Cole 1981). It would take a record of the holdings of many hundreds of libraries to come close to achieving that goal. The *National Union Catalog, Pre-1956 Imprints* (abbreviated NUC), is a beginning of fulfillment of that dream. This massive 754-volume set is a masterpiece representing the combined holdings of most research libraries within the United States. It is still retained by libraries today because not all the entries in it are represented in online databases (Beall and Kafadar 2005).

But it was the shared cataloging system devised by OCLC (which originally stood for Ohio College Library Center, and later became Online Computer Library Center) that really became the de facto national union catalog, and in fact a union catalog for much of the world. It is the largest combined catalog, but it doesn't have everything—far from it. All you have to do is visit bookstores in other countries, search some of the titles you find there in the OCLC database, and you will see how many titles are lacking. Still, the *WorldCat* database has changed the way libraries do business. Catalogers no longer sit at typewriters cataloging individual books from scratch. Records can be downloaded from the OCLC database. Copy cataloging saves time in library technical service departments, as cataloging staff can simply download the appropriate record that has already been created by the book publishers or another cataloger.

Most larger libraries do not even do that, however. With vendors able to supply downloadable catalog records, e-books and print books alike can be loaded into local online catalogs through mass data loads of electronic records.

The OCLC bibliographic database is available for a fee from OCLC through their FirstSearch interface. While the back end of the OCLC database serves catalogers and interlibrary lending purposes, the FirstSearch interface can be used in reference interchanges and for researchers needing to search beyond their local library's holdings.

As of September 2017, the *WorldCat* statistics are truly stunning (table 12.1).

WorldCat has many uses for librarians, both as a reference tool and a collection development tool:

- Provide a way to explore new or unfamiliar topics presented in reference questions to get a sense of what is available in a subject area.

- Find resources in an area that their library is limited in.

Table 12.1. Size of the *WorldCat* Database.

Number of bibliographic records	404,242,755
Number of holdings	2,591,327,999
Percentage of non-English items	56%
Number of languages and dialects	491

Source: OCLC 2017.

- Find resources in a particular format.

- Find everything written by a particular author.

- Determine the availability of materials in nearby libraries before encouraging patrons to make interlibrary loan requests.

- Verify citations (for titles of books, journals, etc.); check publication dates; serial start and end dates, etc.

- Verify problem citations before patrons request them through interlibrary loan, thus saving time by getting things right up front.

- Provide an internal solution if the local catalog is down (assuming local holdings are represented in *WorldCat*).

- Use as a collection development tool by seeing what's out there on a topic, what other libraries own, and what the library might want to purchase.

WorldCat as a Reference Tool

No library can have everything. *WorldCat* allows for discovery beyond the local library to many other of the world's libraries. The FirstSearch interface to *WorldCat* has powerful search capabilities to aid in finding holdings from libraries in all parts of the world. Not all libraries are represented in *WorldCat*, but many are. It is also true that many libraries, especially larger research libraries, do not have everything cataloged. Great strides have been made in cataloging the massive backlogs in some libraries so that library holdings are relied upon by interlibrary lending staff as well as reference librarians. It's always a good idea, however, to also check local online catalog status for materials in remote libraries before recommending that users purchase their plane tickets to access noncirculating items, rare books, and archival holdings. Some libraries are not as diligent at updating their holdings in *WorldCat* as other libraries are.

WorldCat for Citation Verification

Never assume that patron has given you the correct information. Usually something is wrong with the citation. Perhaps they are passing along information that was (wrongly) provided to them by a fellow student or an instructor (often instructors provide citation information from the depths of their memory, which isn't always perfect). *WorldCat* is one of the most useful tools for straightening out bad citations.

Let's take a look at a simple citation problem that WorldCat is easily able to sort out:

Submitted citation: *The Archaeology of Food and Identity* edited by Katheryn C. Twiss (2007)

We don't see this in our local online catalog, so it's off to *WorldCat*. We now attempt to verify this citation by searching *WorldCat*. We do a default keyword search for "The Archaeology of Food and Identity" and retrieve 268 records, of which 144 are books. That title is not on the first page of results, so on to plan B.

Returning to the *WorldCat* search page, we change our search away from the default keyword search to a title search. This retrieves 33 total results, 19 of which are books; but, again, our desired title is not among the results on the first result screen. So now we refine the search away from a general title field search to a more specific title phrase search. Now we retrieve four results, all of which are the desired title. The first catalog record has 88 holding libraries, and the other three each have one to two holdings only. There was nothing wrong with the citation as submitted; it's just that *WorldCat* did not place the title at the top of the search results when searching by the default keyword search or by a general title search.

So why wouldn't we just always do a title phrase search? Sometimes a title phrase search is simply too restrictive. Each of the words searched must be adjacent to each other, and the phrase must be left anchored. But all too often the "known items" we are searching have errors in the titles. In these cases, a general title search rather than a title phrase search would help us target the citations we are seeking.

Let's take the book title *Transforming Pakistan: Ways Out of Instability*. We search our local catalog but find nothing. Then we search *WorldCat* for this title. We find this title in *WorldCat* and quickly notice that there is a series statement: "Series: Adelphi,; 406; Variation: Adelphi (Series) (International Institute for Strategic Studies) ;; 406."

This alerts us to something. We may have this cataloged as a series in our local catalog. We again search our catalog differently: "Adelphi (Series) (International Institute for Strategic Studies)." We see that we have online access through Taylor & Francis to this series. Browsing down to issue 406, we see that we have access online to this title. OCLC *WorldCat* is very helpful in straightening out citations. In this case, the requester did not provide the series information. But that information was critical in gaining access to this work, and OCLC *WorldCat* was the key to resolving the mystery.

One of the characteristics of the *WorldCat* database is that there often exist different catalog records for the same item. There are many reasons for this: a cataloger may have disagreed as to the description of the item, either its physical description or the digital version; the item may have very different subject terms assigned to it (this often happens when foreign-language subjects have been applied, as was the case in one of the four records retrieved in our example); a cataloger has disagreed with previous cataloging and instead of amending an existing record has decided to create a new record; or a vendor record has been loaded and has differing information. A 2003 decision by OCLC allows "parallel records" to exist in the *WorldCat* database. Parallel records are cases where the language of the cataloging used to describe an item are allowed to exist, as in the case of foreign-language subjects (OCLC 2011).

WorldCat and Foreign-Language Searching

To be a good reference librarian working with foreign languages, you don't need to be fluent in the language, you just need to have a bibliographic knowledge of the language. It's helpful to know something about determiners and articles (like the English *a*, *an*, and *the*), as these terms are sometimes omitted from searches.

The Library of Congress's Cataloging and Acquisitions section provides Romanization tables for over 70 languages (http://www.loc.gov/catdir /cpso/roman.html). These are provided to help catalogers with understanding various scripts and orthographies for languages far removed from ours, but they can also be of great assistance to the reference process. For example, being able to transliterate common words for journals, numbers, and bibliographic information assists us in searching in languages we can neither read nor write.

Also useful are foreign-language resources provided by Cornell University Library Technical Services (https://lts.library.cornell.edu/lts/rt/ref/langres) and the music language resources from Yale University's Irving S. Gilmore Music Library (http://web.library.yale.edu/cataloging/music/language -tools).

Google Translate (https://translate.google.com) is about as good as it gets for quick work lookups in nearly every current language. Once you have some clues about using the above resources, you can then search *WorldCat* with more confidence, even when you don't know the language.

WorldCat Search Examples

Let's look at the advanced search interface for *WorldCat* in the First-Search interface. The first thing to notice is that the pull-down menu for type of search differs greatly from what we have seen in article databases, and it also differs from your local OPAC interface.

Keyword

Access Method

Accession Number

Author

>Author Phrase
>
>Corporate and Conference Name
>
>Corporate and Conference Name Phrase
>
>Personal Name
>
>Personal Name Phrase

Language Phrase

Material Type

Material Type Phrase

Musical Composition

Musical Composition Phrase

Notes/Comments

Publisher

Publisher Location

Standard Number

>ISBN
>
>ISSN

Subject

>Subject Phrase
>
>Descriptor
>
>Genre/Form
>
>Geographic Coverage
>
>Named Corporation or Conference
>
>Named Person

Title

>Title Phrase
>
>Series Title

Information placed in these search boxes will search across variable-length fields in *WorldCat*. You have the option of applying limits to the items retrieved. You can use the check boxes to limit before the search, or you can opt to do this after the search results are returned. These limits generally are searching fixed fields in the database.

To make sense out of this huge list of choices, we need to use this form with several search examples. These examples will focus on searches that are often not possible to do in your home OPAC.

Search Example 1: Finding Materials in Other Languages

Librarians are often called upon to do bibliographic research in languages they cannot speak or read. But with a bit of patience, you can search in languages you don't understand and deliver the results to researchers. You already know MARC record structures; you understand how names are cataloged. With keyword searching, your luck will turn to skill over time. Knowing how to convert Chinese Wade-Giles transcription to Pinyin is an easy skill to acquire.

My wife is Japanese. She likes to keep up with political issues in Japan. After a bit of playing around, I discover that the useful Library of Congress subject heading might be "Japan—Politics and Government—21st Century." If I wanted to help her find books she could borrow from libraries in the region, I might frame a search like this:

Search for: Japan Politics and Government 21st Century → Subject
Year: Limit to 2015–2018
Limit to: Language drop-down: Japanese

You should now see a browse screen with results. There is the option of limiting by books (142 results) and several other options. Because we searched in a language with a different writing system, you will see the option from the browse screen to "show non-Roman characters." Click this and you will see Japanese kanji and kana above the Romanized titles.

Now let's amend the search a bit. Going back to the advanced search page, change the type of search from "subject" to "subject phrase." I get zero results. Now change the search type to "descriptor." How many results now? Can you give some ideas as to why the differences? Which of these options would you recommend for future searches?

Search Example 2:
Finding Materials for a Specific Audience

Among the features of the fee-based *WorldCat* is the ability to find materials for a specific audience. Many local catalogs do not have the ability to search in this way, so performing such searches in *WorldCat* is extremely helpful.

Let's assume that you want to find materials for your children. You have a son who is interested in computers, but it can be very difficult to locate juvenile-level reading materials for this topic.

Search for: computers → Subject
Limit to: Books
Limit to: Subtype limits: Juvenile (first drop-down, change from
    "Any Audience"; second drop-down, change from "Any Content"
    to "Not Fiction")

I get over 2,300 results, but all are coded for juvenile level. This kind of limiting is generally not possible in local online catalogs.

Let's take another example. At the University of Denver, we have a rather sizeable cookbook collection. A small subset of those titles is targeted for a juvenile audience, but we want to consider purchasing some of the more recent and popular juvenile cookbook titles.

The first thing we need to do is to find the best subjects for this topic. After looking at several titles, we figure out that *cookery*, *cookbooks*, and *cooking* were used in many of the *WorldCat* records. With that in mind, we fill out the OCLC *WorldCat* search form as follows:

Search for cookery OR cooking OR cookbooks → select Subject
   pull-down
Limit to: Year (put recent years; I put 1990–2018)
Limit to: Language drop-down: English
Subtype limits: Juvenile (change pull-down selection from default
   "Any Audience" to "Juvenile")

We now get a nice focused list of records. As the default result setting in *WorldCat* is to sort by number of holding libraries, the first pages contain the most widely held titles that meet our search criteria.

Because of our search history discussion in chapter 6, I know you are all interested to see the search string executed by *WorldCat* that includes our variable-length terms as well as the fixed-field limits that we put into our search, so here it is:

WorldCat results for: su: cookery OR su: cooking OR su: cookbooks
and yr: 1990–2018 and la= "eng" and mt: juv

You can actually place that search string into one empty *WorldCat* box, and you will retrieve exactly the same results you did when you set up all those pull-down menu selections. That can be a useful tool when trying to retrieve by different dates, languages, and the like.

Search Example 3: Finding Materials by Genre

The Library of Congress defines genre as "a term or terms that designate a category characterizing a particular style, form, or content, such as artistic, musical, literary composition, etc." (Library of Congress 2011). *WorldCat* makes it easy to search by genre. In the full *WorldCat*, you will find "Genre/Form" indented under "Subject" from the pull-down menu.

Given the Library of Congress's definition above, some obvious genres come to mind, such as mystery or science fiction. But there are thousands of possible genres by which to search. What are some examples of authorized genre headings? Here is a very brief list:

Action and adventure films	Digital images
Apocalyptic films	Fairy tales
Artists' books	Diaries
Christian fiction	Ghost stories

Clay animation television programs	Graphic novels
Coloring books	Historical drama
Foreign films	Jazz vocals
Little magazines	Science fiction
New Age fiction	Spy films
Noir fiction	Student newspapers and periodicals
Picture books for children	Television crime shows
Political satire	Video art
Rock music	Women's periodicals

That should get your mind rolling! For a more complete listing of genre headings, I recommend searching the Library of Congress's authorities database at http://authorities.loc.gov. The Subject Authority Headings option (the default option) will search the LC Genre/Form Thesaurus. You can also search using this search form: http://id.loc.gov/authorities/genreForms.html.

For this search example, search *WorldCat* (the fee-based version) by one of the genres from the list above to see how this kind of search can work for you. This kind of search also works in WorldCat.org, but you have to do a general subject search; you cannot just restrict the search to genre/form headings.

WorldCat.Org

WorldCat.org came on the scene in 2006 (OCLC 2015). OCLC has taken their obscure bibliographic database and done a brilliant move: they have opened it up to the entire world. They did so at just the right time, too, because it is given added visibility by Google by including WorldCat.org in its list of resources within Google Books, along with such resources as Barnes and Noble and Amazon. In addition, the interface allows users to see library holdings near them geographically, encouraging the use of local libraries.

Librarians were amazed that OCLC was not charging for this access to data that has been fee-based for so many years. But take a closer look at *World-Cat*. Compare a record from the full *WorldCat* licensed site with the same record from WorldCat.org. (Go ahead, test it out. Pull up a record from the fee-based *WorldCat*, copy the accession number, and in the WorldCat.org advanced search screen, search the number by selecting "Accession Number" from the pull-down menu.) Which fields do you see in the free site? Which fields are missing? While 100 percent of the records from the fee-based site appear in the free site, not all fields are present. This appears to be the way that OCLC is protecting its intellectual property while also opening WorldCat.org to the world.

As an example of the lacking fields, look at accession number 11056816 in the full *WorldCat* database. There you will see that this serial had a preceding title (MARC field 780) and several succeeding titles (MARC field 785). This is important when trying to track down serials that change titles and other elements over time. Yet, when you examine this same record in WorldCat.org, no mention is made of preceding or succeeding titles. I realize that this may be perceived as an extreme example, but reference librarians may want to think twice before saying that they no longer need the full *WorldCat* database.

WorldCat.org Search Examples

Search Example 1: A Known Item Search

Let's say that you were looking for Al Gore's book *An Inconvenient Truth*. Simply search WorldCat.org for "inconvenient truth" (with the books tab selected). From the search results page, you should see the record for Gore's book on the page. Now select "View all editions and formats." When I did this search, I saw 64 records. Regardless of which record I select, I see the same number of holding libraries. It is quickly apparent that *WorldCat* gets around the problem of multiple records in their database by mashing up all holdings together into every record. My screen reads "Displaying libraries 1–6 out of 4692 for all 53 editions." In the traditional *WorldCat* database, each record and format has holdings for only that record. It is important to note the differences between these two holdings displays.

Search Example 2: Using WorldCat.org from within Google Books

Using Google Books (books.google.com), look for a book on searching Google: *Harnessing the Power of Google: What Every Researcher Should Know*. You can search Google Books many ways, but I used this way: "harnessing the power of google brown."

In the left margin, you should see the "Find in a library" link (figure 12.1).

Where do you suppose "Find in a library" points to? That's right! This record for this book in OCLC's WorldCat.org. The problem is that there are multiple records in *WorldCat* for this book. To see all of them, be sure to click the "View all editions and formats" link. You will see some links for print editions and other links for e-book versions. No matter which of these links you click, the holding libraries will be unified. You can see whether there is a library near you that has this book.

Search Example 3: Finding Musical Scores

Let's say you need to find musical scores for a Broadway musical. You could search WorldCat.org like this: "West Side Story vocal selections." I get 601 results overall. In the left-side bar, I now select the facet/limiter that says "musical score." We now have a result set of 61. Clicking on the first result gives me this:

Bernstein, Leonard, Jerome Robbins, and Stephen Sondheim. 2010. West Side Story: vocal selections. Milwaukee, WI: Boosey & Hawkes.

Figure 12.1. Google Books's "Find in a Library" Link. *Source:* Google and the Google logo are registered trademarks of Google Inc.. Used with permission.

I used the cite/export feature to create the citation above. Under the "Find a copy in the library" section of the Web page, we can see libraries that have the item, sorted by closest library.

Local Library Catalogs: Current Trends

After dealing with *WorldCat*, the largest bibliographic database in the world, it seems anticlimactic to discuss local library catalogs, especially as each one of us likely has a different interface from a wide variety of possible vendors. But you need to understand the capabilities of local catalogs to serve your local users in reference transactions.

While we cannot comment on your local library catalog, because we all have such different catalogs from various vendors, I do want to say some things about what we are finding these days in our library catalogs, particularly within academic libraries.

What's the latest in local library online catalogs? For several years, academic libraries have been implementing demand-driven acquisition (DDA) models for purchasing both print and e-book content. This doesn't affect the searching so much as it does the fulfillment—that is, the actual "getting" of the content. Sometimes you will hear this referred to as patron-driven acquisition (PDA). Rather than have a subject specialist librarian do the ordering of books, library catalogs are preloaded with bibliographic records for books that the library does not yet own but will potentially purchase if requested by a user. It has been shown that librarians have historically not guessed well at which books its users would like to access, with only about 40 percent of print titles being checked out once.

The PDA/DDA plans get around that by renting access for the first few accesses but purchasing the e-book after the requisite number of uses. In the case of print books, this likely entails a delay of several days while the book is ordered. In the case of e-books, with many e-book vendors, a user clicks through to content (after authenticating) and never even knows that the book had not been purchased. In some academic library catalogs, there may be tens of thousands of records for books that are not owned by the library, but that are discoverable, at least on the metadata level. The intention of these models is to use diminishing budget funds more strategically.

Google Books and Local Library Catalogs

Even though many libraries load bibliographic records for e-books, whether owned or not, still the OPAC is not a good discovery tool (which we discuss and define in chapter 13). Although most e-books are searchable when reading the text of the e-book or when visiting a vendor's platform, the OPAC itself does not provide full-text discovery. There is an inelegant workaround for this. Again, it is Google to the rescue: Google Books in this case. As a very high percentage of print and e-book content is included in the default full-text searching of Google Books, I often begin with Google Books for searches, initially bypassing the library catalog altogether. When I have located relevant books, I then turn to the library catalog, perform a basic title search, and see whether the book I want is available in print or electronic format.

The Weakest Link

What used to be one of the most powerful tools in libraries—the local online catalog—is now the weakest. In chapter 1, we discussed the development of catalogs in libraries: from the days of card catalogs, where access was by left-anchored author, subject, or title, to the days of the first online catalogs, where you could also search by keyword. These initial catalogs were revolutionary and game changing. They continued to evolve with hyperlinks to online content, the ability to perform back-searches within the catalog, and leveraging existing MARC fixed field and variable field data into facets and limiters. But with all these innovations, the catalog is still searching just the cataloging metadata: author, subject, title, and other fields, like summary, notes, added entries, and so on.

So, what do users today expect? They expect to be able to search the full text. They can do that to some extent with many article databases, but not with the online catalog. We may have a superb catalog with the best *Library of Congress Subject Headings* or *Sears Headings* to capture the "aboutness" of our books, but we cannot drill down into the full text with our catalogs.

Information Access Anomaly

Book content is extremely important to those in the humanities. Yet, the tool that has historically provided access to books, the library catalog, is an extremely weak discovery tool. Known items could be accessed by author or title, and topics could be researched with an educated knowledge of subject headings. But in today's world, where article content can be accessed through full-text searching, the library catalog, through no fault of its own, is more of a library inventory system than it is a discovery tool.

One way of characterizing this phenomenon is through what I have chosen to call the *information access anomaly*. Let us consider a typical print academic book. For the sake of simplicity, let's assume that an average book contains 200 pages of actual text, and that it has an average of 400 words per page (WritersServices 2001). That means that an average book contains 80,000 words. When a library catalog performs a search, it doesn't search the full text of the book, it searches certain parts (fields) of the catalog record. Typically, a catalog keyword search would search all the author fields (personal author, corporate author, and any added author entries); all the title fields (including the title proper, but also series title, spine title, translated title, and any other such fields); subjects fields (whether they be subject headings, subject descriptors, or subject keywords); and the notes field. These catalog records are surrogates; they stand in place of the whole work. If a cataloger/indexer has done an adequate job, the surrogate record should accurately describe the work in terms of physical description and extent, and it should also adequately describe the general "aboutness" of the work. The catalog record, being a brief surrogate, is only able to capture the main topics of the book, but not the details. Some catalog records may contain tables of contents, chapter titles, and subheadings that delineate the book outline in greater detail.

When catalog records are searched through an online catalog, it is generally the author, subject, title, and notes fields, as described above, that are searched. When you total up the indexable words in all the author, title, subject, and notes fields, you may be searching 50–100 words. For the sake of this illustration, let's say that an average of 75 words are searched. This has huge implications in terms of discovery of book information. Thus, a 200-page book, with 80,000 words, would only have 75 words discoverable via the online catalog. This is the information access anomaly. The ratio of indexable words in a typical catalog record (75) divided into 80,000 words of the entire book yields a surrogate record to full-text ratio of 1 to 10,666. This is why students so quickly give up on library catalogs for discovery and go to Google.

Let's look now at the surrogate record to full-text ratio of typical scholarly journal articles. Journal articles are smaller in size than books. Let's say for the sake of argument that an average scholarly journal article is 15 pages in length, with 400 words per page, or a total of 6,000 words. But journal articles no longer need to be indexed to economize space. Instead, these articles are often assigned multiple subject descriptors or subject headings, usually many more subjects than are assigned to books. In addition, abstracts, whether they are author-produced abstracts or added by professional indexers, tend to be several paragraphs in length. For our argument, let's just say that a surrogate record (that is, an index record) for a scholarly article is 300–500 words in length—an average of 400 words. Dividing 400 into 6,000 yields a surrogate record to full-text ratio of 1 to 15.

Table 12.2. The Information Access Anomaly: Assumption of 400 Words per Page.

	Book (Average)	Journal Article	Google (Scholar/Books)
Typical length full text (FT)	200 pages × 400 = 80,000 words	15 pages × 400 = 6,000	
Surrogate record (catalog or index metadata) (SR)	50–100 words (75-word avg.)	300–500 words (400-word avg.)	
SR to FT Ratio	1 to 10,666	1 to 15	1 to 1

Source: WritersServices 2001.

This explains why journals articles tend to be easier to discover than books for most researchers (table 12.2).

Now let's apply the idea of a ratio to Google. Google Scholar generally indexes the full text of nearly all the scholarly articles it has ingested. We can say that Google Scholar has a surrogate record to full-text ratio of 1 to 1. Likewise, even though not every book has been ingested into Google Books, for those that are represented, the surrogate record to full-text ratio is 1 to 1.

Enter Google Books

We don't have time here to go into the history of the development of Google Books (for that, see my other book, *Harnessing the Power of Google: What Every Researcher Should Know* (Brown 2017)). But Google Books performs one element of the search process that the catalog cannot do: it drills down into the full text of a high percentage of books sitting on our shelves. As long as you have your expectations properly set, Google Books will help you. What I mean by that is that there are two aspects to searching and getting: first discovery and then fulfillment. *Discovery* is straightforward: we find the resource that contains the information we are looking for. By *fulfillment*, I mean getting the thing—acquiring the actual book. As long as you realize that, in most cases, Google Books will only perform the discovery and not the fulfillment, you will get along just fine. I encourage students to search Google Books to discover what they might want and then to go to their local online catalog to see whether the book is locally owned. It may be in print format, or it may be online. If it is not locally available, then interlibrary loan may be a possibility.

Library Catalog: Not the Best Discovery Tool

Historically, library catalogs served their purpose. They provided access via well-preened, pre-coordinated subject headings. They kept track of inventory, showed us books that were on order, performed serials check-in of print journals, and showed us when books were checked out and when they were due. But they were (and are) lousy discovery tools. Users today expect more, much more.

A Deeper Search: Augmenting the
Local Catalog with Google Books

A library user is looking for "the OAR portion of the ASTB (navy officer test)." A search of the local online catalog yields no results.

First, you should find out what these abbreviations stand for (even if you don't use this information in your search, it may be important in evaluating whether your results are on target). Doing a regular Google search, you discover that ASTB means "Aviation Selection Test Battery." OAR in this context means "Officer Aptitude Rating." You also discover that these tests are not just used by the navy, but by the marine corps and coast guard as well. You then turn to Google Books and search this way: "OAR ASTB navy officer test." These are the top results:

Officer Candidate Tests for Dummies

Master the Officer Candidate Tests

Barron's Military Flight Aptitude Tests

Searching the local catalog does not turn up any of these titles, but all three titles are held in the local consortium and are available for borrowing.

You can see from this example the power of Google Books in augmenting what the local library catalog can do

---

Online library catalogs presently search only metadata and not full text. This places the library's primary finding aid at a distinct disadvantage when put up against Google Books, HathiTrust, or other databases capable of searching deep down into the full text. The advantage, of course, is that catalogs can discover the "aboutness" of books—the topmost level of what a book is about. But beyond that, users are not able to search deep book content.

This situation often perplexes students. Sometimes users approach the reference desk saying that the library doesn't have any books on their topic. They were searching the non-full-text, metadata-only library catalog. No wonder they think that way.

Here is an actual question from a recent student: "My research is about having energy exchange between Georgia and Azerbaijan. Georgia has more hydropower resources, whereas Azerbaijan has more natural gas resources. My paper is about effective energy trade between these two countries." Doing an initial search in the local library catalog for "Georgia AND Azerbaijan AND "energy exchange"" produced no book results. Although there were article results in the discovery tool, the patron wanted to get books on this topic.

Turning to Google Books, I did the same search as above and retrieved over 8,000 results. Google Books did not allow us to read the desired books, but using it just as a discovery tool, and not expecting fulfillment, we were able to look up several of the books in the local online catalog, having used Google Books as a discovery tools to go far beyond what a local library catalog is currently capable of doing.

HathiTrust

I think of e-book databases in two different categories: historic e-books and contemporary e-books. We have mentioned HathiTrust (hathitrust.org) in connection with e-books in chapter 9, "Humanities Databases," but here we will discuss the project in general and tout some of its features as a bibliographic tool.

The first thing you should notice is that there are two ways to search within the repository, a full-text search and a catalog search (as denoted by the tabbed interface; figure 12.2).

A full-text search will retrieve many more results, but the relevancy rate will be very low. A catalog search does not search any of the text of materials (the particulars including names, places, and other details), only the metadata. It succeeds in reducing the possibilities and occurrences of false drops.

There are many reasons that HathiTrust is a go-to place for reference librarians:

- For pre-1923 works, HathiTrust often comes through with full text of difficult-to-find books. This can allow researchers to read texts when there is no time to wait for interlibrary loan materials.

- HathiTrust materials may allow you to place some microform collections in remote storage.

- As mentioned in chapter 9, most U.S. government publications in HathiTrust, even those after 1922, are fully accessible in full text. Even though entire PDFs cannot be downloaded by nonmember libraries, the entire documents can be read and saved one page at a time.

- HathiTrust includes scans of many rare books and serials.

As noted above, entire full texts are searchable within HathiTrust. Even materials not in the public domain will still show if the search you performed contained "hits." This can help guide you as to whether an interlibrary loan would be worth doing.

The overall statistics for HathiTrust's content are impressive. As of mid-2017, there are nearly 16 million total volumes, nearly 8 million titles, approaching half a million serial titles, with nearly 6 million volumes in the public domain (HathiTrust 2017a). About half of the content is in English, and there is a total of 461 languages, with the strongest showing from Western European languages (HathiTrust 2017b). As long as you are prepared for the fact that you likely will not be able to download entire texts, you will have a very fulfilling experience with the HathiTrust discovery process. Like Google Books, HathiTrust records each contain a link to "locate a print version," which links by OCLC number to WorldCat.org.

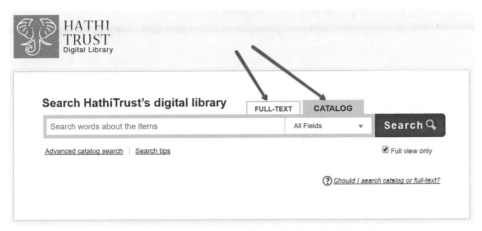

Figure 12.2. HathiTrust with Two Ways to Search. *Source:* HathiTrust.
Used with permission.

Example Search: Suppose you are looking for *Thoughts and Theories of Life and Education*, an 1897 work by John Lancaster Spalding. The local library catalog says that you own this work in microfiche. The catalog record states that this is in the series *Library of American Civilization*; LAC 13592. The good news is that the library owns the item and that it was discoverable in the online catalog. But the bad news is that it is on microfiche. A quick check of HathiTrust shows that this book is available there: https://catalog .hathitrust.org/Record/001734734.

Differences between E-Journals and E-Books

E-journals, for all the various vendors and platforms, are generally easy to use: just open the PDF. You can print it; save it, sometimes save it to a bibliographic management system (e.g., RefWorks, EndNote); or e-mail it to yourself or someone else. But e-books put us in a parallel universe. They are usually fairly easy to "discover": through the vendor's interface, through a local library catalog if the library elects to load MARC records for e-books, or through a discovery tool like *Summon*, *Primo*, *WorldCat Discovery*, or *EBSCO Discovery Service*. But having done so, now what?

Because we are not dealing with a part of a whole (like a journal article) and are instead dealing with an entire thing (a book), issues of copyright and rights management generally come into play. Some vendors, like Springer, allow for downloading of every chapter and even entire books without any further annoyances. Most vendors place limits on the number of pages downloaded, pages printed, and the amount of time e-books can even be accessed via some kind of checkout method.

While we can understand the situation that publishers operate under, it is no less annoying. It seems that, for now, we just have to endure the many and varied models that are imposed on users. Table 12.3 shows some of the contrasts between e-books and e-journals.

Table 12.3. E-Books and E-Journals Contrasted.

Formats	E-Books	E-Journals
	PDF, ePUB, MOBI, AZW	Generally only PDF
Digital Rights Management (DRM)	Commonly used; annoying	Generally no DRM
Printing	Often limits on printing	Usually no limits
Linking	Not usually linked to via OpenURL	Often linked to via OpenURL

Exercises

1. In the early part of this chapter, we mentioned several ways that *WorldCat* can be used in reference transactions. What other uses can you think of?

2. Find some books on fast food (what's the best way—that is, what's a good subject heading—to get books that are really about "fast food" and not about food you can prepare fast?)

3. A patron comes in trying to describe some books she has enjoyed. She remembers the author's name was "something-something Smith," and the books are mysteries, about a female detective in Africa somewhere. Try just searching the author field for Smith and the Genre/Form field for mystery to see whether you can identify this series of books.

4. If you have a favorite author or genre, see if you can use *WorldCat* to find all the records for those works in your local public library branch. (Tip: Use the code look-up screen in *WorldCat* via FirstSearch.)

5. You're at the reference desk on the weekend, and some junior high school kids come in looking for information about corsets and bloomers for a project. A social history type of encyclopedia might really be best; otherwise, books would be a better way to go than articles for this age group. Try searching your local catalog and see what you can find; then try the subscription *WorldCat* database (unless your local catalog has a "juvenile audience" limiter, which would be unusual) and see whether you can find more materials or get some additional ideas that way.

6. *WorldCat* claims to have records for everything from clay tablets to electronic books. See if you can find examples at both ends of this spectrum. (Hints: In each case, use a combination of keywords and limits.) For the clay tablets, note that such things would normally be housed in an archive, thus making them what kind of materials? Learn from your results what a more formal term for *clay tablets* is that you might add as an alternate term to your search. For electronic books, try your favorite author and the "Internet Resources" limit.

(Hint: Look up your author in the Author Phrase index, last name first, to find how his or her name is most commonly entered.)

7. *WorldCat* (FirstSearch) results are sorted, or ranked, by the number of libraries that own the item. There are three other options, but ranking is often set as the default. Why do you think that is? What would be the advantages and disadvantages of the other results display options?

8. WorldCat.org does not have the same sorting or ranking options as the fee-based version. Why do you think there are differences?

9. Now try the searches in exercises 2–5 in WorldCat.org. Do you get the same number of results? Which do you find easier? What are the advantages and disadvantages of searching using the FirstSearch interface versus the WorldCat.org interface?

10. Figure out whether your library, either a public library or an academic library, is linked to from within Google Books. To do this, search your local library catalog and find the title of a book, any book. Then search that title in Google Books, select the "Find in a library" link, and see if it is locally available. (Note that not all libraries have configured their setting to work seamlessly with *WorldCat* and Google Books.)

References

Beall, Jeffrey, and Karen Kafadar. 2005. "The Proportion of NUC Pre-56 Titles Represented in OCLC *WorldCat*." *College & Research Libraries* 66, no. 5: 431–435.

Cole, John Y., ed. 1981. *In Celebration: The National Union Catalog, Pre-1956 Imprints.* Washington, D.C.: Library of Congress. Available via ERIC database, ED261681.

HathiTrust. 2017a. "About." Accessed September 2, 2017. https://www.hathitrust.org/about.

HathiTrust. 2017b. "HathiTrust Languages." Accessed September 2, 2017. https://www.hathitrust.org/visualizations_languages.

Library of Congress. 2011. "Top-Level Element: <genre>." In *MODS User Guidelines* (ver. 3). Accessed August 16, 2017. https://www.loc.gov/standards/mods/userguide/genre.html.

OCLC. 2011. WorldCat *Quality: An OCLC Report.* Dublin, OH: OCLC. Accessed August 8, 2017. https://www.oclc.org/content/dam/oclc/reports/worldcatquality/214660usb_WorldCat_Quality.pdf.

OCLC. 2015. *A Brief History of* WorldCat. Accessed August 16, 2017. Recovered from Archive.li: https://archive.li/iIRhJ.

OCLC. 2017. *Inside* WorldCat. Dublin, OH: OCLC. Accessed November 7, 2017. https://www.oclc.org/en/worldcat/inside-worldcat.html.

WritersServices. 2001. "Matching World Count to Page Size." Accessed 11/6/2017. http://www.writersservices.com/writersservices-self-publishing/word-count-page.

Beyond the Textbook

Carrying on the tradition of the fourth edition, additional exercises, search tips, and tutorials will be available on the publisher's Web site at http://www.abc-clio.com/books.librariesunlimited.com/Librarians-Guide-to-Online-Searching. This will be updated periodically with the inevitable database changes.

13

Web-Scale Discovery Databases

Libraries sometimes become victims of their own success. With online databases available to libraries numbering in the thousands, it's not unusual to see academic libraries with many hundreds of databases listed on their Web sites, in library guides, and however they choose to make these products known to users. But the more databases proliferate, the more confusion is thrust upon the user. Which database is best? Most users do not take the time to ask a reference librarian for advice.

Some library Web sites are better than others at providing advice. Sometimes what happens is that users just go to Google for their information. They may even venture into Google Scholar. Although Google can lead to the discovery of many valuable resources, it cannot go behind pay firewalls into valuable library-licensed content. Users will certainly find many valuable resources from Google, but they will miss much of the pre-vetted material professors expect them to discover via library-licensed resources. Further, Google Scholar will deeply search a very high percentage of academic content, but will users know how to access these resources through library proxy technologies? Will they adjust Google Scholar settings so that they can see which articles they can access from off-campus? Will they realize the many nonscholarly resources that can help them?

Libraries have long realized the need to provide a single point of access to all library resources. There are too many information silos from a multitude of vendors, and that is confusing to users. Each vendor has its own portal to its world. Each of them has its strong features, as we have seen from earlier chapters of this book. But is it reasonable to expect users to search 30 information silos to find information relevant to their research? Some may be okay with that, but most users want a single point of access. Librarians are feeling the pressure to find a way to provide efficient access to the many resources that cost millions of dollars per year. With growing pressure to increase usage statistics to justify maintaining access to databases, the pressure is on to provide seamless access to the numerous primary and secondary resources to which libraries subscribe or own.

From the users' side of things, we cannot expect them to consult multiple information silos to find all the relevant information for their research. Why would users even want to go through the pain of navigating multiple interfaces when they can search Google or another huge search engine?

Let's look at two strategies developed by vendors to help libraries solve the problem of too much information, too many silos to search, and the desire to use a product like Google to find all their information.

Federated Searching in Libraries

In the late 1990s and early 2000s, libraries were seeing a fast increase the amount of content available from publishers and aggregators, but they

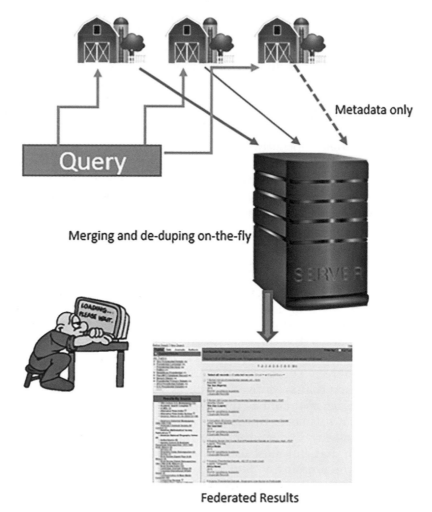

Figure 13.1. Federated Search Model with Querying of Multiple Information Silos and Attempts to Unify Results.

were perplexed with the number of disparate portals available for searching. Surely there must be a better way than searching dozens of portals individually. This is where so-called federated searching came in. By using the technologies available at that time, such as Z39.50 or XML gateway protocols and others, vendors were able to make connections to dozens of databases, pass along log-in credentials, and then pass along search criteria to eventually retrieve results from many of the subscribed remote services. Then a process of merging and de-duplication would take place, and results could be presented to the user—all in real time. Figure 13.1 illustrates this model.

I maintain that what has been called "federated search" is really not that at all; at best, it was "pseudo-federated." What was actually happening was a "disintegrated" *search* with an attempt at federated *results*. There was nothing federated about the search. To be truly federated, the interface should gather together, or federate, records into a single place where they can be searched all at once, which is what the discovery tool models we see today do. As the terminology "federated search" had already been used (and had become associated with tools that were slow, inefficient, and awkward to use), the vendors of the current tools have resorted to such terms as *Web-scale discovery*, or simply *discovery*.

By the mid-2000s, some of the contenders in the federated search market included MetaLib (ExLibris); ENCompass (Endeavor); AGent (Auto-Graphics); Central Search, later named 360 Search (Serials Solutions); and WebFeat (WebFeat and Thomson ISI). These tools had many limitations, such as lack of precision in retrieval, lack of shared searchable fields among databases, problems with phrase searching, keyword as the only available search method, limit features not fully functional, and the inability to incorporate thesaurus or controlled-vocabulary searching (Boss and Nelson 2005).

The "Clinic" Put on by Google

Against the backdrop of librarians and users not being particularly pleased with federated searching, Google came out with Google Scholar in 2004. With some federated searches taking over one minute to connect to remote databases, connect with log-in scripts, pass along search terms, and then merge and de-duplicate results, Google Scholar did two things that hadn't been done to a large scale before: it changed the discovery model to a central index, and it searched the full text of a very high percentage of scholarly content and returned results in under one second. Yes, that's correct, less than a second! Contrast that speed with that of federated search tools of that time: searches often taking more than 60 seconds. Users wanted the Google solution, not the one provided by libraries. Librarians wanted that, too. The vendors knew that they had to change the defective federated search model, and fast.

The Google Age

Without question, most university students begin their research not with the resources librarians have carefully selected, not with the discovery tools that libraries have so thoughtfully invested in, and not with the databases that have been discussed thus far in this book. Most students start their research with Google. Sadly, too many end their quest there as well.

Not that there's anything wrong with Google. As mentioned previously, I wrote a book about how to search Google for academic research purposes (Brown 2017). But students don't have the background information to know what they are finding and, more importantly, what they are not finding when they spend their time exclusively in Google. But what about Bing and other search engines? Why only talk about Google? We could talk about other search engines, but it is Google that has provided Google Scholar and has stuck with the Google Books project for over a decade. The "Three Googles," as I call them, work together as a research suite to provide a definite service to students and their research needs. There are three distinct interfaces with different features and different content focus: Google Web for primary sources, Google Scholar for secondary sources that are generally peer reviewed, and Google Books for full-text searching of a high percentage of book content. These are what make up the Three Googles.

Most people think that they know how to search Google. I maintain that they do not. Google is a database in every sense of the term. It shares many features with databases that have been discussed so far in this book. It just does some of the functions automatically for us in the background, and we have little control over how Google works. For example, Google does not have or use controlled vocabulary in the same sense as the thesauri that have broader terms (BT), related terms (RT), and narrower terms (NT). It does have a sophisticated system of synonyms somehow running in the background that help to match users' queries with massive indexed content. I don't know how Google does it, and it's not something they advertise; perhaps if I did know how they did their magic, I would be a billionaire, too!

Google Scholar will be successful in library research to the extent that your library subscribes to the content indexed in Scholar. Libraries with larger database and online serials budgets will have a higher success rate in terms of "hits," and libraries with small budgets can still make use of Scholar; it's just that more interlibrary loan requests will be necessary.

The central index model used by Google Scholar has provided a model for all the developments since. Google Scholar was able to collect metadata records from publishers. But the big coup for Google Scholar is that it was able to convince publishers to give it more than metadata. To a large extent, Scholar was also able to acquire the full content, the PDFs themselves. With the PDFs ingested into Google, Google was able to run its own OCR, if necessary, and thus index every word of a very high percentage of scholarly content. With the inclusion of older content through such initiatives as *JSTOR*, *HeinOnline*, and other projects that go back to the earliest years of many journals, Google Scholar became an extremely powerful tool.

To add to the already powerful central index model, Google reached out to academic libraries and encouraged them to tell Google what journal content they owned or subscribed to. How could libraries do this mammoth task? At the University of Denver alone, a school of just over 11,000 students,

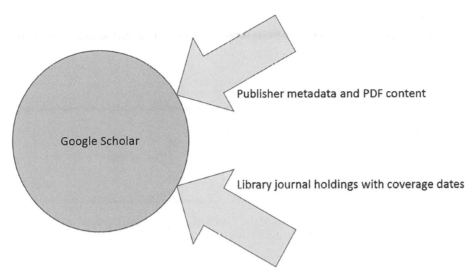

Figure 13.2. Google Scholar Central Index Model.

we provide access to 161,323 electronic journal titles. Of those, 131,521 are unique titles (FY16 data). Fortunately, libraries rely on vendors to provide the XML list that Google needs to add to its central index. So now Google can merge together into the Google Scholar interface (1) metadata for a high percentage of scholarly articles; (2) full text of a high percentage of scholarly articles; and (3) holdings of academic libraries with coverage dates. This is illustrated in figure 13.2.

Now that you have a basic understanding of Google Scholar and how it revolutionized discovery of scholarly articles, let us take a look at vendor responses in the form of library discovery tools.

Discovery Tools Come on the Scene

Discovery tools (sometimes called Web-scale discovery tools) came on the scene around 2010. The paradigm was different from the previous generation of federated search tools. Rather than connecting out to dozens of remote services with various protocols and mixed results, the discovery tools followed more of a Google Scholar approach. They acquired metadata from publishers for books, e-books, magazine content, newspaper content, scholarly journal articles, and multiple other formats and put them into a single searchable "pot" of metadata (a central index). Some of them also included full text in the pot, although this has not generally been the push.

They did not search as deeply as Google Scholar, as full-text searching was mostly lacking. But what discovery tools lacked in depth of searching, they made up in breadth of coverage (figure 13.3), as they searched more types of resources than Scholar. Whereas Scholar was focused (more or less) on scholarly journal content, the discovery tools endeavored to cover the greater breadth of library database content, including newspaper and magazine content, which is not within the scope of Google Scholar.

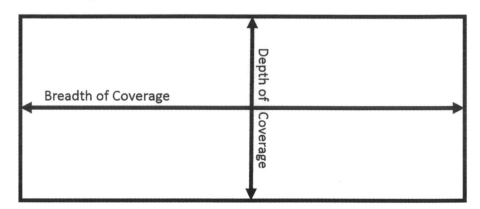

Figure 13.3. Breadth of Coverage = More Types of Resources; Depth of Coverage = Searching the Full Text.

I often hear librarians say that discovery tools search dozens of databases. Often users will ask, "Which databases does the discovery service search?" This question does not reflect the technologies' underlying discovery tools. When searching with discovery tools, you are not searching dozens of databases; you are, in fact, searching a single database, the central index of the discovery tool. I usually tell students that they are not searching databases, they are searching the results of databases. It's as if you took each database, gave it a good shaking, and then poured the contents out into one huge central bowl (as opposed to searching multiple containers). It is not unlike Google Scholar, which searches metadata content and full text given to it by publishers or content it has crawled and ingested into the Google central index from institutional repositories and other sources. Discovery tools likewise search their respective central indexes.

Many of the weaknesses of federated search tools had been fixed by the new model that discovery tools used. No longer were separate information silos being searched. Rather, metadata from those silos was gathered ahead of time, somewhat normalized, and put into a single "pot." It was that single pot of metadata that was queried, rather than dozens of separate information silos from multiple vendors. Wait times, although still not as fast as Google Scholar, were much improved over federated searches. Metadata from the pot could be normalized and results presented in a more even manner that was more principled. Normalization could be performed on records upon ingest into the central index, rather than attempting to instantly react to "on the fly" records coming into a federated search tool. Limiters or facets could be employed in a more meaningful way. Search results could be more easily restricted to library-subscribed content, working even better than Google Scholar's library settings. Figure 13.4 illustrates the Web-scale discovery model.

Major players in the discovery market are Summon (Serials Solutions, and later ProQuest); *EBSCO Discovery Service* (or *EDS*, from EBSCO); *Primo* (ExLibris, recently purchased by ProQuest); and *WorldCat Discovery* (OCLC). Each of these shared the same model of searching a single pot of metadata, thus returning results very quickly, with differences in the way the central index was implemented. All the big aggregator vendors now

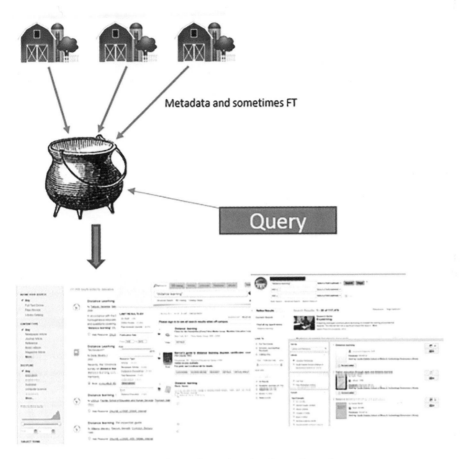

Federated Search and Federated Results

Figure 13.4. Web-Scale Discovery Model of Library Content Searching: The True Federated Search with Federated Results.

regularly share their proprietary metadata with the other competing products, as none of them wants to appear to show bias or to be out of sync with their content. All of them employ either OpenURL or newer technologies to take users to licensed content. They also attempted, with varying degrees of success, to incorporate library catalog results in with article content. The goal was to have a single search for all library content. The "all" is still a pipe dream, but that is the goal (figure 13.5).

It is difficult to have a "one search" for all library content. Think about the challenges: searching for book content has always differed from searching for article content. Not every database is able to be searched through discovery sites. Numerical databases don't lend themselves to searching with discovery tools.

Then there is the problem of full-text searching. Discovery tools need to mimic what Google Scholar does. The problem is that they don't have such an easy time with things. They don't have the resources to acquire all

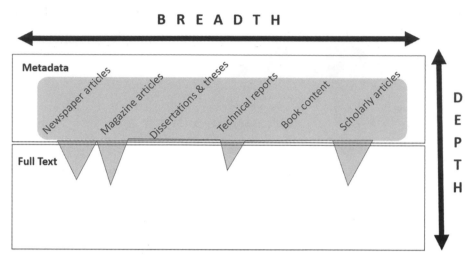

Figure 13.5. Discovery Tools Largely Search Metadata and Rarely Full Text.

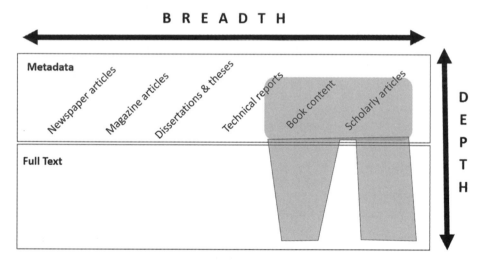

Figure 13.6. Google Scholar: Greater Depth in Searching but Less Breadth.

the full text from publishers. We can only guess that the reason publishers willingly gave article PDFs to the giant Google was to monetize things. And this makes sense. But what would motivate a publisher to give all their publisher content to each of the big four Web-scale discovery services? Instead, the discovery services have to rely on existing full-text availability, that is, that some databases incorporate full text to a limited extent. As a result, very little deep full-text discovery is available in these tools, although it is technically possible. Summon has been the most successful at doing this. While this is a tremendous advance, there still exists a certain unevenness in the search results when discovery is deeper for materials where full text can be searched, but not so deep when it cannot. Thus, there is a degree of full-text discovery, but nothing approaching the deep discovery that Scholar is able to provide (figure 13.6).

Nevertheless, the big four discovery tools are truly revolutionary and have changed the database-searching landscape.

The Unevenness of the Search

The wonders of library discovery services sometimes bring unintended consequences. While discovery tools sometimes include indexing of full text in their central index, those resources tend to be more highly featured (because they retrieval more results) than records with metadata only. As a government documents librarian, I quickly discovered that some discovery tools would pull articles based on keyword matches in the article text, which meant content with full text was producing more results. Meanwhile, government information (which is represented only with metadata records) was becoming backgrounded. In the days when only metadata was searched, you could argue that government information was on par with other information. It was one metadata world against another metadata world. But when discovery tools are able to reach down into selected full text, it so happened that it was never government information that was selected.

This bothered me and motivated me to work with the Government Printing Office (later the Government Publishing Office by late 2014) to see whether the GPO and discovery tool vendors could talk to each other to rectify this situation. I proposed a recommendation to have the GPO collaborate with discovery vendors to expose the full text of *FDsys*, the GPO's full-text discovery interface (Federal Depository Library Program 2014). Hopefully, as discovery tools integrate publisher and aggregator full text into their central indexes, freely available government information will not be forgotten.

Putting Discovery Tools to the Test

Perhaps you want to test discovery tools to see which one is best for your library. This is possible to a large extent. Most installations of discovery tools in academic libraries allow users to perform searches, although they don't allow the "fulfillment" part, that is, actually getting into licensed full text. But in many cases, you can see what the interface and the results look like. This is because discovery tools are a very different model from article databases. The search is performed against the single pot of metadata and generally also includes records from the local library catalog and institutional repository, if there is one.

Determining the scope of discovery tools is not as clear as it is for regular databases, such as EBSCO's *Academic Search*, *ProQuest Central*, or Gale's *Academic OneFile*. This is because of the massive amounts of metadata ingested into their respective central indexes. As previously discussed, scope has two dimensions: breadth and depth. As noted above, breadth is the discovery tools' strong suit, as they cover many document types, but they tend to lack depth, in the sense of searching deep down into the full text. While some discovery tools, like Summon, have a better chance of searching down into the full text, others, like *WorldCat Discovery*, make no attempts to do so.

Discovery tools tend to have stronger representation from secondary sources than from primary sources. This is likely due to several factors:

- Primary sources are not generally tagged as primary sources, usually because the "primary source" means something different in various disciplines. Are historic newspapers primary sources? That depends on the way they will be used in research.

- The significance and potential use of primary source materials is not easily captured in the metadata. How do you adequately capture the significance of works of art? How can you make first-person slave accounts adequately discoverable in the same context as scholarly articles about the mid-1800s?

- Primary sources are harder to identify and load as groups into databases. Journal collections coming from vendors or aggregators are easy to identify because most journals have ISSNs to uniquely identify them. Books have ISBNs. But primary sources such as executive orders, United Nations treaties, works of art, and presidential inaugural addresses each contain very different and distinctive kinds of metadata.

When you are in the market for a discovery service, or for a better discovery service if you already have one, you need to test the other services. If testing such a large, complex product sounds daunting, here are some ideas:

- Test to see how primary sources are covered. Do they have government information? Can archival resources be accessed?

- Take one publisher at a time and test random article titles from that publisher. Use content from *ScienceDirect*, *SpringerLink*, Wiley, Sage, and the like.

- Test selected articles to see whether the discovery tool is able to search down into the full text. Go into a PDF of an article and select some unique text (such as the end of one sentence and the beginning of the next). Test it first in Google Scholar to ensure that the text you selected is discoverable, then test in each of the discovery services.

As you test discovery tools from other institutions, you should not expect to retrieve full text of any articles. The purpose of this testing is not to gain access to content, but to see how content is retrieved and displayed. Listed below are institutions where you can test searches in each of the four major discovery systems.

Testing Summon

Summon is by far the easiest of the systems to test. As Summon is a hosted service that draws on the same big pot of shared metadata for all

Table 13.1. Selected Summon Instances for Testing Purposes.

Institution	Summon URL	Library Home Page
Auraria Library (Denver)	http://auraria.summon .serialssolutions.com	http://library.auraria.edu
Columbia University	http://columbia.summon .serialssolutions.com	http://library.columbia.edu
Cornell University	http://cornell.summon .serialssolutions.com	https://www.library .cornell.edu
Dartmouth College	http://dartmouth .summon .serialssolutions.com	https://www.library .dartmouth.edu
Duke University	http://duke.summon .serialssolutions.com	https://library.duke.edu
U. of Michigan	http://umich.summon .serialssolutions.com	Summon underlying part of bento box
U. of Michigan Library	http://umich.summon .serialssolutions.com	https://www.lib.umich.edu
U. of Southern California	http://usc.summon .serialssolutions.com	https://libraries.usc.edu

subscribing libraries, all you need to know is the library stem—the initial part of the URL, as illustrated in the table below. Table 13.1 shows selected Summon instances, with a direct Summon URL provided as well as the library home page. The reason for both is that sometimes discovery tools change URLs as libraries migrate to newer versions from the vendor, so library home pages are provided as a backup.

Testing Primo

Primo is similar to Summon in that they have a big pot of metadata for vendor content. The difference is that local catalog data is kept in a separate place, not intermingled with vendor content and not mingled with other libraries. Table 13.2 provides selected Primo URLs.

Testing EBSCO Discovery Service (EDS)

EDS differs from the other discovery tools in that it does not make use of a central index for all its content. It becomes evident after observing the way EDS works that EBSCO products are not treated the same as non-EBSCO products. It appears that EDS sends the search two directions: to the central index to search for non-EBSCO content, and a broadcast-like search to a separate EBSCO index, searching both metadata and full text. (Then results from both sets appear to be merged together). This is not so much a publisher bias as an aggregator bias. EBSCO thus treats its results differently than results from the other aggregators, which may result in

Table 13.2. Selected Primo Instances for Testing Purposes.

Institution	Primo URL	Library Home Page
University of Denver	http://primo.library.du.edu	http://library.du.edu
Northwestern University	http://search.library .northwestern.edu	http://www.library .northwestern.edu
Boston University	http://buprimo.hosted .exlibrisgroup.com	https://www.bu.edu/library
Colorado School of Mines	https://mines.primo .exlibrisgroup.com	https://library.mines.edu
University of Tennessee	https://utk-almaprimo .hosted.exlibrisgroup.com	https://www.lib.utk.edu
Purdue University	https://purdue-primo-prod .hosted.exlibrisgroup.com	https://www.lib.purdue.edu
U. of Rhode Island	https://uri-primo.hosted .exlibrisgroup.com	http://web.uri.edu/library

Table 13.3. Selected EDS Instances for Testing Purposes.

Institution	Home Page
University of Georgia	http://www.libs.uga.edu
Santa Ana College	https://www.sac.edu/Library
Mississippi State U.	http://lib.msstate.edu
U. of Central Florida	http://library.ucf.edu
Idaho State U.	https://www.isu.edu/library
James Madison U.	http://www.lib.jmu.edu
Seton Hall U.	https://library.shu.edu

Table 13.4. Selected *WorldCat Discovery* Instances for Testing Purposes.

Institution	*WorldCat Discovery* URL	Home Page
University of Delaware	https://delcat.worldcat.org	https://library.udel.edu
Macalaster College	https://macalester.on.worldcat .org	https://www.macalester .edu/library
St. Louis County Library	https://saintlouiscountylibrary .on.worldcat.org	https://www.slcl.org
University of California Libraries	https://melvyl.on.worldcat.org	http://libraries .universityofcalifornia .edu

favoring their results more highly. And it has not gone unnoticed among librarians (Breeding 2014).

You will often be asked to log in when trying to access an EDS system. Evidently a by-product of their hybrid model, some EDS systems require you to log in to do just about anything, whereas others at least have a guest access provision. Table 13.3 gives selected EDS URLs.

Testing *WorldCat Discovery*

WorldCat Discovery presents results with facets for databases where the hits are found. This method differs from the other discovery tools, where emphasis is on merged metadata. It appears that the search is more of an integrated broadcast search model. Table 13.4 gives selected *WorldCat Discovery* URLs.

Discipline-Specific Databases vs. Discovery Tools vs. Google Scholar

Discovery tools have transformed library research, but they aren't always the best starting place. For those who lack direction on a topic, perhaps a library's single search box discovery tool is the most helpful starting point. But for those who have a specific focus, it may be best to start with the appropriate discipline-specific database. For example, a search for the Tolstoi work *War and Peace* in a discovery tool pulls up 2.5 million results in my local Primo discovery tool. A more constrained search "'war and peace'" limits the results to around 14,000, but that is still a bit unmanageable. But a search in the *MLAIB* for the title phrase brings up just over 700 results, and all of these are in the realm of languages and literatures.

Discovery tools solve the problem of publicizing the many databases to which a library subscribes, but they create their own problems when they draws users away from scoped, specialized subject databases.

You have three kinds of choices now when you do searching for yourself or when you are guiding a patron (or customer, if that's what you call the people you assist) with his or her database questions. It is likely that you will want to use all three of these strategies, and there is no right or wrong answer as to which one to begin with (see table 13.5).

If you were assisting a doctoral student, you would definitely want to start by advising the student to begin with a subject-specific database within his discipline. If you were assisting an undergraduate student who just needed something on her topic, you might want to start her out in your discovery tool (if you have one). If you have a patron who needs primary sources of some kind, you would likely want to get him into the appropriate dedicated database, rather than a discovery tool or Scholar. If you have someone who has a very specific term and it seems that the subject-specific database and discovery tools are coming up short, you would likely want to take her to Google Scholar.

I find myself increasingly starting students out in Google Scholar at the outset, as this can be the quickest way to amass a lot of citations quickly. Then I tell them to "play cleanup" in the discovery tool and subject-specific databases.

Table 13.5. Discovery Features Compared between Discipline-Specific Databases, Discovery Tools, and Google Scholar.

Discipline Database Search	Discovery Tool Search	Google Scholar Search
Controlled vocabulary in many cases	Some vocabulary, but less than total control.	No controlled vocabulary
More chance of normalization of terms	Not as much normalization.	No normalization. Must learn to search with individual author nomenclature.
Scope is easily discovered, well-defined, and restricted	Broad scope. Includes everything from newspaper to peer-reviewed content and e-books.	Narrow. Restricted to peer-reviewed journal content, Google Books "bleed-through," and miscellaneous, sometimes questionable, materials.
Sometimes FT searching	Only occasionally searches FT.	FT searching is the general rule. Rare to find citation-only records.
Strong with primary sources.	Not very strong with primary sources.	Not strong at all with primary sources. Only secondary sources.

This does not minimize the online databases to which libraries pay dearly, but it enhances access by retrieving a greater number of results with Google's mysterious (since they don't tell us how they do it) relevance rankings. It is completely up to users and librarians whether their preference is to begin with the online database interface and all its advantages, like controlled vocabulary; to start with a discovery tool; or to begin with the full-text searching depth of Google Scholar and then go back to discovery tools and discipline-specific databases. It's not a question of either-or, but of using all available searching tools with their various strengths and weaknesses.

The Despair of Depth

One of the reasons students love Google and eschew library database products is that, more often than not, Google can search down into the full text of books and articles, and online databases cannot. Well, sometimes they can, but it is the marked exception.

We can test the depth of searching of individual databases. Let's take, as an example, the *Sage Journals* database. We want to see whether searching within this interface actually retrieves the full text of PDF content or whether it only searches against metadata within the database. To do this, I went to one of their journals, *Acta Sociologica*. Within the full text of one of these issues, I find a feature-length article. The article I selected was the following:

Bakker, Wilma, and Lia Karsten. "Balancing paid work, care and leisure in post-separation households: A comparison of single parents with co-parents." *Acta Sociologica* 56, no. 2 (2013): 173–187.

From page 177 of this article, I selected this text (figure 13.7). Notice that it is desirable to select text that spans across two sentence fragments, as this all but ensures the uniqueness of the selection.

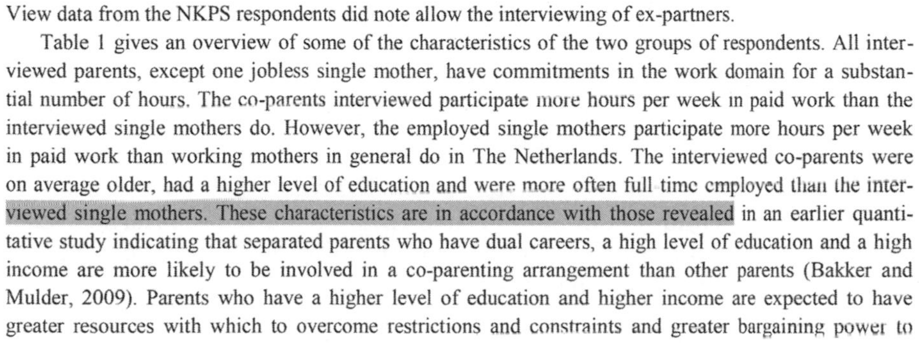

View data from the NKPS respondents did note allow the interviewing of ex-partners.

Table 1 gives an overview of some of the characteristics of the two groups of respondents. All interviewed parents, except one jobless single mother, have commitments in the work domain for a substantial number of hours. The co-parents interviewed participate more hours per week in paid work than the interviewed single mothers do. However, the employed single mothers participate more hours per week in paid work than working mothers in general do in The Netherlands. The interviewed co-parents were on average older, had a higher level of education and were more often full-time employed than the interviewed single mothers. These characteristics are in accordance with those revealed in an earlier quantitative study indicating that separated parents who have dual careers, a high level of education and a high income are more likely to be involved in a co-parenting arrangement than other parents (Bakker and Mulder, 2009). Parents who have a higher level of education and higher income are expected to have greater resources with which to overcome restrictions and constraints and greater bargaining power to

Figure 13.7. Selecting Text for Discovery Tool Testing.

I then pasted this text within the *Sage Journals* interface to see the results. I get many, but they are not the result I am expecting. Then I place the text in quotation marks and do the search: still no relevant results. Can you see the mistake I made? I selected text from a hyphenated word from the previous line. Good indexing will take the hyphenated word and make it a single word. But by eliminating "viewed" and starting my search with "single mothers . . .," I get the result I am expecting. I can test this out in Google Scholar as well. As predicted, Scholar gives me just this article. What we have shown here is that *Sage Journals* does index the full text of its journal content, as does Google Scholar.

This type of depth testing is the same kind of testing I regularly perform with discovery tools because I want to know their capabilities.

Exercises

1. Do you have a discovery system at your library (*Summon*, *Primo*, *EDS*, *WorldCat Discovery*, or maybe a different one)? If so, run some tests to see how broadly your discovery system is able to search.

   a. Search for a newspaper article. Example: "Experts see long-term catastrophe from Colorado mine spill."

   b. Search for a scholarly article. Example: "The Standardisation and Sequencing of Solar Eclipse Images for the Eclipse Megamovie Project."

   c. Search for a government document. Example: "How can the U.S. make development banks more accountable?: Hearing before the

Subcommittee on Monetary Policy and Trace of the Committee on Financial Services" (hearing held in 2016, published in 2017)

   d. Search for primary sources, like archival materials. It's difficult to provide an example search for this category because individual library subscriptions will vary greatly. Try going to a primary source database, perhaps from Adam Matthew or Readex, and see if individual titles are listed in your local discovery tool.

2. If you have a discovery tool, compare your library's tool to those of other libraries. They may be using the same system or a different one. Your task is to design some searches to see which discovery tool produces the most results, the most relevant results, and in which it is easiest to understand the results.

3. Now that you have tested various discovery tools, make a list of strengths and weaknesses of each one. Consider user interface (ease of use), ability to focus searches with facets, and speed of retrieval. Which of the discovery tools do you prefer?

4. Now compare each of the discovery tools you tested with Google Scholar. For this, you need to stay within the realm of scholarly journal articles, as other types of materials are out-of-scope for Scholar. What are the pros and cons of discovery tools versus Google Scholar?

References

Boss, Stephen C., and Michael L. Nelson. 2005. "Federated Search Tools: The Next Step in the Quest for One-Stop-Shopping." *The Reference Librarian* 44, no. 91–92: 139–160.

Breeding, Marshall. 2014. "Discovery Product Functionality." *Library Resource Discovery Products: Context, Library Perspectives, and Vendor Positions. ALA Tech Source* 50, no. 1:5–58. http://dx.doi.org/10.5860/ltr.50n1.

Federal Depository Library Program. 2014. "Recommendations of the Depository Library Council to the Director, Government Publishing Office 2014." Accessed November 14, 2017. http://bit.ly/2igrqBA.

Beyond the Textbook

Carrying on the tradition of the fourth edition, additional exercises, search tips, and tutorials will be available on the publisher's Web site at: http://www.abc-clio.com/books.librariesunlimited.com/Librarians-Guide-to-Online-Searching. This will be updated periodically with the inevitable database changes.

14
User Behaviors and Meeting Information Needs

It's all well and good to know how to search databases, but we really put our knowledge to the test when we match a database to a user's needs. We need to understand user behaviors and how to match appropriate databases to those needs by means of the reference interview. We also need to see the changing role of online databases in the context of providing reference services and to take things beyond merely matching users with information. We need to assist users in using, manipulating, and repurposing the output of databases in formulating their bibliographies.

Users and Their Behaviors

Information-Seeking Behaviors

There is certainly a lot that could be discussed in terms of theories of information-seeking behavior. However, I will not focus on those theories here but will leave that to books like Case and Given (2016) and the countless studies in the library literature of user behavior. Surveys are taken, software is used to track eye movements across Web pages, and Web analytics data is collected and pondered. Instead, I will discuss why users are not knowledgeable about library databases: invisibility, a problem of misinterpretation in the academic setting, and four key elements in users' information-seeking behaviors, based on many years of personal observation.

The Internet has been around since 1969, but it didn't really begin to be adopted by users until after the 1993 introduction of the World Wide Web. For libraries, the mid-1990s were awkward developmental years when databases gradually migrated from print and early electronic formats like CD-ROMs to the robust databases we have today. Today's users seem to share the now universal belief that "everything is on the Web" (even though this is far from the truth), but only a subset of them start from the place where substantial financial resources have been invested on their behalf. Users don't seem to realize that the premium materials, the ones that are poised to help them the most, are behind pay walls and that the way to access these is through their local public or academic library Web site.

It's hard to blame the user. For one thing, the number of online resources has exploded: taking the University of Denver as an example, our database holdings have gone from only a handful in 1997 to 923 in 2017. But libraries generally do not do a great job of promoting these resources. Student's knowledge of technology is generally widespread, but not deep (Dahlstrom and Bichsel 2014).

Adding to the problem, users will rely on guidance materials produced by libraries (OUP 2017), but just as library reference collections and journal indexes have "vanished" into the land of online, so too have library handouts. The popularity of LibGuides (Springshare) and home-grown platforms to host research guides has saved lot of trees, but it has also backgrounded much of the valuable information users want. Libraries continually struggle with how to call attention to these online handouts though their library Web sites.

Another problem can be the misinterpretation of instructions. It's not uncommon for students to approach the reference desk saying that their professor told them not to use the Internet for their research. Some of them go so far as not wanting to be shown any online databases to begin their research. Of course, this is not what the instructor intended (at least, let's hope not). The reason for these kinds of warnings is that students all too often just search the open Web without even consulting curated library resources that will save them a lot of time, direct them to quality resources, and provide citation tools that usually are not found on the open Web.

Thus, the best resources and the guides that might connect users to those resources suffer from a lack of visibility, and sometimes users think they have been told not to use them. So, what do users do instead?

Personal Observations of Library Users

Here are some of my observations on how users approach library research in an online context.

1. **Path of Least Resistance.** Users generally take the path of least resistance. Like water flowing down a mountainside, they tend to bypass difficult obstacles. This is human nature, and we see this in ourselves in our online database usage and in the behavior of library users. If an empty search box presents itself on a library home page, users are quick to type words into it.

2. **No Idea Where They Are.** When users search the Web, they often don't know where they are. Chalk it up to a combination of vendor Web site complexity; OpenURLs taking users to full-text content, but first via a link resolver page; and library proxies taking users to authentication pages before sending them off to a completely different

interface. We can't blame users for being perplexed at the complexity of library resources. University IT folks think that bringing all library Web presence under a single look-and-feel is an easy matter because we are just those people who stamp due dates in books, right? They are blown away when they realize the enormous tasks we have of not only organizing our online library catalog but also our discovery layer, our institutional repositories, and the dozens of contracts we have with outside vendors. When users are linked out to full-text content, they sometimes lose focus on their original starting point.

3. **Keywords.** Users default to keywords. They were searching that way anyway, but then Google and other search engines reinforced this behavior. So now more than ever, there is an almost exclusive reliance on keyword searching. It takes a lot of instruction, encouragement, and motivation to convince students to go beyond keywords and to study and search controlled vocabularies.

4. **Assume Full Text.** "What do you mean there's no full text?" Thanks to the success of databases in incorporating full PDF content into their databases, when users encounter a site with no full text, they are perplexed. Twenty years ago, it was unusual to have any full text accessible via a database. Now databases with no full text at all are more difficult to find.

How many of these four observations are true of you? Do you have other observations or online searching habits of your own that you could add to the list above?

Reference Resources

We've briefly looked at users. The majority of this book has discussed article databases, with several looks at e-books and databases of same. Now we'll discuss a particular variety of database that is part of meeting user information needs: reference resources. But this raises the question, what qualifies a resource to be a "reference" resource? I suggest that a reference tool meet at least one of the following criteria:

- It serves as a gateway or finding aid to locate many other resources (indexes to articles, book reviews, archival materials).

- It is written or published by an authoritative source (associations, governments, international organizations, or a group of respected authors) and is generally not written by a single author.

- It summarizes, simplifies, or creates context (timelines, chronologies, almanacs).

- It provides quick basic introductions to topics (handbooks, guidebooks, subject encyclopedias, subject dictionaries).

- It provides a look-up function (directories, dictionaries).

- It shows marks of permanence. The resource will stand the test of time (authoritative religious texts, canonical literary works, time-tested reference tools of many types).

On a typical day of assisting students in reference consultations, many reference librarians don't need to consult print reference materials. Databases are close at hand to fulfill every reference function, from the quick look-up in a subject encyclopedia to statistical tables to indexes to digital text collections previously held only in microfilm or microfiche.

Table 14.1 shows traditional print reference tools with examples of online formats that fulfill the same purpose.

Reference departments, continually under pressure to minimize footprint and maximize provision of services, are increasingly opting to purchase and subscribe to this content in its online format.

Bringing together multiple types of the reference resources listed above, there are several online tools that fall into the category of *ready reference*. By this term, we mean that they provide quick answers to fast questions. These resources include almanacs, dictionaries (language and subject), encyclopedias (general and subject), statistical compendia, and directories—whatever it took to answer quick questions. What are the online equivalents for these?

Credo Reference. Credo Reference is the name of both the company and the database. Its focus is only on reference materials. The database contains subject dictionaries and subject encyclopedias tied together with topic pages. In addition, some will find the mind map feature helpful in brainstorming and expanding keyword searches.

Oxford Reference. From Oxford University Press, this resource contains topic overviews, timelines, language and subject dictionaries, and subject encyclopedias.

Gale Virtual Reference Library (GVRL). From Gale, *GVRL* was among the first reference e-book collections. Nearly every kind of reference tool is included in the collection.

Libraries will need to consider strategies for making these virtual ready reference tools somehow visible. This may mean scoping or faceting of an online catalog, somehow featuring or favoring them in discovery tool search results, publishing LibGuides or other online guides that discuss individual titles or collections, or creating a separate discovery tool.

The Reference Interview

The reference interview is at the heart of what being a reference librarian is all about. If one has the title "reference librarian" but is not good at the interview itself, then there is a disconnect somewhere. Although reference models come and go, evolving and changing over the years, the reference interview is still the most important part of meeting the information needs of library users. The idea behind the reference interview is to bring library

Table 14.1. Reference Tools: Print and Their Online Equivalents.

Print Reference Tool Categories	Selected Examples of Online Equivalents
Almanacs	*Information Please Almanac* (open source)
Archival Materials	*Archives Unbound* (Gale); *British Online Archives* (Microform Academic Publishers)
Atlases	Perry-Castañeda Library Map Collection
Bibliographies	*International Bibliography of the Social Sciences* (ProQuest); *Bibliography of American Literature* (Chadwyck-Healey/ProQuest)
Biographical indexes	*Biography Index Retrospective* (Wilson/EBSCO)
Catalogs	*WorldCat* (OCLC)
Chronologies	*Hutchinson Chronology of World History* (Ebrary)
Concordances	*A Concordance of the Qur'an* (Oxford University Press)
Dictionaries, language	*Oxford English Dictionary* (Oxford University Press); *Le Grand Robert & Collins Dictionary* (De Marque)
Dictionaries, subject	*Dictionary of Literary Biography Complete Online* (Gale); *Oxford Dictionary of National Biography* (Oxford University Press)
Directories	*Hoover's Online* (Hoover's, Inc.)
Encyclopedias, general	*Funk & Wagnalls New World Encyclopedia* (EBSCO); *Columbia Encyclopedia* (Credo)
Encyclopedias, Subject	*Encyclopedia of Hebrew Language and Linguistics* (Brill); *Garland Encyclopedia of World Music* (Alexander Street)
Gazetteers	*Columbia Gazetteer of the World* (Columbia University Press)
Guidebooks/handbooks	*CRC Handbook of Mechanical Engineering* (CRC/ Taylor & Francis); *Oxford Handbook of Police and Policing* (Oxford University Press)
Indexes	All of the many journal indexing tools
Journal directories	*Ulrichsweb* (ProQuest)
Statistical compendia	*ProQuest Statistical Abstract of the United States* (ProQuest)
Statistical data	*Statista* (Statista); UNdata.org (free)
Style Manuals	*Chicago Manual of Style* (online) (University of Chicago Press)
Thesauri, language	*American Heritage Roget's Thesaurus* (Credo)
Thesauri, subject	*Thesaurus of Psychological Index Terms* (embedded within any of the *PsycINFO* interfaces)
Yearbooks	*Statesman's Yearbook* (Palgrave Macmillan)

resources to meet the needs of users: to match the resource to the question, which is further expanded on below.

Who does the reference interview? Well, that really depends on the public service model of a given library. It may be a librarian. When librarians are on the front lines, we really show the business world how customer service is done. But what business can afford to put their highly paid experts on the front lines? When librarians give top-notch reference service, it gives patrons the impression that they are getting the final answer and won't need to be bounced back and forth to other places for the real answer. Of course, the problem is that most questions as initially asked are not exactly the subject reference type of inquiries. Most of them are directional and don't take a library degree to answer.

It is understandable, from a budgetary point of view, that many (perhaps most) libraries cannot afford to put their highly paid experts on the front lines. For that reason, there are many other models that provide excellent *reference* service and still offer superb *customer* service. Variations of the consultation model allow for paraprofessionals, students, or volunteers to field initial questions, with librarians either on call or available by appointment to spend longer periods of time to assist with the subject-related questions. And speaking of those subject-related questions, a good reference interview is crucial for our next topic.

Determining the Real Question

People ask questions because they don't know the answers. If they knew the answer, then they could frame the question properly. But the fact that they don't already know the answers means that they don't know how to properly ask the questions. This convoluted introduction means that we can't automatically begin to answer the superficial questions that come our way. We have to have a bit of back-and-forth with the asker.

Some people hate asking questions. I just think of myself and how I will do almost anything except ask for help. People make initial judgments about whether to even ask a question and whether the person they are about to ask is the appropriate person, if he or she can be trusted, and if they feel comfortable initiating a conversation.

As you seek to determine the real question, you can use a series of open and closed questions. An open question is one that requires a longer response, like a fill-in-the-blank question. A closed question is just a simple yes/no type response or some other very brief reply. Examples of open questions in a reference context might include the following:

- What resources have you already tried?

- Are there any resources that you have found helpful so far?

- Can you tell me about how you intend to use this information? Is it a short project, or a major one?

- What would your ideal answer look like? What are you envisioning going away with today?

Closed questions might be like this:

- When do you need this information by?
- Are you looking for primary or secondary sources?
- Have you used (particular resource) before?
- Are you looking for current information, or historical?

Determining the real question can be impeded by simple cases of miscommunication: words that have multiple meanings, have been misheard, or are used in unusual ways, as in the following encounter. I remember a time many years ago when I had the evening shift on the reference desk. A woman called on the phone and said she wanted me to look up a couple of titles in the online catalog to see whether the library owned them. I said, "Sure, what's the first title." She replied, "That's not what I meant." "I'm sorry," I said, "why don't you give me the second title then?" "You just don't understand," she replied. By this time, I was perplexed, but I soon came to the realization that her real question was that she was seeking two titles by the linguist Deborah Tannen: *That's Not What I Meant!: How Conversational Style Makes or Breaks your Relations with Others* (1986) and *You Just Don't Understand: Women and Men in Conversation* (1990).

After determining the real reference question, the first thing I try to do is to provide a survey of the possible scope of the answer. I discuss the use of primary sources or secondary sources, searching in various types of databases, from the general/interdisciplinary databases to subject-specific databases. I examine whether a discovery tool or database might be the best starting point. In summary, try to explore "all possible worlds" for answers. You don't want to fall into the trap of making incorrect assumptions about the shape of the response. The user deserves your best response.

Match the Resource to the Question

Doing reference work is all about matching the appropriate resource to the question. This assumes that you listen carefully to the question to make sure you understand the scope of the question; the users project (is it a brief memo, an honors thesis, a doctoral dissertation, a professor's course preparation, a personal novel, or hobby research); and what the desired outcomes are.

Is the patron trying to find everything on a topic or just something? Is a journal article the best source, or is a book? Do a brainstorming session with yourself to find the best kind of resource for the question. (See the "Search Strategies" section in this chapter for more on doing a brainstorming session with yourself.)

Example: I am having difficulty finding material for my research topic, "How social networking negatively affects communication skills." First, consider what kinds of literature would have something to say about this. Let's take one concept at a time, consider resources available to us that cover that concept, and then brainstorm some search strategies.

Social networking: Computer databases such as *ACM Digital*, Pro-Quest's *Computing Database*, *IEEE Xplore*; also try for the concept in education databases (*ERIC*), psychology databases (*PsycINFO*), and sociology databases (*Sociological Abstracts*).

Communication skills: Communication databases such as *Communication and Mass Media Complete* (EBSCO); also *ERIC*, *PsycINFO*, and *Sociological Abstracts*.

It's usually difficult to work ideas like "negative effects" into a search. So, we will look at article titles in the results lists to see whether they can be perceived as negative consequences. Very often, academic literature is more nuanced, with both positive and negative aspects called out. Of course, for all these topics, try the general, comprehensive databases from EBSCO, Gale, and ProQuest.

Let's start with *Academic Search* (EBSCOhost platform). We get 40 results. With this many results, we have nothing to lose. I do a default search (maintaining the "Select a field" option) for the term *negative effects*. I get one result. I notice that the term *negative effects* is coming from the article abstract. This might be an article I want to save or download.

I move on to a communication database, EBSCO's *Communication and Mass Media Complete*. I first notice that there is a thesaurus, so I look for exact descriptors. *Communication skills* is not an authorized term in this thesaurus, but we are directed to use either the very broad term *Communication* or *Communicative competence*. I next see whether *social networking* is a term in the thesaurus. *Social networks* is an authorized term, but the scope note indicates that this refers to interpersonal networks, not computer networks. But the unauthorized term just below, *SOCIAL networks -- Computer network resources*, points us to the authorized descriptor, *online social networks*. Now we feel comfortable putting together a search. The best way to show you how I searched is to copy the search out of the EBSCOhost search history:

SU communicative competence AND SU online social networks

This search retrieved four articles. It's generally not up to the reference librarian to declare whether a resource will or will not work for a student (but we often do make strong suggestions).

Now continue doing the same kinds of things for the other databases from our brainstorming list.

Dismissiveness

Every year in my reference classes, when grading student assignments, I receive answers on student homework that are dismissive. By this I mean that the soon-to-be-librarian is not taking the question seriously and gives off "vibes" that he or she would rather be doing something else. It is not fun being on the receiving end of a dismissive attitude. Have you ever seen a reference librarian who just stays seated when answering questions and never gets up and walks a user over to a section of materials to show them how to locate the information? I have.

Dismissive attitudes can be evidenced in-person, via e-mail, or in chat exchanges. Here are some clear signs of dismissiveness:

- No summarization of topic and delineation of how you intend to respond.

- Brevity and terseness of response.

- No attempt to explain the value of resources you are suggesting and how they answer the question.

- No attempt to mention all the complexities of the question.

Here is an example of a dismissive e-mail exchange:

E-mail question: I need background on the Affordable Care Act. How can I find this? Ken.
Response: Hello Ken, Here are several sources I hope you find useful.
IRS: https://www.irs.gov/affordable-care-act
HealthCare: https://www.hhs.gov/healthcare/about-the-law/read -the-law
Please let me know if you need any further assistance.

How might this have been handled differently?

Virtual Reference: E-Mail and Chat

We now live in a multimodal world. Our modern communication methods could not have been imagined a century ago. Librarians need to adapt to these different communication modes. Instead of in-person walk-ups and answering the phone, it is not unusual for a reference transaction to begin with a chat (immediate need and initial contact; synchronous exchange); morph into e-mail (with screen captures and URLs; slower, asynchronous exchange); and then result in consultation, either in person or virtually over a live video session.

Virtual reference interviews present their own challenges. At least with telephone reference you had auditory cues from the patron, and you gave off cues of your own. But with e-mail and chat, there aren't any of the regular cues we have traditionally used in reference interactions. We can't ignore these interactions, as they are among the most popular ways people interact with reference librarians, but some extra effort is required.

With in-person reference, it is fairly easy to get to the real question first and then offer assistance. But to do so with e-mail tends to frustrate the user. In e-mail reference, the connection is totally asynchronous, and this mode of communication does not lend itself to an ideal reference transaction. You are left to either make assumptions about the question, or you send a reply e-mail and wait for the response. Thus, question negotiation (trying to get to the real question) is more challenging via e-mail because the delays inherent in asynchronous communication make such negotiation too slow and cumbersome. It's best just to send a preliminary reply, asking whether your answer is on point or you missed the point and they intended something different. This initial reply might be accompanied by some database suggestions and a few screen captures just to get things started.

Chat reference, even more popular today, is better, although it lacks the vocal cues that the old-fashioned telephone reference conveyed. In a chat context, you have the ability to ask for clarification before you go off to answer the question. With chat questions, I find myself negotiating the questions more because they are synchronous transactions (in real time).

Let me share some strategies that help with these situations.

- Send back a preliminary reply, clarifying the question that was asked and how you intend to proceed. This question negotiation is similar to that which is done in in-person reference transactions.

- Make some preliminary assumptions, based on your previous experience, and answer accordingly. But include language that says to please let you know if you have missed the mark in understanding the question.

- Ask for clarification: What resources have they already consulted? How do they intend to use the information? This gives clues as to how far you need to delve into the response. If this is just a ready reference, quick-answer kind of thing, then not much time is required for the response. If the person is writing a thesis or major project, perhaps the response will need to be comprehensive.

When I am sure I am answering the right question, I then usually respond to e-mail reference questions with a "chronicling" of my research process, including both the failures and the successes. For example, if I searched the *ERIC* database and didn't find many relevant resources, I state that in the e-mail. I do the same for the databases that really worked for the user's topic. This instructs the user about the places I thought useful enough to search so that they can do the same the next time they have a similar question. It also shows them how much time and effort I exerted on their behalf. In my responses, I endeavor to be as clear as possible. I delineate each search strategy or resource consulted with a number or bullet so that the e-mail is easier to follow.

Important Reminder

With remote users (e-mail or chat), you will need to use what you learned about permalinks (also known as durable URLs) and proxies (assuming that your library uses this technology). Failure to use these when sending along database URLs or links to specific articles will only frustrate your users.

Search Strategies

Size up the question. What kind of resource will help with this question? "I want to find out about the history of social welfare." What works best: a scholarly journal article or a book?

Thinking Like an Indexer vs. Thinking Like a Text

Two approaches to research are presented in this book: a *controlled-vocabulary approach* and a *full-text search approach*. These two approaches are at opposite ends of the spectrum. The first, thinking like an indexer, is more traditional, forcing thoughts of "aboutness" and the big picture. The latter, thinking like a text, is more contemporary, only because it is now possible where it wasn't before. It involves thinking like the writer of your perfect article; it's not so much about the big picture as the constituent parts, the particulars. It's not that one is better than another; it's that both can and should be pursued.

Format-Independent Thinking

Online is just a format. When approaching a reference question, the best practice is to think *format independent*. Too often, we try to answer questions with only online resources. And while that is what this book is all about, it is important to consider all the resources available to you. If the answer is best found on microform reels, then go there. Don't ignore a resource just because you don't like a format.

Have a Brainstorming Session with Yourself

Brainstorming sessions with other people are very important. If you don't have anyone else that understands your topic as much as you do, have a session with yourself. To work with your topic, try the following steps.

Write your question down as a single sentence. What information do you need? In your ideal world, what would that information look like? Would it include scholarly, peer-reviewed journal articles; archival materials; primary sources; statistical or numerical materials; or maps or GIS data? Then run your search through a general database, such as *Academic Search*, *ProQuest Central*, or Gale's *Academic OneSearch*. Do the results suggest additional keywords?

Go to the best database for the field you are searching in (*PsycINFO* for psychology, for example) and use the thesaurus or online index to locate the closest controlled-vocabulary terms. Then search by those terms in that database. Expand your search to discovery platforms (if your library has access to one of them) or Google Scholar. Use Google Scholar to find articles citing the best article you can find and also related articles.

Then determine the scope of the searches you want to do: do you want dissertations or theses, popular literature, scholarly literature, books or book chapters, encyclopedia information, or statistics?

Here are some questions you can ask to get your brainstorming session going:

- What keywords are most closely associated with my topic?

- What disciplines are concerned with this topic? The answer may be many topics or cross-disciplinary.

- Is there a database available to you that has a thesaurus or other controlled vocabulary?

- Are you looking for primary sources or secondary sources?

- Can you consider additional kinds of information sources, such as dissertations or theses, technical reports, government reports, legal materials, newspaper articles, chronologies, and so on?

- When you searched a database, how many results did you retrieve? If you feel you have too few results, consider broadening your search terms, using the OR Boolean operator. If you have too many, consider ways to narrow the search with more specific keywords or controlled vocabulary, ANDing in an additional term, or narrowing the time span.

Modes of Searching: Keyword, Controlled Vocabulary, Citations, Full Text

Which kind of searching are you going to do? Are you going the easy route and doing a default keyword search? If a controlled vocabulary is available in the database, are you going to use it? The answer to these questions will largely depend on the kind of research you are doing and how you intend to use the information. If you are doing a research for a PhD dissertation, you may need everything available on our topic. It is well worth the time investment to study a database completely, how it is constructed and indexed, and whether there are controlled vocabularies or special fields you can leverage to tease out the results, coming as close to that magical "all and only" as you can possibly get.

You may want to search citations to important articles using *Web of Science*, *Scopus*, or Google Scholar. Citation searching provides a different way than keyword or controlled-vocabulary searching and usually results in additional valuable results.

Full-text searching, perhaps best accomplished in Google Scholar and Google Books because of their powerful (and mysterious) relevance rankings, is a favorite among many researchers. Google Scholar offers additional linkages through its "Related Articles" feature. Whether you decide to start here or end up here, you need to be prepared to deal with a few access issues: Google Books is a discovery-only tool in most cases, and you will need to rely on your library to acquire the book or e-book. Articles in Google Scholar may not be available to you through your library subscriptions, so you may need to request interlibrary loan fulfillment in some cases. As long as you are prepared for these issues, these Google tools nicely augment library online databases.

When to Prefer Keyword Searching

Let's face it. No matter how much we study controlled vocabularies, the strengths of field searching, and constructing complex Boolean or proximity search strings, we tend to always favor simple keyword searching most of the time. There are some very good reasons to rely on those simple searches. For example, when searching a database with fields that are not consistent across all records (as in some aggregator databases). Or when searching a database with subject schema from various sources and with back-generated indexes. Modern databases often do what they can to make the best of our humble searches and offer sophisticated search limits to carry the search through to completion.

Make Databases "Your Own"

When I really learned reference skills, I was working at the reference desk in the late 1980s. In those days, reference departments were full of books (what a concept!). I really wanted to learn how each of these tools worked, so when there were no people needing my assistance, I would take a reference work with which I was completely unfamiliar and ask myself a series of questions:

- What is this resource for?

- When would I use it?

- What reference questions does it answer?

For many materials, this was not a difficult task. But there were some resources that were quite a challenge. I clearly remember the most challenging resource being a German-language book review resource: *Internationale Bibliographie der Rezensionen geistes- und sozialwissenschaftlicher Literatur (International Bibliography of Book Reviews of Scholarly Literature on the Humanities and Social Sciences)*. I spent hours trying to master these print volumes, and I finally got it!

The reason I mention this process is that we need to do the same thing with online databases. Don't shy away from a database just because you don't understand it. Master it. Spend time working with it until you own it.

Ask yourself these questions when studying a database:

- What is the stated scope of the database? What subjects are covered? What is the depth of coverage? Is it primary source materials or secondary sources?

- What kinds of materials are indexed (e.g., academic scholarly journal articles, books, book reviews, theses and dissertations, technical reports, government publications, statistical tables, popular literature like magazine articles, or newspaper articles)?

- What populations does this database serve (e.g., general public, undergraduate students, graduate students, or specialized researchers)?

- What is the best way to access the database (e.g., thesaurus entries, keyword searching of metadata, or keyword searching of full text)?

- How do I cite materials in the database? Does it have an automatic citation generator?

- What special features does the database have (e.g., alert system, mapping or visualization features, or links to other databases or full text)?

A New Way to Brainstorm Keywords

Concept maps, or mind maps, have been around for several decades. When I was taking classes at Cornell University, I was influenced by Novak and Gowin (1984). I even took class notes using concept maps and found them to be refreshing and beneficial. They are not for everyone. A while back, there was the search engine called KartOO that used visual representations of keywords to assist in brainstorming and exploration. Not so long ago, EBSCO came out with a concept map in several of their databases. Neither of those tools exist any longer. But now there is a new entrant into the concept mapping space, *Yewno*.

With *Yewno*, over 120 million documents are searched, and results are presented visually. Instead of a list of links, results are visually displayed as concept maps (figure 14.1).

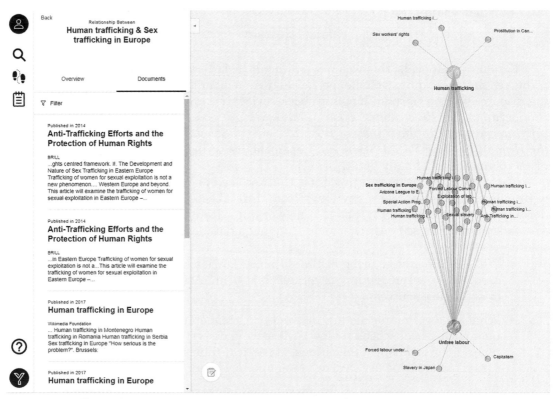

Figure 14.1. *Yewno* Searches by Semantic Connections on a Concept Map.
Source: ©2017 Yewno. Used with permission.

It remains to be seen whether *Yewno* will be able to live up to its hype. The database creators claim that it goes well beyond mere keyword searching and allows for deeper connections. It is likely that this will be more attractive to "right-brained" individuals, those who are visually and artistically oriented. Its strength seems to be in opening up new terms and making semantic connections that wouldn't have otherwise been made, and not so much for discovering "all and only" the results desired.

Going beyond Databases: Using Database Output for Citation Management

We touched on bibliographic citation management briefly in chapter 6 from the perspective of vendor features. But it deserves discussion here in the context of users' needs and their desires. With citation export features often available, databases invite users to repurpose metadata for other tasks. Building up personal bibliographies and merging them seamlessly with finished research papers is a powerful use of technologies to enhance research. Universities often subscribe to RefWorks (ProQuest) or EndNote (Clarivate Analytics) to meet users' needs. But very often users take another path and try to solve the citation management issues on their own. They use tools such as Zotero, Mendeley, EasyBib, or any number of solutions that are available. Mendeley is a crowd-sourced shared body of citations that is strongest in the sciences. Zotero seems to have a dedicated following on most university campuses.

Client-Based vs. Cloud-Based

By client-based software, we mean software programs that have to be installed on a local computer. Cloud-based means software accessed over the Internet. There are strong pros and cons to each of these methods.

Client-based systems, of which EndNote is the most popular, are by far the fastest. When manipulating records, there is no need to wait for a response from the Internet. EndNote has been around since the 1980s, and there is a very strong user base. The import filters and output style formats have been well tested over time. PDF files can be saved within EndNote bibliographies, but saving too many of these will slow down the database response time.

The pros of this are that the PDF is saved along with the citation, making for easy consultation of the actual article. This can be a tremendous time-saver when doing research. On the other hand, some PDF files can be many megabytes in size, especially if they are not source code generated, in other words, if they were scanned from print versions. These can take up a lot of space. If the storage space is local to your computer, as in the case of EndNote desktop, this will slow down the software significantly and make backups difficult. If the storage is Web-based, as in the case of the new RefWorks, there may eventually be space limitations placed on your account.

Word Processor Integration

The ability to insert citations directly into word processing software by installing a plug-in is one of the best features of several bibliographic

Table 14.2. Selected Databases and Citation Export Features.

Database	Supported Systems	Citation Generation
EBSCOhost databases	RIS, EndNote Web, generic, BibTeX, RefWorks, EasyBib	ABNT (Brazil), AMA, APA, Chicago/Turabian Author/Date, Harvard (Australian), Harvard, Chicago/Turabian Humanities, MLA, Vancouver
Gale databases	EasyBib, EndNote, Noodle Tools, ProCite, Reference Manager, RefWorks	MLA (7th and 8th), APA, Chicago Notes & Bibliography
Google Scholar	BibTeX, EndNote, Reference Manager, RefWorks	MLA, APA, Chicago Humanities, Harvard, Vancouver
NewsBank *Access World News*	EasyBib, RefWorks, save to file	Australian Guide to Legal Citation, APA, ASA, BibTeX, Chicago, Harvard, MLA, RIS (for EndNote, ProCite), Turabian
OCLC FirstSearch (*WorldCat*)	EndNote, RefWorks, text	not available
OCLC WorldCat.org	RefWorks, EndNote, Reference Manager, EasyBib	APA, Chicago 15th Author-Date, Harvard, MLA, Turabian (6th) Notes
ProQuest databases	RefWorks, EasyBib, RIS, text	APA 5th and 6th, ASA, BibTeX, Chicago (15th & 16th) Notes & Bibliography; Chicago (15th & 16th) Author-Date; CSE, Harvard, Harvard (British), IEEE, ISO, MLA (6th, 7th, 8th), Turabian (7th & 8th) Notes; Turabian (7th & 8th) Reference List, Uniform, Vancouver
ProQuest *E-Book Central*	RefWorks; EndNote	APA, Chicago/Turabian Notes-Bibliography; Chicago/Turabian Author-Date; Harvard; MLA; Vancouver
Readex All Search interface	None	Only a help guide for formatting MLA and APA styles
Readex interface	Just outputs a simple citation in a tagged format as a generic style	not available
SpringerLink	RIS (for Papers, Reference Manager, RefWorks, Zotero); EndNote; BIB (for BibTeX, JabRef, Mendeley)	Not available

Database	Supported Systems	Citation Generation
Web of Science	EndNote online; EndNote desktop; RefWorks, BibTeX	Not available
Wiley Online Library	Text, EndNote, Reference Manager, RefWorks, ProCite, BibTeX	Not available
HeinOnline	RefWorks, RIS, text	MLA, APA, Chicago (humanities), Bluebook
Nexis Uni (formerly known as *LexisNexis Academic*)	RefWorks, RIS (recheck this)	APA, MLA, Chicago (humanities)

Notes: Chicago has two styles: notes and bibliography, also known as humanities style, documentation I; and author-date, also known as social sciences style, documentation II.
Turabian patterns like Chicago, with a documentation I and a documentation II.
ProCite and Reference Manager have been discontinued, but they are still in use by many.

software solutions. EndNote desktop has Cite while you Write (CWYW); ProQuest RefWorks has Write-N-Cite. Zotero has word processor integration for Microsoft Word and LibreOffice/Open Office. Mendeley has a citation plug-in for Microsoft Office and LibreOffice.

Most aggregator databases and many publisher interfaces have features for exporting/saving results to one of more of these citation management software interfaces (table 14.2). Even if your favorite citation software is not mentioned, there is usually a way to export citations with several additional steps. Some students use Microsoft Word's bibliography features, but I do not recommend this—*ever*! Librarianship is all about standards, and Word doesn't follow them.

It should be noted that databases that contain primary source materials often do not even try to include citation tools. The reason is that primary sources have so many challenges when sorting out the appropriate fields for the various output formats. Thus, ProQuest's *Congressional* database simply lists the fields without having the ability to transform the fields into APA, MLA, Chicago, or any other style. Readex's *Serial Set* will output citations into RIS format for import into any citation package, but given the complexities of congressional materials, it would have been better to format the citation by hand so that focus can be placed in the appropriate elements. Most Alexander Street Press content does not feature citation information formatted in the popular citation styles.

Exercises

1. Imagine yourself seeing a library user who obviously has a question. What would welcoming body language look like? How about unwelcoming?

2. How would you feel if you asked a question at a reference desk, and the librarian responded by turning immediately to his or her computer to start typing?

3. Can you think of bad customer service experiences you have had in nonlibrary contexts? What can be learned from these experiences that apply to library interactions?

4. Have you had many interactions with reference librarians where you were the patron? Which ones do you remember? What do you remember about them?

5. Which bibliographic management software do you use? Does your system work well with the databases you regularly use?

References

Brown, Christopher C. 2017. *Harnessing the Power of Google: What Every Researcher Should Know.* Santa Barbara, CA: Libraries Unlimited.

Case, Donald O., and Lisa M. Given. 2016. *Looking for Information: A Survey of Research on Information Seeking, Needs, and Behavior.* 4th ed. Bingley, UK: Emerald Group Publishing.

Dahlstrom, Eden, and Jacqueline Bichsel. 2014. "ECAR Study of Undergraduate Students and Information Technology, 2014." Research report. Louisville, CO: ECAR. Accessed December 29, 2017. https://library.educause.edu/~/media/files /library/2014/10/ers1406-pdf.pdf?la=en.

Novak, Joseph D., and D. B. Gowin. 1984. *Learning How to Learn.* Cambridge [Cambridgeshire] and New York: Cambridge University Press.

Oxford University Press. 2017. "Navigating Research: How Academic Users Understand, Discover, and Utilize Reference Resources." June. Accessed December 29, 2017. https://global.oup.com/academic/librarians/navigatingresearch.

Beyond the Textbook

Carrying on the tradition of the fourth edition, additional exercises, search tips, and tutorials will be available on the publisher's Web site at http:// www.abc-clio.com/books.librariesunlimited.com/Librarians-Guide-to-Online -Searching. This will be updated periodically with the inevitable database changes.

15
Evaluating Databases

This chapter brings us full circle, as it harkens back to many of the "scope" elements introduced in chapter 1. Here we consider those elements again, and additional ones, to make a detailed list of issues to consider when evaluating a database, either as part of a purchase decision or for writing a review: information to gather, factors to assess, and suggestions for benchmarking. It concludes with advice about how to use this information effectively in putting together a database subscription request.

In real life, you are probably not going to be called upon to do an in-depth formal evaluation of a database that frequently. Institutions tend not to change their database subscriptions that often: getting anything new usually requires cancellation of an existing service (to free up funds), and changing between relatively equivalent products tends to be held in check by the overall community's resistance to change. (Users generally prefer a status quo they are familiar with rather than a change that requires any amount of learning or adjustment in their habits. A replacement has to demonstrate obvious and significant improvements in ease of use or content to be accepted.) It is also likely that you won't be making such a decision alone: you will be part of a team, and thus the whole responsibility will not rest solely on your shoulders. At the same time, you want to remain up to date on new databases in your subject area; therefore, familiarizing yourself with new and changing products may become a fairly steady undercurrent to your job (depending on the volatility of products in your subject area).

Another motivation for doing a thorough study of a database is to write a review of it. Although reviewing is an excellent way to start getting published, it isn't something you do every day. Finally, you obviously want to master a database completely before teaching others about it, even though (as you'll find in the teaching chapter) you want to be judicious in how much of what you learn you choose to pass on to your audience.

This explains the position of this chapter in the book, almost at the end of the sequence rather than at the beginning. It's important, and I hope useful, but much of it is not information that you'll need to work through in its entirety very frequently. The list of factors to consider in chapter 1 should be enough to make you as familiar as you need to be with any database in order to choose and use it based on the information need. This chapter is designed to help you make an informed purchase decision or to write a good review. You will find that you use selected elements from this list regularly in your daily reference activities: factors such as topical coverage, date range, availability of full text, and usability of the interface, you'll find yourself assessing almost automatically, and even memorizing for the databases you use frequently. For those situations requiring an in-depth examination, such as conducting a database trial or writing a review for publication, the following two sections offer a list of categories and associated factors to consider in evaluating and testing databases.

Basic Facts and Figures: Initial Information to Gather

Database Vendor(s)

As with anything else, the same databases are sometimes available from different vendors, and it can pay to shop around. Vendors get the data in a raw format and then format and load it according to how they structure their databases, what fields they want to use, whether those fields are searchable, and so on. The search capabilities (and obviously the user interface) vary depending on the vendor, and you can have a really different experience searching the same database offered by different vendors. If you are seriously looking at a new database and more than one vendor provides it, be sure to try them all. Subscribing to a database is a big investment, and you owe it to your organization, and especially to your users, to get the version that will best meet *their* needs.

Existing Reviews

Before jumping in and possibly reinventing the wheel, stop and check: has anyone already written a review of this database? A thorough database review is a large task, requiring hours of research and testing. Although you may still want to check the latest facts and figures if the review is a few years old, and you will always want to do your own testing, someone else's review is a very useful place to start. If you are using a database such as *Library Literature & Information Science* to locate reviews, searching "Online Databases — Evaluation" or "Information storage & retrieval systems — Evaluation" in the "Subject Terms" field and the name of the database as a keyword should quickly identify any commercially published reviews. The source titles you'll see most often are *Library Journal* and *The Charleston Advisor*, as well as *Booklist, Choice: Current Reviews for Academic Libraries, School Library Journal*, and *Library Media Connection*. All are excellent sources of reviews. If more than one vendor offers the database, look for comparative reviews or individual reviews for the different versions. Electronic versions of reference books are also often thought of as databases and may be reviewed as such. In addition, a specialized resource for reviews of those titles is the *American Reference Books Annual* (*ARBA*; itself available as an online database, *ARBAonline*).

Coverage

There are many aspects to coverage, including subject, material, source, date, and geographic.

Subject Coverage. Subject coverage is also referred to as "scope." What is the subject emphasis of the database—is it devoted to just one topical area or is it multidisciplinary? Especially for a subject-specific database, what is the *level* of the material covered; that is, who is the intended audience? K–12 students? College students? Graduate students? Faculty? Specialists? The lay public?

Material Coverage. What types of material and formats are included? If only periodicals, what types? (Types to look for include popular, scholarly, trade journals, newspapers, and news wires.) Is there one type that is emphasized; that is, are there mostly popular or trade journals, with only a few scholarly titles? For articles containing tables or graphics, are those elements included? If such tables or graphics are included, how are they reproduced? (A formatted table reproduced in plain text can be almost impossible to interpret.) If other kinds of documents are covered, what are they? (Possibilities include books, book chapters, theses, conference proceedings, government documents, speeches, audio transcripts such as NPR interviews, and photos or visual materials such as would be found in an image archive.) For a database consisting of primary source documents, such as those from the Alexander Street Press, what types of documents are included? Are the document types represented equally or is the bulk of the material of one type? What formats are offered for full text: HTML, PDF, or both?

Source Coverage. The *number* of sources is something that vendors love to tout, but, like "database size," this number is almost meaningless nowadays. (Depending on your needs and your audience, numbers that might have some meaning are the number of popular and scholarly sources, if both types are included.) What matters are the specific source *titles* included and the *coverage* of those titles. Are the important journals for the discipline in the list, or has it been padded with a lot of unknown "fluff" titles? Are the publications indexed cover-to-cover or only selectively? Is this policy universal for all titles in the database or does it vary by title? Does the vendor have exclusive rights to any titles; for example, is there a journal whose content you will only find in So-and-So's databaseX? How much information is provided: citations only (unusual), citations with abstracts (like the *Web of Science*), or citations and full text (rapidly becoming the norm)? This is also referred to as the *breadth and depth of coverage*: more source titles would indicate greater *breadth*, and cover-to-cover indexing would provide greater *depth* of coverage.

Date Coverage. Does the database provide only current, or current and retrospective coverage (e.g., how far back in time does indexing for most of the titles go)? Does the database use a "moving wall" date coverage system, wherein titles are covered up to a set number of years in the past? (For example, JSTOR titles are usually covered from the first issue up to issues from three to five years ago. Each year, one more new year is added, but current issues are not available.)

Geographic Coverage. Does the database just index U.S. publications or is the source list international? If it is international, are the materials in their original language? How many and which languages are represented? Are article titles and abstracts (if available) offered in translation? (Is this important to your clientele or not?)

Availability of Sources

For any database that doesn't offer full text for all content, a major consideration is how accessible the material that it indexes will be to your users. How many, or what percentage, of the sources are available in full text? If the database you are evaluating has only partial or no full text, do you have other sources that can provide a significant proportion of those documents, and do you have a way to get users to that material? Interlibrary loan is always an option, but people usually prefer to be able to put their hands on what they want locally and immediately.

Updating and Embargoes

Most databases now add material continuously rather than on a schedule, but it could be worth asking the question: how often is material added? Of more significance is this: are there embargoes on certain titles (e.g., the publisher has decided not to make the most current issues available)? How many titles are embargoed and for how long? (Are they embargoed for weeks, months, or a year or more?) If there are titles that are important to your users that are embargoed for six months or more, this would be a strong red flag.

For example, say you are looking at getting the database *ABI/INFORM* on the ProQuest platform, and you know that the two trade journals *Journal of Investing* and *Journal of Trading* are of particular interest to faculty in your business school. Those two journals show as "full text available," and that coverage is "to present." However, following the word "present" is a note: "(delayed 545 days)." While users can see the list of contents and abstracts up to the most recent issue, full text won't be accessible for about a year and half! In checking the length of an embargo, also take into consideration the type of publication. The *Financial Times*, out of London, is listed in ProQuest's *ABI/INFORM* as "(delayed 1 month)." That doesn't sound bad, but consider that the *Financial Times* is a daily newspaper. This type of reporting probably isn't of much use after a month.

So far, this discussion has mainly focused on periodical databases, but what about a directory database? A list of associations might remain fairly stable, but the corporate world is more dynamic: companies change their names or get bought, sold, and merged into other companies. For both associations and corporations, names of officers, their titles, phone numbers, and so on are likely to change. For any directory or corporate type of database, definitely find out how often it is updated and how the database vendor obtains the information.

Database Aids

Database aids include both online and physical resources that provide help in using the database, teaching others to use it, and promoting it. Investigate the database's online help function: is it easy to find, easy to understand, and easy to use? Is the help context sensitive, that is, different depending on which screen you are on, or always the same? Note that context sensitive is not necessarily always better than static: the system's interpretation of your context may leave you scratching your head and wanting to start at the beginning instead. Also, if this is a vendor supplying many databases, is the help specific to the database at hand, or is it generic, a one-size-fits-all for all the databases they offer? (The latter can be very annoying if you are trying to find out something about a database-specific field or feature.) Is there an online tutorial, and is it useful? Are there quick start or similar brief how-to cards or leaflets that the vendor can provide? Will the vendor send you promotional materials to help market the new database? Most vendors are anxious to provide train-the-trainer services, usually by webinar; this is usually a quick and efficient way to get up to speed.

Cost and Vendor Support

Vendors regularly experiment with new pricing models, and this can be a more intricate question than you might think. In academic situations, the database cost is frequently based on FTE, or how many *full-time equivalent* students there are on campus. Such a charge model usually then means there is no limit to the number of people who can use the database at the same time. At the other end of the spectrum, some databases charge by the number of simultaneous users, or *seats*, that you opt for, meaning that only a limited number of people can use the database at the same time. A database with deep date coverage may be divided into sections, and it might be worth checking to see whether you can purchase only the most recent section (if that would meet your needs).

Price negotiation can be full of wheeling and dealing: discounts might be available based on the number of years that you sign on for or by the number of databases purchased from the same vendor. The price can also depend on how desperate the sales rep is to make the sale. Your institution may be able to drive a harder bargain in December (when the reps are anxious to make year-end quotas) than in July. Again, such a decision will seldom be up to you alone: you will likely be working with a department head or a committee that is familiar with pricing and dealing with vendors.

No matter how you look at it, however, database subscriptions are expensive, often starting at four figures and going up from there (business and science databases can easily run into the $15,000–$100,000 or more range). Many libraries now participate in library consortia, which act together to negotiate pricing with vendors. Because there are so many possible factors, database prices are seldom (if ever) posted on vendor Web sites or listed anywhere. The myriad shifting factors and lack of transparency in pricing is the reason this book makes no attempt to provide pricing information on any of the databases discussed. The best way to determine the cost for a particular database is to start with the collection development or acquisitions librarian in your library. If you are not currently in a library, call the vendor directly and speak with a sales representative.

Vendor Support. It's also useful to explore the kind of support that the vendor offers, in particular for usage statistics. Are usage statistics available? How detailed are they? How do you access them, or can a report be automatically sent to you on a regular basis? For academic libraries, do the statistics adhere to the latest Code of Practice defined by Project COUNTER, that is, are they "COUNTER compliant"? (See http://www .projectcounter.org.) Standardized statistics allow you to really know what you are looking at, what has been counted, and what it means. If you decide to invest the money, it's very important to have some idea of how much the database is getting used.

Other vendor support issues to explore are the nature and availability of technical and search support (by phone? e-mail? Web form? Is it 24/7 and 365 days a year?) and, as mentioned previously, train-the-trainer services. During your database trial period, besides working with the database itself, be sure to test the technical and search support services. Is it easy to reach a knowledgeable person? Were your questions answered accurately and in a timely fashion?

Finally, be sure to try the database under all the current favorite browsers, and on Macs, PCs, and especially handheld devices. If the database is only fully functional under IE on a PC, and most of your users try to do everything on their iPhones, you have a disconnect. (Believe it or not, there are still some databases with such limitations on the market.)

Testing and Benchmarking

As mentioned earlier, prior to initiating a subscription request, you will want to get a database trial (or multiple trials if the database is offered by more than one vendor). This is a key component in your evaluation. I have never encountered a vendor who wouldn't offer some kind of trial access to their products. Do not abuse their good nature in this regard: don't ask for a trial if you aren't serious about the database for some reason (either for purchase or for review-writing purposes) or if you don't have the time to evaluate it properly.

While you have the trial, make good use of it. If necessary, deliberately schedule several time slots on your calendar over the course of the trial to devote to working with the database. As they say, pound on it! You really need to know what you're talking about if you are going to recommend it for purchase. The following section describes aspects of the database to look for, assess, and compare (benchmark) during your database trial.

Testing

Record and File Structure. This topic takes us all the way back to the material in chapter 2. Factors to assess include the following: What fields are available? Are the fields appropriate and useful given the subject matter of the database? When vendors simply apply their standard interface to a new database, the result is often less than optimal. Of the fields you see in a full record display, how many are also searchable? (Some fields may be "display only"; *PsycINFO*'s list of fields clearly delineates which fields are searchable and which are display only.) Another way to think of the field question is, how many ways can you look up the same record? That is, how many "access points" do the records have? More fields aren't always better, but they can be helpful. The questions to keep at the front of your mind while assessing these factors are: Does this make sense for this database? Is it helpful? Does it help get me to better results more efficiently?

Linking is an aspect of record and file structure that you can discover simply by observation. In a record display, are there fields that are linked (e.g., author or subject) that allow you to immediately pull up all other records with that author or subject? Are there other linked fields in the record, and to what do they link?

Indexing and Cataloging Practices: Searchability. Don't be put off by the heading of this section: it is not a suggestion for you to try to find out the interior policies and work practices that the vendor uses. Rather, there are many things that you can observe during testing or find out from the documentation that reveal something about how the vendor has set up the indexes and how much human intervention (cataloging) has been applied to the records. These things can be dubbed *searchability*, and you will find many of them familiar from earlier chapters:

- What limits are available? Are they useful?

- Questions to ask about controlled vocabulary:
  - Does the database use a set of a controlled vocabulary (e.g., subject terms)?

  - Is the subject list a straight alphabetical list of terms, as in Gale's *Academic OneFile*?

  - Or is it a thesaurus: a hierarchical system, with "broader," "narrower," and "related" headings that shows relationships between terms, as you find in *PsycINFO* or *ERIC*?

  - With any kind of list of subject terms, can you browse the list?

  - If subject terms are assigned to each record, how many are assigned? (2 to 3? 5? 10 or more?)

- Do any of the other searchable fields have their own *index* (a list of terms appearing in that field), and can you browse that index? (More and more often, it seems that the answer to those questions is "no.")

- With any browsable indexes, do they offer a "paste to search" function so that you don't have to retype the entry in the search interface? (This saves time and the risk of typing errors.)

- Questions to ask about abstracts and titles:

  o Do the records offer abstracts?

  o Are the abstracts generally long and detailed or short?

  o Are they simply replications of the first paragraph of the article, or are they evaluative or summarizing? (The former are likely to have been machine generated, whereas the latter are more likely to have been written by a person and to be more helpful to users in quickly assessing whether the article meets their needs or not.)

  o If the database offers materials in different languages, are the article titles offered in translation? (Same question for the abstracts.)

- If full text is available, does the database support proximity operators, which are better tools for searching full text?

- Overall, does the database employ features and conventions that are similar to those in other databases? If the answer is "yes," it will enable users to acquaint themselves and start using the new database effectively on their own. You can't teach every single user.

An additional point that bridges both searchability and the next category, user interface, is the idea of search history. This is a user interface functionality that does not have to do with indexing or cataloging practices, but it certainly contributes to a database's searchability. Does the database keep track of your search history? Can you rerun previous searches? Can you combine searches in the history list or add additional terms to a previous search?

User Interface: Usability. Usability is an area that is open to both objective and subjective evaluation, and it can be particularly important in the case of the same database offered by multiple vendors. As you work with the database, keep track of your experiences and reactions to the interface: the *way* you access the content and search functions. In the broadest sense, ask yourself, "Does it work? How well?" When you are comparing vendors, searching the same information through a different interface can feel like a totally different experience. Here are some specific things to look for:

- Does the interface make it clear how to use it, both by layout and by the terminology used? For example, are field names unambiguous?

- If icons are used, are they meaningful?

- Is the interface so bare and simple that it's "naked," or is it cluttered, busy, or mysterious?

- Are there *too many* options (or too many ways to do the same thing)?

- How is color contrast used? Is color used to demarcate functional areas of the screen, or is everything uniform in color?

- Is the interface visually appealing? For instance, is the color scheme easy on the eyes? Are the fonts too small, too big, too hard to read, etc.? Are the colors or fonts adjustable, either on an individual basis by users to suit their personal preferences or globally for the whole institution's account by a local system administrator (or both)?

- How important are the navigation links built into the interface? For example, if you use the back button rather than a "Modify search" link, does it wipe out your search? (This is very annoying.)

- Can you initiate a search by just pressing Enter, or is it necessary to always click a "Search" or "Go" button?

- How easy is it to adjust or modify your search? Do you have to go back to a main search screen, or is the search interface (or other kinds of refine options) available on the results screen?

- Is there an advanced search option? How much more does it offer than the basic? (That is, is it really an "advance" over the basic search?)

- Are functions such as save, e-mail, and download easy to see and understand?

- If the database has a "time-out" function, that is, you get disconnected after a certain period of inactivity, does it provide a warning before disconnecting you? Can the time-out period be adjusted?

- If the subscription is based on a limited number of users, what sort of message (if any) is displayed if all the "seats" are in use when you try to sign on?

- Is there a mobile version of the interface? How well does it mimic the desktop experience?

- If you encounter nonfunctioning tools (i.e., buttons/features that don't work), it provides a good excuse to call the vendor's tech support line and evaluate how they respond.

Treatment of Research. How research is treated is an important factor for any institution that works with students who are writing papers. Terms frequently used for research articles are *peer-reviewed* and *scholarly*. Databases such as ProQuest's *Research Library*, EBSCO's *Academic Search Complete*, and Gale's *Academic OneFile* offer both popular and scholarly articles, and they provide a limit function for "Scholarly" or "Peer Reviewed."[1] Providing such a limit only makes sense when a database includes a wide range of materials. However, databases that consist entirely of scholarly materials, such as the *Science Citation Index* or *EconLit*, do not need this type of filtering functionality, and, thus, you won't see this option.

Based on the discussion above, the questions to ask in evaluating a multidisciplinary database are the following:

- Does the database provide research-level material?

- Is there a limit in the search interface for retrieving only scholarly materials?

- Is there a way to distinguish scholarly materials in search results, even if you haven't used a limit (e.g., by an icon in the record, or by a separate tab in the results display that filters for scholarly articles)?

- Is there anything in the product literature to indicate how many journals, or what percentage of the sources, are scholarly?

- One other point to check: scholarly articles almost always have a bibliography of sources at the end. If the database provides full text in HTML rather than PDF format, check to be sure that such bibliographies are included.

Sorting/Display/Output Capabilities. The amount of control you have over the presentation and output of your results can make a big difference in the usefulness of those results. It affects the extent to which you can easily evaluate them and the ease of working with them. Here are things you may want to assess for each function:

Sorting:

- What are the available sorting options?

- What is the default sort order for displaying results? Can you change the default at the user level? At the administrative level (i.e., for your institution)?

- Is there a limit on the number of results that can be sorted? Some databases only offer a sort option on results sets of, for example, 500 or less.

Display:

- How many results are displayed per page? Can you change that number at the user and/or administrative level?

- Are the search parameters (e.g., words searched, limits used) reiterated on the results list screen?

- Are search terms highlighted in the results display? If they are, is it possible to turn such highlighting off? (Many repetitions of highlighted terms can sometimes turn out to be more annoying than helpful.)

- Are format options indicated for each record, for example, icons indicating HTML or PDF availability?

Output:

- What formats are offered for output, especially of full text? Plain text, HTML, or PDF?

- Can you e-mail records? Does the e-mail function allow you to send actual records formatted as plain text, as HTML, or as a PDF attachment, or does it just send a link back to the record in the database?

- How much can you customize the e-mail: can you enter your email as the return address, put in your own subject line, or add a note? Can you choose to include the search history with the e-mailed results?

- When printing records, do you get to choose what is printed (which fields)? Note the following, especially in databases that provide full text: Can you select a group of records and then print the full records in one continuous stream? Or are you forced to print full-text results one by one?

- If you have reason to believe that many of the people who would use this database use software programs such as RefWorks or EndNote to keep track of their citations, does the database offer an export function for bibliographic management software programs?

Benchmarking

The first three types of benchmark activities listed here are, obviously, most important when you are trying to choose between two databases, especially if you already subscribe to one and are contemplating whether to change to the other. The next point addresses the fact that, in academia, there is always a set of schools with which your school compares itself, and such comparisons are important to administrators.

Source List Comparisons. In choosing between rival databases, a good first step is to compare their lists of sources, that is, which journals (magazines, newspapers, etc.) does each one offer? How much overlap is there? How many unique titles are there? Among the unique titles, which list has more titles that are of interest to *your* institution? Among the titles that are the same in both databases, is the coverage the same? That is, how do the dates of coverage and the availability of full text (if any) compare?

If you can obtain the source lists in Excel format and merge them into one spreadsheet, it can greatly facilitate this comparison process. This comparison is also almost entirely quantitative and objective, which is important in a request for purchase. And you might not have to do this comparison by hand with your own spreadsheets: ask colleagues in the collection development, acquisitions, or cataloging departments to see if any comparison tools are available to you.

Search Result Comparisons. Just as it sounds, you should run the same searches in the databases that you are comparing and see how the number and nature of the hits compare. The number refers to how many results, and the nature refers to the quality of the results: if one database yields 10 more hits on a search, but 8 are from popular magazines or are only brief articles, are you really getting any significant advantage? Absolutely equal searches are somewhat difficult to achieve because each database probably uses different subject terms, the default fields that are searched might be different, and so on, but this is still a very useful exercise to do.

Experiment with keyword searches, phrase searches, and field searches. If there are subject terms that are the same in both databases, those are ideal for benchmark searches. Simply spending some time with the two subject lists side by side on the screen can be useful, too. Try to get a sense of the level of detail of subject terms used and the nature of the language. Even in the realm of controlled vocabulary, there are some that are more formal and others that sound more like natural language. Users are more likely to benefit by accident when the subject terms are less formal (e.g., the terms they type in happen to match the subject vocabulary).

Be sure to keep a record of everything you do while you are benchmark searching: exactly what the search was, the number of results, and comments on the results. Don't count on your memory; by the next day, the similarities and differences will be a blur. Keeping a good log helps this activity stay in the quantitative, objective realm, rather than the gut instinct, subjective realm.

Peer Institution Holdings. As mentioned previously, administrators at colleges and universities are very aware of, and sensitive to, comparisons with other schools that are recognized as peers. It has nothing to do with the intrinsic worth of the database at hand, but if you can show that a significant number of your school's peer institutions already subscribe to this database, that information may be helpful in persuading your administration to fund the purchase.

Making a Request for Purchase

As mentioned at the beginning of this chapter, one of the reasons that you would choose to go through this much work is if you were considering a new database subscription. Now that you've done the work, what can you do to try to make the new subscription a reality? You've done your homework, but keep in mind that administrators, like the rest of us, have limited time and attention spans. They don't want to read 10 pages of detail; they just want to see a succinct argument that shows why database XYZ is necessary, how it will benefit library users, and, quite likely, how you propose to fund the purchase. Most organizations have a process in place for making such requests, but the following list of points probably meshes with, or can be used to enhance, the existing process.

Elements to Include in the Request

What Does This Database Bring to the Institution? Show what material this database offers that is not available from any other existing service (this could include topic areas, material types, specific publication titles, date ranges, etc.). Use numbers rather than text as much as you can. Relate the database directly to the goals of your organization, for example, to specific classes, areas of expansion (new programs), and so forth. If you need to highlight textual elements such as publication titles, provide at most four key titles and list any additional titles you think are important in an appendix. Once you have demonstrated why this database is unique, it is also important to address the next consideration.

How Does This Database Complement the Existing Collection? Although, of course, the database needs to bring something new to your organization (otherwise, why would you be interested in it?), it's also important to demonstrate how the material in this database could complement and extend the existing library collections. For example, if your institution has a strong language program, you could probably make quite a strong case for a database of international newspapers in the original languages, as it would provide a wealth of language content without any of the knotty issues of getting such things in print. Conversely, if you are trying to make a case for a new religion database, but your school doesn't offer any kind of religion degree, you certainly can say it brings something new to your resources; but what exactly would be the point? There would be little complementary material in the collection, and, unless there were popular religion courses offered in another department, it would be difficult to identify a strong user base.

If you are proposing to change from an existing database to a rival product, obviously you'll do many comparisons, as mentioned in the first two types of benchmarking. You'll want to emphasize differences in the new version of the database that are important to your stated audience for it. The next section discusses this key point: the potential database users.

Who Will Use the Database? Who will be interested in the material in this database? How many potential users will it have? If at all possible, try to get some of those potential users involved during the database trial period. Have them test drive the database, or at least take a look at the source list. Comments from users (e.g., "it helped me with a paper," "I needed this for my thesis research," "it seemed easy to use") or, even better, purchase requests from users (i.e., "the library should definitely have this resource") can be very persuasive. If you found a database review that included a strong comment relating to the audience for the database, which matches your potential audience, include it here.

How Will the Database Be Marketed? If you get the database, how will you let people know that the new resource is available? As always, strive for brevity, but try to outline all the avenues you propose to use to market the database: for example, a series of e-mails to department faculty and students touting the new resource, flyers, brown-bag (or better, free pizza) information or training sessions, and so on. Put links to the new resource on as many pages of your Web site as are appropriate. People have a lot vying for their attention, and as vociferously as your users may have said they wanted this new database, you will still need to put out quite a bit of effort to get them to integrate the new tool into their work habits.

In addition, it's a good idea to include how you plan to evaluate database usage after a year. How well did your marketing work? Usage statistics are one obvious measure, but some kind of quick, informal survey (e.g., by e-mail or a Web page) of your target communities shows a bit more initiative on your part. Besides, such a survey has the added benefits of providing additional marketing as well as assessing usage, usefulness, and perhaps gathering feedback.

How Will the Purchase Be Funded? Funding is usually the make-or-break factor: what is the cost, and where will the money come from? With the cost, indicate whether it includes any discounts, which pricing model was used (e.g., if you opted for only two simultaneous users rather than five), or other factors. If you have competing price quotes from multiple vendors, indicate that you've chosen the most economical one (or, if you haven't, why). The money may come from canceling something else (another database or several serial titles) or, if your accounting system permits, from a permanent transfer of funds from a monographic to a serial budget. If you believe your case is strong enough, there is always the option of simply requesting additional funds to be added to your budget line to pay for the new subscription.

What Else? If the database has been favorably reviewed, include citation(s) to the review(s) in an appendix. Particularly useful or pertinent quotes might be included in appropriate sections of the main document. If in the course of your review and testing you have discovered features that you feel are particularly compelling, mention those now. Indicate that you can provide detailed title comparisons or search logs, if requested.

Your overall goal is to present a succinct, clear, and quantitative case as well as a qualitative case. Your first attempt might not be successful, but you will have shown that you can perform a rational and cogent analysis. Your funding agents are more likely to trust you and try to do their best for you when you try again. So, take a refusal like a good sport, and keep gathering data for the next attempt.

Exercises

1. This list of things to consider in evaluating a database is fairly comprehensive (perhaps daunting?), but no list can ever be absolutely complete. You've been working with databases a lot by now. What other points or issues have *you* encountered that you'd add to this list? What points do you think aren't as important or that you wouldn't need to bother with?

2. As a major project, choose a database that is new to you, either from the resources available at your institution or by requesting a trial from a vendor. Do a thorough evaluation of it from the point of view of either writing a review of the database for publication or writing up a purchase request for your management. (If you aren't currently employed in a library or other type of information center, make one up.) Then either write the review or write up the purchase request.

   If you choose the review option, write the review as if you were going to submit it for publication. Include the name of the publication to which you would submit the review, and follow its guidelines in terms of formatting, length, and the like. (See "Instructions for authors" on the publication's Web site.) After your professor has seen it, he or she might well encourage you to follow through with the submission; this is a realistic goal.

   If you choose the purchase request option, include a separate description of your (real or fictional) library or information center to set the scene. Be sure to describe your user community and your institution's overall budget situation. Make it as realistic as possible. If you are currently working in a library or information center, choose a database you'd actually like to obtain. You may be able to put your work here to good use on the job.

In either case, do not feel compelled to work through every single point mentioned in this chapter. Choose the ones that make sense and are feasible for your chosen project.

Note

1. Tip: If a database uses subject headings and includes both popular and scholarly materials but doesn't provide any functionality for distinguishing between them, some subject terms that might help sift out research articles are *methodology, sampling, populations, results, variables,* or *hypotheses.*

16
Teaching Other People about Databases

If the thought of getting up in front of other people and speaking makes your blood run cold, and you were hoping that by becoming a librarian you could avoid having to do that kind of activity, I'm sorry to have to burst your bubble.[1] But *my* hope is that after reading through this chapter and getting some experience, you will change your mind and come to understand that teaching and presenting are a vital part of librarianship. Let us consider the importance and ramifications of presenting for a moment, and then we'll get into some more specific nuts and bolts.

The library profession needs spokespeople and champions. The focus of this book has been, of course, databases, but what good are a group of wonderful databases if you can't convey to others that they exist and how to use them? How long do you think funding for these expensive resources will last if you can't defend them (especially when you are in competition with free resources like Google Scholar)? In the larger scheme of things, it's never too early to get used to the idea of justifying your existence: public, school, and state-employed librarians need to be able to talk to their communities and to local and state legislatures. Academic librarians make points for their libraries in the eyes of the budget controllers by successfully engaging in the academic game: by giving presentations at conferences and holding offices in state and national professional organizations.

Our profession might not be in crisis, but we certainly are challenged by the Internet as almost no other profession is. The Internet is free, and libraries are expensive: we are cost centers, not profit centers. It's difficult to quantify the value we give back. If you've chosen to become a librarian, or are already in the profession, presumably you've made that choice because you enjoy and believe in the library as an institution and librarianship as a vocation. Isn't it worth it to learn to get up in front of people and talk for a short time to ensure that your chosen path has a future? *Any* kind of speaking you do—whether it's an information literacy session for a freshman writing class, an evening program for adults at a public library, a talk at a conference, three minutes of impassioned defense before a state legislature, or even a brief discussion in an elevator—makes a difference. It makes a difference both for libraries in general, and for your own career, to be able to effectively tell others what we do, why our (expensive) tools are useful, and what benefits they bestow.

Teaching often means getting up in front of people and talking. Humans like to communicate (look at the popularity and omnipresence of cell phones), and teaching is just another form of communicating. It's a wonderful improvement that all American Library Association–accredited library schools in the United States now offer at least one class on instruction (Roy 2011), but maybe that course didn't fit into your schedule or maybe library school is a distant memory for you. Still, even if public speaking ranks right up there with getting a root canal on your list of favorite things to do, be assured that it can be done. It gets easier, and you might even enjoy it someday, honest.[2] Maybe you enjoy teaching and presenting already; if so, good for you! And perhaps this chapter will help you become an even better presenter.

Teaching Principles

The following list of eight Teaching Principles are the result of my personal experiences with a variety of teaching and public-speaking opportunities over the course of many years. These experiences have informed my thoughts about what works and what doesn't, and what's important and what isn't, in the process of conveying skills or knowledge from one person to another, from one person to a group, or asynchronously via technology. The process of writing up my thoughts for this chapter included double-checking my instincts against some teaching literature from related subject areas as well as general teaching essays by professors who have been recipients of the undergraduate teaching award at my former university.

These are guidelines that can be applied to any type of teaching, not just of databases, although there are underlying assumptions (e.g., in the emphasis on use of technology) that what is being taught is technical or online in nature. You'll find that the list ranges from the more philosophical "teach to your audience" to the very directive and practical "wait for someone to answer when you ask a question." You will be able to use these principles as a kind of checklist and support system as you strive to acquire all the hallmarks of an effective teacher.

A quote from long ago that is just as true today as it was then declares that "concern for students, knowledge of the subject matter, stimulation of interest, availability, encouragement of discussion, ability to explain clearly, enthusiasm, and preparation" are the qualities that students cite most often in describing effective teachers (Feldman 1976). Those are your goals, and these suggestions can help you achieve them.

Principle 1: Teach to Your Audience

Be very clear who your audience is and keep them firmly in mind as you prepare the session. Make your teaching objectives, materials, and handouts—everything about what you're doing—appropriate to the needs and interests of that audience. It's quite easy to decide what you want to tell people, but it takes a good deal more effort to determine how to deliver your message in a way they will really hear and perhaps remember. Ten-year-olds, undergraduates, lawyers, and the PTA are all very different groups of people, and your approach needs to be different in each case.

Principle 2: Avoid Lecturing

Avoid pure lecture at every opportunity. As Professor Applegate (1999) puts it, "Never miss an opportunity to keep your mouth shut." You probably thought that if you were asked to teach or present, you should fill every moment, but silence truly can be golden. Do not be afraid of silence (Applegate 1999). People need time to process what you're saying, which means that you need to stop speaking from time to time. Give people time to "think about what they have been told" at regular intervals (Felder and Silverman 1988). Something as simple as pausing to write a point on the board, and not talking while you do it, can provide a moment of needed silence. We're lucky in our subject matter, too, in that when you're teaching about databases, you have all kinds of ways you can stop lecturing and give your audience time to use what they've heard as well as think about it. Here are some examples:

- In a hands-on situation, have people start doing their own searching. Try to make the searching, not your lecture, fill the majority of the class time. Talk about one idea, then have people try it. Then go on to another idea and have them try it. Alternate between talking and activity.

- In a demonstration (not hands-on) situation, you might present people with a search statement and then have them work alone or with the person next to them to come up with as many synonyms as they can for each of the concepts in the search.

- Use the projector to display a search request or hand out a paragraph describing a search request, either in the form of discursive text or as a dialogue between a patron and a librarian. Have the class—individually, in groups, or as a whole—figure out one or more search strategies to try. Then have members of the audience come up and type in the chosen searches.

- If you are going over a computer function of some kind (e.g., using the library's discovery service), ask the class if anyone has done it before. (*Wait* for an answer.) Then have one or two volunteers come up and demonstrate how they do it.

- Use questions such as "What are all the uses you can think of for (XYZ)?" to start discussions. To get even the quiet people involved, hand out brightly colored Post-it notes to everyone and have them write their ideas, one per note. Stick them up on a wall or a whiteboard, in categories and start a discussion from there.

In general, look at the list of concepts you wish to get across and come up with alternatives to straight lecturing. More and more, students seem to be averse to learning by lecture, and even faculty have noticed that students learn more effectively from discussing issues with each other (Viele 2006). Small groups, discussion, writing on the board, Post-its, other hands at the instructor keyboard, any kind of physical activity—all of these are lecture alternatives. People learn best when they are developing and putting concepts into practice themselves, so aim for that if possible.

You don't have to come up with all these teaching ideas on your own. Brainstorm with a colleague; it will be fun for both of you.

Principle 3: Wait for Answers

When you ask questions of your audience (which is definitely a good thing to do), first, ask with a purpose, that is, ask a question for which you really want an answer, and second, *wait* for someone to answer. Give your audience a chance to marshal their thoughts and come up with a response. Resist with every fiber of your being the desire to answer your own question. The moment you do, the audience will decide your questioning is all a sham, and they won't bother to make any further effort. You will have no chance of getting them to answer any subsequent questions.

Waiting for someone to answer is definitely one of the hardest things to do in a teaching situation. That silence seems to stretch out forever, but try to remember two things. One, the time seems much longer to you than it does to your audience. Two, the silence will eventually start to bother the people in your audience as well, and they will realize that you really mean it; you *do* want to hear from them. Sooner or later someone will crack and say something. If you really can't stand it, pick someone in the group and push the matter by asking, "What do you think?" in a friendly way.

Of course, the kinds of questions that you ask make a difference, too. Questions that ask people to relate things to their own lives or experience are generally more comfortable and can usually get *someone* to pipe up. Once they do, if you're looking to foster more group discussion, don't immediately respond yourself—look around for someone else who looks on the verge of speaking and give that person an encouraging look, or again, just ask, "What do you think?" Try not to be the arbiter, the touchstone, for every response from the group. It is not necessary to "respond to every response" (Applegate 1999).

Principle 4: Less Is More

Don't overwhelm your audience by trying to do too much. Guided by Principle 1, choose only a limited number of concepts or instructions that you feel will be the most useful information for *that audience*. Take two or perhaps three things you think would be most helpful for that audience to remember or learn and build your presentation around those items. One of the biggest pitfalls for new professors—and this extends to anyone new to teaching—is that they tend to overprepare lectures and try to present too much material too rapidly. Successful teachers, however, present material "paced in a relaxed style so as to provide opportunities for student comprehension and involvement" (Boice 1992).

This may well sound like a recommendation that you set your sights pretty low, and you may feel that it's a disservice to show only a few features of a wonderful database that is loaded with functionality. The problem is, you can't possibly cover as much material in interactive, nonlecture classes as you can if you are only lecturing; such classes aren't very efficient in that sense. If you are adhering to Principle 2, sincerely try to avoid pure lecture (which is the most ineffectual form of instruction anyway) and instead try to foster discussion and engagement and active learning; you can't go over every bell and whistle. It will be frustrating at times. You'll find yourself worrying, "They should know this! They should know that, too! And this other thing!" Consider this, however: if you show them two or three things that get their interest enough so that they go back on their own, don't you think they might discover some of the other "things they should know" on their own? It's likely that they can. Motivated, interested people are pretty smart that way.

Overall, the outcomes of a nonlecture style of teaching can be more useful and rewarding to your students. If you cover only two or three things in an interesting way that show, "here's how this will benefit you," the participants are more likely to remember at least some of the content. And, if you manage *not* to alienate your audience and *not* make the session one they can't wait to get out of, they are more likely to seek you out again for help later in what is probably a more useful one-on-one appointment in your office.

Principle 5: Transparency in Teaching

Don't be inscrutable (Applegate 1999). Lay out clearly the goals and objectives for the class, the assignment, or the exercise—whatever you are doing. Always keeping in mind Principle 1, relate the goals and objectives to your audience. Do your best to make them feel that it's worth their while to be there. Keep things simple, straightforward, and honest. You are not a god(dess) or keeper of keys to special mysteries; you just happen to have some useful knowledge you'd like to share that you believe will make your audiences' lives better in some way. Honesty is important because of the next principle.

Principle 6: You Have the Right to Be Wrong

It is acceptable to be wrong occasionally or to not know the answer to every question. Acting inscrutable is often allied with trying to be infallible, and both are terrible ideas. Of course, you will have done your best to master your material (Principle 8), but it is still inevitable that someone will ask you a question to which you don't know the answer, or that some alert person will point out something you've gotten wrong, pure and simple. Laugh at yourself, thank the person (sincerely) for noticing, make a note to fix it for next time, and get over it. No one is perfect, and most audiences will relate to you more easily if they think that you're human rather than a remote and infallible being. Consider this wonderful quotation:

Arnold Schoenberg wrote in the introduction to his 1911 text on musical harmony that "the teacher must have the courage to be wrong." The teacher's task, he continued, "is not to prove infallible, knowing everything and never going wrong, but rather inexhaustible, ever seeking and perhaps sometimes finding." The more we can involve the students with us in this task, "ever seeking and . . . sometimes finding," the better. (Applegate 1999)

"Ever seeking and perhaps sometimes finding"—what a perfect expression for librarianship. So, don't get upset if you make a mistake; you are in excellent company.

Principle 7: Teaching with Technology

If working with technology of any kind, there are two things to keep in mind: (1) slow down and (2) anticipate technology failure.

When you are working with technology, that is, either a projected computer screen or a hands-on computer classroom, you need to build more time into presentation plans. Especially in a hands-on situation, in which people are looking back and forth from your (projected) screen to their own (and maybe back to yours yet again), *slow down*. It's essential to take more time. You know where you're going, but your audience doesn't. It is all uncharted territory for them. You must give the people who are trying to follow you time to process. Even if they are not trying to replicate what you are doing on their own computers and are just watching the screen, take your speed down a few notches. Don't scroll rapidly up and down, and practice calmly mousing from point A to point B without any additional whizzing around on the screen.

These may sound like small details, but, again, your audience is madly trying to follow you (and might also be trying to take notes); this is new territory for them, and their minds will be doing a lot more processing than yours. Excessive scrolling and mousing in that situation is distracting, if not downright annoying, so work on keeping it to a minimum. Be calm and deliberate in your movements.

The other thing about technology is to be ready for things to go wrong. Plan for how you will handle it if the projector bulb burns out, or you can't get on the Net, or the computer crashes. For example, if you're leading a hands-on session and the projector malfunctions, simply designate one or two of the people in the class as your hands and have them follow your directions while the other students gather around those computers. Invite all the students to help as backseat drivers. They'll probably all have more fun and get more out of it than if things had gone according to plan! If you're presenting in a non-hands-on situation and your projector fails, start a discussion instead. Ask the group something about what you have just been trying to cover. As noted earlier, questions that relate the material to their own experience ("What do you folks usually do when you need to find XYZ?") are good for getting the ball rolling.

If you're presenting somewhere other than your home location and intend to show something live on the Internet, take a PowerPoint file (with screenshots of what you intend to show live) along as backup. It's a fair amount of extra work (depending on the length of your presentation), and you might not need it; but oh, if you do need it, you will be intensely thankful that you took the time. So, take the time. It also gives you a way to rehearse (if you take a laptop with you) on the plane or in the hotel room the night before.

If you're in your home situation and something goes wrong, first, call tech support (if you have it); second, restart the computer; and third, start some kind of discussion.[3] With students, ask them about their assignment (or whatever has brought them to you today), what they've done so far with it, and their familiarity with the library and its systems. In a nonacademic situation, ask them what brought them to the session, what they hope to get out of it, and so on.

Above all, in a technology failure situation, do not betray your anxiety. Don't wring your hands and whimper helplessly. Groaning is permitted, as long as you also laugh. Maintain your aplomb. This is much easier to do if you've rehearsed in your mind what you'll do if the technology lets you down. Because it will: not every time, but at least sometimes. Dave Barry says that your household plumbing makes plans in the middle of the night for how it will go wrong and disrupt your big party. These devices—computers, projectors, servers, etc.—undoubtedly do the same thing.

Principle 8: Practice

There is an old gag that asks, "How do you get to Carnegie Hall?" Answer: "Practice, practice, practice." Practice is essential. If you are not used to presenting or are uncomfortable with it, I cannot emphasize enough the importance of rehearsal. Practice is crucial for several reasons. First and foremost, the time you are allotted will always be limited, and a live run-through is the only way to find out how long the session you have planned actually lasts (and usually you will find that you have more material than you think). Practicing also helps you to become more comfortable, and it can help identify bugs in your presentation, saving embarrassment later. Let's look at the "limited time" issue in more detail.

No matter what sort of group teaching or presentation situation it is (information literacy, staff development, etc.), you will always be working within a specified time limit. Until you have run through what you plan to say—actually spoken the words *out loud*—you won't know how long your presentation really takes. Unless you have a lot of experience, you cannot mentally run through a talk at a slow enough pace to mimic a verbalized version reliably. Especially when a presentation or sample class is part of a job interview, practice it to be *sure* it fits within the time allotted. If you practice and find that your presentation is too long, the only option is reducing the amount of information that you attempt to convey. When in doubt, cut it out.

Talking faster is *not* an option, nor is running over. Both things will irritate your audience. If you simply keep talking and have to be cut off before you're finished, you will look unprepared. Practice by yourself (but aloud!), even if it means talking to the wall and feeling like an idiot. If possible, the best option is to round up some classmates, friends, or family and give your talk to them. Especially if you are trying to simulate a class situation, with questions and back and forth, practicing with friends is extremely helpful in determining your timing and pacing. They can also help identify any non sequiturs or outright errors in your talk.

In a job interview situation, if you teach only one thing but do it well, appear relaxed, interact with your audience, and stay within your time limit; your prospective employers will feel as if you've taught them much more and will, in general, have far more positive feelings about you than if you try to cram in every last nuance, are forced to rush, and lecture the entire time. Unless you are unusually gifted in this area, your audience will almost always be able to tell whether you have practiced.

At the same time, being well rehearsed doesn't mean rattling off your script like, well, like a memorized script. Rather, it means full mastery of your material so that you are talking about your topic naturally and easily, you are able to field questions or take small side trips (or encounter technical difficulties) without getting flustered or derailed from your main intent, and your enthusiasm and enjoyment of your topic come through. If you are suffering, your audience will suffer as well. Take some lessons from Hollywood: rehearse, know your lines, and deliver them with sincerity and enthusiasm. Act like you're enjoying it, even if you aren't. Your audience will enjoy it a great deal more (and you might, too).

This section has tried to impart a lot of advice in a very few pages, and it may come across as somewhat overwhelming. So many things to remember! So many do's, so many don'ts—how can you possibly remember them all *and* the topic of your talk? The answer goes back to Principle 8: Practice. Master your material, remember to smile occasionally (write yourself a note about it if necessary), and breathe. You can't panic when you're breathing deeply and slowly. So, practice, then breathe, smile, open your mouth, and share the wonderful information you have with your audience. You'll be great!

Now let's consider the situations in which you may be using these teaching principles.

Synchronous and Asynchronous Modes of Teaching

The opportunities for teaching or presenting information about databases that you are likely to encounter as a librarian can be summarized as follows. In the "synchronous" mode:

- One on one: working with a person at a service point or by appointment.

- One-off, one-time sessions, often known as *information literacy classes* (or sometimes *bibliographic instruction*) in college and university settings. Presenting such a class is a common part of an academic job interview. In a school library, these are usually referred to simply as *classes* and tend to be quite brief: 15 to 20 minutes. The public library equivalent might be an evening or noontime continuing education session.

- A database introduction or review, such as one would present at a staff meeting or staff development session.

- A sustained, semester-long class.

And the major the major vehicle for *asynchronous* instruction:

- Video tutorials

These are all quite different sorts of encounters, yet you'll find that many of the principles given in the previous section apply to them all. What follows are some thoughts about applying the principles in each case to make your database instruction more effective.

Teaching One-on-One

One-on-one is probably the type of teaching encounter that librarians often find most comfortable. It's intimate; you only have to deal with one person and can focus entirely on him or her. It's also reactive, rather than proactive; the person has *chosen* to approach the service point or make an appointment with you, and after you focus on the topic of the moment, the encounter is over. True, you can't exactly prepare (Principle 8), but that can be a plus: you won't be overprepared. You have your life knowledge, your library science education, and your professional experience, and you simply apply these in various ways to meet each person's individual information needs.

Introducing a patron to a database at a service point or during a research appointment provides an opportunity for a teaching moment, but if you take advantage of that, keep it to a moment. Don't overwhelm (Principle 4, less is more). Pick one or two things to try to teach the patron, such as "This is how you get to the list of databases on (subject X)" and "See this drop-down? If you change it to Subject, the articles you get should be right on target." *Suggest* the power of the database, but don't try to impart all your knowledge. (As Carol Kuhlthau (1988) says in more formal terms, the reference encounter represents the ideal in terms of teaching, because it offers "intervention that matches the user's actual level of information need.") Go through the process with the patron, asking questions about the topic and explaining in a general way what you're doing, but without necessarily going into all the details. In other words, try to be transparent (Principle 5) without being overwhelming or lecturing (Principle 2).

For example: "Let's try this database—it's got psychology articles," rather than "Well, first you should go to the list of psychology databases, and then read the descriptions to decide which one to use." Attempt to engage the patron gently and be quiet from time to time. A good time to be quiet is when you're looking at a list of results together so that the patron can study the screen and process. It's much better to hold back a bit and have the patron ask, "How did you do that?" than to overwhelm him or her with information. Let's face it, not everyone is that interested or *needs* to do this kind of research again (Principle 1: Teach to Your Audience). Dropping a limited number of teaching seeds is more likely to result in further questioning and ultimate skill flowering than 10 minutes of unmitigated, and probably unappreciated, lecture.

Teaching an Information Literacy Session

The classroom situation a librarian is most likely to encounter is really quite the hardest: the one-off, limited time (usually only around an hour) class, whose purpose might range from the typical information literacy, or "library," session for freshman English students, to how to search the Internet in an evening class for adults at the public library. Now you as an instructor are facing a roomful of people who may or may not wish to be there and with whom you will probably only have one class session. You are supposed to have some idea of what makes them tick, make contact with them, communicate, and impart two or three chunks of useful knowledge about a fairly sophisticated topic (i.e., database or Web searching) in the limited time allotted. It is a challenge, but by keeping the principles in mind, you can meet that challenge:

You can still teach to your audience. You will have advance notice that the session is coming, which gives you time to find out something about who your audience is going to be. In any kind of school situation, the teacher or professor should be willing to tell you the reason that he or she has requested an instruction session in the library and something about the class (personalities, skill levels, etc.). In a community education situation, talk to other librarians who have taught such classes before: Who tends to show up? What are they usually most interested in? How are their skills? If you feel you need more information, do some reading; plenty of research has been done on teaching adults (and every other age group). Here's your chance to go to *ERIC* and get "a few good articles."

We'll assume that, based on your research, your session will include some demonstration or hands-on training with one database or possibly two databases, or comparing one (or two) databases to Google Scholar—but that is probably pushing the limits of Principle 4 (less is more). It depends on the point that you are trying to make with each resource. For example, for a first freshman introduction to the library, you might decide that a multidisciplinary database that offers mostly full text is the resource most attuned with their needs and interests, and therefore you will show them the pertinent features of that database. For an upper-level course, you might opt to demonstrate a subject-specific, abstracts-only database (or one of the *Web of Science* Citation Indexes) and how to determine whether full-text is accessible from the library. To get beyond the pesky "Less is More" limitation, you could use self-exploration to great advantage: divide the class into small groups and have each one explore and report back on a different resource, allowing the class as a whole to cover a lot more ground.

No matter who is in your class, one thing you can be sure of is that while they may be vaguely aware of databases, they won't have used them nearly as much as they have Google (or whatever search engine is hot at the moment). Use this to your advantage. You know one thing that represents familiar ground to them, so work it in: compare and contrast the search

---

Don't Reinvent the Wheel

Tip: To find nifty ideas for active-learning exercises to use with undergraduates, simply look at the latest crop of articles in *Library Literature* under "Subject: Library orientation for college students." There are always new great ideas out there. If you'd like to focus on a more specific audience, visit the *Library Literature* thesaurus and browse for "library orientation for," leaving the phrase unfinished. The list of headings ranges from "adults" and "art students" through "college athletes," "gifted children," and "middle school students," to "teachers" and "youth." You'll have a myriad of more specific choices instantly at your fingertips.

---

engine with the properties of databases to introduce what databases are. (What is frustrating is that if you have to explain that there are such things as databases, it uses up one of the precious two to three learning objectives.)

In general, although a brief one-off session can be challenging, it is challenging in a good way.[4] True, you don't have the opportunity to establish much rapport with the group, to see their growth or progress, or to repair any blunders in this week's class next week. On the other hand, you are forced to be really rigorous in developing your one class (draw up your list of learning objectives and then cross most of them out) so that what your attendees receive is a carefully honed, very targeted product. The quality is just as high, if not higher, than that of many of their regular classes, and the session is likely to be more interactive and memorable as well.

If nothing else, the class will come away knowing that (1) you exist, (2) something other than Google exists, and (3) you showed them something that would make their research process easier. If you can leave them with a positive impression, it's more likely that individual students will later seek you out at a service desk, in your office, at your satellite location in their department, or by e-mail, chat, or simply as your paths cross in a hallway.

Mock Instruction Session as Part of a Job Interview. Presenting a class as part of a job interview has been mentioned a few times already, but let me add some specific notes about it here. First, the time will probably be shorter (20–30 minutes) than in any real class. This will tend to force you into more of a lecture style of presentation, which your audience is expecting, but try to surprise them by working in at least one of the interactive, nonlecture approaches suggested under Principle 2. Second, though this may sound obvious, do your homework. The library where you will be interviewing most likely has a Web site. If the library is part of an institution of higher education or a corporation, the organization probably has a Web site. Study these and use them to inform your presentation.

Make the class you create look as if you already work there. Base your presentation on a database available at that library and make your audience a group at that institution (a particular class, with a real class number and professor's name, or a real group within the company or organization). For a public library, study the schedule of classes already on offer and try to come up with a session that would augment or complement an existing class. If you decide that you want to demonstrate a database that is available only at your target library, and not wherever you currently are, call up the vendor and ask for a trial so that you can learn it and use the library's link when you are on site. (Create a PowerPoint as a backup just in case.) Create one or more appropriate handouts to go with your presentation, and, again, don't be shy about copying the library or organization's logo off their Web site to brand your handouts. In as many ways as possible, act like you're already on board. With this kind of preparation, perhaps you soon will be!

A Staff Presentation

Teaching your colleagues about a database is quite different from all the other situations described here. For one thing, knowing your audience shouldn't be an issue; even if you are a new hire right out of library school, you should have a pretty good sense of what librarians are interested in and want to know. Because they are your peers and colleagues (which can make the whole thing both more and less comfortable), it should be much easier to plan and deliver your message. Note, however, that if your group includes members from throughout the library and not just reference librarians, it changes the playing field a good deal. Staff from departments outside of reference, including computer support, may have little or no idea that databases exist or how they are used, and teaching in this situation is more akin to teaching a group of adults from the community. But teaching a group of reference librarians about a database turns many of the formerly stated principles upside down.

- **Principle 2: Avoid Lecturing.** You might be able to get away with more lecture here than in any other situation. It will still be appreciated if you try to break things up, however, and give your audience time to absorb what you're saying from time to time. I think you'll find that a lecture naturally devolves into a more participatory session, for the reason noted in the next point.

- **Principle 3: Wait for Answers.** You probably won't have to wait for answers or need to work at fostering discussion; your colleagues likely will be very forthcoming with comments and questions. This is a group that is truly interested in what you are talking about and eager to explore it with you. (They are glad that you've done the work to master this database so that they can ask *you* questions.)

- **Principle 4: Less is More.** You can set higher goals for the amount of information you plan to impart. Again, this audience is *interested* and does want the details. They are already knowledgeable and will be more interested in salient differences from what they know, rather than the basics. You can start at a much higher level of discussion. However, take some guidance from Principle 4 and don't overwhelm them. A rule of thumb might be to master as much of the database as you can, plan to present 50–60 percent of that (all of which is beyond the basics), and let questions bring out whatever else people want to know.

The other principles do not change much. Principle 5: Transparency in Teaching, still applies. These librarians are likely to have chosen to attend your session, and so they are willing participants. But it's still a good idea to clearly outline the goals and objectives of your talk; that is, give them good reasons to stay and listen. You will very likely get a good workout of Principle 6: You Have the Right to be Wrong. You are talking to a very knowledgeable audience who will undoubtedly catch something or know something that you don't. Don't worry about it! It's a benefit, not a contest.

The two technology points of Principle 7 (go slower, and be ready for it to fail), both apply as in any other situation. Just because they are librarians doesn't mean they can look from their screen to your projected screen (or from your projected screen to their notes) any faster than anyone else. In fact, it may take them longer because they are studying all the details more closely. So, give everyone plenty of time. If the technology fails, you probably will have a whole roomful of people ready to jump in and help, so it's not all up to you. Still, you will want to show that you can stay calm, and have a plan in mind for what to do if the technology lets you down. Of course, Principle 8 applies to every situation: *practice* your database demonstration, in as realistic a situation as possible (e.g., out loud, in front of people if possible), before heading off to your staff development meeting.

If an information literacy session presents the most challenging *format* for teaching, a session for your colleagues undoubtedly presents the most challenging *audience* for your teaching. But again, let it be a good challenge. Learn the database, practice, but don't kill yourself preparing. You'll never remember it all anyway, and you'll just make yourself nervous. If one of your "students" knows something that you don't, let him or her teach you. If someone asks a question that you don't know the answer to, and neither does anyone else in the room, make it an opportunity to explore and find out together. It's really more interesting that way.

The Full-Semester Class

Here at last we have a chance to aspire to what is truly important in teaching, that is, "connection, communication, and the stimulation of critical thinking" (Brown 1999). Instead of one session, you'll see this class over and over, get to know your students, and get beyond the limits of just a few how-tos of only one database. You'll be able to explore many databases and broader philosophical and technical considerations of databases and information seeking. Sadly, these opportunities are quite rare for librarians, so I will not spend much time on this topic. I would like to say enough to indicate that this is a *feasible* project, however. Should you ever get offered the chance to develop and provide such a class, think seriously about taking it on.

A full-semester class, obviously, requires considerable planning, and there are entire books devoted to teaching and curriculum planning (the Suggested Readings include two titles, and a search of *WorldCat* or Amazon.com reveals many, many more). However, it is not an insurmountable effort. Consider these five steps that are recommended in planning a course (Davidson and Ambrose 1994):

- Assess the backgrounds and interests of your students.

- Choose the course objectives (note that these are often set by the department, and you simply need to determine how to achieve them).

- Develop the learning experiences within the course.

- Plan how to seek feedback and evaluate student learning.

- Prepare a syllabus for the course.

You are already familiar with the concept in the first point: know your audience. With a full semester to work with, you can now choose overall course objectives as well as objectives for each session. In both cases, however, you still need to be careful not to overwhelm your students. In each individual class meeting, you shouldn't try to deliver too much, and the sum total of all the sessions ultimately determines the amount of material that you can get through in a semester. You may find it useful to approach a semester-long course as an organizational activity: to work from large overarching ideas, to the components of those ideas, and finally to the steps needed to teach those components. As you work out the steps, you can plan the best learning experiences to support them. As you determine the components, you can then plan ways to assess mastery of them. When all of that is done, you will have enough material to write up a syllabus.

A discouraging aspect of a whole semester's course for many people is that it seems like you have to come up with *so much material*. But, at least in the area of databases and research techniques, the large ideas—the overall objectives—can be broken down into many component parts. If you start analyzing and breaking down the knowledge or skills that you take for granted into a series of intellectually manageable chunks, you'll be surprised at the amount of material this represents. (Students like clearly defined chunks of information.) As you present the course, those component ideas build on each other, heading toward the overall course objectives. Along the way, you are presenting learning experiences to convey those ideas, assessing to see whether the ideas have been conveyed, and giving feedback. It's an organic, iterative, growing process. Go for it.

Video Tutorials for Asynchronous Instruction

Last, some thoughts about a medium for teaching *not* face-to-face. While you can't possibly provide in-person instruction for everyone who needs it (even if they don't realize they need it), providing instruction via video tutorials definitely has its own set of challenges. A well-crafted video tutorial should offer a direct, clear message, in the shortest time possible, using the fewest words possible.[5] You will spend more time creating a good 3-minute learning video than any 60-minute class session, guaranteed (and that's not even counting the time to master the software you decide to use, if you are not already familiar with it). And as soon as you finish it, something about the database will change, and you'll have to either live with it being out of date or redo it.

Still, the hope is that online tutorials may help by relieving library staff from answering the same questions over and over, freeing them up for other activities; saving class time (rather than covering "point X" in the class, point them at the tutorial); and doing a better job of reaching students with different learning styles (visual, auditory, kinetic). (Gravett and Gill 2010, Vaughan 2009, and Dawson, Jacobs, and Yang 2010 all mention all of these points). There is also the perennial argument that it allows students to "learn at their own pace outside of the classroom" (Dawson, Jacobs, and Yang 2010).

While these are all valid justifications, in the spirit of devil's advocate, it is important to note the findings of Lori Mestre's 2012 article, "Student Preference for Tutorial Design: A Usability Study." In it, she reports on her study to test the *effectiveness* of video tutorials as a teaching tool. The four hypotheses she started with were all either disproven or, in one case, unable to be tested due to lack of data. Her findings: "This study indicated that students, across all learning styles, performed much better in recreating tasks when they used a static web page with screenshots than they did after viewing a screencasting tutorial, that they preferred the static web page tutorials with screenshots, and that they preferred the static images over text." The essential problem the students had with the videos (which were only three minutes long) was that it was too hard to go back to a particular point or concept; thus, using the video was *slower*. They found the static Web pages with images faster to use. And for students trying to accomplish a task, speed and efficiency are key (watching funny cat videos on YouTube is a different matter).

Does this mean you should give up on creating video tutorials? Not at all; just approach them differently, not as magic be-all and end-all answers, but as a technique to be used when an animated demonstration is truly the best way to address a particular instructional need. (Otherwise, consider the humbler, but easier and possibly just as effective, static Web page.) Even Mestre concludes,

> Static web page tutorials are generally easier and faster to create and to update than the screencast tutorials. However, to create a balance, as well as to continue to provide multiple options for students, it is recommended that librarians incorporate a variety of multimedia into their tutorials. Students want to be able to pick and choose what is relevant for them and that may change depending upon their needs. By mixing it up and including multiple learning objects (either with links or embedded) on a page (images, charts, video clips, quick games, exercises, scenarios etc.) it may be possible to reach a wider range of students. With multiple options included, the novice and expert can decide how much information they want or which sections they need to review. The kinesthetic learner can try something out, while the aural learner can choose to listen to the process.

Tips for Making Better Video Tutorials. A good video tutorial is a lot like an iceberg: the tip that you can see above the water (the finished product) is only a tiny portion of the whole that lurks below the surface (the bulk of the work: planning and execution). The following is not an all-encompassing list, but rather some thoughts from each end of the spectrum:

elements most frequently mentioned in the literature as well as items that may not be mentioned as often but that I feel are important (and reassuring). For more structured and complete advice, see the articles by Martin and Martin and Weeks and Putnam Davis in the Suggested Readings at the end of this chapter.

First and foremost, keep it short. Keeping it brief—around three minutes—is mentioned repeatedly in the literature (Charnigo 2009; Leeder 2009; Oud 2009; Vaughn 2009; Strom 2011; Mestre 2012; Weeks and Putnam Davis 2017). Set yourself a goal of three minutes or less; if you are creating a tutorial for an involved topic or complicated database, break it up into small chunks: modularize your message. (As it is impossible to "future-proof" the tutorial (Gravett and Gill 2010), keeping it short also makes having to keep redoing or updating it less painful.)

Second, to create such a short, focused message means that before you even turn to your computer, you need to *plan* (Charnigo 2009; Leeder 2009; Meehan and Hylan 2009). Analyze the need (Principle 1: Teach to Your Audience) and determine exactly what goals you are trying to achieve. Write a script, and even follow Hollywood's example: storyboard your movie before you start shooting it. This can be done as simply as a series of quick drawings or more formally by pasting screenshots into PowerPoint.

Include in your planning exactly what effects, if any, you will use. The software packages for creating such tutorials include a plethora of sophisticated options and effects, but as David Strom says, "Resist the temptation to remake *Star Wars* here and just deliver the goods" (Strom 2011). The problem with multimedia is that it puts much higher demands on short-term memory (Oud 2009); keeping your video fairly simple reduces the cognitive load on the user (Leeder 2009). Another important factor to consider is accessibility: Joanne Oud writes frequently on this topic (see Oud 2011, 2016).

If the video is directly tied to something in the students' curriculum, include the instructors of the class(es) in your planning stages and throughout the process. (Dawson, Jacobs, and Yang 2010; Vaughan 2009) This is a wonderful opportunity to engage with the faculty, to ensure the tutorial is meeting the right needs, and to make sure the product of all your hours of work has their buy-in.

Should all videos be accompanied by a narrative voiceover? Let your decision be driven by the nature and content of your video: some ideas or processes may be better conveyed with just a few text balloons inserted in the action; for others, it may be better to talk your users through the process. Another factor is the audience for the video. If you are creating a tutorial for a known, limited audience with whom you are trying to create a relationship (as well as show them how to do Useful Thing X), allowing students to "hear my voice as I narrate the tutorial" provides "one way for librarians to lessen the 'facelessness' of online library services" (Charnigo 2009). But if you are creating some kind of basic how-to for the masses, the silent movie route may be just fine, if not better. (People viewing it on their phone in a crowded room won't create an annoyance for those around them.)

After these injunctions and the hours of work that will likely be involved in creating your video tutorials, my final note in this series of tips is this: do *not* strive for absolute perfection. (In a way, this is Principle 6: You Have the

Right to Be Wrong.) Relax (a little). Unless you are a trained, professional instructional designer, perfection is simply not a realistic goal, and you will spend too much time and drive yourself crazy. As Charnigo wisely says, "My in-classroom library instruction sessions aren't picture perfect, so I think it is okay to allow for a little element of humanness in the final product." I couldn't agree more: it is definitely "okay" to let some of your personality come through. If you can't meet with all your users in person, you still want them to get to know you. As Jamie Price (2010) points out: "A tutorial with a personal touch can make all the difference."

You may be surprised that the topic of *software* occurs last in this section, rather than first. There are two reasons for this. One, software, like interfaces, is a moving target. Names given here may have disappeared by the time you see this book. The second reason is, for me, the more compelling: the most important part of creating any video tutorial is the justification and the planning process. Figure out *why* a video is the right answer, *plan* it, and then decide what kind of software will best execute that project (or what software you have available or can afford).

The most well-known, professional choices at the time of this writing are Camtasia from Techsmith (versions for Windows and Mac) and Adobe Captivate (Windows and Mac). Prices for both are in the three-figure range (Captivate is generally more expensive than Camtasia), but both offer educational pricing that is more affordable. Once you move below this professional level, the names tend to change more quickly. For low-cost or free options, consult with colleagues or, of course, ask the all-knowing Google.

Exercises

1. Think back over all your schooling. Which teachers do you remember most vividly (both good and bad)? See if you can come up with a list of reasons why those instructors either worked (or didn't) for you. Use this information to form your own list of teaching principles.

2. Principle 7: Teaching with Technology includes a strong injunction to *slow down* in any kind of follow-the-leader activity. Prove to yourself how long it takes for people to look at your screen, back to their own and to perform some action, and then back to yours to check that their screen now matches yours by actually timing the process. Come up with an idea for what you want your audience to do (e.g., replicate a search that uses two input fields, one of which is to be searched in a particular field), then commandeer your classroom for five minutes. Have everyone pair up: one person is the timekeeper (most phones or other devices have a timer app), and the other is "the student." Have everyone get to the same screen you are on and tell the timekeepers to start. Enter the search you want the "students" to replicate, have them do it, and indicate to their timer-partner when they feel they have successfully replicated what is on your screen. You will probably be surprised at how many seconds it really takes.

3. One of the most painful but effective ways to overcome any kind of verbal tic is to practice giving a talk in front of a friend who is armed with a bell or some kind of annoying noise-making device. Every time you say "um" or "you know" or whatever your verbal tic is, your friend rings the bell. It's amazing how quickly you will slow down and consider more carefully what is coming out of your mouth, and *that is okay*! (It is also a good deal less painful than watching yourself fumble around on video.)

4. Decide what type of library you would be most likely to apply for a job in, then develop a 20-minute mock teaching session that could be used in your interview. This could be an academic, school, public, corporate, law, or medical library. In real life, outreach is an increasingly important aspect in the services of all these types of libraries (their very survival could depend on proving their value to the overall organization), so even if such a session is not listed as part of your interview schedule, be proactive and offer a session as an added extra to your interview.

5. Think of an assignment you've had where everyone in the class was looking for the same (kind of) thing *or* a database you're familiar with that has a particular quirk that you know from experience needs to be explained. Storyboard a three-minute video to address the issue.

6. You have reached the end of this book: was there something in particular you learned along the way (either from the book, or in class, or in struggling with an assignment) that you'd like to share with other students? Design a conference poster to convey your story. This will involve learning what conference posters are, good design principles for such posters, and so on. Then seriously consider submitting your poster to a major library conference.

References

Applegate, Celia. 1999. "Teaching: Taming the Terror." In *How I Teach: Essays on Teaching by Winners of the Robert and Pamela Goergen Award for Distinguished Achievement and Artistry in Undergraduate Teaching*, 23–36. Rochester, NY: University of Rochester. http://hdl.handle.net/1802/2864.

Boice, R. 1992. *The New Faculty Member: Supporting and Fostering Professional Development*. San Francisco, CA: Jossey-Bass. Quoted in Richard M. Reis, *Tomorrow's Professor: Preparing for Academic Careers in Science and Engineering*. New York: IEEE Press, 1997, p. 276.

Brown, Theodore M. 1999. "Connection, Communication, and Critical Thinking." In: *How I Teach: Essays on Teaching by Winners of the Robert and Pamela Goergen Award for Distinguished Achievement and Artistry in Undergraduate Teaching*, 9–20. Rochester, NY: University of Rochester. http://hdl.handle.net/1802/2862.

Charnigo, Laurie. 2009. "Lights! Camera! Action! Producing Library Instruction Video Tutorials Using Camtasia Studio." *Journal of Library & Information Services in Distance Learning* 3 (1): 23–30.

Davidson, C. I., and S. A. Ambrose. 1994. *The New Professor's Handbook: A Guide to Teaching and Research in Engineering and Science.* Bolton, MA: Anker Publishing. Quoted in Richard M. Reis, *Tomorrow's Professor: Preparing for Academic Careers in Science and Engineering.* New York: IEEE Press, 1997, p. 277.

Davis, Kaetrena D. 2007. "The Academic Librarian as Instructor: A Study of Teacher Anxiety." *College & Undergraduate Libraries* 14, no. 2: 77–101. http://digitalarchive.gsu.edu/univ_lib_facpub/29.

Dawson, Patricia H., Jacobs, Danielle L., and Sharon Q. Yang. 2010. "An Online Tutorial for SciFinder for Organic Chemistry Classes." *Science & Technology Libraries* 29 (4): 298–306.

Felder, R. M., and L. K. Silverman. 1988. "Learning and Teaching Styles in Engineering Education." *Journal of Engineering Education* 77, no. 2. Quoted in Richard M. Reis, *Tomorrow's Professor: Preparing for Academic Careers in Science and Engineering.* New York: IEEE Press, 1997, p. 265.

Feldman, K. 1976. "The Superior College Teacher from the Students' View." *Research in Higher Education* 5, no. 3: 243–288. Quoted in Richard M. Reis, *Tomorrow's Professor: Preparing for Academic Careers in Science and Engineering.* New York: IEEE Press, 1997, p. 261.

Gravett, Karen, and Claire Gill. 2010. "Using Online Video to Promote Database Searching Skills: The Creation of a Virtual Tutorial for Health and Social Care Students." *Journal of Information Literacy* 4 (1): 66–71.

Kuhlthau, Carol C. 1988. "Developing a Model of the Library Search Process: Cognitive and Affective Aspect. *RQ* 28 (Winter): 232–242. Quoted in Edward J. Eckel, "Fostering Self-Regulated Learning at the Reference Desk." *Reference & User Services Quarterly* 47 (Fall 2007): 16–20.

Leeder, Kim. 2009. "Learning to Teach through Video." *In the Library with the Lead Pipe* (October): 1–6. http://www.inthelibrarywiththeleadpipe.org/2009/learning-to-teach-through-video/.

Meehan, David, and Jack Hyland. 2009. "Video Killed the 'PDF' Star: Taking Information resource guides online." *SCONUL Focus* Winter (47): 23–26.

Mestre, Lori S. 2012. "Student Preference for Tutorial Design: A Usability Study." *Reference Services Review* 40 (2): 258–276.

Oud, Joanne. 2009. "Guidelines for Effective Online Instruction Using Multimedia Screencasts." *Reference Services Review* 37 (2): 164–177.

Oud, Joanne. 2011. "Improving Screencast Accessibility for People with Disabilities: Guidelines and Techniques." *Internet Reference Services Quarterly* 16 (3): 129–144.

Oud, Joanne. 2016. "Accessibility of Vendor-Created Database Tutorials for People with Disabilities." *Information Technology and Libraries*, 35(4): 7–18.

Price, Jamie B. 2010. "Screencasting on a Shoestring: Using Jing." *Reference Librarian* 51 (3): 237–244.

Roy, Loriene. 2011. "Library Instruction: The Teaching Prong in the Reference/Readers' Advisory/Instruction Triad." *The Reference Librarian* 52 (3): 274 –276.

Strom, David. September 22, 2011. "Screencasting Tips and Best Practices." Read-Write [tech news site]. http://readwrite.com/2011/09/22/screencasting-tips-and-best-pr#awesm=~oFF90lJQIbNT2N.

Vaughan, K.T.L. 2009. "Development of Targeted Online Modules for Recurring Reference Questions." *Medical Reference Services Quarterly* 28 (3): 211–220.

Viele, Patricia T. 2006. "Physics 213: An Example of Faculty/Librarian Collaboration." *Issues in Science and Technology Librarianship* 47 (Summer). http://www.istl.org/06-summer/article2.html.

Weeks, Thomas, and Jennifer Putnam Davis. 2017. "Evaluating Best Practices for Video Tutorials: A Case Study." *Journal of Library & Information Services in Distance Learning*. 11(1/2): 183–195.

Suggested Readings

Booth, Char. 2011. *Reflective Teaching, Effective Learning: Instructional Literacy for Library Educators*. Chicago: ALA Editions. (This is one of my favorite books on this topic, as it is down-to-earth and full of "news you can use."

Buchanan, Heidi E., and Beth A. McDonough. 2016. *The One-Shot Library Instruction Survival Guide*. 2nd ed. Chicago: ALA Editions. (As noted in the reviews, "concise" and "filled . . . with strategies to guide students utilizing library resources.")

Martin, Nichole A., and Ross Martin. 2015. "Would You Watch It? Creating Effective and Engaging Video Tutorials." *Journal of Library & Information Services in Distance Learning* 9, no. 1–2: 40–56.

Mestre, Lori S. 2012. "Student Preference for Tutorial Design: A Usability Study." *Reference Services Review* 40, no. 2: 258–276. (This article is extensively quoted in the video tutorials section. You owe it to yourself to read the original in its entirety. It is eye-opening and very well done.)

Weeks, Thomas, and Jennifer Putnam Davis. 2017. "Evaluating Best Practices for Video Tutorials: A Case Study." *Journal of Library & Information Services in Distance Learning* 11, no. 1–2: 183–195. (A recent and very thorough review of the literature on best practices for video tutorials, Weeks and Putnam Davis identify 12 best practices that are organized into 5 phases of tutorial creation. They then detail their experiences in applying those best practices to their projects and evaluate theory versus reality.

Notes

1. My opening statement to this chapter is based on years of informal observation and interactions with librarians from many different libraries; an excellent study by Kaetrena Davis provides empirical evidence for it as well. In her survey, she found that, most of the time, people don't go into librarianship specifically with teaching in mind: "more than two-thirds of the respondents (64%) chose librarianship with a desire to help people, followed by a love of reading and literacy (52%)" (Davis 2007).

2. The magic time for jettisoning preclass nervousness and anxiety seems to be between 51 and 60 years of age, according to Davis's study (2007).

3. Tech support people may hate me for presenting these actions in this order, but if you restart the computer and that doesn't solve the problem, you've lost a lot of precious time before initiating contact with tech support, who will inevitably take some time to respond.

4. You might find that you get invited back to give a library session every time the professor teaches the class, so definitely keep your notes and whatever materials you used.

5. David Strom, a professional from outside the library world, provides the useful guidance that "a three-minute video will be about 500 words of script, give or take."

Glossary

A&I databases. Abstracting and indexing databases. It is increasingly difficult to find databases that only include abstracts and not the full text.

aggregator. A database that combines resources from multiple sources. Examples include *Academic Search* (EBSCO), *ProQuest Central*, and Gale's *Academic OneFile*.

altmetrics. Alternative ways of measuring database usage and statistics. This generally refers to social media mentions, downloads, or other nontraditional usage statistics.

AND operator. AND is the narrowing operator. Search terms joined by AND must all appear in the search results.

asynchronous communication. Communication that does not occur at the same time. That is, the sender and the receiver are not in "live" communication with each other. E-mail is an example.

back-generated index. An index that was not built from the ground up by examining individual articles one at a time, but one that was automatically generated by extracting terms (such as subject terms) from all records and built using computational power.

bibliographic formatting software. Software that is used to store bibliographic citations and output them into a standard format, such as APA, MLA, Chicago, or Turabian styles. The software may be client-based (installed on individual computers, like EndNote), or cloud-based (accessed via the Web, like RefWorks).

Boolean operators. Named after mathematician George Boole, the terms AND, OR, and NOT are used in online searching to narrow, broaden, or negate search concepts.

broadcast search tools. Also known as *metasearch* or sometimes *federated search tools*, these tools first establish remote connections with databases through various connection technologies, perform searches, return results, merge and de-duplicate results, and then present the results to the user.

They are not really performing a federated search (as they are searching multiple sources), but they are presenting a federation of results.

broader term. A term used in thesauri to denote a superordinate term.

controlled vocabulary. A principled vocabulary list that is used to control the way database terms, usually subjects, are entered.

database. A collection of information stored and retrieved electronically in fields and records. In the library context, it can be a collection of searchable information about books, journal articles, archival materials, images, sounds, and other types of materials. Databases greatly increase the speed of access and are continually adding features, such as full-text availability, social media connections, and output of bibliographic information.

digital rights management (DRM). This is a control mechanism used by copyright holders to restrict access to their intellectual property.

discovery tools. Also known as *Web-scale discovery tools*. These tools search across a wide range of metadata, usually kept within a single database, providing a single search interface across a wide swath of library content, including local catalog records and subscribed content.

DRM. See **digital rights management**.

durable URL. Also known as a *permanent URL* or *persistent URL*. This is a way to create a link to an object on the Internet, such as a database record or a full-text article, so that the record can be accessed later without reference to a user ID. Durable URLs are also necessary because most databases generate extremely long URL strings that contain session IDs, search preferences, and search parameters.

fields. A field in an online database is a container of information. Fields can have various characteristics, such as textual, numeric, date, currency, URL, etc.

fixed fields. Database fields that contain a set (fixed) value, usually numbers or letters. This is a way databases conserve space and speed up retrieval.

gremlin characters. In a database context, these are hidden characters in an electronic text, such as a soft hyphen, a line break, or even not-so-hidden characters, that may have unpredictable results in searching, such as "curly" quotation marks.

index. In the print world, an index may be a back-of-the-book (inward looking) collection of topics within the book, or it may be a directory of articles or other publications (outward looking), often arranged by subject. In a database context, indexes are compiled electronically for fast computer retrieval.

interface. The front face of a database, including the branding and the look and feel, with which the user interacts.

iterating fields. Fields that are able to repeat. Subject fields in MARC records repeat, as multiple subjects are usually assigned to records. Noniterating fields include field 245 (title field) in a MARC catalog record.

keywords. Words or terms users enter into databases. Depending on the database, records may be retrieved based on those keywords being found in the metadata, controlled vocabulary, or within the full text, if the database searches full text.

left anchored. Access starting place for entries in indexes. As English is read from left to right, it is left anchored. Print indexes cannot be searched by keyword, only by an initial starting point. Personal author last names are inverted in directories, making the last name the left-anchored starting point. In the online database world, left-anchored searching is less common than in the print world. Here, keyword searching is predominant.

Library of Congress Subject Headings (LCSH). A pre-coordinated subject term scheme used in most larger academic libraries.

limiters. Also known as *facets*, limiters are presented as clickable links, usually to the left or right of search results, that enable users to quickly restrict search results to various fixed field or variable-length field features. Limiters commonly restrict to publisher, genre, subject, language, and date.

link resolver. Also known as an *OpenURL resolver*. Developed by Herbert Van de Sompel from 1998 to 2000, the OpenURL framework is a standard (ANSI/NISO Z39.88) that takes metadata from index or catalog records and concatenates it into a URL string that, when run though a resolver, can be passed along to other services to locate full text to which a library subscribes.

medical subject headings (MeSH). Subject headings used by the *Medline* database.

metasearch. A search tool that connects to different remote databases, with various connection protocols, and attempts to unify search results in a single interface. Metasearch is synonymous with broadcast search or federated search.

NAICS. See **North American Industry Classification System**.

narrower term. A term used in thesauri to denote a subordinate term.

nesting. The use of parentheses to control the order of operations in a Boolean statement. Several sets (or layers) of parentheses may be used, or "nested," within each other. Example: ((snowshoeing OR skiing) AND (Breckenridge OR Tahoe)).

North American Industry Classification System (NAICS). NAICS codes officially replaced Standard Industrial Classification (SIC) codes in 1997 and is a more robust system, including newer industries. It also unifies the classification systems of Mexico and Canada as a result of the North American Free Trade Agreement (NAFTA).

NOT operator. NOT is the negating operator. If the NOT term is present, it knocks results out of a search set.

OCLC. Originally stood for *Ohio College Library Center*, but now stands for *Online Computer Library Center*. It is a nonprofit cooperative organization that, in terms of databases, publishes the *WorldCat* database (both under the FirstSearch interface and WorldCat.org) and the *WorldCat Discovery* tool.

OCR. See **optical character recognition**.

online catalog. This is an online version of the old card catalog. Often called the *online public access catalog*, or *OPAC*.

OpenURL. An international standard for passing along metadata so that full text can be discovered across various vendor and aggregator services.

optical character recognition (OCR). This is the process of using software to recognize text on a scanned page. This process is necessary to create digital versions. Without running OCR software, the scanned pages are saved only as graphics (images). In an image, the textual content is not "recognized" and thus cannot be searched or retrieved.

OR operator. OR is the broadening operator. Search terms joined by OR will return results if any term has a hit. A best practice is to always enclose OR statements within parentheses to avoid confusion with other operators.

persistent uniform resource locator (PURL). More commonly *persistent URL* or just *PURL*. It not only shortens the URL, but it also provides a way for updating changed URLs.

postcoordination. Process by which the searcher combines subject descriptors together in a search query.

precision. A measure of the effectiveness of a search query. One that retrieves mostly relevant results is said to have *greater precision*.

pre-coordination. Subject headings that contain one or more semantic notions in the same term (on the same line) so that fewer headings can contain more information. Catalogers and indexers use this method when they create the metadata for subject headings.

proximity operators. Search connectors that go beyond what Boolean operators do and address the relationship of one word or term to another. This may involve adjacency, precedence, or word distance.

proxy. In a library database context, proxies allow for remote users to access databases even though they are not on the same (licensed) network. Logging in to a proxy server assigns the remote user a proxied Internet address.

PURL. See **persistent uniform resource locator**.

query. A user's question. In a database context, it is the search submitted to the database.

ready reference. A subset of a reference collection consisting of frequently consulted reference books.

recall. The number of items found from a query. Formally, it is the number of items found divided by the number of relevant items "out there."

records. In the database context, a record is all the information pertaining to an item being referenced. This may be a bibliographic entity, a sound recording, a video, a still image, or anything being described.

related term. Term used in thesauri to denote a parallel or closely related term.

relational databases. Databases with several tables that are linked together to save space within the database and to allow for one-to-many relationships.

scope. In the database world, the scope of a database is what the database covers, including content, dates of coverage, language of content, and any other information that describes the database.

scope note. A term used in thesauri to describe the descriptor term within a controlled-vocabulary set and how the term is defined.

serials. A publication that is issued multiple times. This includes newspapers, magazines, journals, and annual reports. Also known as *periodicals*.

Standard Industrial Classification (SIC). Usually referred to as *SIC codes*. A classification system developed in 1937 and used by several U.S. government agencies to classify businesses. It was officially replaced in 1997 by NAICS. We still see it used by government entities and several vendors, as it is simpler than NAICS, and users still often ask for data under this system.

subject descriptor. The subject scheme used in most online databases where each term has only one semantic notion.

subject heading. The subject scheme typically used in online catalog records and occasionally in other online databases where each subject term has one or more semantic notions, often separated by dashes.

subject searching. Searches performed in online databases using subject tags or in subject fields rather than the default search settings.

synchronous communication. Communication where participants interact in real time, as in face-to-face communication, telephone conversations, and online chat interactions. In contrast, e-mail is asynchronous communication.

thesaurus. A listing of controlled vocabulary terminology that is usually arranged with references to broader terms, narrower terms, related terms, "used for" terms, and scope notes.

top-level domain (TLD). You are already familiar with .com and .gov for U.S. Web sites, but TLDs exist for every country of the world. The easiest way to find a list of all TLDs is to use Google to search "tld."

truncation. Shortening of a search term to account for alternate endings of terms. Generally, a search character is appended to a word to denote where the truncation is to begin. The most common truncation symbol is the asterisk (*), although some databases use a question mark (?) or an exclamation point (!). As an example, *environment** in many online databases would retrieve the terms *environments, environmental, environmentalism, environmentalists*, etc.

uniform resource locator (URL). Usually referred to as *URL*. This is the Web address.

used for. A cross-reference under a preferred descriptor while making reference to the nonpreferred descriptor.

variable-length fields. Database fields that are not limited to a set number of characters in a particular format (unlike fixed fields).

vendor. A company that sells database products. EBSCO, ProQuest, Gale, Elsevier, Wiley, and Taylor & Francis are examples of vendors.

Web-scale discovery tools. Also called *discovery tools*, these tools are characterized by a central index of metadata (sometimes also including full text) that attempt to provide an index to the contents of many databases. It is important to distinguish these tools from metasearch or broadcast search tools, where individual databases are being searched. With Web-scale discovery tools, a central index is searched, not dozens of databases, making the response time much faster. Examples include ProQuest's *Summon*, ExLibris (ProQuest) *Primo*, *EBSCO Discovery Service* (EDS), and OCLC's *WorldCat Discovery*.

wildcards. Generally refers to a single character standing in place of one or more characters within a word. For example, *wom?n* can be used in some databases to search for both *woman* and *women*. *Colo?r* can be used in some databases to retrieve either *color* or *colour*.

Index